The Handbook of Near-Death Experiences

The Handbook of Near-Death Experiences

Thirty Years of Investigation

Edited by
Janice Miner Holden, EdD, Bruce Greyson, MD,
and Debbie James, MSN, RN

Foreword by Kenneth Ring, PhD

PRAEGER PUBLISHERS
An Imprint of ABC-CLIO, LLC

A B C CLIO

Santa Barbara, California • Denver, Colorado • Oxford, England

Copyright 2009 by Janice Miner Holden, EdD, Bruce Greyson, MD, and Debbie James, MSN, RN

Library of Congress Cataloging-in-Publication Data
The handbook of near-death experiences : thirty years of investigation / edited by Janice Miner Holden, Bruce Greyson, and Debbie James ; foreword by Kenneth Ring.
    p. cm.
    Includes bibliographical references and index.
    ISBN 978-0-313-35864-7 (hard copy : alk. paper) — ISBN 978-0-313-35865-4 (ebook)
1. Near-death experiences. I. Holden, Janice Miner. II. Greyson, Bruce. III. James, Debbie.
    BF1045.N4H36 2009
    133.901′3—dc22   2009011646

13 12 11 10 09   1 2 3 4 5

This book is also available on the World Wide Web as an eBook.
Visit www.abc-clio.com for details.

ABC-CLIO, LLC
130 Cremona Drive, P.O. Box 1911
Santa Barbara, California 93116-1911

This book is printed on acid-free paper (∞)

Manufactured in the United States of America

Contents

Foreword

In the beginning ... was Raymond Moody's word, and the word, hyphenated and multiple though it was, was "near-death experience." Such was the phrase this then-young medical student coined that was shortly to become familiar the world over as the standard term to describe one of the most astonishing and improbable of all human phenomena: the subjective experience of apparently surviving death. Moody's book, aptly titled *Life after Life*, quickly became a worldwide bestseller, and the near-death experience, or NDE, soon became the darling of both the print and broadcast media. The reason: The stories Moody's respondents told were so captivating and enthralling and depicted the experience of dying in such radiantly glorious language that people reading and hearing about it could scarcely believe that what they had always feared as their greatest enemy, when seen up close, had the face of the beloved.

And more—when Moody's interviewees attempted to describe the experience of dying, they often mentioned a light of unceasing supernatural brilliance that exuded a feeling of pure, unconditional, *absolute* love and was associated with such an overwhelming sensation of peace that they sometimes could only liken it to "the peace that passeth all understanding." (One of my own respondents, when pressed to characterize it, could say only this: "If you took the one thousand best things in your life and multiplied by a million, maybe," she allowed, "you could get close to this feeling." I particularly noted that *maybe*.)

No wonder, then, that the experience of dying, as described in Moody's book and subsequently in the media, was thrilling to the public at large. It seemed clear evidence that what our Western religions, at least, taught was true: that life continues after death, that heaven is no fantasy, and that those who die do, indeed, see the face of God.

The year was 1975, and I remember it well because I, too, was one of those people who were immediately drawn to this ravishing phenomenon and were keen to learn more about it. Not long afterward, I began my own research into near-death experiences. A couple of years later, I was to meet Raymond Moody himself, along with what was then a small band of other interested investigators, both academics and physicians. Together, we decided to try to approach the study of this phenomenon, not from the standpoint of religion, but scientifically. As scientists, we naturally had no concern as such with the religious implications of near-death experiences; people were free to think about that as they would. What we wished to do was to subject the near-death experience to critical scientific scrutiny. We were out neither to prove it nor debunk it; our aim instead was only to try to understand it and to encourage other scientists and scholars to do likewise.

Flash forward 30 years. It is now 2005, and a near-death researcher and academic by the name of Jan Holden, who has become the president of an NDE organization that some of us early investigators had established "after" the beginning, is helping to plan a forthcoming international conference on near-death experiences. Jan hits on the idea that after three decades of work on the near-death experience, during which time a massive amount of research and many scores of books had been published addressing this experience, it would be fitting to devote a good part of the upcoming conference to summarizing the main findings and conclusions from this field of endeavor—now called near-death studies—as well as to address the still unanswered questions that such a systematic survey would make clear.

Accordingly, Jan and her colleagues—especially her coeditors of this volume, Bruce Greyson and Debbie James—decide to invite many of the world's leading experts on NDEs to contribute papers on all the major aspects of near-death experiences, researched and understood as of 2005, 30 years after the founding of the field.

The book you now hold in your hand, which is largely based on these definitive contributions, is the fruit of this historic conference of the International Association for Near-Death Studies (IANDS). It was held at The University of Texas M. D. Anderson Cancer Center (TUTMDACC) in Houston in the fall of 2006.

And I used the expression "you now hold in your hand" deliberately, if a bit playfully, because in fact this volume is meant to be, as its title implies, *a handbook* for all those people—scholars, educators, researchers. health care workers, members of the clergy, the public at large, and, yes, of course, near-death experiencers, or NDErs, themselves—with a serious interest in near-death experiences. In short, this book is designed for anyone to use who wishes to know in depth and in searching detail what investigators have learned from 30 years of research into near-death experiences. As such, it is the only book of its kind that draws on the expertise of the world's foremost scholars and researchers who collectively present the most up-to-date and informed summary of the field. Each contributor is an authority on his or her own area of specialization, and each, therefore, has something distinctive to offer the reader, who will come to see through these separate lenses a vision of the whole. Thus, *The Handbook of Near-Death Experiences* is now and is likely to remain for many years the standard reference work for the field.

It is left for me now only to give you an idea of the specific contents of this work, so you can have something of a map at the beginning of your journey through this field of near-death studies. Let me then introduce you to your guides—the authors of this volume—and tell you where they will be taking you.

In Chapter 1, the editors of this volume—professional counselor Janice Holden, psychiatrist Bruce Greyson, and critical care nurse–educator Debbie James—offer a historical overview of the field of near-death studies. They describe both scholarly inquiry into near-death experiences and cases of NDEs in literature prior to 1975. They then review how this field of scholarly inquiry developed over the course of the subsequent three decades.

In Chapter 2, research psychologists Nancy L. Zingrone and Carlos S. Alvarado provide a comprehensive, critical overview of scholarly inquiry into the contents, circumstances, and incidence of pleasurable Western adult NDEs—those dominated by such feelings as peace, joy, and love. They examine the nature, quality, and results of research exploring the range of features that NDErs of this type have reported.

In Chapter 3, one of the pioneer researchers of NDEs, psychiatrist Russell Noyes, along with neuropsychiatrist and NDE researcher Peter Fenwick, and NDE researchers Janice Miner Holden and Sandra Rozan Christian, provides a comprehensive, critical overview of the aftereffects of pleasurable Western adult NDEs. They describe the psychological, spiritual, social, and physical changes in the aftermath of this, the most widely researched type of NDE. They also discuss the extent to which these aftereffects present developmental opportunities and challenges to NDErs who undergo such a near-death encounter.

In Chapter 4, pastoral counselor and NDE scholar Nancy Evans Bush describes the contents and aftereffects of distressing NDEs—those dominated by such emotions as isolation, anguish, terror, and guilt. She analyzes the amount and quality of research into this type of NDE, concluding with areas especially in need of further inquiry. She also reviews philosophical perspectives on the meaning of these experiences for questions about the nature of consciousness and the meaning and purpose of life.

In Chapter 5, sociologist and NDE researcher Cherie Sutherland offers an overview of research findings regarding the NDEs of children and teens. Replete with narratives from her own interviews with child and teen NDErs, she captures both the scholarship and the heart of this topic.

In Chapter 6, Janice Miner Holden, physician and NDE researcher Jeffrey Long, and psychiatrist Jason MacLurg report their comprehensive, critical analysis of scholarly inquiry into the characteristics of NDErs. Addressing the question, "Who has NDEs?" they examine demographic and psychological variables of NDErs, usually compared with non-NDErs—people whose physical circumstances were apparently the same as NDErs' but who have not reported an NDE. They address how well NDEs can be predicted, how NDErs' characteristics inform the current understanding of these experiences, and what may be the most fruitful foci of future research into the characteristics of NDErs.

In Chapter 7, medical sociologist Allan Kellehear analyzes non-Western NDEs cited in the professional literature. Comparing narratives from Asia, the Pacific Islands, and hunter-gatherer cultures of North and South America, Australia, and Africa, he identifies what aspects of NDE contents appear currently to be universal to all cultures and, thus, to humanity across cultures.

In Chapter 8, religious scholar and educator Farnaz Masumian surveys the sacred texts of the world's major religions to identify passages that correspond to the contents of NDEs. Included in her analysis are the Bahá'í faith, Buddhism, Christianity, Hinduism, Islam, Judaism, and Zoroastrianism.

In Chapter 9, Janice Miner Holden addresses the topic of veridical perception in NDEs—apparently nonphysical perception of events that based on the condition and/or position of the NDEr's physical body should not have been possible and yet is later confirmed as accurate. She provides several case examples, describes an analysis of over 100 anecdotes from the professional literature, and reviews the five hospital-based studies researchers have conducted so far in an attempt to capture veridical perception under scientifically controlled circumstances.

In Chapter 10, Bruce Greyson, along with psychologists Emily Williams Kelly and Edward F. Kelly, reviews the models to explain NDEs and, in doing so, analyzes the extent to which each model accounts for all known aspects of NDEs. Their analysis addresses psychological, physiological, and transcendental explanatory models.

And finally, in the last contribution to this volume, Chapter 11, professional counselor Ryan D. Foster, Debbie James, and Janice Miner Holden present a comprehensive review and critical analysis of the scholarly literature concerning the practical applications of NDE research for health care and educational settings. In addition to addressing existing recommendations for medical, psychological, social, and spiritual health care providers working with NDErs, they review the literature on the uses of NDE-related information for work with such special populations as the bereaved and the terminally ill as well as with students in schools and in higher education.

That, then, is a preview of the journey the authors of this indispensable *Handbook* will be conducting. Whether you consult chapters of special interest to you or take the entire tour, you can be sure that you will have been exposed to the most comprehensive summaries yet available dealing with what happens when people die and what we all can learn before we take that final passage for ourselves, which, as the American novelist Herman Melville said, "only an author from the dead could adequately tell."

Kenneth Ring, PhD

Preface

For the people who experience them, near-death experiences (NDEs) are usually emotionally powerful and life-transforming experiences of another reality beyond the everyday, three-dimensional world. Such experiences are transpersonal in nature—transcending experiencers' usual limits of space and/or time and revealing what they perceive to be insights about the nature of consciousness, existence, and the universe. In the contemporary Western world dominated by the scientistic worldview—legitimizing only those phenomena that can be directly and repeatedly observed and measured—and by various religious doctrines, NDEs have been a consistent source of controversy, and the people who experience them have sometimes been discounted, pathologized, and even demonized.

Yet, despite their transpersonal nature, NDEs and the people who experience them—near-death experiencers (NDErs)—can be studied through the scientific method. And for at least two reasons, research into this line of inquiry is vital. On the one hand, non-NDEers' lack of understanding can harm NDErs. On the other hand, NDEers themselves, as well as their personal associates and their health care providers—the medical, psychological, social, and spiritual caregivers who tend to them—along with humanity at large, may benefit from accurate knowledge about NDEs.

When a researcher sets out to conduct a study, the first step is a literature review: a comprehensive, critical analysis and synthesis of all relevant publications that provides the rationale for the study. By 2004, the literature in the field of near-death studies had become vast. As a University of North Texas professor of counseling who had directed several doctoral dissertations, Jan Holden had already seen a few doctoral student researchers create—and re-create—the wheel that is a literature review on NDEs. Anticipating the 30-year anniversary of the opening of the field, she thought it an ideal time to consolidate the findings of that literature into one source that could serve as the foundation for near-death researchers' literature reviews for many years to come. Thus, future researchers could be spared the task of repeatedly re-creating that cumbersome wheel. And that source could serve also to enhance the knowledge of NDErs, their personal associates, and the public at large and to enhance the competence of NDErs' health care providers.

In 2004, Jan was president of the International Association for Near-Death Studies (IANDS), and Debbie James was the organization's long-time conference director. A master's prepared nurse, critical care nurse specialist, and nurse educator, Debbie worked at The University of Texas M. D. Anderson Cancer Center (TUTMDACC) in Houston. One day in the fall of that year, Jan approached Debbie with the idea of a 2006 IANDS conference in which leading NDE researchers would be invited to present literature reviews on 10 major NDE subtopics that would together predominantly cover the field of near-death studies. Synchronistically, Debbie had been thinking of suggesting that IANDS hold an upcoming conference at TUTMDACC. We approached the IANDS Board of Directors, who affirmed the concept. In fall of 2006, those invited presentations comprised the first two days of a four-day conference at TUTMDACC entitled Near-Death Experiences: 30 Years of Research. Recordings of those presentations—available for purchase at http://www.iands.org/conferences/2006_conference_presentations—continue to educate people. The papers on which those presentations were based served also as the basis for most of the chapters in this book.

At the conference, psychiatrist Bruce Greyson, Carlson Professor of Psychiatry & Neurobehavioral Sciences and Director of the Division of Perceptual Studies at the University of Virginia, presented one of the invited papers. He had been one of the founders of IANDS and a past president who had served for more than 25 years as the organization's research director and editor of its scholarly Journal of Near-Death Studies. As a prolific NDE researcher with many publications in peer-reviewed journals, Bruce has the knowledge of information, people, and procedures that made him a shoo-in to coedit this volume.

ACKNOWLEDGMENTS

As with any major undertaking, this volume could not have come into existence without the dedication of many contributors. Most visible are the coauthors whose outstanding work comprises the substance of the book. We coeditors also thank several "behind the scenes" contributors: the University of North Texas for funding Jan's 2006 professional development leave (sabbatical) to organize the original conference; Andrea Curewitz, who provided invaluable final editing of each chapter before initial submission to the publisher; Anneliese Fox, of Fox Computer Systems in East

Windsor Hill, Connecticut, who meticulously created the Index; and our many editors and assistants at Praeger whose devoted attention greatly enhanced the quality of the finished product.

We coeditors have committed to redirect the proceeds from this book to IANDS's Research Fund to provide ongoing support to projects aimed at the discovery and dissemination of new knowledge about NDEs. We hope that this volume will inform members of the public and contribute to health care providers' competent service to NDErs and others interested in NDEs. We also hope that this volume not only will ease the work of scholars already intent on NDE research by providing the foundation for their literature reviews but also will inspire scholars not originally focused on this topic to pursue research on it. Through research, NDEs will be increasingly understood, NDErs and their associates will be competently served, and any potential benefit NDEs hold for humanity at large will more likely be realized and advanced.

Janice Miner Holden
Bruce Greyson
Debbie James

1

The Field of Near-Death Studies: Past, Present, and Future

Janice Miner Holden, Bruce Greyson, and Debbie James

The following chapters provide comprehensive, critical reviews of the scholarly literature through 2005—mostly research studies—on specific subtopics pertaining to near-death experiences (NDEs). This first chapter provides a discussion of the context in which those research findings have emerged, including a history of the development and an overview of the current status of the field of near-death studies.

The field of near-death studies has a rich history, filled with discovery, challenges, and controversy. Most people find NDEs and their implications inherently fascinating. At the same time, people often express strong and widely ranging reactions, finding NDEs to be anywhere from deeply affirming to fundamentally challenging to their own life experiences and deepest-held beliefs.

Although researchers have learned a great deal about NDEs over the 30 years since the phenomenon became a focus of professional attention, far more remains to be understood. One thing is clear, however: Over the course of those 30 years, "near-death experience" and "NDE" have, respectively, become a household term and an acronym in U.S. culture. One indication of this development occurred in 2006 when a major U.S. greeting card company published a birthday card involving a joke that relied on its customers' recognition of the "bright light" in NDEs.

At the same time, after 30 years of scholarly inquiry about NDEs, misunderstanding and confusion about these phenomena is pervasive. One example is the frequency with which members of the media refer to near-death *episodes*—the physical circumstances of being near death—as near-death *experiences*, which encompass the psychological experience of an alternate reality actually reported by only a minority of people who survive near-death episodes.

How awareness of NDEs became integrated into U.S. culture, what has happened in scholarly and professional circles behind the scenes of that development, and the many challenges and promises of the future of the field of near-death studies are among the topics of this introductory chapter.

PUBLICATIONS THROUGH 1975

By the early 1970s, resuscitation technology had advanced to the point where people were being brought back from the brink of death in numbers unprecedented in human history. The conditions they survived were as extreme as several minutes of cardiac arrest. Professionals came to see death not as an instantaneous event but as a gradual process—one that could sometimes be interrupted and reversed (Parnia 2006, 36). During close brushes with death, people were reporting experiences of what, for most of them, was another reality; experiences that, to them, were occurring at the very time they were closest to—or actually in the first moments of—death. For the first time in history, enough people were reporting this type of experience that professional health care providers began to discern patterns in the experience itself and in the aftermath of it.

In 1975, Raymond Moody, then a medical student, published the book *Life after Life*. In it, he coined the term "near-death experience" and the acronym "NDE," and he introduced the phenomenon of NDEs to the public and most professionals. His book marked the opening of the contemporary field of near-death studies. Even in that book, however, Moody noted that writers had recorded NDEs going back as far as ancient texts. It is now clear that accounts can be found in humankind's earliest writings, including the Bible, Plato's *Dialogues*, the *Egyptian Book of the Dead*, and the *Tibetan Book of the Dead*.

As that list of texts suggests, it is also now known that NDEs have been described across cultures, not only in the literature of Western culture but also in the folklore of Native American, South Pacific Islander, and East and Central Asian cultures and in the literature of non-Western cultures. Indeed, accounts of near-death and out-of-body experiences can be found in the oral traditions and written literature of about 95 percent of the world's cultures (Sheils 1978).

More recently, over 150 years before Moody's book, several authors explored the phenomenon that would later be named NDE—some of these people being, literally, explorers. In 1825, Henry Schoolcraft described an account in his book *Travels in the Central Portion of the Mississippi Valley*. In 1872, David Livingstone, of "Dr. Livingstone, I presume" fame, described what we now call an NDE in his book *Adventures and Discoveries in the Interior of Africa*. Just one year later, Samuel Woodworth Cozzens related an account in his book *The Marvelous Country: Three Years in Arizona and New Mexico*. Before 1900, at least six other authors (Barrow 1848; Clarke 1878; Little 1881; Munck 1887; Winslow 1868) published books containing NDE accounts. Among these was Frances Power Cobbe's 1882 book *The Peak in Darien*; in it, she recounted NDEs in which the experiencers encountered deceased people who were not at the time known to be deceased.

In the 19th century, accounts of NDEs also appeared in the Western professional literature of both medicine and psychical research. In the periodical literature, physician A. S. Wiltse published a description of an NDE in his 1889 article in the *Saint Louis Medical and Surgical Journal*. Accounts in the medical literature tended to focus on the effects of these phenomena, with the apparent goals of warning physicians not to declare patients dead prematurely and of helping survivors readjust to life after reviving. Accounts in the psychical research literature tended to focus on accurate perceptions of experiencers while "they" were ostensibly out of their bodies, with the apparent goals of elucidating the relationship between mind and body and providing supportive evidence for the possibility that some part of humans may survive bodily death.

Beginning in the 19th century, Western investigators moved beyond individual case reports into collections of cases, which allowed analysis of features that appeared to comprise consistent patterns across individuals. Among these were Mormon collections of NDEs that were not published for the general public until the 20th century (Lundahl 1979, 1993–94). In Albert von St. Gallen Heim's 1892 article in the *Yearbook of the Swiss Alpine Club*, he described 30 NDEs, primarily from climbers who had fallen while climbing, as he had done. In the first two decades of the 20th century, psychical researcher James Hyslop published a series of articles describing the phenomenology of "visions of the dying." For two decades beginning in 1971, Russell Noyes and his colleagues published a series of articles in the psychiatric literature describing "depersonalization in the face of life-threatening danger," including paradoxical hyperalertness and mystical consciousness. In 1975, German theologian Johann Christoph Hampe published a book describing the primary phenomenological features of NDEs; it was published in English in 1979. Indeed, before Moody's book in 1975, in the scholarly Western periodical literature alone, over 25 authors had published over 30 articles addressing NDEs (Holden and Christian 2005b).

When *Life after Life* first appeared, it quickly became a bestseller. As of 2001, over 13 million copies had been sold, and the book had been translated into 26 languages (E. Russo, personal communication, August 10, 2006). This book ushered in the modern era of near-death research in which NDEs were identified as a discrete phenomenon rather than as a type of depersonalization, a special case of out-of-body experience, or a variety of religious epiphany. In the intervening 30 years, the topic of NDEs has continued to generate curiosity and has sustained interest such that researchers and theoreticians around the world have investigated and written on the topic. Thus, not only have NDEs occurred throughout history and across cultures but also the study of them has become increasingly international.

NDE-RELATED ORGANIZATIONS AND WEB SITES

In 1977, Moody invited a number of scholars who had expressed interest in studying this newly identified phenomenon of NDEs to a meeting at the University of Virginia. His intention was to enable members of the group to coordinate their efforts and share their knowledge, research strategies, and mutual professional support. When the group convened, it became clear that a variety of NDE-related people—not only researchers but also educators, health care professionals, near-death experiencers (NDErs) themselves, and family, friends, and other associates of NDErs— could benefit from an organization dedicated to research and education on NDEs as well as to informational and networking support. In response, a subgroup of the original group, including Moody, medical sociologist John Audette, social psychologist Kenneth Ring, cardiologist Michael Sabom, and psychiatrist Bruce Greyson, formed the Association for the Scientific Study of Near-Death Phenomena. In 1978, Audette, Greyson, Ring, and Sabom drafted bylaws and articles of incorporation and submitted an application for tax exempt status, and in 1981, the organization became the International Association for Near-Death Studies (IANDS).

Among IANDS's products has been its scholarly journal, begun in 1981 as the semiannual *Anabiosis: Journal for Near-Death Studies*, then changed in 1987 to the quarterly *Journal of Near-Death Studies*. Virtually since its inception, Greyson has served as the editor of this publication. Also since 1981, the organization has published a quarterly newsletter and a variety of informational brochures. In the first few years of the 21st century, IANDS cooperated with a research team at the University of North Texas to publish a series of indexes to the complete scholarly periodical literature on NDEs, including most article abstracts and each article indexed by 135 NDE-related topics. For this substantial endeavor to develop an invaluable resource for NDE researchers (Holden et al. 2008), Rozan Christian read and analyzed each of almost 900 scholarly and popular articles on NDEs published through 2005, making her one of the best-read NDE scholars on Earth.

In 1989, IANDS began sponsoring an almost-annual conference; in 2006, the organization held its 15th conference at The University of Texas M. D. Anderson Cancer Center in Houston, Texas. From each conference, IANDS made recordings of presentations by professionals and testimonials by NDErs available for purchase at the organization's Web site (www. iands.org). In addition, IANDS has facilitated the implementation and operation of local interest groups, most of which meet monthly. As of

2005, over 55 of these groups existed, most in the United States and others in Canada, Western and Eastern Europe, Israel, and South Africa.

In 1995, IANDS registered its Web site domain name. Analysis in 2006 indicated an average of 400,000 page hits per month at the site (A. Fox, personal communication, August 10, 2006). Other major English language Web sites dedicated to NDEs included Kevin Williams's near-death.com (www.near-death.com), which he began in 1996, and the Near-Death Experience Research Foundation Web site of Jeffrey Long and Jody Long (www.nderf.org), begun in 1998; by 2006, both sites received about 2.5 million page hits per month (K. Williams, personal communication, August 11, 2006; Jeff Long, personal communication, August 11, 2006). Also in 2006, a Googling of the words "near death experience" yielded results exceeding 76.4 million links.

PUBLICATIONS SINCE 1975

In the first three decades of the field of near-death studies, most books on NDEs were written in English. Most were autobiographical accounts aimed at a general readership, but a few were scholarly works reporting research, comprising edited compilations, or reviewing the current status of research and thinking in the field. Some notable contributions are books by Kenneth Ring (1980, *Life at Death*; 1984, *Heading toward Omega*; 1998, *Lessons from the Light*, with Evelyn Elsaesser Valarino; and 1999, *Mindsight*, with Sharon Cooper, on NDEs in the blind), by editors Greyson and Charles Flynn (1984, *The Near-Death Experience: Problems, Prospects, and Perspectives*), by Margot Grey (1985, *Return from Death*), and by Cherie Sutherland (1992, *Transformed by the Light*), as well as several books by physicians: Michael Sabom (1982, *Recollections of Death: A Medical Investigation;* and 1998, *Light and Death*); Melvin Morse (1990, *Closer to the Light*); Peter Fenwick, with his wife, Elizabeth (1995, *The Truth in the Light*); Barbara Rommer (2000, *Blessings in Disguise*); and Sam Parnia (2006, *What Happens When We Die*). Also noteworthy is the American Psychological Association's (APA) 2000 book *The Varieties of Anomalous Experience: Examining the Scientific Evidence*, edited by Etzel Cardeña, Steven Jay Lynn, and Stanley Krippner—the APA's first-ever publication acknowledging and addressing nonordinary experiences—in which Greyson wrote the chapter on NDEs.

NUMBER AND TYPES OF PUBLISHED STUDIES

The focus in this chapter and this book is near-death studies as a field of scholarly endeavor. Among the many ways to document the history of such a field is to track and analyze the nature of its refereed and professional journal publications. In this field, tracking is facilitated by the aforementioned *Near-Death Experiences: Index to the Periodical Literature through 2001* (Holden and Christian 2005a), which the coauthors updated through 2005 (*Index*; Holden et al. 2008), and which includes a near-exhaustive list of scholarly publications on NDEs. Allowing for unintentional omissions in that document, following are some findings from an analysis of its contents.

From a scientific perspective, an important question is the number of empirical investigations researchers have conducted on the topic of NDEs. One way to categorize such research is to differentiate between retrospective and prospective studies. Retrospective studies involve so-called convenience samples of people who, some time after their reported close brush with death, respond to a researcher's strategy to recruit NDErs; identify themselves as having had an NDE; and volunteer to participate in the research. By contrast, in prospective research, the researchers have information about the NDEr's close brush with death before and during the occurrence. So far, researchers have conducted these latter types of studies in hospitals: For a few months or more, the research team has interviewed every consenting patient who experienced a certain medical condition; so far, that condition has been resuscitation from a near-death episode involving cardiac and respiratory arrest. So, in these latter cases, the medical condition has been monitored and documented, and the sample is more complete, consisting of everyone who survived the first moments of physical death and who agreed to be interviewed. One of the primary advances in near-death research over the first 30 years was a movement from retrospective toward prospective studies.

The two types of studies each have their advantages. Many NDEs occur in the absence of cardiac arrest; these are included in retrospective studies, making them potentially more comprehensive. However, because retrospective studies depend on volunteers, several types of NDErs—for example, those who are shy, whose NDEs seem to them too subtle or too personal to share, or who don't realize their experience "qualifies" as an NDE—might self-select out of volunteering, making the retrospective sample of volunteers nonrepresentative of the complete population of NDErs. One of the important questions about NDEs is whether they are occurring, at least sometimes, when "all physical systems are down"; this question can be answered only in conditions of confirmed and closely monitored cardiac arrest and resuscitation—in prospective hospital studies. Not surprisingly, the two types of studies have yielded some similar and some different findings, a topic addressed throughout this volume. At the same time that prospective studies are a more thorough investigation into a narrower subgroup of NDErs, they are more difficult and expensive to conduct, which is why, as the following analysis reveals, researchers have undertaken such studies much less frequently.

The following analysis is based primarily on listings in the *Index,* with the addition of the few major books that were not reported in the periodical literature. It excludes the numerous individual case studies of NDErs.

Results indicate that in the first 30 years of modern NDE research, U.S. researchers had conducted the largest number of retrospective studies—at least 34 researchers or research teams conducting at least 42 studies— involving sample sizes ranging from four to over 300 NDErs, for a total of over 2,500 NDEr research participants. Of these, 19 studies addressed the experience itself, including its phenomenology/contents, incidence, and correlates; 8 addressed NDE aftereffects—how people had changed in the aftermaths of their NDEs; and 15 addressed both.

Outside the United States, 11 researchers or research teams had conducted at least 13 retrospective studies, most on Western continents of Europe and Australia, with a total sample of over 600 NDErs; 5 retrospective studies in non-Western countries of Asia, with a total sample of over 70 NDErs; and none in South America or Africa. Studies in both Western and non-Western cultures outside the United States addressed the experience, its aftereffects, or both.

At least 10 prospective North American and European researchers or research teams had published as many studies, involving a total of about 270 NDErs. Like retrospective studies, these prospective studies addressed the experience, its aftereffects, or both. As of 2005, prospective research outside these Western culture areas had yet to be published.

Taken together, it is safe to say that between 1975 and 2005, at least 55 researchers or research teams in North America, Europe, Australia, and Asia published at least 65 research studies involving nearly 3,500 NDErs, addressing the experience, its aftereffects, or both. It is primarily the results of these scholarly inquiries that authors reviewed in the chapters of this book.

OTHER PATTERNS IN THE SCHOLARLY PERIODICAL NDE LITERATURE

Shifting perspectives, another approach to the history of the field of near-death studies involves examination of patterns in the NDE-related periodical literature overall; again, these patterns are revealed through an analysis of the *Index.* For example, an overall frequency distribution of scholarly articles published each year in the *Journal of Near-Death Studies* and in other publications combined reveals that scholarly publication on NDEs burgeoned in the 1976–1980 five-year period, peaked in the 1991– 1995 period, and gradually declined but still remained numerous in the decade since 1995. Among the top-ranked periodicals for number of articles addressing NDEs, the clear leader, *Anabiosis/Journal of Near-Death Studies,* produced nearly 15 times the number of articles than the next

Table 1.1
Top 22 Sole or First Authors of Scholarly Articles Addressing NDEs through 2005, Ranked by Number of Articles
and Most Recent Article

Rank	Number of Articles	Author	Most Recent Article	Rank	Current Position/Status
1	37	Greyson, Bruce	2005	1	Professor, psychiatry
2	25	Ring, Kenneth	1997	11	Retired professor, social psychology
3	16	Lundahl, Craig	2001	7	Retired professor, sociology, business
4	14	Noyes, Russell	1989	20	Retired professor, psychiatry
	14	Serdahely, William	1996	14	Chaplain
6	11	Sabom, Michael	2005	1	Cardiologist
7	10	Becker, Carl	1995	15	Professor, philosophy
	10	Kellehear, Allan	1994	17	Professor, sociology, health sciences
9	9	Blackmore, Susan	1998	10	Retired professor, psychology; freelance writer, lecturer
	9	Greene, F. Gordon	2003	6	Independent researcher
	9	Grosso, Michael	2001	7	Retired professor, philosophy
	9	Holden, Janice	2005	1	Professor, counseling
13	8	Morse, Melvin	1997	11	Pediatrician
	8	Stevenson, Ian	1995	15	Deceased professor, psychiatry
15	7	Rogo, D. Scott	1984	20	Deceased freelance writer, lecturer
16	6	Jansen, Karl	2000	9	Psychiatrist
	6	Twemlow, Stuart	1997	11	Medical director, psychiatry
18	5	Gabbard, Glen	1991	19	Director, hospital psychiatry clinic
	5	Gibbs, John	2005	1	Professor, developmental psychology
	5	Hyslop, James H.	1918	22	Deceased professor, philosophy
	5	Irwin, Harvey	1993	18	Retired professor, psychology
	5	Wren-Lewis, John	2005	1	Deceased professor, psychology

highest periodical. Of the other journals that produced the most NDE-related literature, seven could be categorized in the field of medicine, six in parapsychology, five in psychology, four in thanatology, and three in religion. The topic clearly cuts across several major disciplines.

Finally, sheer number and recency of a scholar's publications do not assess quality or impact on the field but are only a crude indicator of who are the leading past and present figures in the field of near-death studies. Still, an analysis of these admittedly crude factors has some value; see Table 1.1. Of course, it's not quite fair to draw comparisons between living, active scholars and deceased or retired ones (several of the latter are represented in this table). Further, some groundbreaking authors in the field of near-death studies are not included in this listing. For example, whereas prospective research has probably had the greatest impact on the field, most of the authors of articles about those studies have been single-publication authors, so they do not appear in this list. This listing is intended to be, not a competition, but, rather, one admittedly limited indication of scholarly productivity regarding the topic of NDEs.

One other interesting observation from the *Index* is the number of articles addressing each of the 135 NDE-related topics the developers used in their content analysis. Of particular interest for this research-focused book is that the most-often addressed topic appears to be *methodology in NDE research*. Happily, the next most frequently addressed topic is *characteristics of NDEs—emotions—pleasurable*. The next three specific topics, in order, are *characteristics of NDEs—autoscopy, out-of-body*; *characteristics of NDEs—light, mystical*; and *altered states and NDEs*. Even though these topics have received a lot of attention, in relative terms, they have not in absolute terms: The actual amount of research published to date has barely scratched the surface of what may, one hopes, someday be a much more comprehensive picture of the NDE.

At the other end of the spectrum, the least frequently addressed topic—with only one citation listed—is *humor and NDEs*. Researchers apparently consider NDEs to be no laughing matter. All kidding aside, at least several of the least-addressed topics already begin to indicate sorely needed areas for further research: *religion and NDEs—Islam* with only two citations, *characteristics of NDErs—psychic abilities* with four, *circumstances of NDEs—combat related* with four, and *religion and NDEs—indigenous cultures* and *religion and NDEs—Judaism* with six each.

That authors in the first 30 years of contemporary near-death studies have published over 600 scholarly articles addressing NDEs attests to the extent of professional curiosity about these experiences, their aftereffects, and their implications. The following section describes conceptual trends and foci that have emerged in the field over the three decades.

RESEARCH FOCI, TRENDS, CHALLENGES, AND QUESTIONS IN THE FIELD OF NEAR-DEATH STUDIES

The "gold standard" of research, involving random assignment of participants to experimental and control conditions, is not currently feasible in the study of NDEs. As intellectually appealing as would be a study along the lines of the 1970s movie *Flatliners* (Douglas and Bieber 1990), in which medical students bring each other to the brink of death and then resuscitate, such a study poses insurmountable technological barriers— imperfect resuscitation procedures—and, for at least that reason, ethical barriers as well. If such experiments could be performed in the future, they would allow the controlled manipulation of variables and concurrent brain imaging considered state-of-the-art protocol in other areas of biomedical research. As of 2005, only certain rare surgical procedures allow for these conditions (Spetzler et al. 1988).

Indeed, as several authors in this volume have affirmed (see Chapter 6), one of the most robust research results about NDEs is that they are unpredictable. Research has not yet revealed why, among people who are apparently equivalent in terms of their personal characteristics and who survive apparently equivalent physically or psychologically disequilibrating circumstances, only a minority will subsequently report an NDE; nor why, among those who do, the nature of their NDEs can vary so extensively. For these reasons, research so far has been limited to the aforementioned retrospective and prospective methodologies.

Conceptualization, Assessment, and Correlates of NDEs

Understandably, the first focus of NDE research was the experience itself. As scholars began collecting larger samples of NDEs, they developed several distinctive ways of conceptualizing them. Some authors conceptualized NDEs as unfolding in temporal stages: Moody (1975) in his original work; Noyes (1972) in his delineation of sequential stages of resistance, acceptance, and transcendence; and Ring (1980) in his sequential stages of peace, leaving the body, entering a tunnel, encountering a light, and entering a transcendent realm. Others conceptualized NDEs as comprising different components that may or may not occur simultaneously: Noyes (1981) in his description of depersonalization, hyperalertness, and mystical consciousness clusters within the NDE; and Greyson (1983) in his description of cognitive, affective, paranormal, and transcendental components. Yet others conceptualized NDEs as falling into distinct types: Sabom's (1982) in his differentiation of NDEs as autoscopic, transcendental, or mixed; and Greyson and Nancy Evans Bush's (1992) in their differentiation of pleasurable NDEs—those dominated by feelings of peace, joy, and love—from distressing ones—those dominated by feelings of

infect a society exposed to secondhand accounts of NDEs? Could such effects be brought about by cognitive information or only by experiential learning? If such effects could be brought about, should they? What is the evidence that doing so might help a specific group as well as global society? Research into questions about helping NDErs and the effect of NDE education on nonexperiencers are among the topics addressed in Chapter 11.

Explanatory Models and Veridical Perception in NDEs

Perhaps the most provocative topic related to NDEs is what they may reveal about the very nature of human consciousness. Perhaps the most provocative subtopic within this discourse is the phenomenon of veridical perception, in which NDErs have reported that during their NDEs, they perceived events from a perspective outside their physical bodies, events they should not have known based on the location or condition of their physical bodies. Investigators have already published many well-documented examples of veridical perception during NDEs, including those that occurred during closely monitored surgical hypothermic circulatory arrest and those in blind experiencers. However, it is difficult in these uncontrolled examples to rule out retrospectively confounding sources of information such as inadvertent sensory leakage, lucky guesses, and after-the-fact errors in reconstructing the event. Prospective NDE research allows the placement of unexpected visual targets in locations where NDEs are likely to occur, under conditions that can eliminate sensory leakage and retrospective misinterpretation and can correct for lucky guesses. Research on veridical perception is the topic of Chapter 9.

To be comprehensive, any theoretical model of NDEs must incorporate everything currently known about these phenomena, including not only the correlates and aftereffects but also phenomena such as veridical perception. The varieties of models that authors have put forth, assessed for their comprehensive adequacy, are the topic of Chapter 10.

CONCLUSION

Readers of this book will learn much of what scholars and researchers have discovered and theorized about NDEs in the first three decades of the field of near-death studies. They also will learn that much more remains to be discovered and understood.

A large body of evidence from a variety of sources points to the independence of mind and brain, collected most recently by Edward Kelly and his colleagues (2007). However, this evidence, as robust as it is, contradicts the mainstream neurobiological model that the mind originates in the brain. NDEs, which appear to reflect the active functioning of the mind while the brain is impaired, may offer key evidence in this conundrum. If it appears that mental functions can persist in the absence of active brain function, this phenomenon opens up the possibility that some part of humans that performs mental functions might survive death of the brain. Indeed, ample evidence that some aspect of humans persists after bodily death comes from centuries of observations of such phenomena as apparitions of the deceased, purported communication with the deceased through mediumship, children who spontaneously claim to remember previous lives, and deathbed visions. But NDEs offer a degree of rigorous observation and perhaps control over key variables that these other lines of evidence do not. And if an impressive body of evidence indicates that human existence does not end with bodily death, that knowledge might affect humankind's values, attitudes, and behaviors, just as individual NDEs appear to affect individual experiencers' values in the direction of more humane personal decisions and more humanitarian public policy and action.

Thus, the future of scholarly inquiry in the field of near-death studies is of vital importance. The answers to remaining questions about NDEs have the potential to yield benefits along a broad spectrum, ranging from the immediate welfare of NDErs to perhaps the most far-reaching ability of the human species to survive in harmony on Earth.

Pleasurable Western Adult Near-Death Experiences: Features, Circumstances, and Incidence

Nancy L. Zingrone and Carlos S. Alvarado

In 1892, classical scholar, psychical researcher, and psychologist Frederic W. H. Myers wrote, "It is possible that we might learn much were we to question dying persons, on their awakening from some comatose condition, as to their memory of any dream or vision during that state" (Myers 1892, 180). At the time Myers wrote, virtually nothing was known about near-death experiences (NDEs) except that they were reported by some people and that they seemed to influence behavior and attitudes. No researchers had, as yet, compiled systematic knowledge of the many important basic questions about these experiences. Perhaps if Myers had been more actively involved in the study of NDEs, he would have been interested in collecting information about the topic of this chapter: What are the features that define the experience, the things people see, hear, and feel while they are in this "comatose condition"? What are the circumstances under which NDEs can take place? How common are these experiences among individuals who come close to death?

Although researchers are still struggling to answer these questions definitively, the situation today is much better than it was in Myers's times because investigators have at their disposal a specialized literature aimed at addressing these issues. As discussed in Chapter 1 of this volume, writers developed this specialized literature late in the 20th century, following a few earlier attempts at case collections (for example, Bozzano 1934/1937; Egger 1896; Heim 1892).

This chapter reviews the modern literature that has addressed the content of the experience, that is, those features that characterize the experience; the circumstances of occurrence; and issues of NDE incidence. Our survey is limited to pleasurable NDEs experienced by adults in the Western cultural context. The emphasis here is on studies of groups of cases, as opposed to studies limited to single case reports (for example, Irwin and Bramwell 1988) or to analyses of very few cases (for example, Walker, Serdahely, and Bechtel 1991). Neither does this survey consider those statistical analyses in which researchers attempted to relate NDEs to other variables (for example, Alvarado and Zingrone 1997–98; Greyson 2000) or those indexes of depth resulting from the scores of NDE scales (for example, Greyson 1983; Ring 1980).

FEATURES OF NEAR-DEATH EXPERIENCES

Studies of Groups of NDE Features

Limiting discussion to 20th-century research, it is interesting to note that compilations of cases of out-of-body experiences (OBEs) such as Ernesto Bozzano's (1934/1937) and Sylvan Muldoon's (1936) did not pay particular attention to features of the experiences that reportedly had taken place in near-death circumstances. Both authors included NDEs in their accounts as examples of OBEs. Similarly, a writer whose work NDE researchers have often neglected, Robert Crookall, combined OBEs and NDEs in his writings, referring to the latter as the experiences of the "pseudo dead." In one of his books, Crookall (1967) listed many features of the experiences, among them seeing mist when leaving the body, occupying a horizontal position over the physical body both at the beginning and at the end of the experience, perception of a "silver cord connecting the disembodied entity to the physical body," the "double" appearing younger than the physical body, and a rapid reentry into the physical body accompanied by a shock.

In 1975, Raymond Moody published a compilation of over 150 NDE cases. He listed such features of the experience as a sense of ineffability, that is, difficulty in describing the experience verbally; experiencers hearing that they were dead; feelings of peace and quiet; hearing noises such as buzzing and windlike sounds; a sensation of being out of the body; passing through a tunnel; meeting other individuals such as deceased friends; encountering a being of light; having a life review; reaching a border that, if crossed, meant the NDErs could not return to life; and finding that they had returned to their physical bodies.

Bruce Greyson and Ian Stevenson (1980) reported a study with a sample of 78 NDEs. Some of the features they identified were having an OBE (75%); passing through a tunnel or similar structure (31%); entering an unearthly realm (72%); encountering beings (49%); reaching a border or point of no return (57%); having somatic sensations such as warmth or analgesia (71%); auditory phenomena such as music and noises (57%);

distortion in the sense of time (79%); extrasensory perception (ESP; 39%); and panoramic memory (27%). Regarding emotional valence of the experience, NDErs described it as positive (15%), mildly positive (40%), neutral or mildly negative (45%), and very negative (0%).

In his book *Life at Death*, Kenneth Ring (1980) presented a pioneering study for which he created an interview schedule of NDE features. He designed the schedule, the Weighted Core Experience Index (WCEI), to measure the phenomenological variety and depth of NDEs through the evaluation of tapes of NDE interviews. Ring believed NDEs consist of stages. He wrote, "In general, the earlier stages of the experience are more common, and the latter stages manifest themselves with systematically decreasing frequency" (39). Feelings of peace, separation from the body, entering the darkness or a tunnel, seeing the light, and entering the light are the features that constitute Ring's core experience. These features appear on Table 2.1, together with the results of other studies.

Of course, the NDE has more than five features, and Ring (1980) himself documented the existence of additional ones. These include, among other features, reviewing one's life (24%), encountering a presence (41%), encountering deceased loved ones (16%), and deciding to return (57%).

Greyson (1983) developed the Near-Death Experience Scale (NDE Scale), an NDEr self-report instrument, through which Greyson and others have collected a great deal of information about the features of the near-death experience (see Table 2.2). In his initial study of 74 NDErs, Greyson reported that the final 16-item version of the scale included four general aspects: Cognitive, Affective, Paranormal, and Transcendental. Among the items Greyson dropped from the final version, because they correlated below .35 with the rest of the scale, were such features as the experience of time stopping or losing meaning (64%), thoughts being unusually vivid (46%), strange bodily sensations (34%), a tunnel-like region (32%), being detached from surroundings (26%), loss of emotions (22%), experiencing

Table 2.1
Core NDE Features Using Ring's (1980) Weighted Core Experience Index (WCEI)

Study	N	Peace	OBE	Tunnel/ Dark Area	Light	Entered Light
Ring 1980	49	60%	37%	23%	16%	10%
Lindley et al. 1981	55	75%	71%	38%	56%	—
Green and Friedman 1983	50	70%	66%	32%	62%	18%
van Lommel et al. 2001	62	—	24%	31%	23%	—

the self as unreal (19%), and senses blurred or dull (8%). The features of
the NDE Scale appear on Table 2.2.

Michael Sabom (1982) presented the features of NDEs reported by individuals who had their experiences in nonsurgical conditions. All experiencers reported a sense of calm and peace, of separation from the body,
and of return. Other features included the sense of being dead (92%), observation of physical objects and events (53%), a dark region or void
(23%), life review (3%), light (28%), a transcendental environment
(54%), and encountering others (48%).

Others authors have reported such varied pleasurable features as illumi-
nated environments (21%), beautiful landscape and buildings (18%),
heavenly music (11%), and feelings of oneness (21%) (Grey 1985); and
sounds of voices (6%) (Gallup and Proctor 1982). In addition, many other

Table 2.2
Features of NDEs Collected Using Greyson's (1983) NDE Scale

Elements and Features of Scale	Greyson 1983	Greyson 2003	Pacciolla 1995	Schwaninger et al. 2002
N	74	27	24	11
Cognitive Elements				
Altered sense of time	64%	18%	—	9%
Accelerated thought process	19%	44%	—	9%
Life review	22%	30%	50%	9%
Sudden understanding	30%	30%	—	18%
Affective Elements				
Feeling of peace	77%	85%	—	100%
Surrounded with light	43%	70%	46%	63%
Feeling joy	64%	67%	—	18%
Feeling cosmic unity/ oneness	57%	52%	—	45%
Paranormal Elements				
Out of physical body	53%	70%	—	90%
Senses more vivid than usual	38%	15%	—	54%
ESP	23%	11%	—	0%
Visions of the future	16%	7%	—	9%
Transcendental Elements				
Another world	58%	63%	—	54%
Encountered beings	26%	52%	—	72%
Mystical being	47%	26%	—	63%
Point of no return	26%	41%	46%	45%

studies have also included features of the NDE (for example, Athappilly, Greyson, and Stevenson 2006; Fenwick and Fenwick 1995; Knoblauch, Schmied, and Schnettler 2001; Pacciolla 1996; van Lommel et al. 2001).

Hubert Knoblauch, Ina Schmied, and Bernt Schnettler argued that NDEs they had collected in West Germany and East Germany differed significantly in such aspects as positive emotions (West 60%, East 40%), negative emotions (29%, 60%), lights (50%, 30%), and tunnels (31%, 45%). Although the authors presented no systematic comparisons, they also argued that German cases were different from American ones:

> Whereas American NDEs include a certain number of elements that seem to follow one another and are typically experienced as emotionally positive, the majority of German NDEs consist of one element or scene without any temporal sequence or events or motifs. They are equally likely to be experienced either positively or negatively. (Knoblauch, Schmied, and Schnettler 2001, 28)

Although the characterization of American NDEs as following a temporal sequence seems exaggerated and dependent on studies such as Ring's (1980), this speculation presents an interesting line for further research.

Studies of Specific Features

Other researchers have focused on single features of NDEs. For example, one author studied NDErs' reports of spirits they encountered during their NDEs (Kelly 2001). In an analysis of 74 cases, Emily Kelly found 129 reports of encounters with spirits. In most cases, the NDErs described the spirits as deceased persons from a previous generation (81%), such as family members. The remainder were individuals from the experiencer's own generation (16%), such as extended family or spouses, and from the next generation (2%), such as daughters and nephews. For 61 of the 129 reports, Kelly was able to assess the emotional closeness experiencers felt to the spirits they reported encountering. She classified 39 percent as very close, 28 percent as close, 13 percent as friendly but not close or neutral, 3 percent as poor, and 16 percent as cases in which the experiencer claimed not to have known the deceased person in life. In comparing NDEs that included reports of deceased persons to those that did not, Kelly found that such reports occurred more often in the context of accidents and cardiac arrest than in other near-death contexts, a difference that was statistically significant. Cases in which NDErs reported having encountered deceased persons also included significantly more experiences of light and of darkness and a tunnel. An additional statistically significant finding was that the closer NDErs were to death, the more they reported seeing spirits of the deceased.

Stevenson and Emily Cook's (1995) analysis of panoramic memory also made an important contribution to understanding NDEs. The authors studied two series of NDE cases: the first from published sources (N = 68), and the second from their own direct investigations (N = 54). Many cases were associated with sudden conditions such as accidents (Series 1, 84%; Series 2, 50%). Whereas the number of cases varied greatly in terms of their evident features, a substantial majority of NDErs described their NDE images as vivid (88%; 84%). The authors classified the sequence of memories as simultaneous/all at once/panoramic (15%; 27%), from childhood to present (62%; 43%), from present to childhood (15%; 11%), and with no particular sequence (8%; 18%). In Series 2, 71 percent of experiencers reported a sense of lack of time, whereas 20 percent reported time going faster and 7 percent slower. The authors noted:

> The most important finding of the present study is the evidence of a wide variety in the life reviews the subjects experience ... The popular picture of the 'whole life' being seen all at once (panoramically) is false as a generalization about these experiences. Some subjects do indeed have this kind of experience, but the majority [do] not. (Stevenson and Cook 1995, 456)

Research has also revealed details about the nature of NDE visual experiences. Janice Holden (1988) reported a study of 63 NDErs who described the nature of their vision of the material world during their NDEs. They described their vision as clear (79%), free of distortion (76%), and accurate in terms of perceiving color (71%). Respondents also claimed to have experienced a complete field of vision (77%), accurate memory of the environment (61%), and the ability to read (57%).

Other researchers have focused on such aspects of the NDE as accounts of tunnels (Chari 1982), encounters with angels (Lundahl 1992), and visions of the future (Ring 1982). Few researchers have studied veridical NDEs—that is, those NDE experiences during which NDErs obtained information they could not have acquired at any time through the normal means of sensory perception or rational deduction—yet the information was later confirmed to be accurate (Cook, Greyson, and Stevenson 1998; Ring and Lawrence 1993; Sabom 1982; Sartori, Badham, and Fenwick 2006). Cook, Greyson, and Stevenson (1998) presented veridical cases in which the NDErs also experienced enhanced mentation and seeing the physical body, but the authors did not compare the features of the veridical NDEs against those that did not involve the claim of veridical perception. Unfortunately, some prospective studies that researchers designed to include the potential of a veridical component—that is, study designs in which targets were placed around hospital areas in the hopes that potential NDErs would identify them within their experiences—have failed because of a variety of problems (Greyson, Holden, and Mounsey 2006; Parnia

2006). For an in-depth discussion of veridical perception in NDEs, see Chapter 9 of this volume.

Patterns of NDE Features

Crookall (1967) claimed there were stages in all OBEs, in which group he included the experiences of the "pseudo dead." He referred to three events in common between "pseudo dead" experiences, OBEs, clairvoyant visions of observers at deathbeds, and mediumistic communications from purported deceased spirits. These events were (1) a mist is seen emanating from the physical body (mainly through the head), (2) the mist assumes a horizontal position over the physical body and forms a replica of the physical body, and (3) the "double" remains linked to the physical body through a cordlike connection. Although more recent NDE researchers also have reported some of these features (for example, Ring 1980), in general, findings of subsequent research have not supported Crookall's hypothesized sequence of events.

Some researchers have explored the possible existence of patterns within the NDE. Ring (1980) suggested the existence of successive stages consisting of feelings of peace, separation from the body, entering darkness or a tunnel, seeing the light, and entering the light. He found that reports of these features became less frequent as the depth of the experience increased. Although Ring described these features as unfolding sequentially, he acknowledged that dividing the experience into stages could be seen as a "matter of convenience for narrative purposes and not a strict experiential reality" (Ring 1980, 190).

In one study, Ring (1980) found that individuals who reported NDEs after suicide attempts did not go beyond the third stage of NDEs. For example, such experiencers did not see or enter the light. However, in a later analysis (Ring and Franklin 1981–82), the researchers did not find confirmation of this pattern.

Sabom (1982) provided an interesting discussion of the patterns in NDEs in his classification of 71 NDEs as autoscopic (29.5%), that is, as experiences in which NDErs reported having observed their physical bodies and the immediate environment from an out-of-body perspective; transcendental (53.5%), that is, as experiences in which NDErs reportedly found themselves in a locale different from the physical world; and combined (17%), a category in which NDErs reported both features. Although Sabom did not perform any statistical analysis to validate his classification, analyses by chapter coauthor Carlos Alvarado performed using Sabom's data can be construed as supporting aspects of his conceptual framework. Among NDErs who saw the area around the physical body, those whose NDEs contained veridical features reported significantly fewer "other-world" features—such as a dark region or void, a transcendental environment, or seeing spirits—than did those whose NDEs did not contain veridical features (Alvarado 1997, 25).

Russell Noyes and Donald Slymen (1978–79) factor analyzed NDEs and reported finding a three-factor solution. They characterized these factors as mystical, such as great understanding, visual imagery, or memories; depersonalization, such as loss of emotion, derealization, or separation from body; and hyperalertness, such as vivid fast thoughts or sharp vision and hearing.

A cluster analysis of the NDE Scale (Greyson 1985) yielded four groups of features: Cognitive, such as time distortion and thought acceleration; Affective, such as feelings of peace and joy; Paranormal, such as extrasensory perception (ESP) or OBE; and Transcendental, such as encounters with beings or having a sense of a border. A more recent analysis of NDE Scale data provided evidence for a single hierarchical dimension of features (Lange, Greyson, and Houran 2004). Based on this finding, the authors asserted that "NDEs indeed appear to form a 'core' experience whose basic structure and semantics are preserved regardless of demographic differences and extreme variation in the intensity of NDE" (Lange, Greyson, and Houran 2004, 173).

Number of Case Features

Accounts of NDEs show that the number of features varies from case to case. Experience reports range from those with a few features, such as being out of the body and seeing the physical body, to those that include many other observations such as the ones included on Tables 2.1 and 2.2. Out of 49 NDEs, Ring considered 45 percent to be moderate in depth, with 6–9 features, and the remaining 55 percent to be deep, with over 10 features. Using the same instrument and criterion for determining NDE depth with a sample of 16 NDErs, Greyson (1986) found 62.5 percent reported moderate experiences and 37.5 percent reported deep experiences. Using the same instrument but a different criterion for depth, Pim van Lommel and others (2001) classified 34 percent as superficial, with 1–5 features; 29 percent as moderately deep; 27.4 percent as deep; and 9.7 percent as very deep, with 15–19 features.

In an analysis of Cherie Sutherland's (1992/1995) data, chapter coauthors Alvarado and Nancy Zingrone (1997–98) found that the WCEI of 51 individuals had a mean of 14.0 features with a range from six to 24 features (SD = 5.38). Further analyses showed that when divided by the median value (14.5), 57 percent of the scores fell below and 43 percent above the median. It should be clear that the number of NDE features per case is highly variable.

Relationship between NDE Features and Other Variables

This section focuses on specific NDE features and not on scores based on counts of features made using the WCEI and the NDE Scale, as such analyses are discussed in Chapter 6 of this volume.

Demographic Variables

Overall, researchers have not found significant relationships between specific NDE features and demographic variables, with the following exceptions. Greyson and Stevenson (1980) found that executives and professionals reported tunnels in their NDEs more often than did laborers and service workers. They also found that women reported entering unearthly realms more often than did men; that NDErs whose experiences occurred at home or outdoors reported encounters with nonphysical beings more often than did those whose experiences occurred in hospitals or other public places; and that the more NDErs reported positive emotions in their NDEs, the more they also were likely to report distortions of time in their experiences. In addition, NDErs who reported feeling that time was slowing during their NDEs were less likely to have used drugs and alcohol on the day of the experience and to report having been relatively more religious before the experience.

Sabom (1982) did not find significant relationships between specific NDE features and age, sex, education, occupation, or religion of the NDErs. The differences he did find were centered on encountering spirits. The NDErs who were women or were employed as laborers or service workers reported more encounters with spirits than did NDErs who were men or were employed as professionals.

In one study, men NDErs reported significantly more experiences with lights and tunnels than did women. Women NDErs also reported sensing presences and seeing colors more often than did men (Morris and Knafl 2003).

Medical Variables and Expectations

Ring (1980) found that NDErs reported panoramic memory more often in the near-death circumstance of accidents (55%) than in the circumstances of illnesses and suicide attempts combined (16%). He also found that no suicide attempters either saw or entered a light in their NDEs, whereas subjects whose NDEs occurred under other circumstance sometimes did. However, a later study (Ring and Franklin 1981–82) did not replicate this finding: Among these subjects, some suicide attempters did sometimes see and enter a light in their NDEs.

In Stuart Twemlow, Glen Gabbard, and Lolafaye Coyne's study (1982), four NDErs who had been given drugs reported bizarre visual experiences.

In addition, the authors noted that individuals whose NDEs occurred in association with cardiac arrest "seem[ed] ... to have experienced out-of-body phenomena at a significantly earlier age than other groups" (Twemlow, Gabbard, and Coyne 1982, 136). However, this study included only 33 cases. Replications of such findings in studies that include more cases are needed.

A few studies have shown differences in the features of NDEs when experiencers believed they were close to death. Gabbard, Twemlow, and Fowler Jones (1981) found more reports of seeing lights and tunnels, hearing unusual sounds, seeing the physical body, and encountering spiritual entities among experiencers who thought they were close to death than among those who did not. In two further analyses, Alvarado (1997) found similar patterns. One of these analyses involved a comparison of cases from Sabom (1982) and Crookall (1961, 1964). Results were that people whose experiences occurred when they were near-death reported significantly more tunnels, spirits, observations of events taking place close to the body, and lights than did those whose experiences occurred when they were not near death. In the other study (Alvarado 2001), the near-death group presented more reports of tunnels, sounds, spiritual entities, OBE with seeing the physical body, and lights than the comparison group, but the differences were statistically significant only with seeing the physical body and the presence of lights.

Other researchers have addressed the relationship of closeness to death and NDE features by examining medical records. They found that in those NDE cases in which records confirmed that experiencers had been medically close to death, significantly more NDErs reported lights and enhanced cognitive function than did NDErs whose records had not fulfilled the medical criteria for closeness to death (Owens, Cook, and Stevenson 1990).

NDE features have occurred in individuals who are not close to death physiologically (Gabbard and Twemlow 1991; Owens, Cook, and Stevenson 1990). For these individuals, "it would seem that among those who were not near death their experiences were precipitated by their belief that they were" (Owens, Cook, and Stevenson 1990, 1177). This finding is clear in those cases in which NDEs take place during falls or accidents in which the experience appears to occur at the time when the person has not yet suffered any physical injury, as when NDErs sees themselves falling prior to impact (for example, Gabbard and Twemlow 1991; Noyes et al. 1977).

Other NDE Features

Justine Owens, Cook, and Stevenson (1990) found a relationship between reported features. Their subjects who reported a light component in their NDEs also tended to report tunnels, enhanced cognitive functions, and positive emotions.

Section Summary

The studies conducted so far have shown that some features, such as OBEs, are common, whereas others, such as hearing music, are less frequent. Considering as a whole the studies that have addressed NDE features, findings are similar enough to support the idea that the NDE is an identifiable phenomenon with a relatively specific array of features. However, because of differences in the feature lists of various studies, no single, clear, uniform pattern of NDE features has yet emerged. Further work conducted with larger samples and aimed at replicating previous results may help to advance a comprehensive understanding of NDE features.

CIRCUMSTANCES OF NDE OCCURRENCE

From early in recorded history, many authors have pointed to conditions in which NDEs took place. Some 19th-century discussions included falling off mountains (Heim 1892) and drowning (Egger 1896). Years later, Bozzano (1934/1937) presented 20 cases of OBEs and NDEs published in the spiritualist and psychical research literatures. His cases that seemed to have occurred in near-death circumstances included two during illness, one while the experiencer was being shot, and one each during smoke inhalation, asphyxia, a fall, and a coma.

Greyson and Stevenson (1980) analyzed 78 NDEs found to have taken place during illness (40%), traumatic injury (37%), surgery (13%), childbirth (7%), and the use of drugs (4%). Forty-one percent of the experiencers believed they had been pronounced dead, and 52 percent believed they were actually dying.

In Ring's (1980) study, he classified 48 NDErs as having gone through illness (60%), accidents (23%), and suicide attempts (17%). In another study of 50 NDEs, researchers found that 48 percent of experiencers were ill at the time of the experience, 44 percent were in an accident, and 8 percent had attempted suicide (Green and Friedman 1983).

Greyson (1983) reported on 69 cases that took place during complications of surgery or childbirth (33%), exacerbation of existing illness or problem pregnancies (23%), accidents (22%), sudden natural events such as cardiac arrest (10%), loss of consciousness from unknown causes (6%), and suicide attempts (6%).

A study by Stevenson, Cook, and Nicholas McClean-Rice (1989–1990) showed that out of 40 cases in which medical records were examined, most of the cases took place during illness, surgery, and childbirth (72.5%). The rest happened during accidents (22.5%) and drug overdose (5%). Whereas

82.5 percent of persons having the NDE believed they had been near death, medical records confirmed their claims in only 45 percent of cases. Another study, this one examining 58 NDErs, used the same categories to group cases; here, researchers found that 71 percent of NDEs occurred during illness, 22 percent during surgery, and 7 percent during childbirth (Owens et al. 1990). Their findings also suggested that medical circumstances were not the only trigger conditions of NDEs, a topic further discussed later in this chapter. In two studies, Noyes and his colleagues found no medical closeness to death at the time of many of the experiences reported (Noyes et al. 1977; Noyes and Slymen 1978–79).

Twemlow, Gabbard, and Coyne (1982) performed a cluster analysis of the medical conditions of 33 NDErs. They found several clusters formed by low stress (16 cases), emotional stress (6), intoxicants (in which drugs were involved, 4), cardiac arrest (4), and anesthesia (3).

Greyson (2003) reported data supporting the importance of cardiac arrest. He wrote that those patients "admitted with cardiac arrest reported significantly more near-death experiences than did patients admitted with other cardiac diagnoses. Near-death experiences were ten times more likely to be reported by survivors of cardiac arrest than by patients with any other cardiac diagnosis."

In Greyson's view, this finding supports the association of NDEs to proximity to death. Sam Parnia, D. G. Waller, R. Yeates, and Peter Fenwick (2001), on the other hand, reported a low incidence of NDEs (6.3%) in a prospective sample of 63 patients who survived cardiac arrest.

A recent study addressed NDEs reported by kidney dialysis patients (Lai et al. 2007). Although conducted outside the Western context to which our review is limited—the patients surveyed were from Taiwan—the study is included here because it presents NDEs drawn from a medical condition heretofore neglected in the Western NDE literature. The authors wrote:

> Although 33 NDEs occurred before the initiation of renal replacement therapy, 16 NDE-associated life-threatening events were associated with uremia (uremic encephalopathy or lung edema) and occurred just before dialysis therapy initiation. The other 6 NDEs occurred within five years before dialysis therapy initiation in the setting of chronic kidney disease. (Lai et al. 2007, 129)

The authors concluded that NDEs were not uncommon in dialysis patients, because 45 out of 710 patients (6.3%) reported NDEs.

Comparisons are difficult with these data because of the different ways various researchers classified the circumstances in question. Some of the categories they used may overlap. For example, in some studies researchers compared the motive to commit suicide with the means (circumstances) of other NDEs, although a suicide attempt may itself involve one of several means, such as drugs or a fall. One opportunity for future research is to establish a standardized way for future investigators to categorize NDE circumstances. Such a system could clarify the categorization of, and relationship between, NDE-related means and motives and would enable more meaningful comparisons of findings.

Section Summary

Research has revealed a variety of circumstances under which NDEs take place. Although some researchers have indicated that severe conditions such as cardiac arrest are particularly important in the production of the experience, this conjecture has not yet reached the status of a well-established conclusion. Some researchers have also found that NDEs can take place under conditions of no actual medical threat to life but in which experiencers may only fear or expect death.

INCIDENCE OF NDEs

Greyson (1998) wrote that "accurate estimates" of the incidence of near-death experiences "would give physicians needed perspective on these anomalous events" (92). As discussed later in this chapter, a variety of authors have attempted to establish these "accurate estimates." But as Greyson (1998) has noted, some facets of researchers' data gathering have diminished the reliability of the estimates they have obtained so far. Therefore, before one can estimate incidence, it is important to set aside those studies in which investigators (1), failed to use adequate methods to identify NDEs, and (2), failed to distinguish prevalence from incidence correctly. Studies that suffer from these problems have been historically important both to the development of the definition of the NDE and to the establishment of the methods by which researchers have assessed the presence or absence of an NDE. Such studies cannot, however, contribute to the reliable setting of an accurate estimate of incidence.

This section also comments on some methodological disadvantages noted by commentators in regard to retrospective studies of incidence that apply also to prospective studies.

Definition and Incidence

In the near-death literature, researchers have defined incidence in various ways, with most researchers employing "working definitions that allow for considerable ambiguity in descriptions of both the phenomenology and the frequency of the experience" (Greyson 1998, 93). As mentioned earlier in this chapter, two investigators have undertaken the main empirical efforts to construct easily administered scales to determine the presence or absence of an NDE: Ring's WCEI (for example, Ring 1980) and Greyson's

NDE Scale (Greyson 1983). Whereas both researchers developed their assessments based on phenomenological examinations of NDE cases, only Greyson (1983) established his scale psychometrically.

In many studies, researchers used definitions of NDEs that ranged widely, from rather uniform to extremely disparate. This range has rendered the results of these studies less applicable to the process of establishing NDE incidence. Among the studies conceptually distant from the phenomenological features covered in the WCEI and the NDE Scale are those in which investigators questioned only experiencers' beliefs about their nearness to death and not the features of their experiences (for example, Thomas, Cooper, and Soscovich 1982–83), addressed experiences not specifically related to being near death (for example, Morse et al. 1986; Morse, Connor, and Tyler 1985; Schnaper and Panitz 1990), defined the experience near death too broadly (for example, Gallup and Proctor 1982), or defined it too superficially (for example, Finkelmeier, Kenwood, and Summers 1984; Tosch 1988; van Lommel et al. 2001).

But what do studies involving an idiosyncratic definition of the phenomena reveal? Without acceptable feature-based criteria such as the WCEI or the NDE Scale, it is difficult to tell.

Prevalence versus Incidence

An additional problem with estimating incidence is the propensity for authors to confuse the terms "incidence" and "prevalence." Although in other disciplines authors have used these terms interchangably, in medicine and epidemiology the terms denote substantially different concepts. In this latter literature, prevalence refers to the lifetime estimate of NDEs in the experience of respondents or patients; it answers the question of how many people are likely to have one or more NDEs over the course of their lifetimes. By contrast, incidence refers to the number of NDEs reported by a specific cohort defined by their recent experience of predefined medically near-death conditions such that it is possible to be relatively sure that the NDE being reported occurred in the context of that condition; it answers the question of how many people under certain medical circumstances are likely to have NDEs. As Greyson has noted, "Prevalence will necessarily be greater than ... incidence". (Greyson 1998, 98). Furthermore, whereas the distinction between the two terms is not relevant in studies that focus on phenomenology, it is relevant in studies aimed at establishing estimates of NDE frequency.

These definitions notwithstanding, a previous review (Greyson 1998) included studies in which investigators had mischaracterized their reported percentages as incidence (for example, Finkelmeier, Kenwood, and Summers 1984; Gallup and Proctor 1982; Green and Freidman 1983; Thomas, Cooper, and Suscovich 1982–83). Because these investigators made no attempt to tie specific experience reports to specific near-death events or to make sure that experiences recounted by a defined cohort occurred during near-death events as the authors had defined them, these investigators were, in fact, sampling prevalence and not incidence. Whereas NDE research can profit from an emphasis on both types of studies—that is, those that provide incidence estimates as well as those that provide prevalence estimates—the latter should not be included in reviews of the former.

Methodological Challenges

In a previous review of NDE incidence, Greyson discussed the representativeness of samples used to establish incidence. He expressed the view that

> samples that are not random or do not comprise an intact cohort may produce estimates of NDE incidence skewed by unidentified variables. This bias is most likely to arise in studies that rely on voluntary subjects who respond to advertisements or on subjects referred by sources familiar with the investigators' interest, and in studies in which large proportions of potential subjects opt not to participate. (Greyson 1998, 95)

Voluntary subjects, Greyson believed, could inadvertently be skewed in one direction or another by the wording of the recruitment advertising and by their knowledge of the investigator and his or her interest in the topic. A number of researchers (for example, Green and Friedman 1983; Lindley, Bryan, and Conley 1981; Ring and Franklin 1981–82) have discussed the likelihood that the content of their initial advertisement biased their results.

Further, Greyson (1998) noted that subjects who were referred to the researcher could have been solicited on the basis of the referring person's knowledge of the investigator's interests. Some authors who have constructed their samples through referrals have, indeed, acknowledged this problem in their datasets (for example, Orne 1995; Ring 1979; Tosch 1988).

For Greyson (1998), an additional complication for the procurement of biased samples was the high refusal rates associated even with surveys that targeted populations identified as having been medically near death (for example, Finkelmeier, Kenwood, and Summers 1984; Green and Freidman 1983; see also Pacciolla 1996). More problematic, Greyson felt, were the refusal rates in surveys of less-well-defined populations (for example, Olson and Dulaney 1993).

Finally, Greyson (1998) noted that social rapport between interviewers and interviewees could have an impact on the accuracy of the incidence estimates obtained (96). In other words, subjects who did not feel rapport with their interviewers might not have disclosed NDEs they actually had

had, or if they did disclose their NDEs, they might have recounted only some of the features they had actually experienced.

Some scholars believe that prospective research obviates the sampling problems of retrospective research, that is, volunteer-based case collections, surveys, and interview studies. In prospective studies (for example, Greyson 2003; Parnia et al. 2001; Schwaninger et al. 2002; van Lommel et al. 2001), an intact cohort of potential respondents is identified by specifying a life-threatening or life-ending medical event in a specific hospital or set of hospitals for a specific period of time. Researchers set up criteria to derive a subset of that cohort who are deemed capable of being interviewed and who, potentially, may agree to participate in the study.

Some scholars (for example, Greyson 1998) have asserted that this prospective method produces unbiased samples that might yield more accurate estimates of NDE incidence. However, prospective methodology reduces but does not entirely eliminate sample bias. First, given that decision points occur at various stages in prospective studies, it is possible that bias could creep in at those points, especially if the potential for bias is not acknowledged and no effort is made to prevent it. For example, specified criteria for "interviewability" of potential subjects may vary from study to study. The resulting levels of discretion that study collaborators have may affect the pool of interviewees presented to the interviewers. In one case, the study by Sam Parnia and his colleagues, the fourth criterion listed for including patients in the pool of interviewees was "agreement to the interview by the medical and nursing staff caring for the patient" (Parnia et al. 2001, 151). Although investigators may assume that such agreement flows only from medical concerns, other aspects of the relationship of doctors and nurses to the investigator or to the patients and their families may influence the decision to agree to or to block inclusion. It is difficult in such cases to be sure that the resulting sample is bias-free. More problematic in this regard are those studies (for example, van Lommel et al. 2001) in which the authors did not describe adequately the criteria they used to obtain the pool of interviewees.

As previously stated, some authors have identified two other retrospective study elements as potential sources of bias in an accurate assessment of incidence: the high refusal rate of convenience samples and the potential impact of social rapport on disclosure of NDEs. Scholars have asserted that these elements are absent in prospective research (for example, Greyson 1998). However, both of these disadvantages apply to prospective studies as well. The exclusion rate appears to be comparable between retrospective and prospective studies. For example, in their prospective study, Janet Schwaninger and her colleagues (2002) identified 174 individuals as members of their presumably unbiased cohort, yet only 30 survived the life-threatening event, were deemed appropriate for interview, and agreed to participate. This is equivalent to a 17 percent response rate when taken as a percentage of the original presumably unbiased cohort. Even more problematic are researchers who did not specify the size of the initial cohort (for example, Parnia et al. 2001); without the ability to calculate "response rate," analysts cannot even begin to speculate as to the possible extent of bias in NDE incidence results.

Finally, researchers must assess the levels of social rapport between the researchers and the medical personnel who decide whether a patient is appropriate for interview and between the interviewers and the patients and their families. Without clear assessment, the extent to which social rapport has biased inclusion in the group of individuals ultimately inter-viewed and has, thereby, potentially biased estimates of NDE incidence cannot be known.

Acknowledging that these methodological complications apply to pro-spective studies as well as to retrospective studies will spur future research-ers to refine the procedures and protocols that investigators have used up to now. Such additional refinements have the potential to reduce further the levels of bias inherent in all types of NDE studies. We believe it is im-portant, however, for NDE researchers to recognize that there is, in fact, no such thing as an unbiased cohort or bias-free study. There are only studies that reduce bias to the lowest level possible given the structure and constraints of the research program at hand.

Reliable Incidence

Greyson's review of NDE incidence presented a table that included 30 studies (Greyson 1998, 84). Ten years ago, an exhaustive table of this kind was very useful in illustrating that incidence estimates had varied widely over the life of the literature, that incidence had been occasionally con-fused with prevalence, and that different types of studies and different types of NDE measurements contributed to variance in the estimates pre-sented. At the present point of development in the field of near-death studies, however, it is important to focus instead on those studies that reli-ably and conservatively estimate incidence.

To this end, our analysis excludes the majority of studies represented on Greyson's (1998) table. Also excluded are three studies in which the non-Western populations surveyed therein are beyond the scope of this chapter (Pasricha 1992, 1993; Zhi-ying and Jian-xun 1992). In addition, eight of the Western studies are excluded because they obtained estimates of preva-lence rather than incidence (Finkelmeier, Kenwood, and Summers 1984; Gallup and Proctor 1982; Green and Freidman 1983; Locke and Shontz 1983; Olson and Dulaney 1993; Ring 1980; Sabom 1982; Thomas, Cooper, and Suscovich 1982–1983). Further excluded are 11 studies because the researchers used questions to determine presence or absence of an NDE that either they did not describe or they described too broadly or too nonspecifically for this analysis to consider their incidence findings reliable (Lawrence 1995a, 1995b; Lindley, Bryan, and Conley 1981; Morse, Conner, and Tyler 1985; Morse et al. 1986; Morse and Perry 1990; Rosen 1975; Sabom and Kreutziger 1978; Schnaper and Panitz 1990; Tosch 1988; White and Liddon 1972). Finally, this analysis excludes two studies because they were case collections of the authors' personal experience and of other subjects whom friends, relatives, and other individuals had referred to the authors (Audette 1979; Grey 1985).

Thus, included on our table of incidence are Greyson's (1998) six remaining studies (Greyson 1986; Milne 1995; Orne 1995; Pacciolla 1996; Ring and Franklin 1981–82; Schoenbeck and Hocutt 1991) and five subsequent studies (Greyson 2003; Greyson, Holden, and Mounsey 2006; Parnia et al. 2001; Schwaninger et al. 2002; van Lommel et al. 2001) that also met our criteria. As can be seen on Table 2.3, of the studies listed, two were retrospective in design, including one with a referral-based sample (Orne 1995) and one in which NDErs were recruited through a newspaper advertisement (Ring and Franklin 1981–82). The remaining nine studies were prospective in design (Greyson 1986, 2003, 2006; Milne 1995; Pacciolla 1996; Parnia et al. 2001; Schoenbeck and Hocutt, 1991; Schwaninger et al. 2002; van Lommel et al. 2001).

The method of determining the presence or absence of an NDE also varied between studies. In two studies (Greyson 1986; Ring and Franklin 1981–82), researchers administered the WCEI (Ring 1980). In two others (Milne 1995; Orne 1995), researchers administered the NDE Scale (Greyson 1983) but did not specify or did not use the accepted threshold score of 7 to determine the presence of an NDE. In another study, the researchers developed their own NDE interview schedule as well as NDE depth criteria that yielded categories ranging from "superficial" to "deep" (van Lommel et al. 2001, 2041). In the remaining six studies (Greyson 2003; Greyson et al. 2006; Pacciolla 1995; Parnia et al. 2001; Schwaninger et al. 2002; Schoenbeck and Hocutt 1991), researchers included as NDErs only those subjects whose NDE Scale scores reached or exceeded the threshold score of 7.

Further analysis of incidence by the method researchers used to determine the presence of an NDE reveals that the NDE Scale with a criterion score of 7 yields an average incidence of 17 percent, the NDE Scale with unspecified criterion score yields 18 percent, the van Lommel and others' (2001) NDE interview schedule yields 18 percent, and the WCEI yields 37 percent. The tendency for incidence estimates to be higher with the WCEI than with the NDE Scale is in keeping with previous findings (Greyson 1998).

The analysis here finds the average incidence estimate of the retrospective studies combined is 35 percent, whereas that of the prospective studies combined is 17 percent. These findings are not out of step with Greyson's (1998)

Table 2.3
Estimate of Incidence in NDE Studies

Study	Population	N	n	NDEs	Incidence	Criteria
Greyson 1986*	suicide attempters	61	61	16	26%	WCEI
Greyson 2003*	cardiac arrest	1,595	116	27	23%	NDE Scale $\geq$ 7
Greyson et al. 2006*	induced cardiac arrest	52	52	0	0%	NDE Scale $\geq$ 7
Milne 1995*	hemodynamic instability	86	42	6	14%	NDE Scale
Orne 1995**	cardiac arrest	—	191	44	23%	NDE Scale
Pacciolla 1996*	various, requiring resuscitation	125	64	24	38%	NDE Scale $\geq$ 7
Parnia et al. 2001*	cardiac arrest	—	63	4	6%	NDE Scale $\geq$ 7
Ring and Franklin 1981–1982***	suicide attempters	—	36	17	47%	WCEI
Schwaninger et al. 2002*	cardiac arrest	174	30	7	23%	NDE Scale $\geq$ 7
Schoenbeck and Hocutt 1991*	cardiac arrest	—	11	1	9%	NDE Scale $\geq$ 7
van Lommel* et al. 2001	cardiac arrest	344	344	62	18%	unspecified NDE interview schedule

Notes:
N = population identified for study
n = sample of interviewees
* Prospective study
** Retrospective study, Referred sample
*** Retrospective study, Advertisement recruitment
WCEI = Weighted Core Experience Index (Ring 1980)
NDE Scale = Near-Death Experience Scale (Greyson 1983)

conclusion that the most reliable estimates of incidence range from 9 percent to 18 percent.

Section Summary

Over the history of NDE research, researchers have made efforts to estimate the incidence of NDEs. Confusion over the use of the terms "prevalence" and "incidence" has diminished: Most researchers now understand that studies that yield counts of lifetime occurrence of NDEs are estimating prevalence, whereas those that yield counts of how many NDEs occurred to a specified group of individuals who have undergone a specified life-threatening or temporarily life-ending event within a stated period of time are estimating incidence. Prospective studies have now become the method of choice for investigators attempting to set reliable estimates of incidence because such studies reduce, but do not eliminate, sampling bias. The measurement of the presence or absence of an NDE through the administration of either the WCEI (Ring 1980) or the NDE Scale (Greyson, 1983) with a threshold score of 7 has become the norm.

Although estimates of incidence still vary, researchers conducting retrospective studies may reasonably expect an average incidence of 35 percent, and those conducting prospective studies may reasonably expect an average incidence of 17 percent. Furthermore, those researchers who use the WCEI to determine presence or absence of an NDE may expect a substantially higher incidence estimate than those who use the threshold score of 7 on the NDE Scale.

RECOMMENDATIONS FOR FURTHER RESEARCH

Features

Many features of the NDE deserve further exploration. NDE researchers should pay more attention to the OBE literature (for example, Alvarado and Zingrone 1999; Green 1968) and study such features as how experiencers perceive themselves during the experience—such as with or without a body, as points of light, or other variants—and why some experiencers find that shocks or jolts accompany their return to their physical bodies (Alvarado and Zingrone 1997). Although Ring (1980) presented some relevant data, these predominantly neglected aspects of the experience may be theoretically important.

For example, Greyson and Stevenson (1980) profitably explored various aspects of the OBE component of NDEs, such a seeing the physical body, the sensation of having a nonphysical body, and the experience of reentry into the physical body. Stevenson and Cook (1995) and Kelly (2001) have also provided detailed explorations of NDE features and the interaction of specific features with other features as well as with other variables. More research along these lines is needed.

The importance of veridical NDEs has been largely overlooked. This feature is very important theoretically because it has the potential to expand explanations of the NDE beyond physiological or psychological processes. Unfortunately, very few researchers have been interested in the veridicality of NDEs. Although several questionnaire studies included reports of extrasensory perception during the NDE (see Table 2.2), very few investigators have attempted to determine whether or not potentially verifiable aspects of the experience actually took place as NDErs had claimed. Still fewer researchers have attempted to determine if information NDErs claimed to have obtained during their experience was wholly unavailable to experiencers through conventional sensory or rational means.

As mentioned before, more researchers should pursue independent and systematic attempts to replicate feature patterns such as the clusters and factors Greyson (1985) and Noyes and Slymen (1978–79) identified. On the basis of the studies that exist to date, such patterns cannot yet be considered established. Difficulties in replicating these findings may arise, although some conditional replication may be possible.

Too few studies of specific features to date also preclude firm conclusions. For example, although NDErs have reported transcendental dimensions (see Table 2.2), no researcher to date has conducted a detailed study on this or other specific features. In a collection of NDEs that included transcendental environments, Sabom (1982) reviewed 28 brief accounts in which images of gardens, clouds, and light predominated. Although this study was a good first step, systematic studies of this and other features are needed.

Finally, other ways to examine features that NDErs report may include examinations of NDE accounts themselves, especially those accumulated in prospective studies that use interview schedules combined with open-ended descriptive questions about the experience. Studies of NDEs occurring in conjunction with medically defined near-death events tend to be reported only in terms of incidence, even when researchers indicate clearly through their methodological descriptions that they have gathered a great deal of additional and specific information. Methods that may be explored in this regard are discourse and conversation analysis and other forms of qualitative treatments of the NDE account as narrative. Especially useful would be studies using these methodologies in which the narratives of experiencers who presented medically confirmed near-death conditions could be compared to the narratives of individuals who only believed themselves to have been near death.

Circumstances

The suggestions for exploring and using diverse methods to gather information also apply here to circumstances. It is important to pursue further research based on existing indications that medical closeness to death is not necessary for an NDE and that fear and expectations of death are important factors in the generation of the experience (Noyes and Kletti 1976; Owens, Cook and Stevenson 1990; Stevenson, Cook and McClean-Rice 1989–90). Assuming it is correct to conceptualize "triggers" of NDEs, it is theoretically important to determine what those triggers are and by what mechanisms they function.

Furthermore, additional studies with individuals in specific circumstances such as those who have attempted suicide (Greyson 1986; Ring and Franklin 1981–82), who are accident victims (Noyes et al. 1977), or who have suffered specific illnesses may profitably be studied to learn more about possible relationships between differing conditions and aspects of NDEs. More discriminating measurements of closeness to death and more comparisons of feature frequency under different NDE circumstances, such as cardiac arrest versus illness, have the potential to enhance current knowledge about NDEs. Despite the amount and quality of research investigators have conducted to date, much remains to be known about the circumstance factor in NDEs. Most notable are questions of what specifically triggers NDEs and what specifically shapes the features that arise in them.

Incidence

As discussed in this chapter and in Chapter 1 of this volume, incidence is probably best researched through in-hospital prospective studies rather than retrospective studies. Although investigators have recently conducted some prospective studies (for example, Greyson, Holden, and Mounsey 2006; Parnia et al. 2001; van Lommel et al. 2001), more research along these lines is needed. In addition, future researchers should include lessons learned from previous studies. By including adequate sample sizes, researchers can conduct meaningful analyses beyond the primary issue of incidence into secondary analyses of correlates of incidence. By carefully describing methodology by which samples are derived, investigators are more able to affirm replication when it occurs and reconcile discrepancies in findings when they occur. By using reliable measures of the presence or absence of NDEs, preferably by adhering to a threshold score of 7 or higher on the NDE Scale (Greyson 1983), researchers ensure results that can be compared between studies. Furthermore, future researchers should take into account the applicability of some of the methodological criticisms of retrospective studies to prospective studies and more clearly define the criteria by which referring physicians and nurses determine whether patients are available for interview. Attention to the need for social rapport between the interviewer and the interviewee should also be incorporated into the methodology of prospective studies.

Retrospective studies and questionnaire surveys of individuals identified in out-of-hospital prospective studies should not be counted out. Indeed, the problematic nature of the response rate of such studies has been overstated. Further, with the proper interview schedule, it should be possible to elicit both incidence and prevalence from large random surveys, potentially updating and extending George Gallup and William Procter (1982).

Similarly, we see a need to expand the existing knowledge of NDE incidence with already explored medical conditions besides illness, cardiac arrest, and accidents. A research focus on other types of patients, such as in the 2007 Chun Fu Lai and others' study of NDEs among dialysis patients, may also be fruitful. This expansion into other conditions may help to compensate for problems such as the use of pharmaceuticals in the treatment of cardiac arrest, which may impair memory of NDEs (for example, Greyson, Holden, and Mounsey 2006).

Finally, large-scale random surveys that produce only prevalence estimates can be very useful in examining the NDE and, if worded properly, may also provide data that investigators can use to estimate incidence. Knoblauch and his colleagues (2001) have illustrated the first point admirably in their interview study conducted in Germany.

CONCLUDING REMARKS

Similar to other areas of scholarly inquiry into what many people consider anomalous, paranormal, or parapsychological phenomena, NDE research is still underdeveloped. Although researchers have made many important methodological advances since the days of Myers and Albert Heim, and although they have amassed much empirical knowledge, much remains to be learned. In reality, scholars are far from understanding many of the basic questions about NDEs. Practical problems hamper the progress of the field, from the dearth of active researchers who investigate the phenomena, to the duration and logistical complexities of high-quality prospective studies, to the cost of well-designed studies involving random samples and the difficulty of obtaining incidence in survey-based studies, to the sheer magnitude of the task of cataloging and accounting for the variation of NDE reports as they appear in formal and informal case collections.

Still, the small number of researchers who have devoted themselves to the topic over the past many decades have done remarkably well in accumulating useful knowledge and refining appropriate methodologies. One can only hope that these researchers will continue to exhibit the same energy and industry in future studies and that new researchers can be recruited to expand the scope of the work. Much remains to be done to understand the phenomena of NDEs.

ACKNOWLEDGEMENT

Carlos S. Alvarado would like to acknowledge a grant from the Society for Psychical Research, which provided support for this review. Both authors would like to thank Dr. Bruce Greyson for the use of his extensive reprint collection and Dr. Jan Holden for her editorial comments, which greatly improved this chapter.

Aftereffects of Pleasurable Western Adult Near-Death Experiences

Russell Noyes, Jr., Peter Fenwick,
Janice Miner Holden, and
Sandra Rozan Christian

From the beginning of modern-day interest and investigation of near-death experiences (NDEs), authors have paid particular attention to their aftereffects. In fact, Raymond Moody (1975), in his groundbreaking book *Life after Life*, listed certain changes in attitudes and values among the characteristic features of these experiences. He noted that people commonly lost their fear of death and came away with a strong belief in survival. Thus, it was evident from the start that the NDE was a powerful force for change, and this observation attracted researchers and scholars for several reasons. To begin with, the changes reported were positive and of great significance, involving personal transformation. Beyond this, by understanding such life-changing effects and the circumstance under which they occur, one might learn how to use them in the care of those likely to benefit, such as dying persons. In addition, the changes might serve to validate NDEs by showing what the experiences meant to those having them. They might also help us to understand NDEs and what they have to reveal about life and death. Finally, in contrast to NDEs themselves, the aftereffects might more easily be studied prospectively and verified by independent observation (Greyson 1989).

This chapter reviews research on NDEs, as defined by Bruce Greyson (1999), conducted over the past 30 years. It deals with the aftereffects of NDEs dominated by pleasurable emotions. The consequences of NDEs accompanied by predominantly distressing emotions are reviewed by another author (see Chapter 4, this volume). It also deals mostly with aftereffects that are positive or life-enhancing in some sense. But because for some individuals the effects of pleasurable NDEs are indeed negative or life-diminishing, any full and balanced review must take negative aftereffects into account, and what determines whether the effects will be positive or negative must be viewed as an important question. This review does not consider the aftereffects of NDEs in children; they appear similar to those in adults (Morse and Perry 1992; see Chapter 5, this volume). The effects of NDEs upon persons other than those who have them, including society at large, are also not considered here although this has been a topic of much interest and speculation (Ring and Valarino 1998; see Chapter 11, this volume).

This review emphasizes studies involving unbiased samples of adequate size using control groups and statistical methods to test hypotheses. The chapter authors identified articles dealing with this subject by searching the *Near-Death Experiences: Index to the Periodical Literature through 2005* (Holden, Christian, Foster, Forest, and Oden 2008). Relevant studies were also identified by one of the chapter authors, Sandra Rozan Christian, as part of her doctoral dissertation. Additional articles and books were identified from reference lists. This review describes the various aftereffects, examines factors that may influence them, considers their development and progression, and reflects upon what they may mean. Finally, it considers some of the limitations of existing research and fruitful directions for future studies.

THE AFTEREFFECTS

Although Moody (1975) described life-transforming effects of NDEs, Russell Noyes (1980) conducted the first systematic study of them. He obtained information from 205 persons who had encountered life-threatening danger. Nearly two-thirds reported a change in attitude toward life or death resulting from their experience. They described a pattern of change that included reduced fear of death, a sense of relative invulnerability, a feeling of special importance or destiny, a belief in having received the special favor of God or fate, and a strengthened belief in life after death. This study, like most examining aftereffects, was based on retrospective assessment of change. Also, people were included who had come close to death regardless of what their subjective experience had been. Some had had NDEs as defined by Greyson (1999); others had not.

Subsequently, Kenneth Ring (1984) compared persons who had had "core experiences" (NDErs) to those who had come close to death without having such experiences (non-NDErs) and those who had never come close to death. For this study, he developed a measure of NDE depth as well as an instrument to assess change after an NDE, the Life Change Questionnaire. The latter consists of 42 items calling for responses ranging from strongly increased to strongly decreased. Using this instrument along with interviews, Ring (1984) obtained reports from his NDErs of greater self-confidence, heightened sense of purpose, reduced fear of death, heightened spirituality, greater care and compassion toward others, diminished value of material possessions, and enhanced appreciation for life. He also obtained corroboration of these changes from informants. His was the first major study of aftereffects using the current definition of NDE (see Chapter 10, this volume) and a design that was to become a standard for the field. However, his study was based on a relatively small and highly selected sample.

More recent studies have used the Near-Death Experience Scale (Greyson 1983c) to distinguish NDErs from non-NDErs. It contains the most important elements of the NDE, and a score of 7 or more approximates the current definition of NDE. These studies have generally examined differences between groups on individual items from the Life Change Questionnaire (Greyson and Ring 2004) but have less often looked at differences in the amount of change (total score) between subjects. It seems clear from available studies that in general, NDErs exceed non-NDErs in the extent of change (Fenwick and Fenwick 1995; Ring 1984; Sutherland 1992). Whether they differ in terms of the type of change is less clear.

Two studies of life change in cardiac arrest patients are especially noteworthy. Both involved consecutive patients who were interviewed shortly after the event, then followed up. Both obtained information using the Life Change Questionnaire and compared NDErs to non-NDErs. In the first, Pim van Lommel, Ruud van Wees, Vincent Meyers, and Ingrid Elfferich (2001) followed up Dutch arrest patients after two years. Thirty-five had had NDEs, and 39 had not. They found significant differences between these groups on 13 of the measure's 42 items, as shown in Table 3.1. Depth of the NDE, as measured by the Near-Death Experience Scale, was associated with higher scores on some items, yet patients who had had superficial NDEs underwent changes that were similar to those reported by patients who had had core experiences. After eight years, all patients, including those who had not had NDEs, reported positive changes including loss of fear of death. The extent of change was greater after eight years than after two years in both groups.

The second study, by Janet Schwaninger, Paul Eisenberg, Kenneth Schechtman, and Alan Weiss (2002) used a similar design to follow up a group of cardiac arrest survivors. Eight had had NDEs and 10 had not. The

Table 3.1

Percent of Cardiac Arrest Patients Showing Positive Change (Increase or Decrease) on Life Change Questionnaire Items after Two and Eight Years[1]

	2 years		8 years	
	NDE n = 23 %	no NDE n = 15 %	NDE n = 23 %	no NDE n = 15 %
Social Attitude				
Ability to express love for others	42	16	78	58
Acceptance of others	42	16	78	41
Compassion for others	52	25	68	50
Understanding of others	36	8	73	75
Involvement in family life	47	33	78	58
Religious Attitude				
Understanding what life is about	52	33	57	66
Sense of inner meaning to my life	52	25	57	25
Concern with spiritual matters	15	−8	42	−41
Attitude toward Death				
Fear of death	−47	−16	−63	−41
Conviction there is life after death	36	16	42	16
Others				
Search for personal meaning	52	33	89	66
Interest in self-understanding	58	8	63	58
My appreciation of ordinary things	78	41	84	50

[1]modified from van Lommel et al. (2001)

authors observed positive changes that were greater among the NDErs. They also found significant differences between groups on over half of the Life Change Questionnaire items. Differences reflecting religious change were the most significant; these included sense of sacredness of life ($p < .001$), inner sense of God's presence ($p < .001$), and sense of purpose in life ($p = .002$). Together these studies show that, in unselected samples, patients undergoing cardiac arrest report transformative change that is greater in those who have NDEs and that increases with the passage of time. Prospective studies such as these are enormous undertakings yet of great value.

Gary Groth-Marnat and Roger Summers (1998) used sophisticated methods to obtain several important findings regarding aftereffects. First, 9 percent of their NDErs and 73 percent of non-NDErs felt their experiences had been distressing or unpleasant; they were among the few to comment on experiences that might lead to negative aftereffects (Greyson and Bush 1992; see Chapter 4, this volume). Second, Groth-Marnat and Summers obtained a correlation between change on the Life Change

Questionnaire and total score on the Near Death Experience Scale of .43 (p < .001). This important observation might be interpreted in two ways. Either deeper NDEs produce greater change, or some individual characteristics that result in greater depth, such as personality traits, also foster greater transformation in those who come close to death. Third, using ratings on the Life Change Questionnaire from significant others, these investigators were able to corroborate the type and extent of observable change.

Major studies have yielded consistent findings with regard to the changes shown in Tables 3.2 and 3.3. What follows is a description of those that are most important. These prototypical changes involve perception of self, relationship to others, and attitude toward life, as well as paranormal phenomena and other alterations in perception and consciousness. Not all people who had NDEs underwent change. For instance, Noyes (1980) and Peter Fenwick and Elizabeth Fenwick (1995) found that change occurred in about two-thirds of those who had come close to death. Nor did all who underwent change report what is about to be described. Nevertheless, from major studies a consistent pattern of aftereffects has emerged (Atwater 1988; Fenwick and Fenwick 1995; Flynn 1986; Grey 1985; Greyson 1992; Groth-Marnat and Summers 1998; Musgrave 1997; Noyes 1980; Ring 1984, 1992; Sabom 1982; Sabom and Kreutziger 1978; Schwaninger et al. 2002; Sutherland 1992, 1995; van Lommel et al. 2001).

Altered Perception of Self

Of the changes listed in Table 3.2, perhaps the most important are those involving the perception of self. *Loss of the fear of death* was reported with the greatest frequency. NDErs have tended to attribute this loss to a new or strengthened belief in survival of bodily death. They often reported that during the experience, their soul had left their body (Sabom and Kreutziger 1978). Beyond this, some said they had experienced death itself, a joyous union with their creator. Thus, their belief in survival was based on firsthand experience, and a belief in heaven—even reincarnation—was often strengthened (Musgrave 1997; Ring 1984; Wells 1993). Although NDErs retained their fear of dying, with its potential for pain and suffering, their experience had reduced the fear of death itself. Such a reduction has been documented in the many studies using the Life Change Questionnaire. Also, by means of the Threat Index, Greyson (1992) found significantly lower death threat among NDErs than among subjects who had never been near death.

Many NDErs reported encountering a Godlike presence, often described as a "being of light" (Musgrave 1997). This presence often showed great care for, and favor toward, the individual during this most profound and meaningful aspect of the experience. This encounter appeared to form the basis of a *new or enhanced spirituality* (Morse and Perry 1992). Cherie

Table 3.2

**Changes in Attitudes and Beliefs Reported by Persons following
Near-Death Experiences**

Perception of Self
  Loss of fear of death
  Strengthened belief in life after death
  Feeling specially favored by God
  New sense of purpose or mission
  Heightened self-esteem

Relationship to Others
  Increased compassion and love for others
  Lessened concern for material gain, recognition, or status
  Greater desire to serve others
  Increased ability to express feelings

Attitude toward Life
  Greater appreciation of, and zest for, life
  Increased focus on the present
  Deeper religious faith or heightened spirituality
  Search for knowledge
  Greater appreciation for nature

Sutherland (1990) reported that a majority of her NDErs—the two-thirds for whom the NDE was spiritual in nature—viewed their heightened spirituality as the most significant change. Although many NDErs had been adherents of one or another religious faith, their direct experience of the light changed them. It made them new persons of God, determined to understand his will for their lives.

Near-death experiencers consistently reported a *new sense of purpose or mission.* Many said that they had been sent back, or had themselves chosen to return to life, because they were needed or because there remained work for them to do. It was not always clear what this mission was, but NDErs recognized it as an important part of a godly plan. This new purpose imparted a strong sense of meaning to individuals' lives and, with it, *heightened self-esteem.* Not only had NDErs received a gift of life, but they had found a divine mission as well. Using the Life Attitude Profile based on Viktor Frankl's existential psychology, Martin Bauer (1985) obtained from a group of NDErs reports of increased life purpose, will to meaning, and death acceptance. Thus, he was able to demonstrate change in a number of core existential attitudes and beliefs.

The change in self included *altered perception of the body.* Many NDErs felt detached or estranged from their bodies as though they no longer belonged, yet were imprisoned, in them (Atwater 1988). Additional bodily changes including increased energy, heightened sensitivity to such things

Table 3.3

Changes in Paranormal Phenomena as well as Alterations in Perception and Consciousness Reported by Persons following Near-Death Experiences

Paranormal Phenomena
　Out-of-body experiences
　Apparitions
　Extrasensory perception
　Precognition
　Healing
　Spiritual, mystical, or transcendent experiences

Alterations in Perception, Consciousness
　Heightened sensation
　Physiological alterations
　Unusual movements, sensations
　Unusual stimulation of special senses
　Mental changes
　Increased energy, decreased need for sleep

as sounds, increased allergic tendencies, and changed energy fields, causing such phenomena as malfunction of electrical devices.

Changed Relationship to Others

Near-death experiencers reported changes in their relationships to others (Table 3.2). They turned away from seeking to advance themselves and toward concern for others. NDErs said they were *no longer concerned about material gain, recognition, or status.* Greyson (1983a) found material and social success less important among those who had had NDEs than among those who had not. Striving for personal gain through competition, which may have dominated their lives prior to an NDE, seemed contrary to their post-NDE outlook. They now experienced *greater compassion for others* together with *a desire to serve them* (Ring 1984; Sutherland 1992). Indeed, these contrasting values—personal gain versus concern for others—were viewed as antagonistic. Personal gain came at the expense of others; material prosperity for one meant deprivation for another. This shift caused some NDErs to look differently upon pre-NDE employment and relationships.

As indicated, NDErs found themselves more compassionate (Flynn 1982). This change meant they were more aware of and sensitive to the problems of others. Their greater sensitivity seemed to have been based on a sense of oneness with humanity arising from their NDEs. Also, they were more accepting, tolerant, and understanding of persons they might have tended to judge in the past. In addition, these NDErs became *more open and free in expressing their feelings* and in caring for those whom they encountered.

New Attitude toward Life

Those who had NDEs reported change in their attitude toward life (Table 3.2). This change often took the form of a *new appreciation of, or zest for, life*. They now regarded the life they had almost lost as something precious. Little things—moments with family or friends, beauty of the natural world—all were experienced more intensely and with greater enjoyment. Many spoke of *living more fully in the moment* without the distraction of planning for the future or concern for the impression they might make. According to John Wren-Lewis (1994), this increasing focus on the moment might help to explain the reduced fear of death. He spoke of a "shift in consciousness whereby life in each moment becomes so vivid that anxiety about future survival ... ceases to be important" (108). Some referred to heightened senses that *enhanced their appreciation of nature* and to greater empathic understanding that contributed to their appreciation of others.

Following NDEs, many experiencers became more religious or spiritual (McLaughlin and Malony 1984). Their encounter had brought them closer to God, and they sought to maintain this closeness through prayer or meditation. Their heightened spirituality also involved reading of religious texts and about world religions. This activity was part of a *search for knowledge*, for understanding the world order that had been revealed to them (Raft and Andersen 1986). Their increased spirituality did not necessarily translate into greater participation in organized religious activities. Indeed, some NDErs reported that these activities seemed less meaningful (Musgrave 1997; Ring 1984; Sutherland 1990). Others described greater commitment to traditional worship services and religious practices.

Many alterations in attitudes and values following NDEs reflected change in the self already described. Among the changes consistently reported (Table 3.2) was a search for self-understanding (Raft and Andersen 1986). NDErs found themselves asking, "Who is this transformed person, and how am I to understand the new spiritual presence in my life?" They sought to learn about themselves in terms of their new spirituality and mission. This quest often meant searching for interests and talents that might be consistent with new values, especially that of serving others. According to Sutherland (1992), some NDErs discovered previously unrecognized or undeveloped abilities such as healing. In other words, they found themselves suddenly transformed and tried to understand what this transformation meant for their lives.

Other Changes

Some NDErs claimed other positive, or in a few cases negative, effects from their experiences. Problems that had existed beforehand were sometimes reduced or eliminated. Some spoke of depression, anxiety, or other forms of psychological distress that were reduced (Greyson 2003a). A few reported that suicidal inclinations had lessened or disappeared. Others described religious conflicts or existential doubts that were overcome. Still others claimed physical healing when the problems that had led to an NDE resolved unexpectedly (Greyson 2001; Noyes and Kletti 1976). On the other hand, some NDErs who had had mostly pleasurable experiences reported persisting distress afterward (Greyson and Bush 1992). A few reported post-traumatic stress disorder symptoms, including intrusive recollections, frightening dreams, and avoidant behavior (Greyson 2001).

Emergent Paranormal Phenomena

As a transcendent or mystical experience, the NDE includes a number of paranormal features such as out-of-body, apparitional, and extrasensory experiences (Greyson and Stevenson 1980). After NDEs, people may continue to report paranormal episodes and periodic alterations in consciousness, as shown in Table 3.3. In a survey of the Association for Research and Enlightenment, Richard Kohr (1982, 1983) found that members who had had NDEs reported more psychic phenomena than did members who were non-NDErs or who had never been close to death. Subsequently, Greyson (1983b), using the same survey instrument, documented substantial, and statistically significant, change in the frequency of psychic phenomena after NDEs. Table 3.4 shows the percent of subjects reporting specified phenomena. In each category, the number of paranormal and related experiences was greater—and, in some instances, significantly (statistically) greater—after an NDE than before it.

Sutherland (1989) reported similar findings. After an NDE, the majority of her sample reported occurrences of paranormal phenomena such as *clairvoyance, telepathy, precognition, intuition, guidance, out-of-body experience,* and *healing ability*. They also reported greater *awareness of dreams, perception of auras,* and *contact with spirits*. Such studies suggest that NDEs render people more susceptible to, or aware of, psychic phenomena. Some researchers have referred to this development as "psychic awakening" and have suggested that greater sensitivity to, or communication with, an alternate reality might be involved (Greyson 1983b; Ring 1984). The altered consciousness during an NDE sometimes remains or reoccurs afterward, either voluntarily or involuntarily. In fact, NDEs may increase experiencers' participation in paranormal-related activities, such as dream analysis and meditation, in order to facilitate such altered consciousness.

Among NDErs, attitudes toward these psychic phenomena varied. Sutherland (1989), for example, found that people took clairvoyant or precognitive experiences in stride, but found out-of-body experiences more difficult to ignore. Some NDErs said they had attempted to suppress or eliminate activities, such as going out-of-body or reading people's minds, whereas others began using psychic abilities for purposes such as healing. As a consequence of such psychic phenomena, many felt more in touch with an "inner source of wisdom" and had a "sense of being guided."

Table 3.4
Percent of Subjects Reporting Various Paranormal Experiences before and after a Near-Death Experience

	Before NDE (n = 69) %	After NDE (n = 69) %	p
Psychic Experiences			
Waking extrasensory perception	24.6	55.1	<.0001
Extrasensory perception "agency"	10.1	29.0	ns
Extrasensory perception dreams	18.8	33.3	ns
Psychokinesis	11.6	18.8	ns
Psi-Related Experiences			
Out-of-body experiences	11.6	43.5	.0001
Encounters with apparitions	13.0	44.9	.0001
Perception of auras	11.6	33.3	.0015
Communication with the dead	11.6	27.5	ns
"Memories of previous lives"	14.5	29.0	ns
Déjà vu	48.5	60.3	ns
Psi-Conducive Altered States of Consciousness			
Mystical experiences	23.2	59.4	<.0001
Lucid dreams	25.0	55.4	.0003
Weekly dream recall	36.8	63.2	.0021
Weekly vivid dreams	26.5	48.5	ns
Psi-Related Activities			
Dream analysis	33.8	72.1	<.0001
Meditation	21.7	50.0	.0026
Visits to psychics	7.2	25.0	ns
Psychedelic drug use	17.6	20.9	ns

Note: Table 3.4 is a modification of a table first printed in a 1983 issue of the now-defunct journal *Theta*. Prior to publication of this book, the first author was unable to obtain a response to requests to reprint this table. The author of the original article, Bruce Greyson, gave his permission for the modified reprint.

Although responses to their psychic sensitivity differed, none of Sutherland's participants saw this as the most significant change resulting from their NDEs.

Alterations in Perception, Consciousness

Many NDErs have reported contact with deceased relatives, friends, and spiritual beings during NDEs (Fenwick and Fenwick 1995; Moody 1975; Morse and Perry 1997; Ring 1980; Sabom 1982), and some have claimed continuing communication of this type. Greyson and Mitchell Liester (2004) obtained reports of "inner voices" or nonpathological auditory hallucinations from 80 percent of a group of NDErs after their experience. Surprisingly, 40 percent reported such voices beforehand. Unlike schizophrenics with whom they were compared, NDErs had a positive attitude toward these communications. Most participants valued them for the inspiration, guidance, and intuitive knowledge they offered. The authors did not report whose voices the NDErs heard or whether they were the same ones encountered during their NDEs.

NDErs also described a number of *varied physical and mental changes* (Table 3.3; Raft and Andresen 1986). Many of these changes occurred for the first time after a near-death encounter and, to a number of observers, resembled changes seen in persons who, following Eastern traditions, practice meditation to achieve alterations in consciousness (Greyson 1993a). Frequently mentioned in this regard has been kundalini, a force that might, if activated, bring spiritual awakening and higher consciousness. Greyson (1993a) compared the lifetime occurrence of *kundalini phenomena* among NDErs, non-NDErs, and persons who had never come close to death. NDErs reported the following phenomena significantly more frequently: assuming strange positions, becoming locked into position, changes in breathing, spontaneous orgasmic sensations, ascending sensations, unexplained hot or cold sensations, internal sounds, intense positive emotions, watching oneself as if from a distance, and change in the speed of thought. Information was not available concerning the frequency with which these sensations had occurred or what relationship they might have had to other aftereffects.

FACTORS THAT INFLUENCE AFTEREFFECTS

A variety of factors may influence aftereffects, including those that come into play before, during, and after NDEs. Preexisting factors might include personality traits, religious beliefs, cultural variables, and individual expectations (Ring 1993). Factors involving the NDE itself might include the circumstances, closeness to death, depth of the experience, or elements of it (Greyson and Stevenson 1980). Factors after the NDE might involve an individual's coping style and response to the experience as well as the response—positive or negative—of others. Of these, one variable—depth of the NDE—appears strongly related to changes occurring afterward (Groth-Marnat and Summers 1998; Schwaninger et al. 2002; van Lommel et al. 2001). For instance, Steven McLaughlin and Newton Malony (1984) observed a positive correlation of .46 between the depth of the NDE and reported change in the importance of religion.

However, it seems clear that coming close to death is in itself responsible for change (Blackmore 1993). In an early study, Dorothy Smith (1979) interviewed survivors of serious illness and elicited from them change in values and priorities related to heightened awareness of death. Among these changes were greater concern for others and sense of community. Since her study, an extensive literature has appeared calling attention to changes in persons who have experienced serious adverse events (Tedeschi, Park, and Calhoun 1998). Such persons have reported a variety of benefits in addition to harmful effects, including changed life priorities, increased sense of self-efficacy, enhanced sensitivity to others, improved personal relationships, and increased spirituality (McMillen 1999). Speaking of such an event, one woman remarked after her husband survived a hemorrhage, "Coming very close to dying ... shakes the very foundation of your existence" (Blackmore 1993, 245). More recently, Richard Bonenfant (2004) observed change in non-NDErs as well as NDErs on a variety of measures. Still, it was the NDErs who appeared to undergo spiritual change.

Some aftereffects seem related to specific elements of the NDE. For example, many NDErs said they know the soul survives the body because they left their bodies during their NDEs. In fact, belief in life after death appears to increase as much after out-of-body experiences as after NDEs (Gabbard, Twemlow, and Jones 1981; Irwin 1993; Tiberi 1993). However, transcendent or mystical experiences, of which the NDE is one, are made up of features that often occur together, and it may be best to regard them as a group of interrelated features or a syndrome and not as individual elements. Because the NDE may be mystical in nature, an encounter with a divine or cosmic force must be the most powerful generator of spiritual transformation (Morse and Perry 1992). Regardless, few efforts have been made to link certain elements to specific aftereffects.

The circumstances of an NDE may influence subsequent changes. For instance, NDEs resulting from sudden, unexpected events, such as accidents, may differ from those related to illness in which death has been anticipated (Greyson 1993b; Twemlow and Gabbard 1984–85). Another circumstance, namely suicide, has been investigated in this regard. When people who had come close to death as a result of suicide attempts were examined, they were found to have had NDEs that were indistinguishable from those resulting from other causes and at roughly the same rate (Greyson 1986; Ring and Franklin 1981–82). In a classic paper, David Rosen (1975) reported interviews with 7 of the 10 known survivors of jumps from the Golden Gate bridge. All had experienced transcendence and spiritual rebirth that had transformed their lives.

Some authors expressed fear that reports of pleasurable NDEs might make suicide more attractive. However, Greyson and Stevenson (1980) found the opposite. Of those who had had NDEs from any cause, over half became more negative in their attitude toward self-destruction. Also, among attempted suicides, those who had had NDEs reported less suicidal ideation afterward.

To understand this change, Greyson (1992–93) surveyed people who had had NDEs and those who had come close to death without having NDEs concerning their attitudes toward self-destruction. To do this, he elicited their responses to statements about changes in attitude likely to deter suicide, such as enhanced self-esteem resulting from belief in postmortem survival or to having been rescued from death. NDErs endorsed 9 of the 12 statements significantly more often than did non-NDErs. He concluded that the enhanced value and meaning of life resulting from an NDE reinforces the wish to live. As one survivor of a jump from the Golden Gate bridge said, "It affirmed my belief—there is a higher spiritual world. I experienced a transcendence—in that moment I was refilled with new hope and purpose of being alive" (Rosen 1975, 291).

Of course, the issue of whether NDEs influence subsequent suicidal behavior would be difficult to test because large numbers and long-term follow-up would be required. Most attempters disavow suicidal intentions after an attempt, so such denial may not be a satisfactory indicator. Early authors even speculated that a near-death encounter might feature in the motivation for attempted suicide. James Weiss (1957) said that for some individuals, the act might be "a gamble with death" or a provocation of fate or God, who might be forced to decide for or against them. He described suicide attempters who, when they tempted fate and survived, experienced a feeling of special importance and exhilaration. Along this line, Stanislav Grof and Joan Halifax (1977) speculated that suicide might be a misguided attempt to achieve self-transcendence. And Robert Lifton (1979) saw in the act a search for vitality and affirmation of meaning.

Any factors associated with the occurrence of a transcendent or mystical experience among people who come close to death might by themselves contribute to transformative effects. Thus, younger age, female gender, closeness to death, and surrender during the process of dying—factors associated with occurrence and depth of NDEs in a few studies—might be associated with more extensive aftereffects (Greyson 1993b, 2000a, 2000b, 2003b; Greyson and Stevenson 1980; Ring 1980; Sabom 1982; Twemlow and Gabbard 1984–85; van Lommel et al. 2001). For example, Greyson and Stevenson (1980) observed that changes in attitude were more frequent among NDErs who believed during their experience that they were dying and those who reported panoramic memory. Also, McLaughlin and Malony (1984) observed less change in the importance of religion after NDEs with increasing age. However, in most studies, demographic variables have had little predictive value (Greyson 2000a).

Personality traits may be related to the occurrence or depth of NDEs and may indirectly influence aftereffects (see Chapter 6, this volume). Several authors have suggested that tendencies toward dissociation and absorption—the propensity to focus on selected sensory experiences to the exclusion of others—might predispose toward altered states of consciousness including NDEs. For instance, Ring and Christopher Rosing (1990) obtained more frequent reports of child abuse and higher scores on a measure of dissociation from people who had had NDEs than from controls. In a similar study, Irwin (1993) also found a higher rate of childhood trauma but no difference in dissociative coping style—that is, the tendency to cope by distancing oneself from one's experience or identity. Greyson (2000b) found the depth of NDE correlated with dissociative symptoms among people reporting such experiences. However, he could not say whether the dissociative tendencies contributed to, or resulted from, the NDEs.

Absorption might also predispose to consciousness alterations. For instance, Stuart Twemlow and Glen Gabbard (1984–85) observed higher attention/absorption scores among NDErs than among out-of-body experiencers. Also, James Council and Greyson (1985) found greater absorption and fantasy proneness among NDErs than among comparison groups, but Ring (1992) found no such difference in fantasy proneness. Ring (1992) hypothesized an encounter-prone personality. As a result of childhood abuse, this personality would develop dissociative tendencies as well as a capacity for absorption in alternate realities. This remains an attractive but unproven possibility (Greyson 2000a).

Cultural and religious factors appear important in shaping NDEs and their aftereffects. Evidence for this hypothesis comes from review of non-Western experiences. Carol Zaleski (1987) compared NDEs from medieval Christian and modern times, and Ring (1993) examined the das-log from Tibetan Buddhist culture. In both instances, the NDEs had forms consistent with the religious beliefs of time and place. Ring (1993) concluded that whereas experiences from diverse cultures are structurally similar, they reflect the imprint of the religious traditions from which they arise. They also tend to support and strengthen existing beliefs. For example, the transformative aftereffects that Zaleski (1987) described were consistent with medieval Christian faith. Hubert Knoblauch, Ina Schmied, and Bernt Schnettler (2001) observed aftereffects in German NDErs that seemed to differ from those of American NDErs. However, it is unclear how these authors defined near-death experience.

A major determinant of post-NDE transformation appears to be beliefs about, and attitudes toward, the experience itself, those of the NDEr as well as others. This observation brings us to consideration of post-NDE factors that influence progression.

EARLY RESPONSES AND THEIR PROGRESSION

The aftereffects of NDEs do not develop all at once. Indeed, although the experience may be a powerful force, whether change occurs depends on the person and one's social environment. Immediately afterward, the experiencer may feel that a profound event has taken place but be stunned and perplexed about its meaning. Also, the experience itself may linger (Atwater 1988). The person has experienced another reality and may not relinquish contact with it all at once or completely. In addition, survivors may continue to experience alterations in time and space. They may have a sense of timelessness and loss of spatial boundaries. At the same time, they may experience a sense of detachment and heightened sensitivity. The feeling of detachment may include not only the world around them but also their bodies, emotions, and sense of self. Heightened sensitivities may include not only the usual senses but also intuition, empathic understanding, and psychic sensibilities.

Attitudes regarding NDEs may interfere with, or slow the progression of, change over time. Some NDErs view their experience as a dream and attempt to put it out of their minds (Hastings 2002). Others are unable or unwilling to make changes and, as a consequence, do not integrate the experience. Still others, when they report it, are met with disapproval or rejection. Medical professionals, family members, and friends often react as though the experience were a manifestation of mental illness, mind-altering drugs, a lack of oxygen to the brain, or even work of the devil, hence of no real significance. Such attitudes—ones often shared by NDErs themselves—may lead to suppression of the experience, its memory, and any positive change it might engender. Changes, when they are forthcoming, may occur rapidly or slowly or, in a few instances, may be delayed. Some early manifestations may fade although the NDE itself tends to remain a vivid memory (Lindley, Bryan, and Conley 1981). Transformation, when it occurs, may do so over months or years and may involve many or most aspects of NDErs' lives.

In interviews with patients soon after cardiac arrests, Roberta Orne (1995) and Linda Morris and Kathleen Knafl (2003) elicited varied responses. Although for most patients survival was a positive, life-affirming experience, the early period was often one of emotional distress, turmoil, and alienation. Patients "realized that something very powerful had just happened to them; however, they did not know how to interpret it" (Morris and Knafl 2003, 150). They showed intense desire to learn the meaning of their experience, yet they were often hesitant to reveal it for fear their sanity might be questioned. The understanding and support of family appeared important during this time of emotional vulnerability. Also, validation of the NDE by health care professionals was important for those who received it.

Sutherland (1992) described what she called an "integration trajectory." Integration begins immediately after an NDE and continues until the experience becomes a part of the NDEr's life. It is an external as well as internal process that involves testing and finding social acceptance. According to this author, the path taken is influenced by a number of key variables, including choice of return (to life), acceptance of being back, attitude toward the experience, societal attitudes, disclosure of the experience, response to that disclosure, and information about NDEs. She described a series of trajectories based on duration and outcome: (1) blocked, (2) arrested, (3) steady, and (4) accelerated. A blocked trajectory occurs among those who regard their experience as meaningless or have this view reinforced when they disclose it. An arrested trajectory may occur in those who do not know what to make of their experience, are afraid to disclose it, or are lacking in social support. Sutherland (1992) speculated that an NDE of greater depth may lead to more rapid and complete integration. However, she did not indicate how frequently various trajectories occur or how important the depth of the NDE might be.

Based on interviews with NDErs, Regina Hoffman (1995) identified five stages in the integration process. These included early shock or surprise, need for validation, interpersonal implications, active exploration, and, finally, integration. She found communication of the experience to be important at each stage. Especially during the validation stage, rejection could be devastating and block further progression. According to this author, disclosure has many purposes depending on the stage. These purposes include a desire to share good news, find validation, explain and negotiate changes, reveal oneself, help others, engage in mutual inquiry, and reexperience the event. Bette Furn (1987) likened the difficulties faced by NDErs to people undergoing culture shock. She noted that the adjustment to a new culture follows a similar and predictable pattern.

The aftereffects experienced by many NDErs, although positive for them, may be disruptive to, and misunderstood by, family, friends, and coworkers (Insinger 1991). A shift in interest and values, such as loss of interest in material possessions, may place a strain on relationships. NDErs have often been criticized or ridiculed for changes in their behavior. Some have been viewed as mentally ill and forced into treatment. Some authors have reported frequent divorce among NDErs (Bush 1991; Groth-Marnat and Summers 1998). For instance, Christian (2005) observed divorce in 65 percent of her NDE research participants compared to 19 percent in participants who had experienced other life-changing events. She found divorce more likely when the NDE caused a couple's values to diverge. Also, new attitudes and values may cause NDErs to reassess their employment or career. From the existing literature, it is difficult to know how frequently various relationship and career changes occur or how extensive they may be.

P. M. H. Atwater (1988), herself an NDEr, described many of the challenges and difficulties survivors face as they return from the reality of an NDE to everyday life. In her book, she detailed the process but did not indicate how common various early changes might be. She spoke of a period between being revived and waking up to reality when "sensations, feelings, thoughts, insights, all toss and jump around until some kind of pattern or sense of order can be established" (109). During this period, "paradox is the only standard. The familiar is now foreign, the foreign is now familiar. It is a period of knowing but not knowing who you are and where you fit in the scheme of things" (109). This phase, she said, may last hours, days, months, or even years. According to her, many NDErs face beginning life anew. This process calls for searching, rediscovering, and redefining oneself and one's life, and it takes time.

According to Atwater (1988), the NDEr's altered perception brings with it benefits but also problems. The experience of cosmic consciousness may result in a sense of oneness but also a blurring of boundaries between the animate and inanimate, the self and others. And the experience of timelessness may bring a new focus upon, and intensity in, the moment but may result in getting caught up in the present at the expense of the future. Some NDErs find themselves more sensitive to their surroundings and other people; senses such as sight, hearing, and touch are more acute, and sympathy for others is intensified. Although beneficial for many NDErs, these changes are sometimes overwhelming.

Such alterations may lessen with time, even disappear, but while they last they may create problems (Lindley, Bryan, and Conley 1981). Some of these problems are minor, but others are of a more serious nature (Bush 2002; Greyson 1997, 2000a). Such problems should not be considered mental disorders even though some NDErs are distressed. NDEs should instead be viewed as life crises that have potential for growth or regression over time (Grof and Grof 1980; Kellehear 1996). Psychiatric classification (DSM-IV-TR) includes a nonpathological designation of "religious or spiritual problem" to cover such difficulties (American Psychiatric Association 2000; Greyson 1997). Greyson and Barbara Harris (1987) described a series of intrapsychic and interpersonal problems that may follow NDEs. These complications and the interventions that may be required to deal with them are described in detail elsewhere (see Chapter 11, this volume).

MEANING OF AFTEREFFECTS

In terms of explanatory models, the pattern of positive life change described appears to reflect rebirth. NDErs report that they—however briefly—experienced their own death and that this experience shattered their assumptive world (Greyson 2000a). It revealed to them a transcendent reality and brought them face-to-face with a divine presence. Their experience materially altered their view of themselves and their world, and subsequent changes reflect the new reality. Because their original selves or egos had been survival oriented and based on fear of death, they may have blocked earlier recognition of this reality (Blackmore 1993; Grof and Halifax 1977; Wren-Lewis 1994). In the course of a mystical experience, the individual may undergo dissolution of this original self (Pennachio 1986; Nielo 1997). Therefore, it seems correct to say that NDErs experience their own deaths, not in the physical sense, but in terms of the experiencing self and its identifying characteristics (White 1997). A variety of circumstances, including major life crises and transitions, may cause this type of alteration in consciousness (Kellehear 1990; Parkes 1971).

The point here is that in a very real sense, NDErs die and are reborn. Near-death experiencers often refer to themselves in just such terms

(Noyes 1980). It is as though the creator of the universe has given them a precious gift of life, and this life takes on special importance and is endowed with a unique mission. NDErs often believe that they survived because God willed it and had a divine purpose in bringing them back. They have experienced the love of God and been changed by it (Grosso 1981). The most important aftereffects reflect rebirth, and this concept helps to draw the various changes together. When persons who have not come close to death celebrate a birthday, they may marvel at the gifts they were given: yet unlike NDErs, they do not see the event as part of conscious memory, nor does the event necessarily have spiritual significance for them. Grof and Halifax (1977) used the phrase "death-rebirth" in describing the mystical experience that sometimes occurred with the drug LSD, and this transition from death to life seems appropriate in making sense of NDE aftereffects.

Many NDErs have overcome death and subsequently experience life in its fullest expression. The concepts of vitality and stasis or of "aliveness" and "deadness"—qualities of existence apart from the biological state of the organism—may contribute to an understanding of this transformation (Noyes 1982–83). For many experiencers, the result of an NDE has been greater vitality or aliveness. They have described a sense of invulnerability and of special importance or destiny, and some believe they have received the special favor of God, together with a firm belief in continued existence. Many have come face-to-face with a personal God with whom they continue to maintain a loving relationship. In doing this, they might be said to have experienced heaven. For according to Christian tradition, heaven is not reserved for the afterlife; it is now: "Truly, truly, I say to you, he who believes has eternal life" (Gospel of John 6:47). Certainly, some NDErs view life from this mountaintop.

Death is one of humanity's ultimate concerns, and fear of death may be seen as the most basic and potent source of anxiety (Yalom 1980). This anxiety is so powerful that it may rob a person of the life he or she is afraid of losing. It may create a form of "death in life," or psychological death. As Seneca, the Roman Stoic philosopher said, "He who fears death will never do anything worthy of a man who is alive" (Seneca 1928, De Tranq. An. XI.6). Near-death experiencers consistently report a reduction or loss of this fear. This change stems largely from their experience of survival, for if there is no personal annihilation, then there is no death. Two other factors appear to contribute as well. The first is a sense of having been rescued by a divine or cosmic force for a purpose. This aspect implies a continuing relationship and protection. The second is a sense of being special and, consequently, less vulnerable. Freed from this all-encompassing fear, many NDErs are likely to find themselves relieved of existential disturbances and other forms of psychopathology that may arise from them.

The NDE represents a powerful confrontation with death that has two important consequences manifested in its aftereffects (Grof and Grof 1980). One is an existential crisis that forces individuals to question the meaning of life and reexamine their values (Yalom 1980). For a few NDErs, this crisis may bring heightened fear of nonbeing, of meaninglessness (Greyson and Bush 1992). But for most, it results in a lessening of worldly striving for wealth and power that seems less important from the perspective of finite existence. The other is a spiritual encounter. A few NDErs may feel abandoned or that no God exists. In the face of death, they may look for a godly presence yet find none. But for most, the result appears to be spiritual awakening. The NDE often brings with it spiritual certainty and an intense desire to conform one's life to divine will. The new relationship with what is often a personal God becomes central to the NDErs' lives.

Changes that occur after an NDE are part of the whole; they are a reflection of, and serve to validate, the experience. Elements of the experience are clearly represented among its aftereffects. Consequently, alterations in consciousness that are without such transformative effects are unlikely to belong in the category of NDEs. It has been suggested that temporal lobe seizures and rapid eye movement intrusion might be responsible for NDE phenomena (Britton and Bootzin 2004; Nelson et al. 2006). Yet, neither is associated with aftereffects of the kind described. On the other hand, some experiences resulting from the administration of drugs like LSD and ketamine are like NDEs, and their aftereffects strongly resemble those that typically follow NDEs (Corazza 2006; Jansen 1990; Krupitski and Grinenko 1997; Richards et al. 1972). These, then, appear appropriately categorized as NDEs. Such experiences are probably not produced by the drugs; rather, the drugs bring about changes that facilitate their occurrence.

LIMITATIONS AND FUTURE DIRECTIONS

The investigation of aftereffects is well underway but generally suffers from some of the same limitations found in the study of NDEs themselves (Greyson 2000a). Of course, NDEs are difficult to study. They are infrequent and unpredictable events, so that assessment of the individual beforehand is difficult; and because the experience itself is subjective, it is difficult to verify—hence the advantage of studying aftereffects. Still, most studies of these effects suffer from reliance on small, biased samples and retrospective reporting of change. If volunteers are sought from among known NDErs, it is likely that participants will differ from nonparticipants, especially if they know what the investigator is looking for (Roberts and

Owen 1988). Too often, careful description of recruitment and selection methods is not reported, making judgment about potential biases difficult. Small and self-selected samples are unlikely to yield a true picture of the range and variability of change. Of course, retrospective recall can be unreliable, especially after 5 to 10 years have elapsed since the NDE, as is the case with many studies.

Several strategies have proven useful. One is the comparison of NDErs with persons who have come close to death yet have not had NDEs. These groups may, however, differ with respect to pre-event characteristics that render them susceptible or resistant to certain aftereffects as well as to NDEs themselves. After all, research has shown that premorbid psychiatric history, child abuse, and family psychiatric history render victims of trauma more susceptible to post-traumatic stress disorder, a pathological aftereffect (Brewin, Andrews, and Valentine 2000; Ehlers 2000; Holeva and Tarrier 2001). The severity of the trauma is important, but so is the preexisting vulnerability. A number of aftereffect studies have relied on the comparison of NDErs and non-NDErs and shown major differences. Yet, their interpretation remains in some doubt, in part because non-NDErs also undergo change. Assessments made immediately after the NDE perhaps have the best chance of capturing important pre-NDE characteristics.

Future studies need to include informants to verify the aftereffects NDErs report. Structured personality interviews, such as the Structured Interview for DSM-IV Personality (SIDP), routinely rely on informant information in arriving at overall ratings (Pfohl, Blum, and Zimmerman 1997). Using such standard assessments, researchers might compare NDErs with controls matched for age and sex from the non-NDE population. Measures of change that ask paticipants to compare themselves before and after NDEs are subject to a desirability or halo bias. Someone who has had a religious transformation is likely to rate positively many items relating to that event. The Life Change Inventory should continue to be used but supplemented by standard measures of such factors as personality, attitudes, spirituality, values, life satisfaction, and self-esteem. It would be helpful to document differences using relevant but nonspecific measures. One might, for example, hypothesize certain differences on basic personality dimensions such as neuroticism and extroversion.

The aftereffects themselves appear to have various dimensions, and it would be valuable to identify these by means of factor analysis so that relationships between them and various predictive variables might be examined. The Life Changes Inventory–Revised has proven especially valuable and has been widely used (Greyson and Ring 2004). However, there have evidently not, been studies of the measure's psychometric properties. Instruments used to measure post-traumatic growth, such as the Stress-Related Growth Scale and Post-Traumatic Growth Inventory, might be considered in studies of aftereffects as well (Park, Cohen, and Murch 1996;

Tedeschi and Calhoun 1996). It would also seem worthwhile to develop an instrument assessing current attitudes, values, and beliefs that might be used to compare across groups. Such an instrument may already exist, or a new instrument may need to be developed for the assessment of existential attitudes and concerns. The Life Attitude Profile is one candidate (Reker 1992).

Some different strategies might prove useful. Community surveys are possible given the rate of near-death encounters—15 percent in two surveys (Gallup and Proctor 1982; Kalish 1969). A nationwide telephone survey would be relatively free of self-selection bias and might well provide somewhat more diverse findings as did a recent German study (Knoblauch, Schmied, and Schnettler 2001). Also, in studies of persons exposed to life-threatening danger, assessing the traumatic aftermath might profitably be expanded to include positive as well as negative outcomes. Research into post-traumatic stress disorder—risk factors, nature of the trauma, long-term course—is ongoing and might yield information about risk factors for NDEs and predictors of beneficial aftereffects (Brewin, Andrews, and Valentine 2000; Nemeroff et al. 2006). Finally, mystical experiences are surprisingly common in the general population—30 percent superficial and 10 percent deep—and findings with respect to experiences of this kind occurring in other than near-death circumstances might nevertheless apply to NDEs as well (Hay 1994; Hay and Morisy 1985).

When personality changes following NDEs are investigated, organic factors should be considered. Studies of patients who have experienced serious illness events, such as cardiac arrest or hemorrhagic shock, should be evaluated by means of MRI, EEG (sleep deprived), and neuropsychological testing. Brain injury can lead to changes in such functions as impulse control, memory, and judgment. For those who have come close to death but not lost consciousness, comprehensive gene testing might be considered. Early studies suggest that expressed genetic profiles change after traumatic events. It would be of interest to know what genes are expressed after pleasurable experiences.

Clearly, the pleasurable NDE is a potent force for change and may, like other such forces, have injurious as well as beneficial affects—often in the same individual. Distressing experiences and their aftereffects (see Chapter 4, this volume) have been neglected in part because of lesser frequency (Greyson and Bush 1992; Kalish 1969). But because they may be devastating, even traumatic, they warrant greater attention (Greyson 2001). When researchers examine factors that influence NDEs and their aftermath, they should identify those that determine negative as well as positive outcomes. For instance, brain damage is an important cardiac arrest complication that may interact negatively with other changes (Granja et al. 2002). In Egyptian and Tibetan traditions, efforts were made to prepare people for their encounter with death. Such efforts arose from recognition of the real and serious challenges that often confront dying people. For some people facing impending death, the response may be helplessness or hopelessness. How can such final outcomes be avoided, and how might individuals prepare themselves, if not for an NDE, then for death itself?

CONCLUSION

The past 30 years have seen considerable progress in understanding NDE aftereffects. Yet, in some areas, there is need for refinement of methodology, and in others, attention to aspects that have been relatively neglected. A good deal is now known about the aftereffects themselves but less about how they are produced and not much at all about how they might be made available to others who might benefit from them. But interest remains high and the future promising for investigators of courage and determination.

4

Distressing Western Near-Death Experiences: Finding a Way through the Abyss

Nancy Evans Bush

What kinds of beings are we, that we can feel in such a profound way that *the feeling alone makes for heaven and hell?*
—Mishka Jambor (1997, 163; emphasis in original)

Who knows what lies behind and beyond our images until we trust them enough to ride them fully even into the darkness and into the depths like a seed in the soil? Perhaps we will never know the gift that our images are until we ride them through to the other side, and only from that perspective will we see them for the first time.
—Matthew Fox (1983, 204)

THE DARK CLOUD

In the early years—the Eden of near-death studies—the accounts that made news were blissful narratives of radiant near-death experiences, and the world listened, transfixed. That was shortly after the publication of Raymond Moody's *Life after Life* (1975), the book that introduced the term "near-death experiences" (NDEs). But as Kenneth Ring would describe it years later, "In 1978, a dark cloud of chilling testimony began to penetrate into the previously luminous sky of reports of near-death experiences" (Ring 1994, 5).

Ring was referring to the work of cardiologist Maurice Rawlings (1978) and Rawlings's lurid depictions of hellish near-death experiences. Ring's words point to the most common assumption about harrowing NDEs: that while radiant experiences are welcomed, these others are considered at best distasteful, at worst a dreadful portent that something like a literal hell might actually exist. With that assumption, other conjectures begin tumbling over each other, most especially that having such an experience must be a deserved consequence of prior wrongdoing, an indication of deficiencies of character or competence, perhaps even a tinge of evil.

Whatever their reasons, most researchers and the public alike turned their backs. In the winter of 2002, the *Journal of Near-Death Studies* featured an article entitled, "Afterward: Making Meaning after a Frightening Near-Death Experience" (Bush). It described what is known about harrowing NDEs, how experiencers respond to them, a framework for interpretation, and suggestions for coping after such an event. It was a fairly substantial article, the first of its ilk. The response was one letter from a friend and one note that an experiencer had found the article helpful. Otherwise, there have been no questions, no argument, not a word of commentary.

Why?

Transpersonal psychologist Arthur Hastings told a story of "a curious incident" involving a group of consciousness experts discussing the likelihood of consciousness after physical death. A case was presented of an NDE that was an instance of apparent *consciousness in the absence of brain function*, evidence of enormous importance to those professionals; yet their reaction was—not a word. Hastings wrote, "There was the sense ... of a feeling of avoidance. I was struck by the idea that there may also be *the will not to believe*, or perhaps *the resistance to belief* ... even though one of the principles avowed in scientific theory is to be neutral and let the evidence speak for itself" (Hastings 2002, 2).

The will not to believe. The resistance to belief. A dark cloud of chilling testimony...

It was George Gallup Jr. who noted wryly, "As might be expected, hell is not a very popular concept among the general public" (1982, 73). It is not very popular with researchers, either. The persisting difficulty, however, is that as with any reductionism, ignoring distressing NDEs or diminishing their impact or number does not make the reality go away; the *fact* of these experiences remains stubbornly somewhere in psychic orbit, awaiting resolution.

A dark cloud of chilling testimony—what could it mean but something like hell? It is imperative to discover what it could mean, without falling immediately into assumptions of guilt and punishment and suggestions of evil. Traditional shamans, the world's mystics and practitioners of meditative traditions, and others know that there is more to spiritual experience than a naively uninformed view that only stories of radiance are meaningful.

Speaking from decades of work with the deep psyche, psychiatrist Stanislav Grof observed that

> these mythologies and concepts of God, heaven and hell, … are an intrinsic part of the human personality that cannot be repressed and denied without serious damage …. For the full expression of human nature, they must be recognized, acknowledged and explored. (Grof 1980, 31)

It is past time to recognize and explore the dark side of spiritual experience in NDEs.

In references to the work of other authors, this chapter uses their terminology for the experience—such as "frightening," "negative," or "hellish"; inmy own text, the term "distressing NDEs" (dNDEs) indicates the category of experiences dominated by disturbing emotions.

DISTRESSING NDEs IN GENERAL STUDIES

Studies with No Reported Distressing NDEs

Studies of radiant experiences dominated by pleasurable emotions such as peace, love, and bliss have been the major influence in the field of near-death studies. Moody himself claimed never to have heard an account featuring the archetypal hell (1977, 169); and in eight studies since then, some of them formative, researchers reported no unpleasant or distressing experiences of any kind.

The earliest of those studies, after Moody's, was the 1980 publication of *Life at Death*, the first quantified analysis of NDEs, by social psychologist Kenneth Ring, of the University of Connecticut. His study sample of 49 participants with NDEs of at least moderate depth yielded only pleasurable experiences. Ring noted that despite occasional feelings of fright or confusion near the beginning, no one had described a mainly unpleasant experience (Ring 1980, 192–193). Further, he said, "[Frightening] features appear to have been, in the main, *hallucinatory visions*, which were *qualitatively discriminable* from the core experience itself" (195, emphasis in original).

In his second book, *Heading toward Omega*, Ring echoed Moody in the claim that although "a few [distressing] experiences have been described in the literature … I have never personally encountered a full-blown, predominantly negative NDE" (1984, 44).

In Australia, a three-year search by sociologist Cherie Sutherland (1992) resulted in more than 200 contacts with experiencers across that continent. Using a modified format of Ring's protocol for *Heading toward Omega*, she personally interviewed her final sample of 50 and found no distressing experiences.

Since so many people close to death in Western countries are in hospitals, it seems only logical that hospitals would be productive settings for near-death research. The first such report came from cardiologist Michael Sabom, who, with medical social worker Sarah Kreutziger, designed a carefully objective study of patients who survived cardiac arrest or other near-death crises. Of 116 participants in the study, 78 reported an NDE, none distressing. Sabom said of them, "In each case in which unpleasant emotions ... were encountered ... they were perceived to be but a momentary impression in an otherwise pleasant NDE" (Sabom 1982, 20).

Over a span of 23 years, researchers have conducted four more influential hospital-based studies (Greyson 2003; Parnia et al. 2001; Schwaninger et al. 2002; van Lommel et al. 2001). All four studies involved only survivors of cardiac arrest and were designed according to rigorous methodological standards. Like Sabom (1982), these researchers reported no distressing NDEs.

Studies with Reported Distressing NDEs

During the same time period as those studies, however, other investigators were discovering quite different outcomes.

In 1978, three years after Moody's *Life after Life* and two years before Ring's *Life at Death*, Maurice Rawlings, a Tennessee cardiologist, published his first book about NDEs, *Beyond Death's Door*. In it he recounted numerous accounts of hellish and otherwise terrifying NDEs told to him by his patients. Rawlings took the position that only conversion to conservative, biblically literal Christianity would save readers from a similar fate.

Almost everyone in near-death circles looked the other way. Academia discounted Rawlings's work because too many easily verifiable facts such as names and affiliations were carelessly presented and sometimes downright wrong, statistical information was absent, his descriptions were often lurid, and his perspective not only lacked objectivity but also was biased by a strong born-again Christian proselytizing. With the central truth of Rawlings's disclosure obscured by methodological sloppiness and his theological stance, readers conveniently bypassed his point: The near-death experiences of some people do not conform to the classic, peaceful pattern. Some people believe they have gone to hell.

The following year, psychologist Charles Garfield (1979) reported 47 NDEs of cancer patients, including some with descriptions of images that alternated between blissful and terrifying, the latter including unbounded floating in the Void, or constriction in a tunnel, or both. Gracia Fay Ellwood (2001, 91) later observed, "Garfield found almost as many 'negative' visions as blissful ones."

Three years after Rawlings's first book and a year after Ring's *Life at Death*, James H. Lindley, Sethyn Bryan, and Bob Conley published a careful interdisciplinary study out of Evergreen State College, Washington. In what came to be known as the Evergreen Study, the researchers defined "negative" experiences as containing extreme fear, panic, or anger, possibly with visions of threatening or taunting demonic creatures. The experiences, they concluded, usually transform "into a positive experience in which all negativity vanishes and ... peacefulness is achieved" (Bryan and Conley 1981, 113). Of the 55 NDEs in that study, 11 (20%) were "negative," although only 1 was considered hellish.

Next to mention frightening experiences were Gallup and William Proctor, whose *Adventures in Immortality* in 1982 was based on a Gallup Poll. The authors augmented statistical findings with discussions of traditional interpretations of afterlife issues and were generous with quotes from participants.

Among the 15 percent of participants reporting an NDE, the Gallup survey found both classic accounts and "featureless, sometimes forbidding faces; beings who are often merely present but aren't at all comforting; ... emotional or mental unrest; feelings of confusion about the experience; a sense of being tricked or duped into ultimate destruction; and fear about what the finality of death may involve" (Gallup and Proctor 1982, 83–84).

Probably the single most-quoted finding of the Gallup study has been that only 1 percent of the NDEs included "a sense of hell or torment." Many later writers have misinterpreted this to mean a 1 percent *total* of distressing NDEs, although the text reads, "The picture is more complex than that ... [I]t does seem clear that many of these people [in the sample of experiencers] ... were reluctant to interpret their experience in positive terms" (Gallup and Proctor 1982, 76–77).

The first report of near-death experiences in children appeared the following year, with a review of 17 accounts. It included a conversation with the distraught mother of a kindergartener who had nearly drowned but who later described an encounter with "a man" the youngster identified as God. The mother reported the child had no religious upbringing, but told her:

> God said it wasn't my time yet and I had to come back. I put my hand out and God put his hand out, and then God pulled his hand back. He didn't want me to stay. On the way back, I saw the devil. He said if I did what he wanted, I could have anything I want,... but I didn't want him bossing me around. (Bush 1983,187)

Despite the child's remarkable self-possession when describing this Faustian experience, the emotional cost was high: "God didn't want me," he told his mother, "but the devil did." Severe behavioral disruptions emerged, and the youngster was subsequently referred to a psychologist, who refused to discuss the NDE: "You know children and their imaginations" (188). A few years later, the mother reported that they had still found no psychologist willing to talk about the experience and that the parents were moving the family to another town, hoping that a change of scene would help ease their son's continuing distress.

Eighteen years after that article, psychologist and medical researcher Richard J. Bonenfant (2001) wrote about the NDE of a six-year-old who also reported encountering both God and the devil. The devil in this case, "composed of rotting, putrid flesh," was trying to "suck" the child away from God. The boy reported being terrified and that he "desperately tried to keep his faith in God" (Bonenfant 2001, 90). He believed that God rescued him but could not say how.

The parents reported that for months the boy experienced anxiety and nightmares and had become more interested in religious matters. Unlike the child Bush (1983) described, the child Bonenfant (2001) described showed no evidence of lasting emotional problems.

In 1985, British psychologist Margot Grey reported on the earliest general study to look seriously at distressing NDEs. Her research sample consisted of 39 experiencers—32 British and 9 American—of whom 12 percent reported terrifying experiences. Because those in her own sample were so few, she incorporated distressing accounts from other studies into her thinking (though not into her study data) so as to understand them more clearly.

Grey had looked carefully enough to notice the distinction between a "negative" and a "hellish" experience and to recognize that radiant and distressing experiences share similar elements but with differing details and emotions. Her explicit definitions included virtually all elements to be found in a population of these distressing NDEs:

> ... a feeling of extreme fear or panic ... emotional and mental anguish, extending to states of the utmost desperation ... a great sense of desolation ... the brink of a pit ... the edge of an abyss ... being tricked into death and [needing] to keep their wits about them to prevent this from happening.
>
> The hell-like experience ... includes all [those] elements ... often a definite sense of being dragged down by some evil force ... visions of wrathful or demonic creatures ... [or] unseen beings or figures which are often faceless or hooded ... intensely cold or unbearably hot ... sounds that resemble the wailing of "souls" in torment ... a fearsome noise. (Grey 1985, 58)

Despite Grey's clear witness to the existence and range of unpleasant NDEs, it would be seven years before the next publication about them in the near-death literature.

In the spring of 1992, P. M. H. Atwater announced that despite claims about the rarity of unpleasant NDEs, her interviews showed "an abundance of such cases: 105 out of the more than 700 I have queried" (Atwater 1992, 150). Like Grey, she had noticed a similarity of patterns in distressing and radiant experiences and offered a comparison (Atwater 1992, 154; see Table 4.1). If there was anything controversial in the Atwater article, it was the flat-out certainty with which she couched her conclusions about why a distressing NDE may occur: "It is usually experienced by those who seem to have deeply suppressed or repressed guilts, fears, and angers,

Table 4.1
Comparison of Heaven-Like and Hell-Like NDEs

Heaven-Like Cases	Hell-Like Cases
friendly beings	lifeless or threatening apparitions
beautiful, lovely environments	barren or ugly expanses
conversations and dialogue	threats, screams, silence
total acceptance and an over-whelming sensation of love	danger and the possibility of violence, torture
a feeling of warmth and a sense of heaven	a feeling of cold (or temperature extremes) and a sense of hell

and/or those who expect some kind of punishment or accountability after death" (Atwater 1992, 156).

A century of psychology indicates the likelihood that *everyone* has deeply suppressed guilt, fear, and anger; but in the absence of a control group, Atwater did not demonstrate how people with distressing NDEs might differ from the population at large or from people with pleasurable NDEs. Further, individuals who expected judgment after death or were likely to be feeling guilt, fear, or anger—as, for example, suicide attempters—have reported blissful NDEs (Greyson 1991; Rosen 1975). Although logic, intuition, or culturally based expectations may suggest such links, the literature so far has shown no quantitative evidence to support them.

In a 1995 article, William Serdahely, a professor of health science at Montana State University, reported that of 12 NDErs, 33 percent considered the experience "frightening, scary, unpleasant" but without specifically hellish images. He also heard two secondhand accounts of NDEs that he says were considered hellish (Serdahely 1995, 188).

In 2001, a Swiss professor of religious studies, Hubert Knoblauch, and two master's-level researchers from German universities, Ina Schmied and Bernt Schnettler, working with a professional research organization, published the first study of NDEs in Germany. From their national survey sample, 82 respondents (4%) reported NDEs. Although the ideological separation of East Germany and West Germany did not seem to affect the *occurrence* of NDEs, "among West German NDErs, 60% reported positive emotions and 29% negative; while amongst East German NDErs, only 40% reported positive emotions and 60% negative" (Knoblauch, Schmied, and Schnettler 2001, 25). The authors concluded that not only the interpretation but "also the very content of what is experienced ... *is culturally constructed*" (Knoblauch, Schmied, and Schnettler 2001, 28)—an interesting contrast to the findings of Alan Kellehear (see his chapter in this volume), who found some NDE features to be universal across cultures, whereas other features are culturally unique.

Knoblauch, Schmied, and Schnettler (2001) also found that fewer than 50 percent of respondents claimed to have been in life-threatening situations when experiencing their NDEs, and only 6 percent claimed to have been clinically dead (Knoblauch, Schmied, and Schnettler 2001, 22). With such a percentage of NDEs not linked to biological death, the question arises: If a distressing NDE isn't about an afterlife "hell," what is it about?

Why Are Results So Different?

In all, although 9 studies with 459 experiencers found no accounts of distressing NDEs (0%), 12 other studies involving 1,369 experiencers produced the accounts of 315 people (23%) who reported NDEs ranging from disturbing to terrifying or despairing. Why are the results so different?

Unreadiness to Disclose

People who have had a terrible NDE are notoriously reluctant to talk. In my own experience, they make contact but do not answer callbacks; they cancel appointments; they disappear. Medical social worker Kimberly Clark (now Sharp) observed in 1986 that "there's lots of problems with a negative experience ... People will call and begin to talk about them, but then change their mind and say, 'Goodbye, I have to go.' And they often won't tell you who they are when they call ... [and] sometimes I won't hear from them ever again after they related it to me" (Flynn 1986, 87).

In a different context (1984), Clark had noted that it is important "not to pressure patients who are not ready to talk about [a distressing NDE]." She continued, "I have come to appreciate how critical timing is in approaching near-death experiencers, and I no longer push while people are in the hospital" (Clark 1984, 246).

Even with pleasurable experiences, she observed, "it is most common ... to hear about patients' NDEs after they are already out of the hospital and have returned for a follow-up clinic visit. Many people just are not ready to deal with the experience until some time has passed" (Clark 1984, 248).

With distressing NDEs, any problem of disclosure is compounded, so even the best-designed study will not bring out an account unless the person is ready to disclose. Invaluable reading on NDE disclosure generally is Regina M. Hoffman's (1995) "Disclosure Habits after Near-Death Experiences: Influences, Obstacles, and Listener Selection."

What Are the Questions?

Distressing NDEs are likely to remain buried if questions are not designed to draw them out. Carol Zaleski (1987) observed that "the interviewer—whose line of questioning is designed to be reassuring and upbeat ... is unlikely to elicit disturbing testimony ... [and some researchers] pursued a line of questioning that drew explicitly on [pleasurable] imagery from *Life after Life*" (Zaleski 1987, 149).

Who Is Asking? The most complete information appears to come when NDErs are interviewed well after the experience, in an informal setting, with no time constraints, and by a person they trust. Cherie Sutherland (1997) was clear that trust is essential for the revelation of intensely personal confidences (Sutherland 1997, 54). The empathetic physician Barbara Rommer (2000) could report that by her 20th interview she was already finding "accounts that were very frightening" (Rommer 2000, xx), whereas Carol Zaleski (1987) noted the comment of one of Sabom's NDEr participants: "I'll be damned if I share my feelings about death and dying with anyone who makes 2-minute U-turns at the foot of my bed" (Zaleski 1987, 148).

What Does the Asker Want to Know? Zaleski (1987) has commented on the difficulty of avoiding all researcher bias. Bruce Greyson, editor of the *Journal of Near-Death Studies* for two decades, has been quoted as acknowledging, relative to distressing NDEs, that in the early studies, "we didn't try to find them because we didn't want to know" (Atwater 1992, 150).

DISTRESSING NDEs AS A SCHOLARLY FOCUS

Studies of Distressing NDEs

The extreme difficulty of finding individuals who, at least in the early years, were willing to share a distressing experience is indicated by the fact that 12 years elapsed from Rawlings's (1978) "chilling testimony" to the first evaluative study of distressing NDEs. In 1992, Greyson and Bush reported that in a 10-year collection of accounts of nonpeaceful NDEs, most were brief to the point of abrupt, but 50 contained sufficient detail to identify three distinct phenomenological types (Greyson and Bush 1992).

In the first type, which represented the largest subgroup in the sample, the elements of a classic NDE were interpreted as terrifying. Loss of control appeared to be a significant factor in the fear, as suggested in this fragment: "I was flying, and drawn directly into the vortex or funnel. At the end the lights were blinding, and crystal flashing was unbearable. As I neared the very end, I was reaching for the sides, trying to stop myself from falling off the end into the flashing crystal" (Greyson and Bush 1992, 99).

The second type of experience involved "a paradoxical sensation of ceasing to exist entirely, or of being condemned to a featureless void for eternity ... Sometimes ... a sense of despair that life as we know it not only no longer exists but in fact never did, that it was all a cruel joke" (Greyson and Bush 1992, 101). Of this group, people would sometimes try to argue their way out logically and, following their NDEs, were often left with feelings of terror and a persisting sense of emptiness and desolation.

The third type, represented by the smallest number of accounts, featured graphic hellish symbolism such as threatening demons or falling into a dark pit. None of these accounts converted to a peaceful one with time (Greyson and Bush 1992, 105).

Following Maurice Rawlings's *Beyond Death's Door* by 22 years, internist Barbara Rommer published *Blessing in Disguise* in 2000. She reported that of 300 experiencers she had interviewed, 17.7 percent had a *Less-Than-Positive* (LTP) experience. She suggested that fright about the perception of an externally judged life review might constitute a fourth experience type, noting, "The only time that an interviewee has felt judged by anyone but themself [sic] was in a Less-Than-Positive Near-Death Experience" (89).

Possibly related to that fear is Rommer's (2000) observation that "until a person is able to work through why an LTP occurred, the experience acts as a thorn in his side" (25). That the "thorn" is significant, is evident: "Once the individual explores (often through therapy) the 'why' of the LTP, then suddenly all the dots become connected, a picture forms, and the healing begins" (98). Rommer's assertion is a rare reference to the possible need for psychotherapy or spiritual direction following many distressing NDEs. Beyond those observations, the book is a combination of experiencer accounts and Rommer's heartfelt and highly positive explanations of them.

Although the Rawlings and Rommer books shared the same topic and both authors were physicians, the tones of the two books could not have been more different. Rommer's slant was no less ideologically insistent than Rawlings's perspective. However, Rommer's was New Age metaphysical and optimistic rather than fundamentalist: a cheery assurance of happy endings in contrast to Rawlings's hortatory warnings of damnation. It is difficult to assess many of the conclusions in Rommer's study because they are so interwoven with statements of belief that do not lend themselves to a response other than metaphysical concurrence or outright rejection. Despite the book's significant flaws of logic and evidence, it remains to date the strongest collection of distressing NDEs in professional near-death literature.

PUBLISHED COMMENTARY ON DISTRESSING NDEs

How They Work: Phenomenology, Physiology, Psyche

In *Life at Death*, Ring (1980) described distressing NDEs as infrequent "hallucinatory visions" (195). In *Heading toward Omega* (1984), he reported that according to the literature, they appear "exceedingly rarely" (44). For a decade, he did not waiver from these assertions. Then, in 1994, Ring took an entirely different approach: Distressing experiences do seem to occur, he wrote, but they have no real ontological status (22). Citing as primary evidence *A Course in Miracles*, Ring (1994) argued, first, that of the experience types Greyson and Bush (1992) identified, the "inverted" Type I and hellish Type III, are variants of the prototypical radiant NDE, and that if the experiencer were to let go of the ego's hold on illusory identity, the NDE would transform into the hoped-for peace of the classic near-death experience.

In Ring's words, "According to the *Course*, what's real—and the only thing that's real—is what NDErs call 'the Light.' ... What's illusion, on the other hand, is your idea of yourself, your ego ... If, however, the person begins to let go, or simply surrenders to the Light ... one then becomes permeated by the Light—Reality itself ... Frightening NDEs, therefore, though they are by definition scary, aren't real" (Ring 1994, 15–16).

Shifting to the Void experience, Greyson and Bush's (1992) Type II, Ring (1994) argued that since ketamine and LSD commonly produce images similar or identical to those of NDEs, "experiences of the Void— though highly real—are not true NDEs as such but are essentially emergence reactions to inadequate anesthesia" (20–21). He concluded that "frightening NDEs merely reflect the fact that hell is actually the experience of an illusory separative [sic] ego fighting a phantom battle" (22). He would reiterate this stance two years later (Ring 1996).

In that same 1994 issue of the *Journal of Near-Death Studies*, Ring's article was followed by a response from Christopher M. Bache, a professor of philosophy and religious studies at Youngstown State University, Ohio, trained in the psychedelic and holotropic work of Stanislav Grof. Although he agreed with Ring that resistance to ego death causes distressing NDEs, Bache maintained that "all three forms of frightening NDEs— inverted, hellish, and meaningless void—are better understood as rooted in the perinatal level of consciousness [hypothesized by Grof]" (25), which is "both the basement of personal consciousness and the beginning of transpersonal consciousness" (38). Therefore, "a frightening NDE is not an alternative NDE but an incomplete NDE. It is not necessarily a reflection of the individual's moral character but represents instead an encounter with some of the deepest structures of the psyche, structures that are universally distributed among persons" (41–42).

Citing St. Teresa of Avila, who considered her many frightening experiences "helpful to her spiritual development," Bache observed that "the descent into hell is simply an extreme instance of a large set of arduous experiences that are a rather common feature of the mystic's journey" (43).

Writing from a physiological perspective, behavioral neuroscientist Todd Murphy (1999, 2001) has pointed out that the human brain's temporal lobe and its limbic system, long recognized as associated with emotional states, seem likely to be involved in NDEs. Especially relevant to distressing NDEs is Murphy's mention of the seeming "affective lateralization" of the temporal lobe, the theory positing that the right temporal cortex is specialized for positive emotions and the left for negative emotions such as fear, sorrow, and dread. A harrowing experience occurs when "the positive affect of most NDEs, originating in the right temporal cortex, is replaced by negative affect from the left temporal cortex" (109).

Greyson (personal communication) has pointed out that the separation of pleasant and unpleasant emotions into the right and left amygdalas "is not quite as clear-cut" as Murphy has suggested. However, Greyson affirms that the affective component of NDEs does seem attributable to activity in the amygdala and related brain centers, and it remains a promising area for continued investigation.

Elsewhere, Murphy (2001) has noted that "when we consider how young (and poorly funded) the field of NDE research is, it seems reasonable to assume that there are determinative influences still waiting to be discovered" (115). Speculation about temporal lobe lateralization, mentioned in Murphy's 2001 article, is pursued at length on his Web site (http://www.shaktitechnology.com/neurotheology.htm).

What They Are: Archetype, Faith, Persistence, Suffering

As early as 1983, philosophy professor Michael Grosso was calling for an interdisciplinary approach to NDEs, pointing to Carl Jung's theory of archetypes as being central to that perspective. His view encompassed distressing as well as blissful NDEs, quoting Jung that "just as all archetypes have a positive, favorable bright side that points upwards, so also they have one that points downward, partly negative and unfavorable, partly chthonic" (186). In content, the dark encounter, especially the hellish experiences with their lakes of fire and demonic figures, "more clearly resembles the mythical and religious accounts of the afterlife … The clearer this resemblance, the clearer the case is for the archetypal nature of the NDE" (Grosso 1983, 186). Although exploration of archetypes and the near-death images of both blissful and painful NDEs seems like a potentially rich resource, it has received surprisingly little attention in the literature, other than from Grosso.

The 1987 book *Otherworld Journeys: Accounts of Near-Death Experience in Medieval and Modern Time* is, in my opinion—and in the opinion of several other scholars (Basford 1990; Fox 2003; Matlock 1989; Zimdars-Swartz 1990)—a scholarly classic on the topic of near-death experiences. In it, Carol Zaleski, a professor of religion at Smith College, described otherworld journeys in the history of world religions, medieval near-death narratives, and modern NDEs. She looked at religious underpinnings, scientific theories, skeptics' objections, the force of culture, and the role of the researcher. In other words, what she brought to the exploration of NDEs was a perspective unprecedented in its breadth.

Zaleski (1987) identified four types of near-death experience (26–42):

- common in the *Dialogues* of Gregory the Great, *miracle* stories attesting to the ongoing activity of signs from heaven, the bringing back of information or messages. Today's more sensationalized autobiographical NDE paperbacks are of the same type;
- accounts like those of the eighth-century Anglo-Saxon Bede, with a pattern of *death, revival, and conversion,* as with St. Paul and seen in contemporary accounts like that of Howard Storm, where there is a drastic life turnaround (Cressy 1994);
- journeys of *apocalypse,* the NDEs of revelation, of wonder and amazement and future scenarios, such as that of Tom Sawyer (Farr 1993); and
- accounts of *pilgrimage,* of travel involving many scenes and landscapes, like that of George Ritchie (Ritchie 1983).

Zaleski is noteworthy for her recognition that modern NDE reports are strikingly empty of unpleasant scenarios. Whereas medieval and older folkloric and mythological stories are replete with images of both ascension and fall, one leading to salvation, the other at best to purgatory, she observed that "modern accounts tell us that despite the differences in individual experiences, all move in one direction from darkness to light, from death to heaven" (122).

Certainly, anyone venturing into near-death studies thinking to be objective should read Zaleski on the role of near-death researchers, since her section on the interplay of personal beliefs and reporting is especially perceptive. It is the researcher who determines the questions, designs the scales, does the interviews or trains those who do them, and helps to determine the final shape of near-death testimony. She asserted, "We have seen that the vision story is formed in an inner dialogue between the visionary and his culture and develops in the telling and retelling, until it finally comes into the hands of an author who shapes it further for didactic, polemic, or literary use" (153).

Another accomplished religious scholar is Gracia Fay Ellwood, whose "Distressing Near-Death Experiences as Photographic Negatives" appeared in the *Journal of Near-Death Studies* in 1996 before expanding into the 2001 book *The Uttermost Deep: The Challenge of Near-Death Experiences.* Ellwood's subject in these works is the types, themes, patterns, and interpretive frameworks surrounding NDEs and how they may contribute to a coherent theory of survival, of life after death. She examined the near-death literature but expanded her horizon to include a range of historical

and religious perspectives on survival, including contributions from parapsychology. To those readers who may be put off by the mention of parapsychology, I say, "Don't quit yet." To leave her book because of possibly
uncomfortable ideas would be to miss a rich background of information
simply not available elsewhere in one place. Ellwood's book is one of the
best anywhere for its breadth.

Some of Ellwood's distinctions smash cherished preconceptions about
NDEs, such as when she noted that "we have not yet pinpointed the reasons why some are painful. Besides, some persons have had painful and radiant experiences in quick succession with no noticeable change of heart
between them, and occasionally experiences will begin with peace and
happiness then become painful, or vice versa" (95).

Ellwood is at her best in the overview of interpretations of NDEs, as in
this scholarly and graceful comparison of two interpretations of frightening
NDEs:

> In the full projectionist position only the Ultimate, the Light, is really real …
> Thus to the NDEr enduring tormenting beings or chaos or cosmic loneliness,
> and to the story's anxious listener, the projectionist response is: When you see
> with clear consciousness, there is nothing to fear; the situation isn't real; you
> are already "home."
>
> For some whose approaches are essentially gradualist or initiatory, how-
> ever … conscious beings are more than projections; they have an existence
> in their own right. They may be aware of their Creator/Source, or may be
> ignorant or partially asleep. Their decisions make a difference; they can
> become evil, can do harm to others and themselves. They can suffer terribly;
> they can help and heal. But there is a cosmic pattern to which they belong,
> a … story with a happy ending. From these perspectives the response to evil
> and to the prospect of cosmic pain is: With your eyes on the prize, control
> your fear, choose to love; you will be "home" in the morning. (264–65).

Returning now to Ring's (1994) assertions that because experiences
induced by ketamine and LSD may contain imagery identical to that of a
Void experience, the latter "are not true NDEs as such but are essentially
emergence reactions to inadequate anesthesia" (20), one must surely dis-
agree with Ring's conclusion (Bush 1994).

The first reason for disagreement is that Ring discounted only childbirth-anesthesia experiences of the Void, not childbirth-anesthesia experiences that were radiant. Moreover, the pharmacological dismissal of NDEs
had been rejected by the near-death research community years earlier;
Ring himself (1980) had said that "although anesthetics may not preclude
phenomena associated with near-death experiences, such experiences cannot be explained by them" (211). In response: "If the pharmacological
theory is inadequate as explanation of radiant NDEs, it is difficult to

understand how it should now be considered sufficient as explanation of one type of frightening experience" (Bush 1994, 48).

Regarding the concept of "an illusory separative ego fighting a phantom battle" (Ring 1994, 22), one must plea for an existential approach: "At the level at which the horrific experience is brought into daily living ... exploration of symbol, metaphor, and meaning will certainly be more productive as a starting point than dismissal" (Bush 1994, 53).

By the 40th anniversary of my own near-death experience, I thought perhaps I had enough information to attempt a summary, presented in "Afterward: Making Meaning after a Frightening Near-Death Experience," a lengthy article (Bush 2002). Here I briefly mention only its major points.

First, in the years since Bruce Greyson and I identified three distinct types of experience, I had also noticed three ways in which people appear to make sense of this type of event in their lives (Bush 2002):

- The *conversion* response, the most common: "people who interpret their NDE as a warning, who are able to connect it with previous behaviors they identify as unwise or downright wrong, and who then find avenues by which to modify their lives in satisfying ways" (104).
- The *reductionism* response, what most people mean when they say, "It was only ..." To quote a young experiencer: "There are actual rational explanations for what I experienced. British researcher Susan Blackmore says [it is endorphins and cortical activity]. In the 1930s, a University of Chicago scientist, Heinrich Kluver, PhD, determined that ... [it is anoxia] ... It's all very scientific" (107).
- In the third category are "people who, years later, may still struggle with the existential implications of a frightening NDE" (108). This response often, but not exclusively, follows an experience of the Void. *What did I do to deserve this? What is the truth about existence? What is there that I can't identify about myself, that this should happen? What are the rules, if the rules I lived by don't work?* Not for a long time, if ever, do they lose their fear of death (110).

  These were the people most likely to have sought counseling, often unsuccessfully. There are too many stories of medications prescribed to mask the questioning; of therapists who will not address the matter, or who leave the client feeling blamed, or who romanticize spirituality and cannot deal with its dark side; and of clergy who have no idea what to say or who reject the experience outright (109).

A second major point was that I noted a curious-seeming inversion of interest in radiant and distressing NDEs. The literature contained abundant discussion of the aftereffects of radiant NDEs but virtually none about how a person's prior mental or emotional state, disposition, or upbringing might have contributed to the experience. The exact opposite was the case with distressing NDEs, about which the literature contained virtually no mention of aftereffects but offered abundant assumptions that negative mental and emotional states, general disposition, and upbringing had contributed to such an experience (Bush 2002, 111). The implication is clear though perhaps unwitting: The writers assumed something was "wrong" with these experiencers.

Third, based on my own struggle in interpreting a painful NDE and its implications, I wanted to point out the differences in Eastern and Western thinking about ego and the self/no-self question and to note the difficulties that the idea of an illusory self poses for many Westerners. Western religious traditions have been grounded in concepts of personal identity and personal relationship, and Christianity has been called "the most psychological of all religions because of ... the important role which it assigns to the ego as the bearer of consciousness" (Bush 2002, 114). (This difference is illustrated in a different sense by Ellwood's projective and initiatory interpretive frameworks.) I introduced the idea of cultural adaptation of counseling strategies with a quote from depth psychologist Lionel Corbett (1996):

> Even the most sublime wisdom is of no value if it is given at the wrong time, to the wrong person or in the wrong manner. We may need to make a personal choice between Buddhism's assertion that there is no self in the sense of an entity (*anatman*), and the Judaeo-Christian and psychological assumption that such an entity exists. (115)

A fourth central idea (Bush 2002) was that although so much attention has been directed to the physiological precipitants of and cosmic theories *about* NDEs, little has been given to the actual remembered *experience:* the images with their associated emotions and how their interpretation reshapes a person's worldview. In a secular time in which literal meanings are better understood than metaphor and in which journalism trumps symbolic language in public value, individuals have little cultural support when trying to make useful sense of a disturbing NDE. Ultimately, my search for healing metaphor led to the (really quite obvious) observation that "just as the Biblical story of Eden reflects the archetype of the earliest phases of human and individual development into consciousness, so the constellation of elements in the hero's journey forms the template of the dark NDE" (121).

The final section of the article (Bush 2002), lists approaches that might be helpful in interpreting, and thus integrating, a distressing NDE.

In this section, the last word on the hypothesized phenomenology of distressing NDEs belongs to Mishka Jambor, a Polish philosopher now living in Australia whose field of interest is transcendent experiences. The most helpful approach to the mystery of distressing NDEs is a matter of asking the right questions—and her questions are breathtaking. Her 1997 article "The Mystery of Frightening Transcendent Experience" moved the discussion and my understanding of NDEs to an entirely new level.

"Let us explore then transcendent experiences," she said, explicitly considering both frightening and pleasant experiences "transcendent" because they move beyond ordinary waking consciousness toward something experientially more real. Given their similarity, Jambor wondered, "Where do all of these experiences come from?" And with that she arrived at her central question: "What kind of beings are we, that we can feel in such a profound way that the *feeling alone makes for heaven and hell* (for otherwise the experience would only be judged cognitively as unusual and interesting)?" (Jambor 1997, 164).

She called the overwhelming emotional forces "deep-feeling" and asked, "What is its origin?" If the pleasant deep-feeling—that of a radiant NDE—originates in "ultimate reality," what of the frightening deep-feeling, which, she said, "deserves the name 'abyss': What is that force, an abyss, into which mundane and transcendent events plunge us?" (Jambor 1997, 166).

The testimony of spiritual traditions and mystics is that "the true Beyond" is beyond any pair of opposites; so Jambor (1997) finds it unlikely that ultimate reality would be constituted by an element, bliss, that has an opposite, horror/pain. She put forward the idea that the first breakup of the nonduality of the Beyond lies in "awareness-in-bliss and awareness-in-horror"—the "primordial building blocks of the manifest world: desire and aversion, enjoyment and pain, and even attraction and repulsion devoid of consciousness are the ground rules of the world of individuation" (168).

Radiant, inverted, and hellish NDEs belong to "a class of experiences with supersensory components" (Jambor 1997, 170). Although supersensory, the reality they access is "clearly not the ultimate state beyond space and time, beyond distinctions, and beyond form" because experiences develop in sequence (time), with discrete events and spatial characteristics; yet they are a step *toward* the Beyond (167). On the other hand, some transcendent experiences, whether pleasant or frightening, surpass the sensory level but retain emotional content from the cognitive level; as example, she mentioned the meaningless and painful, lonely void.

Jambor (1997) touched on the dynamics of affliction and suffering, referencing the work of Simone Weil and suggesting how surrender may evolve from submersion in horror and pain. Interestingly, Jambor's model seems complementary to Todd Murphy's description of affective lateralization and the function of the amygdala.

Summarizing, Jambor (1997) said:

> So far near-death research has labored under the schism between the metaphysical and existential aspect of NDEs. This need not be so. We require a

metaphysics that delivers straightforwardly the existential advice of taking both radiant and frightening NDEs equally seriously. Certainly the scenario of the Beyond and bliss/abyss duality goes part of the way toward such a metaphysics. (174)

As a model, Jambor's (1997) proposition feels balanced and inclusive. She concluded her article by saying, "We need a series of questions to inspire a new theory, or a refinement of ones already in existence" (174). She then posed seven questions, which conclude the literature review section of this chapter:

1. [Echoing Bache] When so many people are frightened of death and ego dissolution, why are so few of them propelled into frightening NDEs?
2. Why is there such a narrow thematic content of frightening NDEs? Bache's answer—that perinatal experiences, including frightening NDEs, activate a level of the psyche where universal motifs prevail—seems quite satisfactory, but perhaps there are alternative explanations.
3. Is ego death enough to transcend horror and pain? Or does ego-death make more room for both pleasant and frightening transcendent realities to be fully encountered?
4. If ... the transcendence of valuation [is] the sublime task beyond the immersion in bliss, how could it be carried out or lived?
5. What is the essence of spiritual surrender? Has it got anything to do with facing abyss?
6. Is the traditional Christian and Buddhist view of pain as purification valid? What is being purified? Is purification another name for detachment from sensory and conceptual components of one's life, such as beliefs and worldview?
7. And finally, at what point are we filled with true love and compassion? Could near-death research contribute to the longstanding philosophical enquiry into the nature of good and evil? (174–75)

CONCLUSIONS

A generation of inquiry has provided at least a sketch of the outlines of frightening and otherwise distressing near-death experiences.

What Can Be Concluded with Relative Certainty

Although the list presented here seems to represent facts about distressing NDEs that can be concluded with relative certainty, this is one person's view; its constitution and wording are open for discussion:

• Near-death experiences, both radiant and distressing, are not a unique type of event but belong to a family of experiences of the deep psyche, including experiences of prayer, meditation, shamanic initiation, near-death, and other circumstances; in this list, "NDE" refers to any of these experiences.

- A conclusion about the meaning of an NDE is initiated by the predominant emotional tone within the experience.
- Some NDEs are marked by intense terror, guilt, panic, loneliness, despair; as radiant NDEs represent the heights of spiritual experience, these distressing NDEs represent the depths.
- Whether blissful or harrowing, the general pattern of NDEs is similar: a sense of movement, possibly an out-of-body experience, intense emotions, ineffability, light or darkness, encounter with nonmaterial beings, life-changing messages, sometimes transcendent elements such as symbols and archetypal images.
- Any NDE may remain emotionally consistent, or it may move from distressing emotions to pleasurable or from pleasurable emotions to distressing.
- Whereas the *content* of an experience may be to some extent culturally conditioned, certainly post-NDE *interpretations* are culturally derived.
- Some temporal lobe involvement seems central as a physiological mediator of the affective component of NDEs, whether or not the experiences originate from, or occur independent of, brain function.
- Distressing NDEs are more common than has been thought, with a percentage possibly in the mid- to high teens.
- Distressing NDEs are underreported out of fear, shame, social stigma, the sense that the experiencer cannot burden others with such horrific information, avoidance of reliving the experience, and other reasons.
- Distressing NDEs fit no *single* description but may be catgorized as at least three general types (inverted, void, hell-like), in addition to the single case of a condemnation-laden life review that Rommer reported.
- Distressing NDEs occur in both life-threatening and non-life-threatening situations.
- Distressing NDEs may produce long-lasting emotional and psychospiritual trauma.
- After experiencing a distressing NDE, a person may find meaning through conversion or reductionism, or may struggle to come to resolution.
- There is *no evidence* that these experiences are punishment for wrong beliefs or unacceptable or evil behavior, nor does evidence show that NDEs happen only to bad people.

What Is Relatively or Completely Unknown

What 30 years of scholarly inquiry has not yet revealed is why NDEs occur. Most authors of the still-scanty professional literature on distressing

NDEs display widely held cultural assumptions about the people who have these experiences—but without concrete evidence to support their assertions and, indeed, in the face of evidence that contradicts them. These questions need answers:

- *Who experience distressing NDEs?* Are there, in fact, contributing personal factors in terms of temperament, life history, behaviors and beliefs, religious upbringing, and related influences that contribute to the occurrence of harrowing experiences? Are the people who have distressing NDEs uniquely guilty, hostile, angry, unloving, rigid, ego-bound, God-denying, controlling, or fearful as has been commonly reported? Do their characteristics actually differ substantively from individuals who have had a pleasurable NDE or from the population norm?
- *Is there a relationship between prior behaviors and occurrence of a distressing NDE?* In those experiencing distressing NDEs, is there evidence of genuinely maladaptive behavior beforehand that is different from the behavior of people experiencing radiant NDEs or who represent the population at large, or is the perception of such behavior an artifact of the interpretation and resolution of the experience?

What Remains to Be Investigated

Resistance to Distressing NDEs

Resistance to the subject of distressing experiences remains an issue to which there is no clear answer. However, this matter is important, for attitudes about distressing NDEs have implications for all experiencers, especially in support groups and in the language of researchers.

One manifestation of resistance is terminology with negative connotations that deny, devalue, and stigmatize distressing NDEs and those who report them, even when writers and speakers are unconscious of those potentials. For example, in a work very early in his career in the field of near-death studies, Ring (1980) described disturbing NDEs as the slums of a city, created by "the nature of the minds that are interacting to create this reality" (249). However unintentionally, this descriptive analogy displays the same kind of linguistic shading found in stereotypes about poverty or racism: Distressing experiences are "the slums of a city," the lowest level of urban environments, from which privileged travelers—those with pleasurable NDEs—are protected. It is "the nature of their minds" that relegates some individuals to the "lower domain." The challenge for NDE authors, speakers, and discussants is to find analogies and terminology that illustrate and describe differences without devaluing diverse types of NDEs or their experiencers.

It is likely an aspect of human nature to recoil initially from distressing phenomena. It also is a manifestation of maturity to overcome that initial impulse, especially in the service of enhanced compassion and the promotion of greater well-being—both one's own and others'. A study of resistance to the subject of distressing NDEs would make an interesting and useful focus of scholarly inquiry.

Is It Really Hell?

With Barbara Rommer one can say, "I believe with all my heart," but surely the greatest healing to be offered is, not to comfort while ignoring the pain, but to enter all kinds of NDEs fully and to see them with new eyes. About distressing NDEs, a conventional, literal afterlife interpretation is certainly possible, with efforts to love vying with claims of damnation and eternal suffering; however, that interpretation, unexamined, limits the range of tones to negatives: guilt, torment, an assumption of evil. Other perspectives can broaden and clarify even a literal understanding, and reframing may help mitigate the dread of addressing the images within frightening experiences. Images of fire, for instance, traditionally signify purification, not only punishment; the Void that terrifies a beginner in spiritual practice may be the long-sought objective of the accomplished mystic.

What about the experience is so profoundly disturbing? We need to ask the question, and keep asking it, until we can label the source, both personally and as a discipline. What is frightening, and why? Almost a quarter-century ago, Michael Grosso (1983) observed that "it is possible, as Jung argued, that 'modern man' ... has lost touch with the healing symbols and energies of the deep psyche that help us to cope with death and dying" (5). We need more information to help reestablish that touch—from depth psychology about *discerning* those healing symbols in NDEs and *how* energies of the deep psyche help us to cope with death and dying, examples of how dreamwork techniques can be helpful, how the sacred literatures offer insights, and more from practicing psychotherapists and spiritual directors about interventions that are helpful in resolving difficult experiences.

Who Knows What?

When as a layperson I first began looking for information about frightening NDEs, there was simply nothing to go on: There were no index listings, no library references, no cross-references. I once asked, with embarrassing naiveté, "Isn't there something in the Bible about these things?" and from the response one might have suspected that perhaps I was delusional. It was as if near-death experience were a field unto itself, with no antecedents, no siblings, no referents.

A brilliant Jungian scholar much later said to me, "These experiences are crying for integration." Of course, he meant that in a psychodynamic sense, but it applies also to the field of near-death studies and its near relatives. It is past time to integrate more of what other disciplines know into the framework of near-death studies. The *Journal of Near-Death Studies* continues its long tradition of excellence as a forum; through the *Journal*, cross-pollination has been under way, but there is so much more to say.

- What is the connection between near-death and what *transpersonal psychology* calls "nadir" experiences—a good name that could be adopted at least to characterize the most distressing NDEs?
- The *meditative traditions* have centuries of experience and information to share. For example, as mindfulness meditation teacher Shinzen Young (2005) has said, "À propos of images of decay, destruction, personal mortality and being assailed or devoured: Two traditions describe these in great detail as stages associated with spiritual growth, Shamanism and Buddhism ... Such phenomena are best interpreted as part of a natural process of release from the deep archetypal levels of the mind. In Shamanism, they are a common feature of the ordeal that the shaman must pass through."
- It would be helpful to hear more commentary on *mysticism*, including its hazards, and how contemporary visionaries incorporate frightening experiences into their lives and understanding.
- It would be helpful to hear more from the fields of *depth psychology* and *mythology* about practically anything, but especially about symbols. How does the psychological realm of distressing and hellish NDEs relate to human suffering as is now happening in the external world, in torture, war, sexual violence, and enslavement?
- As the work of sociologist James McClenon (1994) demonstrates, an experience-centered approach to the *sociology of belief, medicine, religion, and folklore* offers a virtually untapped mine of insights and data.
- Practical information could come from *psychotherapy*, such as how interventions for post-traumatic stress disorder may be helpful for some distressing NDE experiencers.
- As a field, near-death studies is overdue for exploration of the concerns of the religious institutional community, which has been largely silent about NDEs. *Pastoral care* has been virtually ignored in the NDE literature, as have the *theological* and sociological difficulties mystical experiences present to religious institutions. What studies might broaden both religious and secular comprehension of these experiences?
- What have *hospice and palliative care* professionals observed about frightening experiences of the dying, and what can be said about them?

- As always, continued reference to and from the *neurosciences* and *physics* is essential to further exploration and understanding of all NDEs.

If people from the italicized disciplines do not volunteer their insights to near-death studies, interested researchers can investigate the fields identified on the preceding list to find abundant resources that bear on both pleasurable and harrowing NDEs.

What Can Be Said about Resistance to Surrender?

Surgeon Bernie Siegel used to tell his audiences a list of proofs that God is love. One proof that God is love, he said, is that *blood clots*. Like all creatures, humans are built for survival, for living, for holding on. How, then, are ordinary experiencers to understand the spiritual imperatives to let go, to surrender? Should one prepare for surrender, as Jambor suggests (Question 3)? Further, if, as William James (1902) observed and Todd Murphy's (2001) algorithmic model postulates, the experience is beyond the individual's control, how is it possible to make a decision to surrender from within the experience? What if the force confronting the experiencer appears to be evil? How can a success-driven culture address issues of surrender? Given differing worldviews, an informed and thoughtful discussion about these questions would serve readers well.

How to Talk about Distressing NDEs in Ways That Bridge Interpretive Frameworks

In writing for diverse communities of belief, authors would do well to recognize their statements of faith and to distinguish them consciously from hard evidence. What appears incontrovertible from within one model may be perceived quite differently from outside it. Although authors will continue to speak from those positions—of faith, of religion, of spirituality, of speculation—clarity requires that they not conflate or confuse beliefs with quantifiable evidence and that they communicate to their audiences that they know the difference. Discussion of these challenges would be helpful.

Palliative Care

The question has been posed, what do these findings about distressing NDEs suggest for people in a palliative care setting? At first, it seemed an oxymoron. Certainly, these NDEs can be transformative, but the evidence suggests that this process can take years, and people needing palliative care do not have that luxury. What can one say in these circumstances?

- Listen.
- Tell them something of what is known, that this kind of experience has happened to many people throughout time—to holy people and saints, as well as to other good people. The experience is not permanent. It does not reflect their essential "goodness" or "badness."
- Tell them that sometimes experiences just like theirs, those that go on longer, become peaceful and light-filled and loving.
- Reframe the context of a distressing experience; for example, think of purification rather than punishment, of unfamiliar creatures as guides rather than demons.
- Tell the wonderful stories of radiant NDEs.
- Tell them to look for and ask for the light that is, according to those who have experienced it, pure love.

Five thousand years of near-death and similar shamanic accounts have described the otherworld journey as potentially glorious but fraught also with terrors and challenges. From the *merkabah* tradition of early Jewish mysticism comes the story of four worthy rabbis who made the perilous ascent to Paradise (Couliano 1991, 170). One rabbi looked and died; a second looked and lost his mind; another became a heretic; and one entered in peace and departed in peace. May we come to these mysterious, painful near-death experiences in Rabbi Akiba's peace, holding in our minds this question: What kinds of beings are we, that we can feel in such a profound way that the *feeling alone makes for heaven and hell?*

5

"Trailing Clouds of Glory": The Near-Death Experiences of Western Children and Teens

Cherie Sutherland

Not in entire forgetfulness,
And not in utter nakedness,
But trailing clouds of glory do we come
From God, who is our home:
Heaven lies about us in our infancy!

—William Wordsworth
Ode: Intimations of Immortality from Recollections of Early Childhood
(Quiller-Couch 1919)

For more than 30 years now, since Raymond Moody published his pioneering work *Life after Life* in 1975, people have been fascinated by the phenomenon he named "the near-death experience" (NDE). Quite apart from the more general public and media interest generated by the release of Moody's book, many researchers embraced the challenge of further investigation.

By 1982, interest in NDEs had become widespread, although the NDEs of children and adolescents rarely rated a mention even in the professional literature. It was not until 1983 that the spotlight was focused for the first time on child near-death experiencers (NDErs) when Melvin Morse published the now well-known case of a seven-year-old near-drowning victim. Morse had resuscitated this child, whom he later called Katie, in the emergency room of a nearby hospital. Two weeks later during a follow-up appointment, when Morse attempted to identify the circumstances of Katie's near drowning by asking what she remembered from the experience, she replied, "Do you mean when I visited the heavenly Father?" She then became embarrassed and would go no further with her story.

One week later, however, during another visit, Katie described traveling through a dark tunnel, which became bright when a tall woman "with bright yellow hair" appeared. This otherworldly guide, Elizabeth, accompanied Katie into heaven, where she encountered deceased relatives and even two souls awaiting rebirth; and then she met "the heavenly Father and Jesus." After being asked if she wanted to see her mother again, she said yes and woke up in her body. Despite being amazed by what he heard, Morse later wrote that she had told her story in such a "powerful and compelling" way, he believed her implicitly (Morse and Perry 1990, 7).

Soon after the publication of Morse's article, Nancy Evans Bush (1983) reported 17 accounts of NDEs in children, and in 1984, Glen Gabbard and Stuart Twemlow—who, himself, had had an NDE as a child—published three more cases in *With the Eyes of the Mind*. Even in 1990, at the time Morse with Paul Perry published *Closer to the Light*, the number of child NDE accounts was still small (Herzog and Herrin 1985; Morse et al. 1986; Morse, Conner, and Tyler 1985; Serdahely 1987–88, 1989–90, 1990; Serdahely and Walker 1990a, 1990b).

Because *Closer to the Light* was the first book devoted exclusively to the NDEs of children and provided a source readily available to the media and wider public alike, its contents were both enthusiastically welcomed and vigorously debated. By that time, the general appetite for the subject seemed to have become insatiable. There was even a growing interest in child NDErs among researchers such as Gabbard and Twemlow (1984) and Harvey Irwin (1989) because it was believed that the accounts of children, especially very young ones, would be relatively free of cultural influence. Other books with a focus on this population soon followed (Steiger and Steiger 1995; Sutherland 1995), further adding to the pool of child NDE accounts.

By 2006, several hundred child NDErs were mentioned in the literature, yet in some cases the lack of recorded detail rendered them of little use to future research. It has also been frustrating to find that over a series of publications, a particular child's case can be presented by the same author under different names, with different ages, and even with different versions of distinctive features of the experience. In a bid for clarity, I suggest it would be useful for authors to refer consistently to their cases, at the very least, by a particular name, and for their age to be noted—at both NDE and interview—so that individual cases could be tracked over time from publication to publication. In addition, it is always helpful for an author to report the circumstances surrounding the NDE and, of course, where relevant, the aftereffects. However, leaving aside other fundamental research concerns such as study design, sample selection, secondhand reports, and impressive statistical analysis of inadequate samples, a return to the NDE itself always seems warranted.

PHENOMENOLOGY OF THE NDE

Moody (1975), in his popular first book, outlined what he called a theoretically "ideal" NDE that embodied all the common elements of the experience in an order he'd found to be typical. Ring's (1980) research strongly supported Moody's findings, but Ring found that the earlier stages of the "core" experience were far more common than the later ones (Ring 1980, 39–66).

Many others have corroborated these early findings, and some researchers have since turned their attention to classifying NDEs into particular types or categories. For instance, in an early paper, Bruce Greyson (1983) introduced the NDE Scale; and in 1992, Greyson and Bush made the first serious attempt to distinguish between a variety of frightening or distressing experiences. Researchers, handicapped as they were by the small number of cases available for comparison, at first believed that children did not have distressing experiences at all or that they occurred only in teens (Atwater 1995, 10). Neither did they believe children had life reviews, frightening or otherwise (Bush 1983; Morse et al. 1986). However, as the number of child and childhood cases grew, these conclusions were subsequently shown to be incorrect.

In order to consider these issues, as well as others, we must return to the raw material at the center of all this research activity and give a voice to the NDErs themselves because it is in their stories that the evidence and the answers are often to be found.

COMPARISON OF ADULT AND CHILD EXPERIENCES

There is no doubt that every NDE is unique. However, underpinning this unique expression are the deep structures of the typical NDE pattern. It is particularly interesting to see this pattern played out in the multiple experiences of people who have had NDEs as both children and adults. As they relate their stories, it becomes clear that the form or complexity of the experience has no discernible relationship to the age of the experiencer. One example is the case of Hannah, reported in *Children of the Light* (Sutherland 1995). Hannah had four NDEs: two in early childhood, one as a teenager, and another at age 20 during childbirth. Hannah related her story as follows:

> I was born a Jew in Germany probably some time in late 1937 ... My first experience happened when I was 3 or 4 years old. I remember being taken out of my house by my father and a soldier ... I looked back and saw my

mother yelling ... an SS officer went over to her ... and shot her in the head with his pistol ... I screamed ... He turned, raised the pistol and pointed it at me. I turned to run and was shot in the back. I experienced a shock ... Then I heard music. I can't describe it in earthly terms. I was in darkness, then the darkness changed into a passage and then it was light and peaceful, like being in a big smile. I heard voices and ... in the light I saw "beings" ... I tried to reach out to one. Tears were in his eyes ... At that moment the pain started, and I must have slipped into a state of sleep or unconsciousness. (Sutherland 1995, 142–43)

Upon regaining consciousness some time later, Hannah realized she had been taken to the nuns, who were looking after her. Doctors began to operate on her back. She said,

I faded out. It was blue-black then a roaring black, then once again there was peace. This time there was no music, no lullaby. I saw two people I knew but I don't remember their relationship, and I also saw three "beings." The third "being" then sent me a message of hope, love, and caring. He sent me messages of a future without pain. (Sutherland 1995, 144)

Hannah assumes she then returned to her body because later, while strapped in splints, she remembers the building being on fire and being rescued by being thrown out the window.

Before the end of the war, Hannah was taken to New Zealand as an orphan; and her next NDE occurred when she was about 15 and in a bicycle accident. This time she had no awareness of any darkness or pain, but while out-of-body she observed the people who were gathered around her. She said, "I floated happily, watching myself and them for a very long time" (Sutherland 1995, 144).

Five years later, at 20, while afflicted with pneumonia and heavily pregnant, she was rushed to the hospital. Her child was born "in a great hurry." She said, "I could see her, myself, and the doctors and nurses, and then I traveled through the tunnel until I was presented with the choice of rest or going back" (Sutherland 1995, 145). The next thing she knew, she was in the Intensive Care Unit, and three days later her daughter died.

RELIABILITY OF RETROSPECTIVE ACCOUNTS

The earliest of Hannah's NDEs was recounted to me 50 years after the event. This time lapse raises two fundamental questions: (1) How reliable are such retrospective accounts? and (2) How affected by cultural conditioning and social expectations are their contents?

Many investigators have disputed the "cultural conditioning" argument (for example, Bush 1983; Gabbard and Twemlow 1984; Morse 1983; Serdahely 1991). And I have come across several cases myself in which the children specifically commented on how *different* certain aspects of their experiences were from what they were led to expect from their religious or cultural background. For instance, Daniel, 14 years old, who was born with serious birth defects—the esophagus not joined, an imperforate anus, spina bifida, and others—shocked his mother when, at four years of age, he insisted that Jesus didn't look anything like the illustration she was showing him in a religious book. His mother said, "As he explained it, Jesus had a black flowing cape" (Sutherland 1995, 99). Daniel added, "I remember his hands, they were soft, but they didn't bleed like the picture on the wall" (Sutherland 1995, 100).

Even more unusual was the description of Jesus that Morse (1992) heard from Jamie, a seven-year-old who came close to death as a result of bacterial meningitis. Jamie saw not only Jesus wearing a red hat and having a round belly like Santa Claus but also people waiting to be born—neither of which corresponded in any way to what she had been taught in Sunday school (Morse 1992, 126).

In Western societies, in our present secular age, the level of religious training received by young people is often rudimentary at best. It is for this reason that researchers have taken an interest in the NDEs of young children. However, even in the two cases previously cited, in which both children had some religious instruction, the images reported were very specific but quite different from what the children had been taught. As Richard Bonenfant (2001) pointed out, "Children's accounts are often informative simply because they report exactly what they see without great concern over the rational interpretation of their observations" (Bonenfant 2001, 95). Their accounts seem untainted. Implicit in this thinking, however, is the questionable notion that the accounts of adults are substantially different from those of children and *are* overly determined by religion and culture.

In the case of Hannah, who reported both childhood and adult NDEs, there is no evidence that she embellished her childhood experiences over time to conform with adult notions of rationality or cultural acceptability. Indeed, I found that adults often described their childhood NDEs in childlike terms. One of my interviewees, Barbara, described the amazement she felt while out-of-body:

> I was floating on the ceiling and I was just so, so happy ... and my first thought was, "How mean of them not to tell me about this before!" ... And then I began to look around. There were two old-fashioned wardrobes in the room, and I thought, "Oh gee, Mother doesn't dust the top very well. I can write my name in this." I was enjoying just bouncing around ... But then I thought, "Now I'm going!" (Sutherland 1993, 25)

Barbara told me the feeling she had was better than "all the birthday parties" she'd ever been to. This is not a child speaking but, rather, a 62-year-old woman who, as a 10-year-old child, had been critically ill with pneumonia. Her childlike curiosity and thoughts, the emotion in her voice, and the tears in her eyes as she related her story convinced me absolutely that she was presenting the account exactly as she had experienced it so many years before.

Serdahely, in his comparison of retrospective and contemporary accounts of childhood NDEs (1991), concluded that adult retrospective accounts were indistinguishable from contemporary pediatric NDEs (Serdahely 1991, 223). This finding supported earlier work by Bush (1983). Indeed, in discussing his own results, Morse wrote, "Unlike ordinary memories or dreams, NDEs do not seem to be rearranged or altered over time" (Morse 1994b, 142).

THE NDEs OF VERY YOUNG CHILDREN

It has often been supposed that the NDEs of very young children will have a content limited to their vocabulary. However, it is now clear that the age of children at the time of their NDE does not in any way determine its complexity. Even prelinguistic children have later reported quite complex experiences. For instance, Marcella, who was 10 years old when I interviewed her, described the NDE she had on the first day of life when born prematurely, one of twins, and dangerously tiny. She said,

> I remember ... I saw a light ... and there was this head in the light. And behind me there was this other man who was trying to get me to go back to reality. But he [the head in the light] was trying to make me stay. Then I saw this girl walking into the light and this man told me, "Why don't you be like her ... When you get to the end you'll find a surprise." So I decided I'd walk behind her.
>
> In the background of the head ... were all these little bubbles full of light and every time he moved one of them burst ... and all this gold and coloured air came out. I was frightened at first but then ... I wasn't scared any more. I would have liked to stay.
>
> But before I got right into the light ... there was some type of force that was taking me back. I could see the colours coming towards me ... and then that's all I remember, I just went back into my body. (Sutherland 1995, 82–83)

Several other authors have also found NDEs in very young children. For example, Serdahely (1995) mentioned in passing the case of Melissa, a four-year-old child born three months prematurely, who apparently had her NDE while still in the incubator (Serdahely 1995, 187). Also, with Barbara Walker (1990a), Serdahely reported the NDE of Sara, whose NDE occurred at the time of her birth when she was strangled by the umbilical cord (Serdahely 1995, 178).

In *Lessons from the Light* (2000), Kenneth Ring and Evelyn Elsaesser Valarino explored research on perinatal memory reported by David B. Chamberlain, a psychologist and perinatal researcher. As a result of his extensive inquiry, he became convinced absolutely that birth memories are often genuine recollections of actual experiences (Ring and Valarino 2000, 117). According to Chamberlain, objections based on assumptions that the brains of newborns are insufficiently developed to process such memories are unfounded (Ring and Valarino 2000, 116).

Ring and Valarino related the story of Mark Botts, who, aged 9 months, suffering from severe bronchiolitis, had his NDE during a full cardiopulmonary arrest. It apparently took more than 40 minutes for doctors to revive him, and afterward he was in a coma for an additional three months. One day, more than four years later, totally without warning or previous reference, he surprised his parents by talking about "when he had died." He described how, during his experience, he left his body and crawled through a dark tunnel into a bright golden light where he was greeted warmly by some "white clouded figures." He then glided down a golden road until suddenly a being whom he understood to be God appeared in front of him. They conversed telepathically until Mark was sent back (Ring and Valarino 2000, 108–12).

Interestingly, while out-of-body, Mark saw things that could subsequently be verified. He observed the doctors and nurses working on him, and he watched his grandmother wandering through the hospital corridors looking for his mother. As Mark's mother said, commenting on the cynicism she faced when talking about Mark's experience, "How can you not believe him when the things he said happened?" (Ring and Valarino 2000, 112).

In another case (Walker, Serdahely, and Bechtel 1991), a boy aged between 1and 2 years swallowed a marble that then stuck in his throat. He remembered leaving his body and traveling toward a brilliant white light that told him he had to return. As Walker and her coauthors commented, "Communication was instantaneous and comprehensive, despite the apparent barrier of age, developmental reasoning, and lack of formal language skills" (Walker, Serdahely, and Bechtel 1991, 194). This is a very significant point, according to Peter Fenwick and Elizabeth Fenwick (1995), because it means that "the NDE does not depend on the maturation and development of the brain" and possibly that NDEs "reflect some fundamental features of experience to which the dying brain, *at any age*, has access" (Fenwick and Fenwick 1995, 182–83).

THE CIRCUMSTANCES

Just as age does not seem in any way to affect the content of the NDE, neither does the nature of the near-death crisis appear to be a significant determinant. Some researchers who conducted hospital-based studies have focused on a particular precipitating factor, such as cardiac arrest (Greyson 2003; Holden and Joesten 1990; Parnia et al. 2001; Sabom 1982;

Schwaninger et al. 2002; van Lommel et al. 2001) or meningococcal disease (Shears et al. 2002), but most research has drawn on people who have had their NDEs in a diverse range of circumstances: illness, surgery, accidents and drowning, suicide (Colli and Beck 2003; Rosen 1975; Sutherland 1993); and violence, such as war traumas (Sutherland 1995; Valent 1993); sexual abuse (Serdahely 1987–88, 1992, 1993); and physical abuse of various kinds (Sutherland 1995).

One episode of physical abuse led to an NDE for Naomi when she was only 12 months old. Aged 38 at the time of interview, she engaged all her senses to describe the feeling of sitting in her highchair while her mother tried to force her to eat:

> There was the feeling of the spoon at the back of the throat and me being resistant. Then the feeling of fingers on my throat, the feeling of choking, and the sound of her screaming, and the sound of me screaming. And then I must have become unconscious.
>
> The next thing I remember is the feeling of going down this tunnel. At first it was silent but then there started to be the sound of ringing. Then there was the feeling of standing at an all-enveloping, very bright light. This was when the sound changed too from that piercing ringing to this almost ethereal sound. And then I was drawn into the light ... And when I came through I was in this space where ... I felt really enveloped by this sense of peace and joy and being connected to everything ... It was lovely being there ... Then the next thing I remember is the jolt of coming back ... By the time I came to I was lying flat, and I could see the kitchen table legs.
>
> After that, all through my childhood I used to have dreams of going down tunnels ... and sometimes I had a dream of looking into a light. I certainly had a lot of ambivalence about it ... but now I realise the ambivalence I felt was about the circumstances. I didn't ever talk about it with anybody—not in my family. (Sutherland 1995, 136–41)

In *The Omega Project*, Ring (1992) asserted that NDErs are more likely than others to have had a history of child abuse and other childhood traumas (143). This claim has been widely discussed (Hoffman 1998; Irwin 1993; Morse 1994a; Morse and Perry 1992, Serdahely 1992, 1993). In an earlier article, Ring and Christopher Rosing (1990) postulated that such a background of abuse or trauma would tend to foster a defensive "dissociative response style" and in near-death crisis situations promote sensitivity to NDEs (Ring and Rosing 1990, 231). Here, of course, the authors were referring specifically to NDErs who had a *history* of abuse rather than to children, such as Naomi, who had her first NDE *during* an episode of abuse. However, if the violence is ongoing, as it was in Naomi's case, the history could already have been there, too. If, in later life, a person such as Naomi were to find herself again in a near-death crisis, she would be expected, according to Ring and Rosing, to move easily into an NDE—as she in fact did, aged

20—and be more likely to remember it because of her prior familiarity with nonordinary states and her capacity for deep psychological absorption. In Ring and Rosing's terms, "Such persons are what we might call psychological sensitives with low stress thresholds, and it is their traumatic childhoods that have helped to make them that way" (Ring and Rosing 1990, 232).

Ring (1991) further suggested that the NDE might at times be seen as a "compensatory gift" conferring upon such people "both a heightened sense of compassion and an extended range of intuitive perception" (Ring 1991, 12). P. M. H. Atwater (1995) dismissed this idea as a "myth" (Atwater 1995, 12); but other authors, such as Bruce Horacek (1997), have embraced it. Indeed, as Naomi told me, "Despite the incredible level of violence in my family, I always had the ability to see the good in people, and to have compassion towards people, including those not behaving in the most correct way. And I think that's probably the product of the near-death experience" (Sutherland 1995, 141).

THE CONTENT OF NDEs IN CHILDREN AND TEENS

Erin was 10 years old when I first met her, just 12 months after her NDE. At that point, she still showed some physical signs of the brain damage she had sustained as a result of a cardiopulmonary arrest during an acute asthma attack. These disabilities included a slight Parkinsonian disorder, limited use of her left hand, and difficulty with walking. Erin had the luminescence I often observed in child NDErs, and I found her to be extremely intelligent and highly articulate. According to her father, Erin had been clinically dead for perhaps three minutes, and after a critical period of about five days she finally came to—blind and with no movement at all. It was some months after this episode that Erin first spoke about her NDE. He said at the time it was "a humbling experience" to be given "the most believable description of life after death" by his daughter, a child of nine years of age (Sutherland 1995, 89).

I met with Erin and her parents three times over a six-month period. On that last visit, I found the level of her recovery astonishing; and as she and I sat together on her bedroom floor, she was even more full of fun and good humor than usual while drawing what she had seen during her experience. On all three occasions, I found her story to be consistent. She said:

> When I was in the ambulance I was looking down at myself and thinking, "Oh my God! Oh my God! What's going on?" And then I was on top of the ceiling looking down at myself thinking, "Oh, this is radical!"
>
> And then all of a sudden I saw my mum and dad. They were crying their eyes out. Then something pulled me through the ceiling and I was flying down this cloudy white tunnel. Then I saw this beautiful magnificent light. And I stopped there. It was so nice and peaceful. And then somebody spoke

to me and it was a familiar voice. It was Vanessa, one of my best friends who had passed away. She had light around her ... and she looked quite pretty. And then I saw God. He was standing in a light. Boy was he good! God had a body but he wasn't male or female, and he had like billions and millions and millions and trillions and billions and billions of heads—all the heads of the whole galaxy. I was searching around to find my head, but my head wasn't there. It must pop off when you die! Then God gave me three choices: to get reborn, or to stay in heaven, or he said I could go back to my body, but my body would be damaged and I would have to fight. I chose to fight. *Bad* choice!

I'm full up with all these memories! I saw Jesus too. And whenever you see pictures of him you get really fed up because that's not what he looks like.

There were millions of people there ... There was the "reincarnating" line, there was the "staying" line ... And I was right there on the "fighting" line. It was spooky. I've been trying to block it out of my mind ... But this is the toughest bit. When I [had to fight], the devils had weapons and I didn't.

CS: How did you fight them then? [She looked astonished that I could be so ignorant.]

Erin: With my heart! (Sutherland 1995, 87–95)

AFFECT

The most commonly reported feature of NDEs is a sense of peace and well-being—all-encompassing love and tranquillity. However, as can be seen in Erin's story, there can also be moments of excitement, elation, fun, curiosity, puzzlement, and even fear.

Distressing experiences first appeared in the NDE literature in 1978 in cardiologist Maurice Rawlings's *Beyond Death's Door*; but because this book was unabashedly written from a fundamentalist Christian perspective, several authors have expressed doubts about the legitimacy not only of his reports but also of his theory and his evangelizing conclusion (see, for example, Atwater 1992; Irwin and Bramwell 1988; Ring 1980). Much more characteristic, however, are pleasurable feelings (see, for example, DenBesten 1978). These more typical feelings are evident in the childhood NDE of Bruce Low, who described falling from a bamboo bridge into a stream and being carried by the current into a lagoon in front of the family house. He wrote:

The strangest thing was that I did not panic .... I was 6 years old and could not swim. I simply sank slowly, with my eyes open, towards the bottom of the lagoon. In fact the experience was wonderful. My body felt light and I heard soft music. Then, all of a sudden, I saw a baby—and realized it was me—sitting in an old-fashioned pram. I saw the eyes of my mother—at once concerned and full of pride—as she watched me taking my first tottering steps on my own. I saw my rocking horse whose tail was missing. I saw my ever-cheerful father, our cook, and the gentle old man who looked after the garden. Everyone looked happy and full of smiles. I had absolutely no fear, and felt totally safe and secure. (Sutherland 1995, 4–6)

LEAVING THE BODY

Typically, as a feature of the NDE, the out-of-body experience is often the NDEr's first indication that something is wrong. Hence, Erin was at first alarmed at being out of her body but soon became quite excited. Another child, Tommy, was eight years old when he suffered a ruptured spleen and closed head injury during a car accident. The damage affected both sides of the brain but mostly the right. He was on life support for 21 days and then in a coma for three months. Five and a half years after his near-death crisis, he still suffered considerable physical disabilities, his speech was still affected, and his mental development had been retarded. Nonetheless, he was keen to describe his experience of being out-of-body. He said:

> I felt like the inner part of me, I felt like my inner part in me was up like a ghost and I felt like my inner body was taken out of me. I felt like I was going out, like my inner body was going out of me and I felt like, I felt like a dummy almost, that my body was like a dummy and I was outside it. (Sutherland 1995, 68)

Elisabeth Kübler-Ross (1983) maintained that "children who are in a coma are out of their physical body most of the time, and during this time they can hear all communications that people may have with them" (Kübler-Ross 1983, 59). During the months Tommy was comatose, his parents communicated with him constantly—hopeful he *would* hear them and be comforted—yet they were not prepared for how much he had observed while out of his body. Nine or ten months after the accident, once he had begun to speak again, it became clear he had actually observed many things that could be verified. And two years later when he visited the Intensive Care Unit where he'd been, he went straight to the right section (one of three) and even knew which bed he'd been in (Sutherland 1995, 66–73).

MOVING THROUGH THE DARKNESS
TOWARD THE LIGHT

Once out of the body, typically the experiencer will travel through the darkness toward a light. Hal, 56 years old, who had his NDE during a cardiac arrest when he was 14, moved very quickly through a dark tunnel into the other world (Sutherland 1995, 25). Alice, who was 10 years old when she had her NDE during a bout of pneumonia, described *floating* through "a black area." She said, "It was soft, substantial—supportive and cosy" (Sutherland 1995, 26).

Even preverbal or nonverbal children may give some indication that they have traveled through the tunnel. David Herzog and John Herrin (1985) recounted the story of an infant of six months who had been admitted to the Intensive Care Unit. They noted that some months later, "she had a panic reaction when encouraged by her siblings to crawl through a tunnel at a local store." Apparently this "tunnel panic" reaction had occurred on other occasions, too. Then, three years after the child's hospitalization, when her mother was explaining the imminent death of the grandmother, the child asked, "Will Grandma have to go through the tunnel at the store to get to see God?" (Herzog and Jerrin 1985, 1074).

IN THE COMPANY OF "ANGELS"

One of the distinctive features of children's NDEs is that the children are often accompanied as they travel through the tunnel into the light. Daniel Shears and his coauthors (2005) noted that one of the children in their study—a three-year-old boy interviewed three months after recovering from meningococcal disease—revealed he had been accompanied into a celestial landscape by an adult angel and a little boy angel who held his hand (Shears et al. 2005, 630). This type of "angelic company" is not restricted to very young children either. Morse and his coauthors (1986) reported on the NDE of an adolescent boy, 16 years of age, who described traveling very quickly through a dark tunnel, accompanied by a being "about eight feet tall, with long hair and a white robe," who the boy thought might be an angel taking him to Christ (Morse et al. 1986, 1112).

These loving beings are not always specifically described as angels. Serdahely (1987–88) reported on the childhood NDE of a woman who was aged 10 or 12 at the time of a life-threatening episode of sexual abuse. She recalled that she had left her body and gone into the darkness, where she was met by a "beautiful lady" (Serdahely 1987–88, 130). In another article about pediatric NDEs, Serdahely (1990) reported that Natalie, 15 years old, was accompanied through the tunnel, hand-in-hand, by two friendly "light figures" and that Mike, four years old, sensed the touch of a warm hand on his shoulder and was comforted by a loving male voice that told him it was not his time. In another interesting manifestation of divine guidance and comfort, seven-year-old Pat was greeted not by an "angel" or a "beautiful lady" or even by friendly "light figures" but by two much-loved family pets who had died four years prior to his near-drowning (Serdahely 1989–90, 1990).

Atwater claimed that over 70 percent of children's NDEs feature "angel visitations" (Atwater 2003, 49). Although it is not clear how she arrived at this figure, there is no doubt that light beings or presences of one kind or another do quite often appear at some point during child and adolescent NDEs. Some form of loving light being often accompanies the child through the tunnel, as we have already seen, and such beings are certainly present once the child arrives in the "world of light." However, a presence may also be in attendance as the child experiences a life review, wherever this review takes place.

LIFE REVIEW

Helen, 38 years old, had her life review during an NDE precipitated by a severe asthma attack when she was 15. She not only saw a replay of events from her life but also, in the company of a loving presence, experienced feelings of empathy for her siblings. She said:

> Suddenly *whoosh* I was going up through this tunnel ... And then the next thing I knew, I was out in this gray misty place ... And then this man came towards me—like a misty light-filled-in outline—and he said, "Come with me and I'll show you your life." The thing I most remember having pointed out to me was when I was throwing stones at my brothers and sister. I was about 9 or 10, and I was really angry and frustrated ... and they were really upset. [Seeing this] I was ashamed, and then he took me away from that ... and I heard music. (Sutherland 1995, 148)

Typically, as in the case of Helen, it seems the presence of a "light being" or other such companion during a life review is more for the purpose of encouragement and instruction than for judgment or blame.

Some children also receive a message about the future during their life reviews—a phenomenon Ring called a "personal flashforward" (Ring 1984, 183). Often the flashforward occurs while the experiencers are deciding whether or not to stay in the other world. For instance, Natalie, 15 years old, was shown how sad her mother would be if she died (Serdahely 1990, 35). And Lisa, 34, who was four years old at the time of her NDE, recalled seeing both parents and grandparents "grieving badly." She said, "I couldn't let them go through that" (Walker, Serdahely, and Bechtel 1991, 191).

Another common flashforward is for the child to be given a "mission." Adult NDErs often return to life with a strong sense of purpose—even if they are not exactly certain what that purpose might be. Imagine how much more puzzling it must be for a young child to receive such a message. For instance, Dorothea, 51, was only five years old when she nearly drowned. After hearing the Bible story of St. Peter walking on water—possibly a reference to Matthew 14:29—she had walked into a canal to see if she, too, could do it. She said:

> I immediately went under the water. I didn't feel either frightened or disappointed ... I saw instantaneously four or five events—important events—that had already happened to me in my short life ... As I recall there were also some thoughts about my first communion which was still two years in the future. And I heard a voice say to me, "I have work for you." (Sutherland 1995, 29)

Dorothea told me that she had never forgotten this message and had always had it at the forefront of her mind when making choices at various times throughout her life. These choices had led her to train as a nurse and move from Holland; and when I first met her, she had already been working for some years with aboriginal people in an isolated desert community.

ENCOUNTERING OTHERS

As in Dorothea's case, the encounter can sometimes be auditory rather than visual; however, in the NDEs of many children, the voice is also embodied in some form, particularly once they reach the "world of light." The spiritual beings most frequently reported by children are angels or light beings, as we have already seen, deceased relatives or friends, Jesus, and The Light or God.

Brad Steiger and Sherry Hansen Steiger related the story of a nine-year-old boy, Edward Cuomo, who encountered several deceased relatives during his NDE, including his sister Teresa, who, as far as his family knew, was still alive. It was not discovered until the next day that Teresa had been killed in an automobile accident just three hours before Edward's fever broke (Steiger and Steiger 1995, 42–46). And Serena, a woman I met at a meeting of the International Association for Near-Death Studies (IANDS) group in Australia, told me that during her childhood NDE, she had encountered two little girls, one of whom introduced herself as Olivia. Afterward, when she told her mother what she'd seen, she was surprised at her mother's emotional response. It was some time before she discovered that Olivia was the name of an older sister who had died before she was born (Sutherland 1995, 31).

Several of the children I interviewed described being in the presence of God. We have already seen that Erin saw God as a being with "all the heads of the whole galaxy," whereas Tommy said God was a voice, a being, a feeling, not a human. "He was just there" (Sutherland 1995, 71). Helen, who was 15 at the time of her NDE, had several interactions with God. She said:

> I thought, "Well, if this is supposed to be heaven, then where's God?" Then suddenly I felt this presence all around and I felt that it was just looking at

me to see what I could fathom of it. I understood that it was some sort of force—it didn't have any sort of gender and it occupied all this space. And it *was* the space. It was pleased with my understanding this and then it just went away. (149)

Dennis Stone, who was 13 years old in 1938 when he had an NDE during an attack of meningitis, said he suddenly found himself in another, beautiful, world. There he felt a powerful presence close by, and a deep, resonant voice spoke reassuringly to him. He said, "I then knew I was in the presence of God, though I could not see him. He then covered me with an invisible force field, which felt so warm and safe" (Fenwick and Fenwick 1995, 175).

COMING BACK

All these children at some point returned. Some chose to come back, others were sent back, and some just suddenly found themselves back in their bodies. For those who remember being *sent* back, the feeling of rejection can, at first, be overwhelming. For instance, Denise, 41 years old, was 17 when she was critically injured in a road accident. During her NDE, she found herself in the presence of an indescribably beautiful light she took to be God but was told she could not stay because she had "a life of service" in front of her. She said, "I felt a deep sense of regret at that, but I knew I couldn't argue ... I felt very rejected at first ... I felt great disappointment and a profound sense of loss" (Sutherland 1993, 87–88).

Children and teens in such circumstances often wonder what is wrong with them: Why are they being sent away? Why are they being punished? To be abruptly torn away from an experience of bliss and returned to a painful body can be overwhelming. And if their attempts to talk about their experiences are dismissed, the repercussions can be long-lasting.

TELLING OTHERS

Many children try to tell someone about their experience quite soon after the event, and the response they receive appears to greatly influence how they subsequently think about it. If they are believed, this acknowledgment can help begin the integration process and provide an impetus for ongoing change and personal growth (Sutherland 1992).

Joe Ann Van Gelder suffered a series of illnesses between the ages of 15 months and 10 years, during which she had a number of NDEs that as a child, she took to be "natural and normal" because her mother had also had an NDE and understood (Atwater 2003, 42). Unfortunately, not everyone is so blessed. Many children, if rebuffed, end up keeping silent. For instance, Hal, who was 14 years old when he had several cardiac arrests, said: "I tried to tell my mother and was told, 'Don't be silly.' I tried to tell my scoutmaster and my local Methodist minister. They seemed to be embarrassed. So I just stopped.... I just didn't tell anyone about it after that" (Sutherland 1995, 186).

Carol Jean Morres, who was 14 years old when she had her NDE, said, "Because others cannot accept my experience as real, I have had to keep it locked up inside me for the most part, and that creates a feeling of isolation and loneliness" (Atwater 2003, 95). Atwater stated that children are six times more likely than adults to "tuck away" their experience (Atwater 2003, 111). Although it is unclear how Atwater came to this conclusion, there are indeed many cases in the literature of children either totally forgetting their NDEs or putting them on hold until something triggers their memory or suddenly helps them come to an understanding of it (see, for example, Gabbard and Twemlow 1984, 157; Sutherland 1993, 89; 1995, 186). However, even if children have never told anybody about their NDEs, the many aftereffects that reverberate through their lives may well reveal their status as NDErs.

THE AFTERMATH

Probably the most universally experienced aftereffect among any population of NDErs is the decline in death anxiety following their NDE (for example, see Ring 1980; Sabom 1982). In my own study of 50 NDErs ranging in age from seven years to 76 years at the time of their experience, 98 percent reported no fear of death following their NDE (Sutherland 1992, 87). Morse and Perry wrote that this change is "simply because they have been there and know what to expect" (Morse and Perry 1992, 64).

In a study comparing the aftereffects reported by NDErs and non-NDErs, Bonenfant (2004) found that the majority of NDErs spoke of multiple aftereffects that were ongoing and, in some cases, even increased over time. He even found statistically significant differences on spiritual and paranormal measures.

Most experiencers maintain that their NDE was spiritual in nature, and researchers have generally found that the majority of NDErs—whatever their prior level of religiosity—tend to consider themselves spiritual rather than religious after their experience. Typically, the distinction made is between church-connected formalized religion and an ongoing *direct* experience of God requiring neither mediation by institutions such as the church nor interpretation by the teachings of any one denomination or tradition (Sutherland 1990, 30). In my own study of aftereffects, 76 percent of my sample of 50 NDErs claimed to be spiritually inclined rather than religious after their NDEs (Sutherland 1992, 99).

Paranormal aftereffects are also very common (for example, see Ring 1985; Sutherland 1992). These phenomena can range from the enjoyable and playful to the quite disturbing. Some children have ongoing contact with deceased relatives (Sutherland 1995, 41), and some speak of "guardian angel" figures that communicate with them (Atwater 2003, 34; Liester 1998; Morse and Perry 1992, 11). Some children are aware of things before they happen. This precognition can range from the easy-to-live-with knowing who is on the phone when it rings, to having dreams or visions that can be so distressing that the experiencers may want to have their ability removed (Fenwick and Fenwick 1995, 147; Steiger and Steiger 1995, 76). Some children have out-of-body experiences (Sutherland 1995, 23), and some report knowing things about other people and reading minds (Sutherland 1995, 41).

Child and teen NDErs also describe a number of other strange phenomena. For instance, some find that lightbulbs pop when they are angry (Atwater 1996, 10) or that they can never wear watches because they always break (Morse and Perry 1992, 11). There can be an unusual sensitivity to light and sound and a generalized sensitivity to anything electrical (Atwater 2003, 83). For instance, Nicole—aged 12 at the time of her NDE—said: "Sometimes I can get quite strong feelings off a place or an object ... My senses have always been through the roof. I even have buzzy fingers. But there's a really neat side too—like experiencing music with its patterns and colours" (Sutherland 1995, 108).

In addition to Nicole's particular experience of synesthesia, Bonenfant found many others, such as "feeling colors, tasting words or smelling sounds" (Bonenfant 2004, 163). He found the incidence of such sensory confusion to be surprisingly high—two-thirds—among a population of NDErs ranging in age from 10 to 76 (Bonenfant 2004, 171).

Yet, however surprising or confusing many of these specific aftereffects may be for child experiencers, they still appear to be just additional symptoms reinforcing their overall feeling of being different when they come back—different from how they were before *and* different from everybody else. Many children describe feeling estranged from their peer group because they no longer share the same interests (Greyson 1997; Sutherland 1995, 40). They tend to be indifferent to materialistic and competitive success and status (Flynn 1986). They have often had an experience of being "all-knowing" or "at-one-with-everything" and return with an overwhelming thirst for knowledge and meaning that can set them apart. As one mother said, "It's like sending in a six-year-old and getting back a 36-year-old" (Corcoran 1988, 37). Emily, 10 years old, who had her NDE when she was five, actually said to her mother that she wished she could "spend a day in some other child's body just to know what it felt like to be normal" (Sutherland 1995, 79).

For some families, dealing with a child NDEr can be extremely challenging. My first contact with Emily's mother occurred when she wrote to me seeking advice on how to handle the turmoil in her family caused by

Emily's NDE and its aftermath. She wrote that when Emily told her about her experience, she was shocked. She continued:

> But considering the changes in her I wasn't surprised. She was very different from the small child I knew before the illness but I had no idea why ... Last year Emily had a very bad time ... Up until that point she had been a loner but that awful year led her to depend more on her peers, and it upset her to discover just how different she was from other children. Her behaviour deteriorated, school and sports performances nosedived and her health declined. (Sutherland 1995, 74)

Emily's mother then related how she had begun reading to her daughter from one of my books and had discussed "many key bits" with her. As a result, she wrote, "Acceptance has begun to replace her confusion, self-doubt, low self-esteem and feelings of mental instability as she now knows she is not alone" (Sutherland 1995, 75).

The experience of Emily's mother strongly suggests that parents—and perhaps others such as health care professionals, or indeed anyone who is knowledgeable about NDEs and their aftereffects—can critically influence the relative amount of distress or peace of mind or even developmental enhancement a child will experience in the aftermath of an NDE.

HELP FOR THE DYING AND THE GRIEVING

Beliefs and knowledge can also have a major influence on the nature and duration of the grieving process (see Sutherland 1997). Many bereaved parents contacted me after the publication of my first book to tell me that the NDEs of children gave them solace following the death of their child. Marja, whose five-year-old son had died in a drowning accident, told me that when she serendipitously came across Bruce Low's account of his childhood near-drowning NDE in a German magazine, she felt totally exhilarated. Bruce Low had been virtually the same age as her son when he died, and the circumstances were almost identical. From that day on, she read everything she could find about NDEs, and, she said, "with each new account, the bottomless, black despair I had felt for so long receded, and a wonderful new hope was born somewhere deep within me" (Sutherland 1995, 6).

Bruce Horacek (1997), describing the NDE as a "healing gift," outlined several situations in which having an NDE, or knowledge of NDEs and other death-related visions, can be helpful in facing one's own death or the death of a significant other. Indeed, many childhood NDErs have told me that as adults they have gone on to work with the dying or grieving. Having no fear of death themselves appears to give NDErs the confidence to ease that fear in others.

Knowledge of NDEs even has the potential to help health care professionals who work with terminally ill children. As Morse (1994a) suggested, if health care providers took into account NDEs and other death-related visions, rather than viewing death as a professional defeat and doing everything possible to prevent it from happening, they could drastically reduce the heroic measures they often put in place—utilizing expensive, intrusive, dehumanizing medical procedures on dying patients without any real hope of prolonging life (Morse 1994a, 82). He wrote, "Spiritual visions carry with them an understanding that the process of dying can be joyous and spiritual and that death is not to be feared" (Morse 1994a, 83).

HELPING CHILD NDErs

The NDE is a profound, emotionally powerful experience. As illustrated in the case of Emily's mother, perhaps the best way to be of service to a child experiencer is simply to be informed, aware, sensitive, interested, and willing to give support. However, the importance of validating the experience cannot be overemphasized because such acknowledgment is an important first step on the child's integration trajectory (Sutherland 1992). Nowhere has this principle been more clearly demonstrated than in the case of David, a nonverbal quadriplegic adolescent who was assisted over a period of many months by social worker Rick Enright (2004) in the arduous task of revealing his NDE. Enright concluded that this revelation—and having it acknowledged—was for David an incredibly important process that "brought about significant changes in his emotional state, helped return personal control over his life, and ultimately led to his peaceful and fulfilling death" (Enright 2004, 95).

CONCLUSION

So what have we learned over the past 30 years about the NDEs of children and teens? First, it is clear, as Abraham Maslow suggested so long ago, that "even young children are capable of peak moments of lasting impact" (Hoffman 1998, 1). We now know that children of all ages are capable of having, *and remembering,* NDEs. And there can no longer be any doubt that these peak experiences "leave profound and transformative effects in their wake" (Hoffman 1998, 2).

In terms of NDE content, even though every experience is unique, the NDEs of children and teens follow a consistent pattern that appears to be little different from the pattern experienced by adults—including the presence of a life review. Neither do children's experiences appear to be affected by cause of near-death crisis, age, gender, religiosity, or any other demographic variable. One distinction appears to be that children are almost always accompanied into the light. Although adults do also sometimes have the sense of a presence with them early in their experience, children seem far more often to see, and even to have their hand held by, a luminous being of one kind or another as they move together into the other world. We know that children—even very young children—can have distressing moments in their experiences; yet overall, as in adults, the experience is primarily a pleasurable one.

In terms of aftereffects, the range is so wide and varied—including physiological, neurophysiological, psychological, emotional, social, behavioral, attitudinal, spiritual, and paranormal—that it is impossible to make a blanket statement about them, other than to say that people around child and teen experiencers frequently comment on how changed those children are after their NDEs. Overall, despite an initial period of turmoil and problems of adjustment, many of the aftereffects *are*, over time, successfully integrated and experienced as positive.

Despite the fact that very young NDErs do not have a "before and after" reference point, most child and teen experiencers do comment on aspects of their NDEs that have caused them to view the world differently and have different priorities from their peer groups and families. How measurable these changes can be, is questionable. Yet, as a researcher more practiced in qualitative rather than quantitative research and someone who finds the subjective far more interesting than the objective—the messy mystery of a lived experience far more fascinating than neat columns of statistical analyses—I have found the NDEs of children to provide an endless source of inspiration, speculation, and data for future research. However, the way children integrate their experiences—and how that process can be facilitated—is still of concern to me, and I suggest it as a topic for further research. Unlike many people, I do not consider knowledge of NDEs in the wider community to be a contaminant; rather, I see that knowledge as a facilitator of integration. Validation of the experience is the first step on that path, and the chance of children having their NDEs validated today is, thankfully, far greater than it was 30 years ago.

Although it has now been shown that childhood NDEs related by adults many years later are reliable—not distorted or altered to fit in with cultural or social expectations—to hear those same stories from a child is a special privilege. One can learn again and again from their accounts that there is no need to fear death because death is not an ending but a transition into another realm. Morse (1994b) wrote, "The scientific evidence clearly suggests that NDEs occur when they are subjectively perceived as occurring, at the point of death. As such they must represent the best objective evidence of what it is like to die, regardless of which neurotransmitters or anatomical structures mediate the experience" (143).

Be that as it may, I'd like to give the final word to some of the children: Marcella, aged 10 years, who had her NDE in the first day of life, said, "When you die it's like you're still alive" (Sutherland 1995, 86). And Marc

Beaulieu, aged nine years, suffering from incurable leukemia, said, "The life that's inside is infinite, it never ends" (Ring and Valarino 2000, 120). Finally, Daniel, aged 14 years, who was born with severe birth defects and had 17 major operations and many NDEs in his early years, said, "Death's all right. I know I could die any time so I just live each day. I'd say to people who are dying, 'Don't be afraid. It's a beautiful place'" (Sutherland 1995, 105).

6

Characteristics of Western Near-Death Experiencers

Janice Miner Holden, Jeffrey Long, and B. Jason MacLurg

Many investigators have studied characteristics of near-death experiencers (NDErs), occasionally as a primary focus of study, but more often as part of a broader investigation of near-death experiences (NDEs). Their purpose has often been to answer two questions: (1) What characteristics might differentiate the substantial minority of people who report NDEs following near-death crises from the majority who do not report NDEs following apparently identical crises?; and (2) Of those who report NDEs, what characteristics might be related to the NDE features—whether the experience was predominantly pleasurable or distressing, which specific NDE elements were included—and/or to the aftereffects the NDErs experienced?

Following is a review of scholarly peer-reviewed literature and books published from 1975 to 2005 pertaining to the characteristics of Western NDErs, including the occurrence, incidence, contents, depth, and aftereffects of their NDEs. *Occurrence* addresses whether people in each subcategory of a characteristic have reported NDEs: For example, regarding sex, have both males and females reported NDEs? *Incidence* refers to the frequency with which people in the characteristic subcategory have reported NDEs: Have males, females, or neither subgroup reported more NDEs than the other? *Contents* refers to the reported presence of certain NDE elements: Do more males, females, or neither more often report the presence of unearthly light, a tunnel sensation, and so forth, in their NDEs? *Depth* refers to the reported number of contents of NDEs: Do males, females, or neither report more elements in their NDEs? And *aftereffects* refers to the relationship between subcategory affiliation and physical, psychological,

social, or spiritual changes following NDEs: Do more men, women, or neither more frequently report a reduced interest in materialism following
their NDEs? Occasionally, we authors supplement the results of published
research with references to previously unpublished data from the Near-
Death Experience Research Foundation (NDERF) Web site (www.nderf.
org), where members of the public may register their NDEs. In addition,
we briefly compare non-Western NDErs with Western NDErs.

We present the most significant literature regarding the characteristics
of Western NDErs and acknowledge not having been completely comprehensive in our discussion of the scholarly literature on this topic. For
example, we typically excluded studies involving five or fewer NDEr
research participants. All studies described herein were conducted in the
United States unless otherwise specified.

This review of the literature emphasizes studies suggesting possible similarities or differences in the characteristics of NDErs compared with non-NDErs
regarding their predisposition to have NDEs at the time of crises. The discovery of differences between NDErs and non-NDErs might allow prediction of
individuals predisposed to have an NDE and potentially suggest a cause of
NDEs. Conversely, discovery of no discernable differences between NDErs
and non-NDErs would suggest that NDEs occur independent of the influence
of a variety of demographic variables, preexisting characteristics, and prior life
experiences. This finding also suggests individuals predisposed to have an
NDE cannot be predicted, and the cause of NDEs may be unrelated to known
biological, psychological, and sociological factors.

DEFINITIONS

The term "Western" as used in this chapter, consistent with the dictionary definition, includes areas of the world with a predominantly Judeo-
Christian heritage. The great majority of NDE literature references Western NDEs. The term "characteristics" as used here pertains to a variety of
distinguishing traits of NDErs, including various demographic features, psychological characteristics, and prior life experiences.

There is no universally accepted definition of "near-death experience."
The literature we reviewed was published over a 30-year span. The definition of "near-death experience" varied substantially among different
authors and during different time periods. For the purposes of this review,
we accepted each author's definition of NDE as used in their publication.
This variability in definitions of NDE is a limitation of this review.

METHODOLOGICAL CONSIDERATIONS

Throughout this chapter, we refer to "retrospective" and "prospective"
studies of NDEs. In retrospective studies, researchers first meet their NDEr

participants after the NDEs—often years after. Not having known the NDErs prior to their NDEs, researchers could not have conducted an assessment then. Thus, all data consist of NDErs' retrospective reports. In the matter of NDEr characteristics, this fact is less a problem with relatively objective factors that NDEs have been found not to change, such as age, sex, and socioeconomic status (see Chapter 3, this volume).

However, regarding psychological characteristics, retrospective research is more problematic. Following near-death experiences, NDErs commonly undergo dramatic and lasting changes in their beliefs, values, and relationships. When researchers conduct retrospective studies on the psychological characteristics of NDEr participants, they cannot know for certain whether the characteristics they find characterized the NDErs prior to their NDEs—that is, whether they preexisted the NDEs—or are the aftereffects of the NDEs—that is, developed following, and presumably as a result of, the NDEs. The most researchers can do is ask NDErs to report retrospectively their memories of those psychological characteristics prior to their NDEs. However, the following example illustrates the potential inaccuracy of retrospectively asking about psychological characteristics. Research on marital satisfaction shows that when researchers study couples and find them nondistressed in their marriages, but then years later the couples become distressed and the researchers study them again, at that later point the couples describe themselves as having been distressed at the earlier time (Buehlman, Gottman, and Katz 1992). Thus, married people tend to reconstruct their past based on the nature of their present psychological state.

The same could be true of NDErs: Their post-near-death reports of psychological characteristics prior to their NDEs could be colored by the aftereffects of the NDEs themselves. Though Bruce Greyson (2000a) was speaking of one psychological characteristic in particular, his statement could apply to all characteristics: "The question of cause and effect can be answered only by a prospective study in which [characteristics] are assessed in individuals before and after their NDEs" (Greyson 2000a, 462). We recommend readers keep these issues in mind while reading the following material.

REVIEW OF THE LITERATURE

Age

Occurrence

The age of NDErs is an almost universal demographic reported in the near-death literature. Even a cursory familiarity with that literature reveals that people of all ages have reported NDEs.

Extremely elderly people have reported NDEs. Although the great majority of published NDEs occurred in adults, we found scant research on NDEs in the elderly. However, in the largest prospective U.S. study by Greyson, the mean age of 27 NDErs was 56 years old (Greyson 2003, 272), and in the large-scale prospective Netherlands study by Pim van Lommel, Ruud van Wees, Vincent Meyers, and Ingrid Elfferich (2001), the mean age of the 62 NDErs was 58.8 years (2042). An extreme example of an NDE in the elderly was one occurring when the NDEr was 97 years old (Near-Death Experience Research Foundation 2008a).

Extremely young people also have reported NDEs. Cherie Sutherland (1995) found Australian children under five years of age who, once able to talk, reported to their parents NDEs that corresponded to medical crises the children were known to have survived. She found reference to an NDE in a nine-month-old infant, and she personally interviewed a man who believed his lifelong recurring dream was actually a memory of an NDE at the time of his very difficult birth. Peter Fenwick and Elizabeth Fenwick, in their large-scale retrospective study in the United Kingdom, quoted a letter from a woman claiming memory of an NDE at birth (Fenwick and Fenwick, 183–84). P. M. H. Atwater also reported a case of an NDE recalled from birth (Atwater 1999, 12–13), as well as cases of other very young children.

The reliability of later verbal accounts of earlier preverbal NDEs may be especially open to question. Very young infants, especially those less than one and a half years old, may not have well-developed short-term memory. In their prospective research with adults, van Lommel and his colleagues found that "good short-term memory seems to be essential for remembering NDE" (van Lommel et al. 2001, 2043). This finding might explain the dearth of reported NDEs in infants less than one year old. Approximately three and a half times as many children die before the age of one than the total of all deaths in children between the ages of one and nine years (Social Security Online, Period Life Table 2004). Although death statistics may or may not reflect the incidence of near-death events, the mortality data suggest more NDEs would be expected in the age group of less than a year old than has been reported in the professional near-death literature.

Conversely, research in adults indicates that unlike accounts of other experiences, NDE accounts remain virtually unchanged even over the course of years (van Lommel et al. 2001). Focusing specifically on child NDErs, William Serdahely compared 47 NDE characteristics between five childhood NDEs disclosed by children with five childhood NDEs disclosed as adults. Serdahely concluded, "This study ... supports the claims of previous researchers that adults' retrospective reports of childhood NDEs are not embellished or distorted" (Serdahely 1991, 219). These latter findings lend some credibility to NDEs recounted once a child becomes verbal.

A question that plagues the study of adult NDEs is how an NDEr can know events that occurred when the brain was apparently inactive (see

Chapters 9 and 10, this volume). A similar question plagues the study of NDEs in very young children: How can a very young child remember coherently an experience that occurred when the brain was at an extremely early stage of development? Answers to these questions suggest a possible nonbiological cause of NDEs, which is addressed further in the conclusion of this chapter.

Incidence

In one of the largest retrospective studies conducted so far, Fenwick and Fenwick found that of over 350 NDErs in the United Kingdom, 78 percent were age 19 years or older at the time of their NDEs, and 9 percent were 10 years or younger (Fenwick and Fenwick 1995, 2). Gary Groth-Marnat and Roger Summers (1998) compared 53 NDErs to 27 research participants who had come close to death without an associated NDE; they found no significant difference in the age represented in the two groups. Prospective research on adult NDEs reveals further insight.

In a prospective study of Netherlands patients resuscitated in hospital (van Lommel et al. 2001), 52 percent of 62 NDErs were under age 60 as opposed to 34 percent of 282 non-NDErs, a significant difference. In Greyson's (2003) prospective study of patients admitted to cardiac inpatient services, the mean age of 56 years among 27 NDErs was eight years younger than the mean age among 1,568 non-NDErs, a significant difference. Because most of the NDErs in Greyson's study were resuscitated from cardiac arrest, they were similar to the sample of van Lommel and his colleagues.

In retrospective studies comparing participants who had come close to death, both Kenneth Ring (1980) and Greyson (2000a, 2003) found that those who reported NDEs tended to be younger. Similarly, Atwater summarized from her own inquiries that "children who brush death, nearly die, or who are pronounced clinically dead but later revive have a much higher incidence of ... NDEs than do adults" (Atwater 1996, 5).

It is tempting to conclude that the younger a person in a life-threatening situation, the more likely that person is to have an NDE. However, as Greyson (2003) noted, all studies, both retrospective and prospective, are studies of reported NDEs, which may or may not correspond to actual NDEs. It may be that NDEs actually occur equally in people of all ages, but younger people are more able to remember them or are more willing to disclose them. Greyson (2003) hypothesized that NDErs may be younger on average because older patients are more likely to have reduced blood flow to the brain during cardiac arrest and, consequently, to lack recall of the events surrounding the arrest. Even among recalled NDEs, younger NDErs may be more willing to disclose their memories out of greater trust that they will not be ridiculed or judged mentally ill. Among people who face a life-threatening situation, the available data appear to justify the conclusion that younger people are more likely to report NDEs and to suggest, but not to justify, the conclusion that younger people are more likely to have NDEs.

Contents

Regarding age and NDE contents, we found no study in which the researcher analyzed specific NDE elements in adults by ages of research participants. Most discussion in the NDE literature has addressed a comparison between the contents of childhood and adult NDEs.

In 1983, Melvin Morse published the first case report of a childhood NDE, after which several authors published studies of childhood NDEs. Whether the participant sample consisted primarily or exclusively of adults reporting their childhood NDEs retrospectively (Bush 1983; Gabbard and Twemlow 1984; Herzog and Herrin 1985) or of children reporting their NDEs soon after they had them (Morse et al. 1984), researchers concluded that elements of NDEs in children seemed similar to those of adults.

In their retrospective study of 350 U.K. NDErs, Fenwick and Fenwick (1995) included a detailed comparison of 24 content elements of childhood and adult NDEs (184–85). Their descriptive statistics revealed substantial similarity.

In a literature review of childhood NDEs, Pamela Kircher, Janice Holden, Atwater, Morse, and the International Association for Near-Death Studies (IANDS) Board of Directors concluded that "the same features reported by adult NDErs have been reported also by child NDErs." However, these reviewers did identify a few differences in children's NDEs, including (1) fewer elements; (2) more concrete and less complex content; (3) more deceased pets or other animals; (4) relatives the child does not recognize at the time (but might later recognize in old family photos the child had not previously seen); and (5) more often seeing people who actually were alive at the time of the NDE (IANDS 2003).

Over the first three decades of NDE research, investigators have published findings on several hundred childhood NDEs. NDEs in children appear to be accurately remembered, even if shared years later in adulthood. The contents of children's NDEs appear similar to those of adults and do not appear to be substantially affected by age. Sutherland (Chapter 5, this volume) concurred with these conclusions. Because infants and very young children are less influenced by culture and life experience, NDEs in this age group remain an important focus of future research.

Aftereffects and Summary

As in the case of NDE contents, we are unaware of systematic studies addressing the relationship between age and specific NDE aftereffects, and most researchers have compared aftereffects of adults and children.

Though hampered especially by children's inexperience, inability to think abstractly, and inability to metacognize—imagine asking five-year-olds how their attitudes toward religion have changed since their NDEs—researchers have drawn conclusions. Sutherland, for example, in a study of 51 NDErs, including 10 whose NDEs occurred when they were under the age of 18 years, asserted, "The impact of an NDE on an adult is immense ... in the case of children, it is no less dramatic" (Sutherland 1995, 78). Other investigators have concurred (Atwater 1996; Morse and Perry 1992). Most of these investigators have emphasized that in the aftermath of NDEs, children may be especially prone to confusion and other psychosocial challenges that likely call for skilled response.

In summary, research has provided some insight into the relationship between NDEr age and the occurrence of NDEs: People of all ages, from infants to the elderly, have reportedly experienced NDEs. Regarding incidence, when facing life-threatening events, younger people appear to be more likely to report NDEs. The specific hypothesis that children are more likely to report NDEs than are adults in similar near-death circumstances awaits confirmation through systematic study. Regarding NDE contents, the same elements appear in NDErs of all ages, though the exact nature of certain elements may vary somewhat by age. Regarding NDE aftermath, child NDErs may be in particular need of help understanding and integrating the contents and aftereffects of their NDEs. (For an in-depth discussion of children's NDEs, see Chapter 5, this volume.)

Sex

As with the variable of age, even a cursory review of the NDE literature reveals that both males and females have reported NDEs. Several researchers have investigated the relationship between NDErs' sex and the incidence and contents of their NDEs.

Regarding incidence, two retrospective studies (Greyson 1990; Groth-Marnat and Summers 1998), one meta-analysis of 12 other studies published between 1975 and 1996 involving a total of over 500 NDErs (Audain 1999), and two later prospective studies (Greyson 2003; van Lommel et al. 2001) included analysis of NDE incidence by sex. They all revealed no significant difference, indicating males and females are equally predisposed to have an NDE.

The first analysis of NDE contents by NDEr sex we found was Michael Sabom's study (1982). Focusing on 10 NDE elements, he found no significant differences between groups except that females were more likely than males to encounter others during their NDEs. The only other study we found that included analysis of these variables was van Lommel and others' prospective Dutch study (2001), in which the research team found that "women, who were significantly older than men, had more frequent deep experiences than men" (van Lommel et al. 2001, 2041). We found no studies in which the researchers analyzed a relationship between NDEr sex and NDE aftereffects.

In summary, numerous studies so far indicate that NDEs occur in both sexes, and the incidence of NDEs appears to be about equal between them. However, women might more often encounter others during their NDEs and might have deeper NDEs. Both these latter findings and the absence of data on the relationship between NDEr sex and NDE aftereffects call for further investigation, such as through meta-analysis of existing studies.

Race and Ethnicity

Research addressing the occurrence, incidence, content, or aftereffects of NDEs by race or ethnicity is scant. Many researchers have not reported race or ethnicity among their participants' demographics. However, at least four researchers or research teams did.

Sabom's (1982) sample of NDErs included only European-Americans ("Whites"), although his non-NDEr group included African-Americans ("Blacks"). However, Ring's (1980) and Richard Bonenfant's (2004) retrospective studies, together with the prospective study of Janet Schwaninger and associates Paul Eisenberg, Kenneth Schechtman, and Alan Weiss (2002), also included African-Americans and Asian-Americans. Although the latter studies involved small samples and possibly biased methodology, their results combined with those from the few studies of non-Western NDEs (see Chapter 7, this volume) indicate clearly that members of every race and numerous cultures have reported NDEs.

Beginning with Sabom (1982), researchers have acknowledged that small numbers of non-Caucasian NDErs among their samples have precluded further analysis of possible factors of race or ethnicity as related to the incidence, contents, and aftereffects of NDEs. These questions remain ripe for research. In addition, future NDE researchers could enhance understanding of these questions by including race and ethnicity among the reported demographics of their participants.

Socioeconomic Status

Socioeconomic status also is a demographic that researchers have reported infrequently. Sabom (1982) analyzed differences among 78 survivors of near-death crises in hospital settings that could provide some limited insight into socioeconomic status: size of home community (rural, <10,000, 10,000–100,00, >100,00) and occupation (laborer-services, clerical-sales, and professional). His interviews yielded representatives of each category in each of the two variables. He found no significant difference between NDErs and non-NDErs in percentage representation in categories of either variable. In addition, among NDErs, Sabom found no significant relationship between categories of either variable and any of 10 NDE elements, with one exception: A greater number of laborer-services workers than professionals reported encountering others during their NDEs (Sabom 1982, 57–60, 194, 206, 207).

Ring (1980) conducted structured interviews retrospectively with 102 research participants who had survived a near-death crisis: 49 NDErs and 53 non-NDErs. Without defining the four social-class categories that were part of the demographic aspect of the interviews, including whether Class 1 or Class 4 was upper or lower, he found representatives in each class and similar percentages between NDErs and non-NDErs in each class.

In a more recent study, Richard Bonenfant studied 40 patients who had survived clinical death in a medical setting. Although he did not specify whether he categorized participants or they categorized themselves, he reported that five subjects were defined as financially secure, meaning that they would be able to survive loss of income for an extended period of time; 17, as middle class, defined as having dual income plus savings and assets; 10, as working class, defined as being entirely dependent upon a weekly salary; and 8, as disadvantaged, defined as requiring social assistance (Bonenfant 2004, 162).

Bonenfant did not compare those frequencies to national norms. However, comparing his percentage findings to Leonard Beeghley's (2004) U.S. class membership percentages, respectively, yields 12.5 percent versus 6 percent of the rich or superrich, 43 percent versus 46 percent of the middle class, 25 percent versus 45 percent of the working class, and 20 percent versus 12 percent of the poor. It is interesting to note that the working class appears to have been overrepresented in Sabom's small sample but underrepresented in Bonenfant's.

The evidence regarding a relationship between socioeconomic status and NDEs is sparse. It can be concluded with confidence that members of every status have reported NDEs. The little existing evidence suggests that NDErs represent each status proportionately to that status's proportion of the overall population and that no specific relationship exists between socioeconomic status and NDE content, but these hypotheses await confirmation through further research. The relationship between socioeconomic status and aftereffects is another area for further research.

Education

Though equally rarely reported as many other demographics, NDEr education level has yielded consistent findings in two retrospective and two prospective studies. In interviews of 78 survivors of near-death crises in medical settings, Sabom (1982) was the first investigator to find no significant difference in the education levels of NDErs and non-NDErs. Groth-Marnat and Summers (1998) found the same result.

Similarly, in their prospective research, Schwaninger and her colleagues found all levels from "less than high school" to "attended college" represented, with no significant difference in education level between 11 NDErs and 19 non-NDErs (Schwaninger 2002, 220, 221). In their prospective Dutch study, van Lommel and his colleagues (2001) found no significant difference between the education levels of 62 NDErs and 282 non-NDErs.

Regarding a possible relationship between education level and NDE contents, Sabom (1982) found NDErs' education levels to be unrelated to the frequency with which they reported any of 10 NDE elements. Van Lommel and his colleagues (2001) found no significant relationship between education level and depth of NDEs.

We found no study that included analysis of a relationship between education level and NDE aftereffects. Research addressing the demographic of education level supports the clear conclusions that people of all education levels have reported NDEs and that those with different education levels are equally likely to have NDEs in which they report comparable elements and depth. The dearth of inquiry into the relationship between NDErs' education levels and incidence, contents, and aftereffects of NDEs calls for additional research.

Religious Affiliation and Religiosity

Because most NDErs describe their NDEs in spiritual or religious terms (Greyson 2000b), a number of NDE investigators have studied the religious affiliation and the religiosity—that is, the extent of religious involvement—of NDErs. Regarding occurrence, people of every religious affiliation have reported NDEs, including Buddhists (Carr 1993), Christians of all denominations (Fenwick and Fenwick 1995; Lundahl 1981–82; Ring 1980; Sabom 1982), Hindus (Pasricha and Stevenson 1986), indigenous religious adherents (Schorer 1985–86), Jews (Fenwick and Fenwick 1995; Ring 1980; Sabom 1982), and Muslims (Suliman 2004). Religious nonadherents have also reported NDEs, including agnostics, atheists, and people who describe themselves as spiritual but not affiliated with an organized religion (Fenwick and Fenwick 1995; Ring 1980; Sabom 1982).

Most studies of religious affiliation and religiosity of NDErs have included primarily Christians and religious nonadherents with some Jews. Several researchers have found no relationship between NDErs' religious affiliation or nonaffiliation prior to their NDEs and either the incidence (Ring 1980; Sabom 1982; van Lommel et al. 2001), contents (Sabom 1982), or depth (McLaughlin and Malony 1984; Ring 1980; van Lommel et al. 2001) of their NDEs. Though researchers have defined religiosity in various ways, such as reported frequency of attendance at a place of worship (Sabom 1982) or responses to a more detailed questionnaire about religious involvement (Ring 1980), they have found no relationship between that variable and incidence, contents, or depth of NDEs.

In a study of 61 individuals who attempted suicide, Greyson (1991) found 16 (26%) reported an NDE. Comparing the NDErs and non-NDErs, he found no evidence of any differences between the two groups with regard to prior religious affiliation or religiosity.

Regarding the relationship between preexisting spirituality or religiosity and NDE aftereffects, researchers have focused primarily on two phenomena: how NDErs interpret their NDEs and post-NDE changes in spirituality or religiosity. Ring both cited previous researchers and reported his own findings indicating that NDErs who are religious tend to interpret their NDEs in religious terms (Ring 1980, 134). In other words, two NDErs with different religious backgrounds who both describe what appears to be an essentially identical NDE element, such as entry into an all-knowing, all-loving light, are likely to use their respective religious terms and concepts to describe and interpret that experience.

Several researchers have examined the relationship between religious orientation prior to and following participants' NDEs. In his retrospective study of 111 NDErs representing a variety of religious affiliations, Ring (1984) found that participants tended to shift away from affiliation with a specific religion and toward spiritual universalism. In her retrospective study of 50 Australian NDErs, Sutherland (1992) found a strong tendency for participants affiliated with Jewish and a variety of Christian organized religions prior to their NDEs to be nonaffiliated following their NDEs but more engaged in spiritual practices and experiences such as prayer, meditation, a quest for spiritual values, and a sense of being spiritually guided. Sabom (1982), however, found among his participants the strongest tendency for them to become more involved in their pre-NDE religions following their NDEs. And Margot Grey, in a study of 41 British NDErs, found change to more intense religious feelings among 44 percent representing Protestant, Catholic, and "Other" pre-NDE religious affiliations; change to alternative religious beliefs among 27 percent of NDErs representing Protestant pre-NDE affiliation; change to nondenominational philosophies among 20 percent representing all pre-NDE religious affiliations (Protestant, Catholic, Other, and None); and no change in religious beliefs and affiliations among 10 percent representing Protestant and Other pre-NDE affiliations (Grey 1995, 110).

The absence of a clear pattern of pre- and post-NDE religious affiliation and religiosity may be the result of methodological differences between the studies or may indicate simply that in the aftermath of an NDE, for reasons research has not yet revealed, some NDErs' beliefs and involvement in their pre-NDE religions deepen, some change in beliefs or involvement to other religions or to nonreligious spirituality, and some remain unchanged. Further research on this question is clearly warranted.

In summary, atheists, agnostics, and the conventionally religious representing a full range of affiliation and devoutness have described NDEs. Very young children have reported NDEs despite being too young to have established religious beliefs at the time of the NDE. A consistent finding in multiple studies is the lack of association between NDErs' prior religiousness and the probability of an NDE occurring or the content or depth of the NDE. However, some investigators found that NDErs' prior religious belief systems markedly influenced their interpretations of their NDEs. Further, although religious affiliation and religiosity often change following NDEs, research has not yet clearly indicated whether or how NDErs' religious affiliation and religiosity, as well as other factors, prior to their NDEs are related to those changes.

Sexual Orientation

Individuals with gay, lesbian, bisexual, or transgender (GLBT) sexual orientations have reported NDEs. Liz Dale (2001) presented the only major study of this population in her book *Crossing Over and Coming Home: Twenty-one Authors Discuss the Gay Near-Death Experience as Spiritual Transformation*. We found no observable differences between the contents of NDEs in the literature at large—presumably those of predominantly heterosexual NDErs—and GLBT NDEs. Consistent with heterosexual NDErs, GLBT NDErs were often quite spiritually transformed following their NDEs (Dale 2001); thus, sexual orientation does not appear to be a factor in the transformative aftermath of an NDE. Being based on one study, these observations, of course, call for further investigation.

Physical Disability

People with blindness have reported NDEs. This population includes both people born blind and those who became blind some time after birth.

NDErs born blind are an especially interesting group in terms of NDE research. Such individuals are totally unable to perceive visually, so, for them, the ability to see is an abstract concept. They understand the world only from their senses of hearing, touch, taste, and smell. Even their dreams do not include vision, although they may include other senses such as sound and touch.

In 1998, Ring and Sharon Cooper (1998) published a study of NDEs and related experiences in the blind, and they presented their findings in greater detail in a book the following year (1999). The study included 31 blind or severely visually impaired individuals who had NDEs or out-of-body experiences (OBEs). Of the 31 research participants, 10 were not facing an imminent life-threatening event at the time of their experiences, and 25 reported at least some visual impressions during their experiences.

This study included 14 individuals who were blind from birth. Nine of these 14 individuals had visual impressions during their experiences. In case reports from this study, NDErs blind from birth had highly detailed visual NDEs with typical NDE elements consistent with NDEs in people with physical sight.

Two noteworthy case reports involved a different physical disability: quadriplegia and inability to speak. Serdahely and Barbara Walker (1990) reported the case of man with congenital quadriplegia and cerebral palsy who, as an adult, reported his NDE at age two-and-one-half years; and Rick Enright (2004) reported the case of a 10-year-old boy with congenital cystic fibrosis whose quadriplegia and inability to speak were the result of brain trauma from surgical complications at age eight—the same complications associated with his NDE. The authors communicated with the NDErs through yes/no questions. In both cases, the authors considered the NDEs typical of others they had encountered in the professional literature.

It appears that people with disabilities also have NDEs. The small number of studies and research participants precludes any firm conclusions about the incidence, contents, and aftereffects of NDEs among people with disabilities but the studies suggest they are comparable to those of NDEs among people without disabilities.

Occupation

A number of NDErs have reported NDEs while performing duties associated with their occupations. It is reasonable to assume that occupations with the greatest probability of encountering a life-threatening event would be associated with a higher likelihood of NDEs. Perhaps the riskiest occupation is combat duty in the armed forces. Most documented combat-associated NDEs are anecdotal or case reports, but Robert Sullivan (1984) conducted a preliminary study of 24 combat-associated NDEs. The NDEs reported in this study seemed to have the typical NDE elements. The author discussed the unique challenges of studying combat-associated NDEs.

As previously discussed, Sabom analyzed differences among 78 survivors of near-death crises in hospital settings by three occupation categories. His interviews yielded representatives of each category, showed no significant difference between NDErs and non-NDErs in percentage representation in the three categories; and among NDErs, indicated no significant relationship between the three categories and any of 10 NDE elements, except that a greater number of laborer-service workers than professionals reported encountering others during their NDEs (Sabom 1982, 57–60, 194, 206, 207). Groth-Marnat and Summers (1998) also found no difference in the distribution of occupations at the time of a life-threatening event between 53 NDErs and 27 non-NDErs.

People representing every major category of occupation have reported NDEs. Very few researchers have included occupational categories among their demographics. We are not aware of any study suggesting occupation is associated with either the probability of an NDE occurring or its contents, depth, or aftereffects, though these foci are appropriate for further research.

Marital Status

Few researchers have reported the marital statuses of their research participants. In a small-scale study, Susan Schoenbeck and Gerald Hocutt (1991) found one single, one divorced, and nine married people among a convenience sample of 11 NDErs, mean aged 56.8, who had undergone cardiopulmonary resuscitation. Their findings reflect our conclusion in perusing the NDE literature: NDEs occur in people representing every marital status.

Regarding NDE incidence and marital status, we found only one study. Groth-Marnat and Summers (1998) found no significant difference in the proportion of marital statuses represented at the time of a life-threatening event between a group of 53 NDErs and a comparison group of 27 non-NDErs. Their findings suggest that marital status is unrelated to the incidence of NDEs under life-threatening circumstances.

Regarding aftereffects, the only factor we found addressed in the NDE literature was the question of NDErs' quality of marriage following an NDE. Atwater (2000) observed that the majority of childhood NDErs enjoyed long-lasting marriages, whereas among adult NDErs married at the time of their NDEs, over three-fourths ended in divorce in about seven years. By contrast, Groth-Marnat and Summers (1998) found no difference in marital interaction or incidence of divorce in their comparison of adult NDErs and non-NDErs married at the time of their NDEs. However, they did not report the number of such participants, the lapsed time since participants' NDEs, or the actual degree of difficulty in marital interactions in each group. Also, as they pointed out, the non-NDErs, having come close to death, may have suffered from "posttraumatic reactions or problems adjusting to chronic illness" (119) resulting in interpersonal difficulties; they suggested that comparing both groups with individuals who had not come close to death might reveal a difference in marital distress or stability.

Sandra Rozan Christian's (2005) research provided some possible further insight. She compared 26 NDErs married at the time of their NDEs with 26 non-NDErs using their most life-changing, nonparanormal or non-mystical event during married life (LCE) as a before/after referent. She found that the 65 percent incidence of divorce among the NDErs was significantly higher than the 19 percent among the comparison group. She also found among NDErs some cases of marriages that became stronger following the NDE of one of the spouses. Her findings indicated that if the NDE resulted in a divergence of values between the spouses, the marriage was likely to end; whereas if it resulted in a convergence of values, the marriage was likely to become more satisfying and stable. Unfortunately, her study was flawed by a disproportionate number of LCErs whose experiences occurred since 2000 (n = 11) compared to NDErs (n = 2); more LCErs had less time to feel the effects of their experiences and possibly divorce. Nonetheless, Christian's findings were suggestive of support for Atwater's observation regarding overall greater marital dissatisfaction and instability among married adult NDErs. Christian's findings also point to a possible role of *spouse* characteristics in the aftereffect of degree of marital satisfaction and stability: If the spouses' values already compare favorably to the values to which NDErs tend to gravitate—or if the spouses somehow are able to adopt similar values—such that their and their NDEr spouses' values converge following the NDE, the couple might realize greater marital satisfaction or stability.

Marital status is a rarely reported demographic in large-scale studies. The fact that children, as well as adults of all marital statuses, have reported NDEs indicates that marital status is not related to NDE occurrence; the little existing evidence indicates also that it is unrelated to NDE incidence; indeed, it is unlikely that marital status is related to NDE contents, though this hypothesis awaits research. Likewise, research on marital status and aftereffects is virtually nonexistent. Yet several tantalizing prospects for future research exist. For example, a researcher could study the relationship between the convergence/divergence of spouses' values and their marital satisfaction and stability among three groups in which one spouse had not come close to death and the other spouse was one of the following: (1) an NDEr, (2) a non-NDEr who had come close to death, or (3) a non-NDEr who had not come close to death. Christian's findings (2005) would be confirmed if spouses' values diverged and if marriages were correspondingly less satisfying and stable among the first group compared with the other two groups. A more challenging study would be to find and compare couples in which their NDE/non-NDE statuses were mixed, such as a first-time NDEr married to a previous-NDEr spouse. As Christian (2005) found, cooperation of the divorced spouse of an NDEr may be impossible to garner, posing a substantial challenge to research in this area.

Life History

Knowledge of NDEs

A legitimate question is whether knowledge of NDEs increases their likelihood. Less than seven years after NDEs came to widespread public attention, Sabom (1982) found so few of 61 NDErs reported previous knowledge of NDEs that the number was insufficient for further statistical analysis of how such knowledge might be related to NDE contents. Fifteen years later, when NDEs had presumably become much more widely known, Greyson (1991) found that among 61 suicide attempt survivors consecutively admitted to hospital, 88 percent of the 16 NDErs reported previous knowledge of NDEs, and 87 percent of the 45 non-NDErs also reported previous knowledge of NDEs.

Thus, NDEs occur to people both with and without prior knowledge of NDEs, and such knowledge does not appear to influence NDE incidence. How such knowledge might relate to NDE contents, and especially whether prior knowledge about NDEs might be helpful in the aftermath of an NDE, awaits further research.

Prosocial and Antisocial Acts

Whereas the great majority of NDEs are pleasurable experiences characterized by feelings such as peace, joy, and love, a small percentage of NDEs are distressing experiences characterized by feelings such as fear, isolation, guilt, or confusion (see Chapter 4, this volume). These latter emotional states may be in response to terrifying NDE imagery that may include profound isolation, fearsome beings, frightening landscapes, or even hellish scenery. Harvey Irwin and Barbara Bramwell (1988) and others have found that NDEs may have both pleasurable and distressing components. Though a review of research on distressing NDEs reveals a rather broad range, these types of NDEs are less frequently reported (see Chapter 4, this volume).

Scholars, health professionals, and members of the public alike have questioned what NDEr characteristics might be associated with having one or the other type of NDE. In addition to the other characteristics we address in this chapter, some people have speculated that NDErs with a history of prosocial acts might experience pleasurable NDEs and antisocial acts distressing NDEs.

A few individual cases undermine this hypothesis. Ring (personal communication, 1990) gave an example of a physically abusive prostitution solicitor ("pimp") who had a pleasurable NDE—and was subsequently reformed. There also is the case of an NDEr with a history as a military assassin who reported a pleasurable NDE (Brinkley and Perry 1994). And Bonenfant (2001) reported an NDE that included the distressing element of an encounter with the devil—in a five-year-old boy with no atypical history of antisocial acts.

Barbara Rommer (2000) presented the largest study of frightening NDEs with dozens of case reports in her book *Blessings in Disguise*. She referred to all types of distressing NDEs as "Less-Than-Positive (LTP)" NDEs and concluded:

> In summary, there are basically three reasons why a Less-Than-Positive experience occurs instead of, or in addition to, a blissful light NDE. First, the LTP event is an impetus to reevaluate previous choices, actions, reactions, thoughts, and belief systems. Second, an LTP event may occur because the person's mindset immediately prior to the experience was less than loving. Third, I feel many of the examples have proven that an LTP may occur secondary to negative programming during childhood. (Rommer 2000, 196)

Rommer also noted, "Everyone has the potential of having an LTP" (Rommer 2000, xxii). Other researchers of distressing NDEs have drawn the same conclusion (see Chapter 4, this volume). It appears not to be the case that "good" people have pleasurable NDEs and "bad" people have distressing NDEs. To our knowledge, no study has addressed specifically the relationship between history of prosocial or antisocial acts and the incidence, contents, depth, or aftereffects of NDEs; such research is needed.

Abuse and Trauma

In 1990, Ring and Christopher Rosing undertook a study to address a variety of psychological factors as they relate to NDEs, including a reported history of childhood abuse or other major trauma. They compared 74 NDErs with 54 participants who were interested in NDEs but had not had one. They found NDErs reported a higher incidence of childhood physical, psychological, or sexual abuse; neglect; or negative home atmosphere (Ring and Rosing 1990, 219). NDErs also scored higher than the comparison group on a measure of psychological dissociation, "a form of psychological fragmentation in which one portion of the individual splits off, like an autonomous entity, from the conscious self" (Ring and Rosing 1990, 213), a recognized response to trauma. The authors raised the possibility of an NDE-prone personality involving "the capacity to shift into states of consciousness that afford access to nonordinary realities coupled with strong tendencies toward psychological absorption" (Ring and Rosing 1990, 235); the latter defined as "the tendency to become deeply involved in sensory and imaginative experiences" (Ring and Rosing 1990, 212).

Irwin (1993) expressed concern that Ring and Rosing may have overlooked the possibility that dimensions of childhood trauma might be intercorrelated. If this were the case, Ring and Rosing's series of univariate tests might not have been the optimal statistical approach. Using alternate analyses, Irwin did find that NDErs were more likely to report a prior history of childhood trauma but found no evidence that NDErs were more prone to dissociation.

Another consideration is that in the instrument Ring and Rosing used to assess childhood abuse and trauma, with 38 items comprising five sub-scales and a response range from 0 (never) to 4 (always) for each item, the possible range of total scores was 0 to 152: The NDE group's total mean score was 9.53, and the comparison group's score was 7.61, a statistically significant difference. Though Ring and Rosing did not report ranges of total scores, the mean scores suggest that many NDErs scored as low as many comparison group members. Thus, although childhood abuse and trauma may contribute to NDEs, it appears not to be a precondition. Indeed, Fenwick and Fenwick (1995) found that 50 percent of their more than 350 U.K. NDErs described their childhoods as "happy" or "very happy."

Another possibility is that the aftereffects of NDEs might promote healing from childhood abuse and trauma, accompanied by a greater willingness to disclose such a history. This possibility could explain why, in retrospective studies such as Ring and Rosing's (1990), NDErs would report a higher incidence of childhood trauma and abuse than would non-NDErs. The possibility that people with a history of childhood abuse or trauma might be more likely to experience an NDE when they encounter near-death crises would best be determined by prospective NDE research comparing NDErs, non-NDErs who had experienced similar near-death crises as NDErs, and non-NDErs who had never come close to death.

Although NDErs might report childhood abuse, neglect, and other trauma more frequently than non-NDErs, such life experiences clearly are not universal among NDErs. At most, they may facilitate NDEs, but they certainly are not preconditions of them. An understanding of the relationship between childhood history of abuse, neglect, or other trauma and the incidence, contents, depth, and aftereffects of NDEs awaits research, particularly prospective research.

Psychological Characteristics

Several researchers have sought to ascertain whether certain psychological characteristics are overrepresented among NDErs, a finding that might help to explain the occurrence, incidence, content, and aftereffects of NDEs. This section reviews much of the research about these characteristics.

Psychopathological Characteristics

A basic question about NDErs is their mental health. Greyson (2000b), citing consistent findings from the retrospective studies of Ring (1980), Sabom (1982), Thomas Locke and Franklin Shontz (1983), Glen Gabbard and Stuart Twemlow (1984), Irwin (1985), and Greyson (1991), concluded that NDErs are indistinguishable from a variety of comparison groups regarding mental health. From a prospective viewpoint, if NDErs were over-representative of people with mental illness, prospective researchers—those conducting long-term hospital studies of cardiac resuscitants—would have been expected to observe and report this trend, yet none have done so. Thus, NDEs appear to occur to people representing a range of mental health profiles—mostly mentally healthy, as is the general population—and with no greater NDE incidence related to any mental health profile. Another way of stating this finding is that NDErs are no more likely to show psychopathology (mental illness) than are comparison groups of non-NDErs.

Regarding depth of NDE, however, several researchers have found a trend. People with psychiatric disorders tend to report less elaborate NDEs (Gabbard and Twemlow 1984; Greyson 1991, 2000a, 2001; Greyson and Liester 2004; Irwin 1985; Locke and Schontz 1983). The dynamics behind this finding are a topic for ongoing research.

Over the history of the field of near-death studies, some researchers have focused particularly on two possible psychopathological dynamics among NDErs: depersonalization and dissociation. (Both are discussed later in this chapter.). An important consideration for readers to keep in mind is that in finding a comparatively higher or lower incidence of any psychological characteristic in NDErs through retrospective research, it cannot be determined whether that difference preceded the NDE or was a result of it.

Russell Noyes and Roy Kletti advanced one of the earliest psychological models, suggesting NDEs were a type of depersonalization by the NDErs. They defined depersonalization as "a subjective mental phenomenon having as its central feature an altered awareness of the self" (Noyes and Kletti 1976, 375) involving feelings of detachment, strangeness, and unreality. Noyes and Kletti suggested that NDEs protected NDErs from the threat of death by inducing feelings of detachment and unreality.

Some years later, Gabbard and Twemlow (1984) published a careful comparison of the subjective experiences of depersonalization versus OBEs that characterize NDEs. They found several fundamental differences. Whereas the subjective experience of depersonalization often includes unpleasant feelings and a sense of loss of reality, most NDEs are profoundly pleasurable and involve a sense of absolute or hyperreality. Depersonalization also involves a sense of detachment from the body that is subjectively different from the experience of near-death OBEs. Gabbard and Twemlow concluded that NDEs are distinctly different subjective experiences than depersonalization.

Irwin concurred with Gabbard and Twemlow's conclusion but asserted the possibility that NDErs may be more prone to dissociation, which Greyson (2000a) defined as "the separation of thoughts, feelings, or experiences from the normal stream of consciousness and memory" (Irwin 1993, 460). In two separate studies, Ring (1990) and Greyson (2000a) found that NDErs scored higher on a dissociation scale than did members of comparison groups. Both researchers found the degree of NDEr dissociation was not consistent with a diagnosis of a pathological dissociative disorder. Greyson (2001) concluded that NDErs may respond to severe stress with adaptive dissociation that is not pathological.

Nonpathological Characteristics

Psychological Absorption and Fantasy Proneness   Ring (1992) suggested that NDErs might be prone to NDEs by virtue of psychological absorption, a term that Auke Tellegen and Gilbert Atkinson (1974) coined to describe "the propensity to focus one's attention on imaginative or selected sensory experiences to the exclusion of other events in the external environment" (Greyson 2000b, 323). Greyson related this concept to that of fantasy-proneness, a concept Sharon Wilson and Theodore Barber (1981, 1983) described as "a strong investment in fantasy life, vivid hallucinatory ability, intense sensory experience, and excellent eidetic memory" (Greyson 2000b, 324). Though researchers before (Lynn and Rhue 1986, 1988; Wilson and Barber 1983) and since (Gow, Lane, and Chant 2003) have found higher levels of absorption and fantasy proneness among NDErs, including a small positive correlation between NDE depth, as measured by the NDE Scale, and both variables (Council and Greyson 1985), Ring (1992) did not find higher fantasy proneness among NDErs as compared to people interested in NDEs. Greyson concluded that "empirical data regarding absorption and fantasy proneness among near-death experients have been suggestive but not compelling" (Greyson 2000b, 325). These tendencies may contribute to NDEs—or at least the ability to perceive and/or remember NDEs—but appear not to account fully for them.

Expectations about and Surrender to Death   Another possible factor in NDEs is NDErs' expectations about death or the dying process. At least one study yielded a negative finding in this regard. In Greyson's (1991) research with suicide attempt survivors consecutively admitted to hospital, he found no differences between 16 NDErs and the 45 non-NDErs with regard to their expectations of what death or dying might be like.

Another factor that might increase the likelihood of an NDE during a life-threatening event is an attitude of surrender. Greyson (1993) asked 187 NDErs and 59 non-NDErs if they had "let go and surrendered to the dying process" at the time of their life-threatening event. He found that 82 percent who answered in the affirmative reported NDEs, whereas only 60 percent who answered in the negative reported NDEs. This difference was statistically significant. Greyson concluded:

> Surrender to the process of dying and to the possibility of death appears to be strongly associated with the near-death experiences and their affective

and transcendental components. This relinquishing of control by the ego may be an important step, not only permitting the subjective experience to unfold, but also in producing some of the therapeutic effects of the experience. (Greyson 1993, 398)

A question remains regarding what factors contribute to a willingness to surrender at the time of a life-threatening event.

Psychic Experiences   In the aftermath of NDEs, experiencers often report an increase in psychic experiences, including telepathy and precognition (see Chapter 3, this volume). Some researchers have addressed whether NDErs already evidenced a higher incidence of such experiences prior to their NDEs, suggesting a possible predictor of NDEs under near-death circumstances.

Results of this inquiry have been mixed. In an early study of 78 NDErs, Greyson and Ian Stevenson found "prior experiences suggestive of extrasensory phenomena were less common" than among control populations (Stevenson 1980, 1193). Similarly, Sutherland found in a retrospective study of 40 NDErs that those interviewed "reported no more psychic phenomena before the NDE than the general population. There was a statistically significant increase following the NDE in 14 of 15 items examined" (Sutherland 1989, 93).

One later study yielded different results. Greyson (2003) surveyed 1,595 patients admitted to a tertiary care center cardiac inpatient service. The 11 percent of patients who reported an NDE "did in fact report more prior purportedly paranormal experiences" than did non-NDErs matched for diagnosis, sex, and age.

> That difference may suggest that persons who believe they have had paranormal experiences in the past are more likely to report near-death experiences; or it may suggest persons who have near-death experiences are more likely retroactively to interpret past experiences as paranormal. (Greyson 2003, 274)

Other   Researchers have investigated several aftereffects that they suggested might not have appeared for the first time following an NDE but might have characterized the NDEr prior to the experience and "merely" have increased noticeably following it. For example, the physio-kundalini syndrome is a complex biological process known in Eastern traditions as kundalini. Physical symptoms include powerful experiences of energy and heat; mental symptoms include increased belief in the existence of a higher power and increased morality. In a study of 153 NDErs, experiencers reported more symptoms of the physio-kundalini syndrome than did non-NDErs, especially with regard to motor and mental symptoms (Greyson 1993). Greyson noted he could not rule out the possibility that

NDErs might exhibit kundalini features even *before* the NDE, thus indicating a possible preexisting and perhaps predisposing factor rather than only an aftereffect.

In another study, Greyson and Mitchell (2004) found that 80 percent of 73 NDErs reported auditory hallucinations that they found predominantly positive, containing inspiration, guidance, and other life-enhancing value. Of these, 40 percent reported such hallucinations prior to their NDEs, suggesting, again, the NDE as a point in time when, for some NDErs, aftereffects were increases of preexisting phenomena.

In a rare study comparing electroencephalogram (EEG) readings in 23 NDErs and 20 non-NDErs, Willoughby Britton and Richard Bootzin (2004) found NDErs had significantly more epileptiform activity than comparison participants, which was nearly completely localized in the left hemisphere of the brain. They also found among NDErs more paroxysmal EEG activity during rapid eye movement (REM) sleep, a longer latency period before the onset of REM sleep, and fewer REM sleep periods. The researchers noted they could not determine whether these differences between the NDEr and comparison groups were present in the NDErs before they experienced their NDEs or were aftereffects of the NDE. The authors cautioned that the NDErs in this study might not be representative of all NDErs. An additional finding of this study was that "the near-death experience was not associated with dysfunctional stress reactions such as dissociation, posttraumatic stress disorder, and substance abuse, but rather was associated with positive coping styles" (Britton and Bootzin 2004, 254).

Summary

For people who experience a life-threatening event, some psychological factors do not appear to influence the likelihood, content, or aftereffects of NDEs. These include expectations about death and mental health profile—with the exception that people with psychiatric disorders are likely to report less elaborate NDEs. Other factors might contribute to, but clearly do not determine—nor does their absence prohibit—the occurrence, nature, and aftereffects of an NDE. These include surrender to death, psychological absorption, fantasy proneness, and a history of psychic experiences, kundalini features, life-enhancing auditory hallucinations, and left-brain hemisphere epileptiform activity.

Culture

Although an entire chapter in this volume is dedicated to examination of one NDEr characteristic—that of membership in a particular culture (see Chapter 7 by Allan Kellehear)—this important topic is also addressed briefly here. Kellehear found possible noteworthy differences between the contents of non-Western and Western NDEs. He attributed these differences to the influence of culture. The similarities and differences that may exist between Western and non-Western NDEs merit further examination.

In one large study of non-Western NDEs among Chinese earthquake survivors (Zhi-ying and Jian-xun 1992), researchers used medical criteria to determine NDErs' closeness to death and the NDE Scale (Greyson 1983) to confirm the existence of NDEs. They found that 32 survivors, or 40 percent of those close to death, had NDEs. This percentage was significantly higher than typical percentages of 10–20 percent in similar Western NDE studies (Greyson 2003; Parnia et al. 2001; van Lommel et al. 2001). Consistent with studies of Western NDErs, these Chinese researchers found that "age, gender, marital status, educational and occupational level, personality, brain trauma, and prior knowledge of NDEs and belief in spirits, ghosts, God, and destiny did not significantly affect NDE contents." They also found that the contents of NDEs were not related to "alterations in state of consciousness, duration of loss of consciousness, and prior views of death" (Zhi-ying and Jian-xun 1992, 47).

Jeffrey Long reviewed approximately 25 non-Western NDEs submitted to the NDERF Web site (Near-Death Experience Research Foundation 2008b). In most cases, the NDEr submitted the account personally, many in English and some translated into English. Long considered the experiences to be NDEs if they included a lucid experience occurring at the time of an imminent life-threatening event, regardless of the Greyson NDE Scale score. He found their contents quite similar to those of typical Western NDEs, suggesting at least some non-Western NDEs are similar to Western NDEs.

Several problems have plagued the study of non-Western NDEs. Western NDErs usually find it very difficult to describe their NDEs. Assuming this ineffability is universal, the problem of accurate description would only be compounded by an English account from an NDEr for whom English is not the first language or one from a translator. Many researchers have not assessed or reported how close the NDErs were to death. In addition, NDErs' self-selection in these retrospective studies, along with NDEs published in the popular rather than scholarly literature, may yield NDEs that are not representative of all NDEs from the non-Western culture. Furthermore, non-Western NDE accounts are still quite few in numbers; a history of the field of near-death studies reveals that researchers identified certain less frequently reported characteristics of NDEs, such as NDEs dominated by distressing emotions, only after many years of investigation that yielded sufficient numbers to make the characteristics evident.

Any one or a combination of the preceding issues might explain many of the apparent differences between Western and non-Western NDEs that Kellehear found. More research will be necessary before it can be reliably determined if non-Western NDEs are truly different from Western NDEs, and if different, the extent of such differences.

RECOMMENDATIONS FOR FURTHER RESEARCH

Throughout this chapter, we have made recommendations for further research. Following are some reiterated and additional recommendations to yield findings that clarify the role of NDEr characteristics in the occurrence, incidence, contents, and aftereffects of NDEs.

- Retrospective studies with larger samples and samples representing diversity of NDEr characteristics, perhaps using the Internet
- Prospective studies
- In both types of studies, detailed documentation of NDErs' demographic and, when possible, life history and psychological characteristics
- Consistent use of the NDE Scale (Greyson 1983) as the measure of occurrence and depth of NDEs; validated translation of that scale into other languages and research into the validity of that scale for assessing non-Western NDEs
- Clarification of the similarities and differences between NDEs and related phenomena, such as deathbed visions
- More objective means to assess the variable of nearness to death. Researchers have found nearness to death affects the content of NDEs (Kelly 2001; Owens, Cook, and Stevenson 1990). This variable could be assessed through medically trained professionals' review of NDEr research participants' medical records, when such records are available. It also could be specified through Owens, Cook, and Stevenson's rating method (Owens, Cook, and Stevenson 1990, 1175) or through Karnofsky Scores (Karnofsky and Burchenal 1949) of 100 (no physical compromise), to 10 (moribund) to reflect unconsciousness, to 0 (death) to reflect convincing evidence of a cardiopulmonary arrest associated with the NDE. Because researcher assessment of nearness to death may involve subjectivity, assessment by multiple reviewers would be advisable to establish interrater reliability.

CONCLUSION

This chapter has reviewed research on the characteristics of NDErs. Researchers so far have tended to find that most hypothesized predictors of NDE occurrence, incidence, contents, and aftereffects are not reliable. Studies have revealed a few possible predisposing factors; as of the writing of this chapter, these factors remain in the domain of possibilities, awaiting further elucidation through future research.

Theoreticians over the past 30 years have proposed various models to explain NDEs. From our review of the characteristics of Western NDErs, we found little evidence to support previously proposed biological, psychological, or sociological explanations as the sole cause(s) of NDEs. Another hypothesis is that NDEs are spiritual and transpersonal experiences, possibly with a contribution from known or unknown biological, psychological, or sociological factors. Most Western NDErs believe their experiences were real and were actual encounters with another realm of existence. Visual NDEs in blind experiencers, including those blind from birth, provide strong evidence of the insufficiency of biological, psychological, or sociological hypotheses, either individually or in combination, to explain NDEs. Converging lines of evidence support the hypothesis that the cause of NDEs involves some component(s) other than or in addition to biological, psychological, or sociological factors alone.

For now, the best answer to the question, "Who has NDEs, how often, what kind, and with what aftereffects?" is probably that NDEs appear, for the most part, to be equal opportunity transpersonal experiences. Though people with certain characteristics might be more prone to report NDEs during near-death episodes, or to report deeper NDEs or particular aftereffects, research has not yet revealed a characteristic that either guarantees or prohibits the occurrence, incidence, nature, or aftereffects of an NDE. Perhaps the conclusion of research so far—that everyone is a potential NDEr—is the most mysterious, provocative, and important message for readers to take away.

Census of Non-Western Near-Death Experiences to 2005: Observations and Critical Reflections

Allan Kellehear

The majority of near-death studies research has focused on white, Anglo-European respondents. Not surprisingly, the highly similar cultural backgrounds of these populations have resulted in highly consistent clinical presentations of near death experiencers' (NDErs) descriptions of their experiences to researchers and health professionals. This similarity of presentations has led to claims about the universality of near-death experience (NDE) features (Atwater 1988; Grosso 1981). This chapter argues that features such as the life review and the tunnel sensation in clinical presentations of NDEs are not universal and, therefore, that the development and general application of biological theories of causation is premature. In other words, a demonstrated absence of certain NDE features from some cultures supports the hypothesis that NDE content is influenced by NDErs' cultural learning histories rather than that it is the result of some inherent human physiological process. The research bias toward biological explanations over simpler cultural ones is regrettable if only because sufficient transcultural material exists to warrant reverse priorities. A review of the case material in this area demonstrates the importance of exploring cultural factors more thoroughly before turning to biological factors.

This chapter is organized in the following way. First comes a preliminary discussion of the main features of the NDE as researchers have described them in clinical literature. Then follows non-Western case material. This review of case material from different cultures illustrates the diversity of the clinical phenomenology of the NDE, particularly between areas dominated by historic religions such as Christianity and Buddhism and those characterized by "primitive" or animistic religions.

Although reliable accounts from Pacific areas (Melanesia, Micronesia, and Maori New Zealand) and hunter-gatherer societies (Native North and South America, Aboriginal Australia, and Africa) now total 39, I repeat my observations made in previous surveys. Because of global Westernization and modernization processes now underway, many of these cases are historically unique. Because of these processes, accounts from hunter-gatherer and cultivating and herding peoples are particularly difficult to collect in their traditional forms. This small but significant sample may, therefore, represent important empirical and historical evidence that certain Western features of the NDE are probably culture-bound. Certainly, substantial changes to these cultures in the direction of Westernization will progressively obscure these findings in the future, making their present identification and discussion of NDEs important and unique. Finally, I conclude by discussing the qualifications, limitations, and criticisms of surveys addressing cultural variations of the NDE, including the one presented here. The review in this chapter is an update of earlier surveys (Kellehear 1993, 1996) and integrates the published cultural data that have appeared in the literature over the past 10 years since my earlier work but also including some earlier overlooked work.

NDEs IN THE WEST

In its most popularly understood form, the NDE is triggered by a physical crisis that brings the person close to death, usually by accident, misadventure, or illness. However, researchers have also found that certain social crises—for example, being a castaway after a shipwreck—may also produce the basic NDE phenomenology (Kellehear 1996; Morse and Perry 1993). The sensations of peace and being out of the body, so that one may observe the accident or resuscitation scene as an observer, is the first major feature of the NDE. This experience may be followed by the sensation of traveling into a darkness or void often described as a tunnel, at the end of which one may meet a bright "being of light." At this point a life review may commence, sweeping across major and minor events of one's life. This is an educational evaluation rather than a judgment. Some time afterward, one may enter a transcendent world where deceased relatives and friends are met in another society similar to that of the individual (Lundahl 1981–82). Not all NDErs report these events. Indeed, clinicians Bruce Greyson and Ian Stevenson (1980) and Michael Sabom (1982) have distinguished two or three variations, some of which do not include an experience of darkness or visiting another realm beyond death.

Yet, despite common internal variations in the order of unfolding experiences, the extent of the experiences, and the proportion of experiencers who report the different types of experiences, the mentioned images well represent the composite Anglo-European experience and the clinical understanding of the NDE. Some of the basic features of the NDE, such as visits to a supernatural world, seeing the dead, and experiencing feelings of euphoria or horror, have a long history in the Western world reaching back through medieval times (Zaleski 1987) to the Greco-Roman period (Walker and Serdahely 1990) and even as far back as the Stone Age (Kellehear 2007). The modern Western form of NDE, however, seems both more and less than a simple otherworld journey. It is more because other elements are described in it such as out-of-body experiences (OBEs), life reviews, and return to life; and it is less because unlike most otherworld journeys, the otherworld that modern NDErs describe is frequently lacking in detail and in tests, trials, and judgments.

Notwithstanding these broad differences between NDEs and otherworld journeys, non-Western cases of NDE differ in important ways from their Anglo-European counterparts. In the following material, I review only the NDE phenomenology associated with illness for two reasons. First, these circumstances are the main type clinicians are likely to encounter. Second, these circumstances characterize the NDE in the popular imagination. This focus is also a good starting point to show that culture, rather than physical processes, seems to provide the critical influence in these experiences.

Furthermore, despite certain anthropological parallels between the clinical NDE and, for example, the social phenomenology of shipwrecks and other rite-of-passage experiences, distinguishing between the two phenomena seems important. Although it is clear that similar social experiences may evoke similar psychological processes, it does not follow that these have a singular or even an overlapping set of physiological correlates.

For example, reviewing one's life consciously may have different physiological correlates from reviewing one's life as part of a clinical NDE while unconscious. In both cases these life reviews involve similar psychological processes, but each might involve different brain areas and their respective functions. Which, if either, of the underlying physiological correlates is causative or derivative of these psychological processes is not crucial here. However, to focus on the NDE associated with illness, I will not complicate matters by conflating its phenomenology with anthropological parallels that may have a different underlying etiology. In this respect, assessing the universality of the life review or tunnel sensation across all types of human experiences is *not* the purpose of this chapter. Instead, the more modest question of their presence cross-culturally in clinical NDEs is the focus of the following review.

NON-WESTERN NDEs

As of 2005, authors of a total of 16 refereed journal articles had described approximately 275–350 non-Western NDEs, which here are grouped by three culture areas: Asia, Pacific Area, and hunter-gatherer cultures (see Table 7.1). This section provides a critical analysis of the NDEs

Table 7.1
Summary of Findings Regarding Features of Non-Western NDEs by Culture Category and Culture

Culture Category	Culture	Published Cases	Tunnel	OBE	NDE Feature Life Review	Beings	Other World
Asia	China	100–180	maybe	yes	yes	yes	yes
	India	109	no	yes	yes	yes	yes
	Thailand	10	maybe	yes	yes	yes	yes
	Tibet	16	no	yes	yes	yes	yes
	Area total	235–315					
Pacific Area	Western New Britain	3	maybe	maybe	maybe	yes	yes
	Hawaii	1	maybe	yes	no	yes	yes
	Guam	4	no	yes	no	yes	yes
	Maori New Zealand	1	maybe	yes	no	yes	yes
	Area total	9					
Hunter-gatherer	North & South America	14	no	yes	no	yes	yes
	Australia	1	no	no	no	yes	yes
	Africa	15	maybe	no	no	yes	yes
	Area total	30					

described in each publication for the presence or absence of five NDE features: tunnel sensation, OBEs, life review, supernatural beings, and otherworldly location.

Asian NDEs

China

Contemporary accounts of Chinese NDEs in the academic literature are fragmentary and piecemeal. What is known about Chinese NDEs comes primarily through the historical work of Carl Becker (1981, 1984) and the more recent empirical work by Feng Zhi-ying and Liu Jian-xun (1992). Becker reviewed three traditional biographical accounts of well-known Chinese monks who were important to the founding of Pure Land Buddhism. Each monk experienced a serious illness that resulted in either an NDE or a deathbed vision while still reasonably conscious. In each of these accounts, no tunnel experience was reported, although one person proceeded "through a void" (Becker 1984, 163). Neither the OBE experience nor the life review was mentioned in these accounts. Encountering other beings, usually religious figures, and observing supernatural environs, usually interpreted as the paradisical "pure land," are consistent throughout the three narratives. In a later work, Becker (1984) provided a secondary analysis of the works of Saeko Ogasawara (1963) and Whalen Lai (1996). Ogasawara documented about 20 accounts of deathbed visions, and Lai documented up to 100. Becker argued that the analysis of deathbed visions reveals features of the NDE that are strikingly parallel, an observation made earlier by the parapsychologists Karlis Osis and Erlendur Haraldsson (1977). Once again, though, there is no report of a tunnel sensation. However, emerging from a "dark tubular calyx is reported" (Becker 1984, 64). There was no report of an OBE, but one person reported a life review of "sinful deeds" (Becker 1984, 64). Once again, supernatural environs and beings of light were witnessed.

Physicians Zhi-ying and Jian-xun conducted a study of Chinese NDEs (1992). They interviewed 81 survivors of the Tangshan earthquake of 1976 and found that 32 of them reported NDEs. They found that most of the Western NDE phenomenology was present in their sample, including OBE, the tunnel sensation, a sensation of peace, life reviews, meeting deceased beings, and sighting of an unearthly realm of existence. Unfortunately, they did not include descriptive cases that can be analyzed for content; thus, observations about their data cannot be scrutinized further.

Finally, an early survey some colleagues and I conducted in China (Kellehear, Heaven, and Gao 1990) indicates that the Chinese experience and understanding of the NDE may not be different from that of the Anglo-European. Similar to Zhi-ying and Jian-xun, we presented a typical Anglo-European vignette of an

NDE to a sample of 197 Chinese in Beijing. Twenty-six of these respondents claimed to have had an experience similar to the one described in that survey. Overall, it seems that from the historical and survey evidence available, the Chinese NDE may be very similar to the Anglo-European NDE.

India

The first major report of NDEs from India came from the work of Osis and Haraldsson (1977), who interviewed 704 Indian medical personnel about their experiences with the dying. In this sample, 64 participants reported having witnessed NDEs, whereas the remaining reports concerned near-death visions. More recently and directly, Satwant Pasricha and Stevenson (1986) reported 16 cases of NDE from India. In the majority of cases (10), the authors directly interviewed the NDEr, whereas in most of the other cases they interviewed a "firsthand informant." In later studies, Pasricha (1992, 1993) uncovered another 29 cases of Indian NDE.

In a total of 45 cases, then, Pasricha (1992, 1993) and Pasricha with Stevenson (1986) found no evidence of a tunnel sensation. They reported one case of an OBE. Their participants regularly reported a life review, but this experience took the form of others reading the record of the NDEr's life rather than the form of a panoramic review that Anglo-Europeans commonly mention. According to the authors, the belief that a person's record will, in death, be read is a traditional Hindu belief that most people of India either hold or know. Finally, these NDE reports included observing religious figures and deceased beings in a supernatural world with features that resembled the traditional view of the "other realm."

The Indian NDE accounts that Pasricha and Stevenson (1986) collected do not seem to exhibit tunnel and OBE features. However, in interviews with Indian health personnel, Osis and Haraldsson (1977) found several reports of OBEs in Indian patients near death. Susan Blackmore (1993) claimed to have found cases of tunnel sensation in Indian NDEs in her survey of eight respondents. On closer inspection, however, all three of those who supposedly reported tunnel sensation actually reported a sensation of darkness. One respondent agreed that her experience of darkness was "tunnel-like" only after accepting this leading suggestion from Blackmore (Kellehear et al. 1994).

Life review and observing a transcendent world in Indian NDEs have parallels with Anglo-European accounts. However, deceased acquaintances aside for the moment, the figures observed in this world are those suggested by traditional Indian or Chinese mythology. Nevertheless, as Pasricha and Stevenson (1986) warned, social variations in another realm, if it exists, should be expected just as they exist in our own world. The appearance of familiar cultural images may be psychological, but it may also be sociological. In other words, either a projection may account for the visions, or the visions may actually be observations of another "reality" that resembles the world of its "expatriate" inhabitants.

Thailand

While living in Thailand, Todd Murphy (2001) obtained 10 published accounts of NDEs. Similar to accounts from China and India, the Thai NDEs appear to be heavily influenced or stylized by Buddhist beliefs and ideas.

Murphy's (2001) material included one report of an OBE. Although an OBE can serve as evidence of the NDEr's death, Murphy argued that the appearance of Yamatoots—guides sent on behalf of Yama, the Lord of the Underworld—more often served this function. No NDEr reported a tunnel or tunnel-like sensation, although a report of an otherworld journey contained reference to a tunnel. In this context, Murphy observed that "tunnels are rare, if not absent, in Thai NDEs" (170).

Clearly, Thai NDErs report encountering supernatural beings, first the Yamatoots and sometimes the great Yama himself. Although Murphy (2001) stressed that no Thai NDEr reported meeting with a "being of light," nevertheless Yama and Yamatoots perform nearly all the same or similar roles to "beings of light" for Westerners: guiding, supporting, or facilitating or accompanying a life review.

Life review is also present in these Thai accounts, but the culture-specific variation to note here is that the review is not panaromic; that is, it is not usually a review covering one's entire life or even a major slice of that life. Rather, the review examines one particular incident in one's life, and the discussion is couched in terms of merit (boon) or sinful action (baap). Such terms relate to an overall view of karma that is for many Thais somewhat simplified into the principle, "Do good; receive good. Do bad; receive bad" (Murphy 2001, 168).

Tibet

Lee Bailey (2001) reported 16 NDEs drawn from accounts of Tibetan *Delogs*. For at least two reasons, these are ambiguous accounts. First, it is not entirely clear that these are NDE accounts as such accounts are understood in Western clinical terms; that is, these NDEs are not genuinely mystical experiences emerging from critical illness or near-fatal accident. Some of Bailey's participants, for example, reported "dyings" regularly on fasting days such as the 10th, 15th, and 30th of each month (143). Second, local observers of these experiencers and their NDEs seem to view them and their experiences as epileptic. People may encounter the otherworld through their epileptic seizures, or an encounter with the otherworld is evidenced by such seizures. Either way, these are not the usual ways that people knowledgeable about NDEs would ordinarily view them.

Notwithstanding these reservations, not all of Bailey's (2001) accounts display these background features. Some of the NDE accounts do seem to conform to a major period of illness, do not occur predictably, or do not seem to be associated with epilepsy. For the sake of completeness and to avoid the risk of overlooking a potentially important cultural source of NDEs, these accounts are included here. Bailey drew from 16 NDE accounts derived from 12 written accounts from the Tibetan Library of Works and Archives in Dharamsala, India, and 4 interview-based accounts from the anthropologist Françoise Pommaret (1989).

In all these accounts, no experiencer mentions tunnel sensation, but some report OBEs, meeting supernatural beings, and experiencing a form of life review. These accounts are strikingly similar to those already discussed from China, India, and Thailand. Perhaps these similarities can be attributed largely to the influence of Buddhist beliefs and ideas on the supernatural beings and environments encountered.

Pacific Area NDEs

Guam

School psychologist J. Timothy Green (1984) reported four cases of NDE among the Chammorro of Guam. Green conducted two interviews directly and collected the other two cases from a local man who was interested in the subject of NDEs.

Like the NDEs gathered in India and China, the Chammorro cases include visits to a paradisical place of gardenlike appearance. Here the NDEr is met by deceased beings, some of which are relatives. Unlike the Indian and Chinese cases, however, Chammorro cases included OBEs; the respondents recounted flying "through the clouds" (Green 1984, 6) and making invisible visits to living relatives in America. The accounts included no mention of any sort of life review or tunnel experience. Indeed, the transition from the ill and unconscious state to the OBE appearance was unexplained. Respondents suddenly found themselves flying through the sky or walking on a road. The emphasis of the narrative was on the social experiences while unconscious, that is, of meeting deceased relatives or experiencing a flying visit to living ones.

Hawaii

I reported one case (Kellehear 2001) of a Hawaiian NDE identified from an old published source from Thomas Thrum's *Hawaiian Folk Tales* (1907). One of these stories is a report of Kalima, a woman who "died" in Kona, Hawaii. She had been ill for weeks before appearing to die and revived only when she was placed alongside her soon-to-be grave for her funeral rites.

Kalima reported an OBE at the commencement of her remarkable account. But instead of then turning toward a light or tunnel, she simply reported that she turned and began walking out of her house and then her own village. She eventually came across another village with many people—in fact, thousands. Her next surprise was that everyone she met that she once knew was actually a person who had previously died.

Kalima continued her walk, now apparently understanding that she was *compelled* to walk and was apparently heading unerringly toward Pele's Pit—a traditional volcano site for the jumping off of souls of the dead. However, before she was able to reach that point, she encountered a small group of people who informed her that it was not her time yet and that she must return to her people in life. Reluctant to do this, the crowds in this otherworld drove her back to life.

Once again, this account included no reference to either a tunnel or a life review. However, if Kalima had leaped into the volcano, perhaps she would have described that experience as tunnel-like. Even so, the journey through darkness came at a sequential location in the NDE that was different from most Western accounts—at the beginning—and this difference suggests that *if* a tunnel were described, it would be, as it was in one Thai account, part of the otherworld geography and not a feature of the journey there.

Western New Britain

Dorothy Counts (1983) reported three cases of NDE among the Kaliai as part of her 1981 anthropological fieldwork. Once again, these experiencers reported visiting other realms and meeting deceased relations and friends. The afterlife environment, as in previously described accounts, had a strong physical and social resemblance to the NDEr's usual world. So far, these two features of the NDE—encountering other worlds and deceased beings—are steady, recurring features of NDEs. As shall be seen in other non-Western cases, this trend will continue.

Two points about these particular Melanesian cases are particularly noteworthy. The first is the single report of a life review; the second is the absence of an OBE or tunnel experience. However, the picture is somewhat more complex than these first impressions may suggest. Although one person reported a life review, this respondent stated that he also witnessed a review of someone else's life: a sorcerer. The NDEr narrated this review as a visit to a place where sorcerers are placed "on trial." Each person stands on a series of magnetic "manhole covers." If these hold the person fast, so that others must assist him in freeing himself, then he is called to account. If his explanation is unsatisfactory or unforthcoming, a series of punishing events occurs, ending with burning by fire. This is an unusual account, for as Counts noted, "there was no pre-contact notion of judgment of the dead for their sins" (Counts 1983, 129).

However, Counts noted that the Western New Britain area had been "missionized" by Catholicism since 1949. Many of the Kaliai were at least nominally Catholic, although traditional and Christian ideas often existed side by side. These conditions may account for the life review in this case. This is not the first case of mixed cultural imagery in an NDE. Pasricha and Stevenson (1986) reported the experience of an American follower of Sai Baba, an Indian holy man, who almost died in a hotel. His NDE featured the Indian life review of having his life record read by others.

Although no Kaliai NDE contained a report of an OBE, Counts (1983, 123) reported one case that may be a vivid dream, hypnagogic imagery, or an OBE. Its nature is difficult to discern in that account because the experiencer neither observed a dead or sleeping body nor identified a new astral-type body. An ability to see unusual sights and travel vast distances is connected with characteristics of the spirit world. The question of OBE among the Kaliai, then, must be left open. There is a possibility that interpretations of similar experiences by Westerners may favor an OBE explanation, whereas those of the Kaliai may not.

Finally, in no case did an experiencer report a tunnel experience. All informants reported the early part of their NDE as walking on a road. However, in one case the NDE began in darkness, which gave way to a walk in a field of flowers. Only after this part of the experience did the walk continue onto a road (Counts 1983, 119).

Maori New Zealand

In an autobiographical exploration of New Zealand white culture and its encounter with the native Maori culture, Michael King (1985) recounted a Maori NDE. Nga was a Maori woman who encountered her first white person when she was "a girl just over school age" (92). A favorite story of Nga's was apparently one about the occasion when she believed she had died.

> I became seriously ill for the only time in my life. I became so ill that my spirit actually passed out of my body. My family believed I was dead because my breathing stopped. They took me to the marae, laid out my body and began to call people for the tangi. Meanwhile, in my spirit, I had hovered over my head then left the room and traveled northwards, towards the Tail of the Fish. I passed over the Waikato River, across the Manukau, over Ngati Whatua, Ngapuhi, Te Rarawe and Te Aupouri until at last I came to Te Rerenga Wairua, the leaping off place of spirits. (King 1985, 93–94)

At this sacred place she performed the ablutions expected of the departed. Ascending to a ledge, she gazed down at the entrance to the underworld. After performing a dance, she prepared to descend into the subterranean passage leading to the realm of the spirits. At this point, she was stopped by a voice that informed her that her time had not come and that she must return until called again. She then returned to her body and awoke to see her anxious living relatives.

In this Maori account, the NDEr made no mention of a tunnel; instead, Nga flew to the land of the dead after her OBE—specifically, "I had hovered over my head then left the room." However, the story of Nga included traveling to the entrance of a subterranean underworld, and this, had she entered it, may have constituted a tunnel experience. This subterranean passage is a common feature of some Pacific cultures (Panoff 1968) and may mean, for the purpose of this review, that a tunnel experience cannot be excluded. If the experience had lasted longer, perhaps Nga would have descended to that underworld place through the traditional dark passage. So the absence of a tunnel sensation must be seen as a conditional matter that may relate idiosyncratically to this single account. Nevertheless, another characteristic, such as the life review, is unequivocally missing in this account.

Hunter-Gatherer NDEs

Native North and South America

C. E. Schorer (1985) reported two cases of NDE from Native North Americans, and more recently Jenny Wade (2003) described 11 cases. Schorer found his accounts in H. R. Schoolcraft's 19th-century work *Travels in the Central Portion of the Mississippi Valley* (1825). In these accounts, NDErs reported OBEs and encountering other realms and deceased beings. The other realm, as in all previously discussed cases, was similar to the NDEr's former world. Absent from these two accounts were any reference to a tunnel experience or a life review. Drawing from an assortment of early ethnographic and historical documents, Wade provided both a critical analysis of the earlier Shorer accounts and a nuanced and more reliable account of another 11 NDEs from six different Indian cultures in North America. She, too, observed the absence of descriptions of tunnel-like experience and life review. The emphasis in these stories appears to have been on walking journeys and the encountering of trials and tests, as well as meeting deceased friends and relatives in a supernatural environment.

Similar to the accounts from Guam and Western New Britain, Native American NDErs emphasized their journeys. The narrative was a series of tales about what happened to them after they discovered that they were dead. This pattern was repeated in the only account to appear from South America. Juan Gómez-Jeria reported a single NDE account from the Mapuche people in Chile. In this account, an old man named Fermin was considered by his family and friends to be dead for two days. When he finally woke, he reported having visited another realm.

He said that all his dead acquaintances, his own parents, his children, his wife, and other children that he did not know were all in there. There was also a German gentleman reading and writing in big books. When the German saw him, he asked Fermin what he wanted.

"'I am following my son,' said the old man.

'What is his name?' asked the German gentleman.

'Francisco Leufihue.'

He called the guard and ordered him to inform Francisco."

After passing through a series of noisy gates, Fermin was reunited with his son, who told him that it was not his father's time. "'When the time comes, I myself shall go to the side of the house to look for you. Then you will come. Now, go away'" (Gómez-Jeria 1993, 220–21).

The absence of tunnel sensation or life review is, again, noteworthy. The NDE reported here contains a visit to other worlds and the meeting of deceased beings. Gómez-Jeria (1993) asserted that the presence of the German gentleman is an indication that culture "contributes in part to shaping the content of mental experience" (Gómez-Jeria 1993, 221). This manifestation may be true for certain structural elements such as, for example, *the presence or absence* of review phenomena, but caution should be exercised *in explaining every small detail of NDEs in cultural terms if cultural analysis is to avoid falling prey to reductionist tendencies*. Clearly, NDErs meet an assortment of social beings, and their previous experiences shape their *interpretation* of the identity, function, and meaning of these beings. Only in the presence of strong evidence that these NDE accounts are purely subjective, like dreams, would it be justified to link even small details of the NDE content to culture and biography. At this time, such evidence does not exist.

Aboriginal Australia

An isolated account of an NDE among Australian Aborigines has appeared in several ethnographies during this century. It is, by all accounts, an unusual story in aboriginal terms because it is not a mythical account that can be interpreted as part of the Aboriginal "dreamtime." (For an excellent description of the Aboriginal afterlife, commonly interpreted as part of the Aboriginal dreamtime, see William Ramsay Smith's example [1970, 173–82]). However, the most interesting feature of the anomalous story provided here, of which there are several versions, is that it is a historically real account of a human being who visited the land of the dead.

Lloyd Warner (1937) retold a version of the account as "Barnumbi—and the Island of the Dead" in A Black Civilisation. More recently, Ronald Berndt and Catherine Berndt have reported the same story told to them as "Yawalngura dies twice." According to the Berndts, "The story is now quite old and part of a long oral tradition" (Berndt and Berndt 1989, 376).

The account is a long one, so only the main elements are summarized here. Yawalngura was out gathering turtle eggs with his two wives. He ate some of the eggs, after which he lay down and "died." Later, his wives returned from their own search and found him dead. They returned his body to the main camp and, with others, built a mortuary platform for him. After this, Yawalngura revived and told others that he had become curious about the land of the dead. He decided to build a canoe so that he could travel there to visit. This he did and set off on a journey lasting for several days and nights. Finally, he arrived at an island where he met traditional spirits, such as the Turtle Man Spirit, and deceased beings who recognized that he was alive and had to return. These spirits then danced for Yawalngura and gave him gifts, such as a Morning Star emblem and yams for his return journey.

> Yawalngura took those things which were given to him. All the spirit people danced at that special spring (well), and they told Yawalngura that he had to return: "You have to return, you're not dead properly; you've still got bones. You can come back to us when you die properly." (Berndt and Berndt 1989, 381)

Yawalngura returned and told others of his fantastic epic journey. "Two or three days afterwards," however, Yawalngura died again, "only this time he did so properly" (Berndt and Berndt 1989, 381).

In this account, the NDEr visited deceased beings and a land of the dead. Again, both the people and the place had traditional mythical qualities. However, accounts of his experience included no tunnel experience and no life review. Although the OBE is regarded as common in Aboriginal Australia, especially during sleep and dreaming, this NDE account included no mention of an OBE. These features appear also in the final accounts presented here, those from Africa.

Africa

In their work *Transformed by the Light*, Melvin Morse and Paul Perry (1993) related 15 accounts of NDEs. These accounts came from informal correspondence from a medical colleague in Zambia. Although Morse and Perry described these accounts as emerging from "deepest Africa" (Morse and Perry 1993, 120–26), their cases were not entirely unambiguous in a cultural sense. In other words, some of the cases may have been influenced by Western and local cultures. Nevertheless, they are included in this census because they appear to be basically consistent with other NDE accounts from the hunter-gatherer societies mentioned earlier.

Morse and Perry described accounts from a truck driver, dentist, clerk, and charcoal burner, but they drew other accounts from unknown occupational groups such as a "grandmother," "widow," and child. Each of these accounts emerged from NDEs from illness or accident. The NDErs described walking journeys; some experiences of darkness; meeting deceased people, some of these in white robes; and supernatural beings—in one case, Jesus. One NDEr described being caught inside the hollow shell of a gourd from which she tried to extricate herself, eventually successfully.

Morse and Perry (1993, 124) argued that these NDEs have all the basic features of Western NDEs, even tunnels. However, a close scrutiny of their text and cases presented in the book reveals neither evidence nor words that describe tunnels. The authors appeared simply to assume that the darkness experienced in two NDEs qualify as "tunnel" sensation. Furthermore, although Morse and Perry argued that life review is a basic feature of NDEs, that feature was not presented in any of their 15 cases from Africa. OBEs also were absent from the cases they presented.

Summary of Non-Western NDE Features

A summary of the preceding review of non-Western NDEs features appears in Table 7.1. It shows features that seem cross-cultural, those that appear to be culture-specific, and those in which the question of universality remains ambiguous.

In every case discussed, NDErs encountered deceased or supernatural beings. They often met these beings in another realm, variously described as the "land of the dead," the "island of the dead," the "pure land," and so on. Consistently, the other realm was a social world not dissimilar to the one from which the NDEr came or, in the case of many Asian accounts, not dissimilar from the one the percipient would have expected in the "underworld." The major difference is that the supernatural world is either often much more pleasant socially and physically or is much less appealing. Clearly, the consistency of these reports from highly diverse cultures suggests that at least these two features of the NDE are, indeed, cross-cultural.

The evidence is less clear regarding the feature of the OBE. Members of some cultures, such as the New Zealand Maori, Native American, and Chommorro, clearly experience some kind of OBE with their NDEs. However, the African accounts did not include this feature. Finally, the sole Australian Aboriginal account did not include an OBE, despite the fact that OBEs are known in this culture. In fact, OBEs are known in the vast majority of cultures (Sheils 1978), but these phenomena may not necessarily occur, or occur consistently, in NDEs in these cultures. The apparent randomness of the finding concerning OBEs makes conclusions about them in relation to the NDE ambiguous. On the basis of the present data, it seems unclear whether OBEs are cross-cultural or culture-specific features of NDEs.

However, clear patterns emerge when the life reviews and tunnel experiences are examined in the different non-Western cases. Life review was a definite feature of the Chinese and Indian NDE accounts. In at least one Chinese account one's "sinful deeds" were observed, and in several Indian accounts one's life record was read from a book. This reading of incidents or the moral weighing of incidents from one's life was also a feature of Thai and Tibetan accounts. A life review was also noted in connection with a Melanesian account, but this finding was equivocal. The life review described in the Melanesian account contrasts sharply with traditional—that is, pre-Western-contact—notions of death and judgment. This particular feature and case may be better explained as a function of Western influence. Because many of the Kaliai people are under Catholic influence, this factor may have altered either the experience or the narrative. This possibility gains some support from the observation that judgment is not part of the precontact Melanesian beliefs about death.

Life review was absent in all accounts from Guam, Native America, Aboriginal Australia, Africa, and Maori New Zealand. In other words, except for one ambiguous case in Melanesia, all published accounts from hunter-gatherer, primitive cultivator, and herder cultures do not exhibit the feature of life review. Accounts from India, China, Thailand, and Tibet, however, definitely do exhibit this feature.

Finally, the tunnel experience does not seem to be a feature of most non-Western NDE accounts. The published cases from Native America, Guam, and India give no indication of a tunnel experience or sensation. There is, however, some suggestion that a tunnel experience may occur to those NDErs if their experiences are prolonged. This suggestion attaches conditions to any conclusion about this finding in the New Zealand case, as already noted, because the Maori—and possibly the Hawaiian NDEr—traveled through a subterranean entrance to the land of the dead. Had she traveled to that place, she might have experienced a dark tunnel-like experience, and this feature would have occurred after her OBE—as it does in some Western accounts.

In the Australian Aboriginal account, much detail may have been lost in its development into an oral tradition. For example, the visit to the land of the dead occurred after the percipient revived rather than during the time he was unconscious and "dead." It is difficult to speculate about what message or meaning is intended in this interesting turn to the story. Perhaps, having been dead, that person inherited special privileges or powers as a result of the experience that enabled him to travel while "alive" to the land of the dead. Perhaps the account has simply been altered in its oral transmission through the normal passage of time and embellishment. In any case, the trip to the land of the dead reportedly included a journey of successive "nights," which indicates the importance in the account of light and darkness. This theme is also important in other aspects of the account, particularly when a struggle takes place over a "star."

In the Western New Britain accounts, most of the NDErs described how they suddenly appeared on a road. In one account the individual emerged from darkness into a field of flowers but did not describe the darkness as a tunnel. And in China, there exists at least one report of emerging from a similar darkness described as a dark void or "dark, tubular calyx." This throatlike part of a flower complements the lotus imagery of much Pure Land Buddhist narrative. In any case, Zhi-ying and Jian-xun (1992) reported several accounts of tunnel sensation in their study of Chinese NDEs. There are also ambiguous reports of darkness and emerging from a dark gourd in African NDE accounts. These experiences may be interpreted as "tunnel-like" as, indeed, these authors seem to describe them.

Overall, then, the present review has revealed that the major cross-cultural features of the NDE continue to include encounter with other beings and other realms on the brink of death. Life review and the tunnel experience seem to be culture-specific features. Life review seems to be a feature of Western and Asian NDE accounts. Cases published so far from hunter-gatherer, primitive cultivator, and herder societies have not exhibited this feature. The tunnel experience has not been described in most non-Western accounts, though an experience of darkness of sorts has often been reported. The present review has revealed no major pattern in reports about the OBE in non-Western NDE accounts; therefore, this finding must be viewed as inconclusive.

DISCUSSION

The universality of NDEs and visions, in which individuals purport to see new worlds and beings beyond death's door, is not a particularly new or interesting finding. In relation to this recurring feature of death or NDEs, there has been a long tradition of medical social science literature, as well as similar concerns in the humanities and in religious thought generally. The conclusion is either that such visions represent observations of another empirical reality or that they are simply hallucinations. Suffice to say that the universality of such human experiences has created, and will continue to generate, fierce, complex debate. Culture-specific findings are somewhat more modest in their demand for explanation, and let us now turn our attention to these.

Tunnels in NDEs

Blackmore and Tom Troscianko (1989) asked two questions about the tunnel feature so often reported in Western NDEs. First, why is the tunnel so often a regular feature of the NDE? Second, why do other symbols not appear, for example, gates or doors? In the review presented in this chapter, I have not found tunnel experiences in any of the non-Western case material. However, there were several mentions of darkness described as a void, a calyx, or simply darkness. This finding suggests that tunnel experiences are not cross-cultural but that a period of darkness may be. This darkness is then subject to culture-specific interpretations: a tunnel for Westerners, subterranean caverns for Melanesians, and so on. Near-death experiencers who do not report darkness may not view this aspect of the experience as an important part of their account or narrative.

Because an account of an event is a social exchange based on mutual expectations about what is or is not important information, recall may sometimes be selective and shaped to the perceived requirements of the listener. This phenomenon may be an important methodological point for a review such as this because the sample of cases is too small to enable assessment of whether darkness is important or unimportant in all regional accounts. On the other hand, unless appropriate images can be selected that may convey traditional meanings about darkness, no image at all may be chosen to explain the experience. The first question that Blackmore and Troscianko (1989) asked must now be reformulated as follows: Why is the frequently reported sensation of traveling through darkness by Western NDErs so often described as a tunnel experience? In other words, why do many Western NDErs choose the term "tunnel" to denote their experience of darkness?

The term "tunnel" has two major meanings in the English-speaking world, and both of them are relevant to the NDE (*Oxford English Dictionary* 1989). In a literal vein, tunnels are shafts or structures similar to the inside of a chimney. They may resemble subterranean passages or they may denote tubes, pipes, or simply deep openings that channel partway into other structures. Kevin Drab (1981) argued that tunnels have specific properties that make them enclosed spaces whose length is greater than their diameter. This definition emphasizes the technical but in doing so omits the metaphorical, representational, and symbolic. This omission would not be important except that, in social communication terms, such dimensions must be viewed as equally influential in a person's choice of words. This point is even more significant when one considers that the NDE is often described as ineffable, that is, beyond words. Excluding the symbolic meaning involves excluding the figurative meaning, and the figurative meaning may be the most critical.

As a figurative term, "tunnel" may also denote a period of prolonged suffering or difficulty, as embodied in such expressions as "light at the end of the tunnel." Tunnels are often viewed as experiences of darkness that lead to other experiences. This representational view is well grounded in common experiences of the Western workaday world. It may begin in childhood as, for example, with such stories as Lewis Carrroll's *Alice in Wonderland* (1965), in which Alice falls down a dark rabbit hole that signals the start of a journey into a wondrous and confusing adventure. Or it may begin with accounts of Santa Claus, who is expected to appear at the bottom of the family's chimney every December. From a child's kaleidoscope to the adult's experiences of gazing through telescopes, microscopes, and binoculars, Western people have grown accustomed to seeing strange new worlds through the dimness of tunnels. Through dark tunnels, and in the light that appears at the end of them, people leave the ordinary momentarily to experience the strange and unfamiliar.

Furthermore, tunnels are common images for the idea of transition, of traversing from one side to another. Drab (1981) objected to this notion of transition, arguing that often the tunnel in NDEs does not lead anywhere. However, this point ignores the social fact that people may believe or *expect* the tunnel to lead them somewhere. Social experiences can rarely be understood in terms of concrete events separated from their interpretations, and these interpretive processes are constructed from attitudes, beliefs, expectations, and assumptions. If NDErs are moving along in a shaft or space of darkness, some may choose a term that commonly denotes that experience. The tunnel is a symbol that in Western industrial societies is readily associated with that kind of experience. This observation relates back to Blackmore and Troscianko's (1989) second question: Why a tunnel and not other symbols such as a gate, door, or bridge?

However, gates, doors, bridges, and many other symbols do appear as images in the NDE, as Blackmore and Troscianko (1989) readily admitted, but frequently they appear alongside or after experiences of the tunnel. They rarely seem to substitute for tunnels, and this should be no mystery. The most obvious reason why gates or doors seldom substitute for tunnels is that NDErs are attempting to describe some kind of movement through darkness. It is the tunnel, therefore, rather than gates or doors, that best captures this experience. This experience of movement is a further problem with a technical definition of tunnels that relies on shape as its primary characteristic. Shape reflects architecture rather than experience, but it is the experience that NDErs are describing. Because the experience is difficult to communicate, the descriptions will always be rich in interpretations that lean more toward metaphor than toward measurement.

Life Review in NDEs

The life review is the second feature of the Western NDE that seems to be limited in other cultures. Indian and Chinese NDEs seem to exhibit features of the life review, but NDEs in Australia, Africa, the Pacific, and Native North America do not. This difference might be explained by the scarcity of cases from these areas. A larger sample from these areas might turn up NDEs with life reviews. There is, however, much in the medical and anthropological literature to suggest that such will not be the case.

Robert Butler argued that life review is always something of an identity search. He used the mirror as an example of an identity search metaphor that recurs in Western literature. In the Narcissus myth, the story of Snow White, stories from the *Arabian Nights,* and also in the preoccupation of adolescents and the aged, the mirror reveals the face, the life, and the person. The mirror and the life review "serves the self and its continuity, it entertains us; it shames us; it pains us. Memory can tell us our origins; it can be explanatory and it can deceive" (Butler 1963, 75).

This sense of self as interior, as inwardly responsible, driven, and reflective from within, is a social construction of identity recently born in the development of what Robert Bellah (1976) called *historic religions.* In historic religions, such as Buddhism, Christianity, Islam, and Hinduism, two worlds exist: the material and the divine. The self and the material world are devalued. Human nature is flawed and in need of rehabilitation and redemption, and the material world is mere illusion. The responsibility for rehabilitation lies in the action of the self. In "primitive" (see a useful discussion of this term in Douglas 1966) and archaic religions such as those of Native Americans, Australian Aborigines, and many Pacific cultures, the distinction between self and the world is less explicit. "Mind" as a store for social experience is not paramount, for experience is also drawn from the animistic world of animals, vegetation, rocks, landforms, and climate. The mythological and actual worlds are not sharply separate but heavily overlapping. Individuals are no more responsible than the world. Anxiety, guilt, and responsibility are in-the-world properties or characteristics, not located purely within the private orbit of an individual's makeup.

Géza Róheim (1932) observed that the psychology of the Australian Aborigines, for example, was based on much less internalizing of social sanctions. They have a very good opinion of themselves, are easygoing, and fear the social consequences of transgression much more than private guilt, remorse, or anxiety. Laws are obeyed because transgressors fear being caught.

Róheim (1932, 120) discussed what happened when Christian missionaries began their proselytizing practices among the Aranda Aborigines. These early missionaries observed that the Arunda were all basically "sinful" and "wicked" and needed forgiveness before God. In response to this rather novel view, the Arunda retorted with understandable indignation. "Arunda inkaraka mara," they declared; the Arunda are *all* good people. These were hardly a people who would seek a life review in evaluative terms or be impressed by a biographical review of their individual deeds.

So, although Indian and Chinese cultures may appear quite different from Anglo-European ones, in terms of social custom and language they are broadly similar in terms of religious development. Historic religions, whether Hindu or Christian, emphasize the cultivation and development of the moral self vis-à-vis the divine world and its demands. Historic religions actively appeal to the notion of individual conscience. And conscience places great importance on past thought and action in the process of self-evaluation. As Max Weber has asserted, when belief in spirits is transformed into belief in god, "transgression against the will of god is an ethical sin which burdens the conscience, quite apart from its direct results" (Weber 1965, 43).

Because these religions link death with conscience, and conscience with identity after death, it is little wonder that some kind of life review takes place in near-death circumstances among people from these cultures. In a different worldview altogether, members of Aboriginal and Pacific cultures may not review their past personal lives in search of sense of identity. As mentioned earlier, the store of social experience is contained not within the self but, rather, in the animistic and communal life of the physical and social world. Once again in this census, I repeat: There is probably little private use or function for a life review in individuals from this type of society.

LIMITATIONS OF THIS CENSUS

Several limitations in the preceding review render any conclusions drawn from this discussion tentative and subject to further investigation. All the cases were collected by different researchers, using different methods, sensitive to different aspects of the NDE, and in highly different societies. Whereas Becker (1984), for example, noted the issue of life changes following an NDE, this focus played no part in the investigations of Pasricha and Stevenson (1986) and many others.

Language translation is also a problem. Not all words or phrases have an English equivalent. Indeed, not all social experiences are translatable, particularly outside their contexts. Even Western NDErs struggle to find words in their own language to describe their experiences. A further complication is the lack of a widely agreed-upon definition of the NDE, an issue explored further in the next section.

The features of the NDEs presented in this chapter are drawn from descriptive conventions of writers primarily from psychology and medicine. For some of these writers, features such as time distortion or subsequent life changes are an important characteristic of the NDE; for others, they are not. Furthermore, as argued in the following section, social circumstances play an influential role in the appearance or absence of certain features of the NDE. Thus, the social experiences of the NDEr are crucial in understanding psychological states underlying the NDE.

The current census of cross-cultural case material, however, strengthens the association between the social and psychophysical factors and suggests even broader links. For example, because tunnel symbolism, life review, the meeting of supernatural beings, and time distortion may occur separately or together in a variety of non-illness contexts, there is a critical need for cross-cultural research linking and comparing these contexts to clinical presentations of the NDE. These data will help investigators to arbitrate systematically and empirically on the difficult issue of whether similar social and psychological processes have similar or separate physiological etiologies.

Such comparisons will also invite discussions about whether the clinical phenomenology of NDE is merely part—a subset of experiences, as it were—of the general social and psychological features of crisis and transition in ordinary human affairs. The review in this chapter has identified cultural differences in the clinical presentation of NDEs particularly in regard to the tunnel sensation and life review. But one certainly cannot claim that tunnel symbolism and life review do not exist in other contexts for each of the cultures discussed. The question of the cultural factors that promote these processes in the psychological life of the individual in one circumstance, such as dreams, but not in another, such as near death, is still open.

The limitations noted must not be thought to subtract from the current analysis or conclusion. On the contrary, they underscore the main purpose of the review itself. The review of cross-cultural clinical NDE material demonstrates that physiological theories of the NDE that do not incorporate a cultural theory of their context are methodologically weaker for that omission.

BROADER CRITICAL CONSIDERATIONS

Visions of another world beyond death have a long history and appear in most cultures. This census and earlier ones indicate that these visions seem to be cross-cultural phenomena, part of the store of human possibilities that are not dependent on local influences of culture and socialization. Other features associated with these visions in Western accounts have had a deep and dominating impact on the way psychological processes in human beings at the brink of death have been understood. Authors of the clinical literature on tunnel and life review experiences have assumed a universality that seemed to point to some biological quality, character in the psychological construction of the self, or feature of some alternate reality. But, as argued here, it seems that tunnel and life review experiences may be features of a certain type of human development in culture and psyche.

In Western reports of a tunnel experience near death, this development materializes in the common shapes and symbols mentally associated with modernity and technology. If this conclusion has any validity, NDE darkness should be described as tunnel-like *mostly* in such modern, industrialized countries as the United States and Great Britain. This description should be used *far less often* in Asia or the Pacific regions and should be *rarely employed* in hunter-gatherer societies. My current observations do seem to support this cultural explanation. In the case of life review, religions such as Hinduism, Buddhism, and Christianity have cultivated an ethic of personal responsibility and conscience; therefore, this feature of identity seems to appear more in the NDEs of cultures under these religious influences.

However, the whole framework of this current census rests on tracking and documenting a handful of characteristics of NDEs that are largely chosen because the features are ones most analyzed and debated in the literature. Tunnel sensation, life review, encountering supernatural beings, or OBEs occupy the lion's share of argument and theorizing in near-death studies. But it is well known that those are not the only characteristics of the NDE.

As early as 1975, Raymond Moody identified 15 "experiences" of dying. Other characteristics listed, but receiving far less attention from theorists, are experiences of ineffability, feelings of peace and quiet, auditory sensations such as ringing inside one's head, and encountering borders or points of no return. The widely publicized changes in NDErs' lives—both the depth and character of these changes—have also received little or no cross-cultural assessment.

German researchers Hubert Knoblauch, Ina Schmied, and Bernt Schnettler (2001) reported yet other features among their sample of 82 NDErs. These features include "horrible feelings," full mental awareness and clarity, meeting nonhumans, and meeting living humans. Some of these features, such as meeting nonhumans, have been reported by child NDErs, whereas horrible feelings are known to be associated with distressing NDEs (see Chapter 4, this volume)—another divergent form of NDE that has received little cross-cultural assessment. Janet Schwaninger, Paul Eisenberg, Kenneth Schechtman, and Alan Weiss (2002) reported yet other features: lack of fear, time distortion or absence, and painlessness. Once again, few of these features have undergone cross-cultural identification and assessment. Such diversity of possible NDE features underscores a further problem with any attempt to chart the prevalence and nature of NDEs across different cultures. So-called basic features of the NDE may not be basic, after all.

These features may not actually be basic enough to single out the NDE from dozens of similar, perhaps identical altered states of consciousness. On the one hand, if one ties the NDE to medical circumstances of resuscitation, then one can have a significant amount of academic amusement theorizing its similarity to other post-truama, post-resuscitative, or post-unconsciousness psychological sequela—as does the recent work of Geena Athappilly, Greyson, and Stevenson (2006). Unfortunately, neither the psychological, medical, nor social features of the NDE, however they are characterized, are confined to these circumstances. The NDE, broadly or narrowly defined, has long left the hospital and has been officially sighted almost everywhere.

On the other hand, there is an abundance of reports of all the so-called basic psychological experiences of tunnel/darkness, life reviews, encounters with supernatural beings, OBEs, sensations of peace, ineffability, clarity of thought, and radically altered social values post-NDE. These experiences have been reported by trapped coal miners, castaways at sea, and shamanic initiates; in the lives of saints, monks, and other holy people; and also by ordinary people experiencing severe depression or bereavement. Some of these features are associated with deathbed visions, visions of the bereaved, EMDR (Eye Movement Desensitization and Reprocessing) experiences, meditation, and drug-induced experiences. In other words, some of or all these experiences occur to people in conscious and unconscious states, in situations of illness and health, with or without drugs, near-death or in the prime of life, among the religious and secularized, and among those threatened by death and those not.

None of this information is particularly a problem unless one narrows the framework into which one wishes to pour our data. In other words, if the point of theorizing is to reduce the experience to a medical or supernatural phenomenon associated with death—in order to provide evidence of a new organic syndrome associated with death or to push open a new window to the possibility of an afterlife—then a narrow framework for this task is essential. Both purposes tie the data to death itself. But this is a flawed approach.

The old word coined for such experiences—the unsolicited review of our lives, the experiences of darkness and light, meeting supernatural beings, ineffable experiences and emotions, sensations of deep peace or deeply disturbing visions—was "mysticism." Now a vastly unpopular and underrated word, it is currently unpopular because of its unashamed association with religion, religious studies, and the sociologically uncomfortable idea that the world itself—rather than solely the afterlife—is enchanted.

For those who want to chase a so-called scientific reply to the skeptics, humanists, atheists, and their materialist friends among the positivist, empiricist, academic establishment, this word will undoubtedly disappoint. For this epistemological game, played by empiricist rules and values, one needs to keep the NDE close to a hospital, where all the prospective studies desired can be performed. One will also have to employ models of proof that will disqualify the conclusions to which one aspires simply because among other things, these models were not originally designed to evaluate nonempirical phenomena. That won't be a problem if the assumption is made that beings of light are citizens of another world just beyond the last set of traffic lights before hitting the northern border of New Jersey. For those with a less nominalist, literalist, and physicalist sense of the problem that theorists are up against, there are more fruitful directions to explore.

Mystical experiences are unusual psychological, perhaps supernatural experiences that occur to people under special types of social, that is, interpersonal, circumstances. People may be at an important existential crossroad in their lives as a result of a bereavement, illness, job loss, or initiation-time of their child or adult development. Or they may instead be experiencing major social isolation, self-imposed or as an exile through accident or political or religious force. That loose set of suggested social factors (social settings) may induce a psychological attitude or orientation (mindset) that can permit human beings to see, hear, or otherwise feel experiences that are strange, alien, and foreign but may also be frightening or uplifting.

True, some of these experiences can be drug induced, but it is important not to be naïve about pharmacology here, either. The pharmacological properties of drugs alone—heroin, cannabis, or even simple analgesics—are highly mediated by the mindset of the drug-taker; that mindset, in its turn, is mediated by the interpersonal surroundings—the social setting (see Zinberg 1984). So even when drugs influence bodily processes in the service of creating delusions, hallucinations, simple feelings of pain relief, or euphoria, influences such as social setting and attitude play major, perhaps crucial roles in their production. An adrenalin rush can produce fright, aggression, or happy thrills depending on whether it occurs during a high school exam, a roller-coaster ride while on holiday, or in combat in Afghanistan. Neither the physiology nor the social situation alone explains what is happening to the individual without a scrutiny of both dimensions.

At best, a census such as the one presented here can show the importance and value of combining the forces of the biological and social sciences in pursuing sound explanations for experiences near death. At worse, such journeys distract both investigators and humanity at large from acknowledging that NDEs are neither bound nor defined by their proximity to death but, rather, are connected to a wider class of experiences. Indeed, *all* the features of NDEs, basic and not so basic, suggest an urgent need to update our understanding of human perception and social experience to include the extraordinary in everyday life. To follow this path means letting go of narrow surveys of cultural difference, such as the one presented here, and to look among our daily lives and their settings to see how simple social choices and accidents in those lives open humans to the unexpected—moment to moment, day after day, even to the very end of our lives.

8

World Religions and Near-Death Experiences

Farnaz Masumian

A close examination of the scriptures of many Eastern and Western religious traditions reveals striking parallels between religious and near-death experience (NDE) accounts of afterlife, including both the dying process and the nature of ongoing existence following death (Masumian 2002). This chapter presents brief summaries of the afterlife teachings of Hinduism and Buddhism from the Eastern traditions and Zoroastrianism, Judaism, Christianity, Islam, and the Bahá'í Faith from the Western tradition. Furthermore, this chapter examines the extent to which those teachings accommodate the various features of typical NDEs and the extent to which each religion's values align with NDE aftereffects. (For a thorough discussion of NDE aftereffects, see Fenwick, Noyes, Holden, and Christian, this volume.) The findings could promote greater mutual understanding and further collaboration among religionists and scientists.

HINDUISM AND NDEs

At the center of the eschatological beliefs of most Hindus are the twin doctrines of *karma*, that a person reaps what one sows, and *samsara*, the transmigration or rebirth of an individual's soul. According to these intertwined doctrines, each person is reborn countless times and lives through different types of existences. The quality of one's current life is a reflection of one's past and present karma. Therefore, if a person enjoys a comfortable life, this outcome is the reward for good deeds performed in past and present lives.

The author wishes to thank her husband, Bijan Masumian, for his contributions to this work.

On the contrary, when one experiences misery, one can only blame oneself for evil deeds one is committing in the current life or has committed in previous lives. Thus, each person is held completely responsible for the quality of his or her current life, and pointing the finger of blame at external forces such as demons, deity, or fate is not acceptable (Nigosian 1994). The ultimate goal in the life of a Hindu is breaking the cycle of rebirth and attaining *moksha*—liberation from transmigration.

Rig-Veda and NDEs

In the *Rig-Veda*, the most ancient and sacred of Hindu scriptures, accounts of afterlife reveal several commonalities with NDE episodes. Following are a few examples.

Realm of Light The *Rig-Veda* indicates that the deceased will enter a place of light;

> ...Place me in that deathless, undecaying world
> Wherein the light of heaven is set.
>
> (Griffith 1926, 381)

Many people who have experienced a deep NDE reported entering a realm of light (Bryson 1997; Greyson, 2000).

Listening to Singing and Flutes In the *Rig-Veda*, righteous souls are depicted as enjoying a happy life in a world of perpetual light. "The sound of singing and the flute is also among the delights available" (Keith 1971, 407). Some near-death experiencers (NDErs) have reported a similar experience: "There were no sounds of any earthly thing. Onlye the sounds of serenity, of a strange music like I had never heard. A soothing symphony of indescribable beauty blended with the light I was approaching" (Ring 1984, 54).

Seeing the Forefathers and Yama According to the *Rig-Veda*, the dwellers of heaven will be reunited with their forefathers. They will also meet Yama, the King and Judge of all the dead:

> Go forth, go forth upon the ancient pathways whereon our sires of old have gone before us ... Meet Yama, meet the Fathers [dead ancestors]. (Griffith 1926, 399)

During the course of an NDE, many subjects similarly have described encounters with religious figures and their deceased relatives (Greyson 2000; Moody 1975).

In 1986, Satwant Pasricha and Ian Stevenson (1986) conducted a survey, which included 16 cases of NDE in India. Eleven were male and five were female. The main features of their NDEs included "messengers" and mistaken identities.

Yamdoots ("messengers")   The typical Indian NDEr was taken by hand by "messengers" called Yamdoots in Hindu mythology (Pasricha and Stevenson 1986). Many American NDErs have described a somewhat similar experience when they reported encountering angels—a term that literally means "messengers." Individuals who have had NDEs reported or implied that the function of these angels was to guide, inform, and protect the NDEr (Greyson 2000).

Cases of Mistaken Identity   A clear difference between Indian and American NDEs is cases of mistaken identity found in the former (Pasricha and Stevenson 1986). For instance, many Hindu NDE accounts contained experiences of someone who lived in a different but nearby village or a person of the same name but a different caste who, instead of the NDE subject, should have died and been brought to the "next world." Such cases of mistaken identity frequently lead to the eventual revival of many Indian NDErs.

In contrast, many Western NDErs reported they *chose* to return to physical existence because of their love for their living family members. Others report they were "sent back" by departed persons who told them their "time has not yet come" (Pasricha and Stevenson 1986).

Life Review   Both American and Hindu NDE accounts included life reviews. Yet, unlike Western accounts in which the NDEr typically have seen a panoramic life review, Indian subjects have reported a life review during which others read a record of the NDEr's life to the NDEr. The reading of one's life record is part of the Hindu traditional belief system (Kellehear 1993).

Meeting the Deceased   Some Hindu NDErs have reported meeting friends and relatives in the "other world." However, unlike most Western NDE cases, deceased individuals in Hindu NDEs have had nothing to say or do about the prematurity of the NDEr's death or a need for the NDEr to return to earthly life (Pasricha and Stevenson 1986).

Meeting Religious Figures   Some Western NDE subjects have reported seeing angels and religious figures or feeling the presence of God (Ellwood 2000). Likewise, Indian subjects have, at times, described meeting religious figures such as *Yamraj*, another term for Yama (Kellehear 1993) or *Sakkthi*, a Sanskrit term for "Holy Power" (Pandarakalam 1990). These reports appear to support the view that cultural factors contribute to NDE accounts (see also Chapter 7, this volume).

The Hindu Belief System and NDE Aftereffects

Certain parallels exist between the Hindu belief system and the character transformations most NDErs undergo as a result of their NDEs. The most important of these are respect for life, selfless service, and nonviolence.

Respect for life is an ancient Hindu belief that is deeply rooted in the Atman-Brahman doctrine taught in the Upanishads—Hindu scriptures that are commentaries on the Vedas. The Upanishads include the concept that all beings, including human souls (atman) are, in reality, manifestations of Divinity (Brahman). Based on this doctrine, a true Hindu treats all beings with respect. A traditional Hindu greeting, *nemaste*, means "the God within me greets the God within you" (Canda and Furman 1999, 135).

Another fundamental belief in Hinduism that has its parallel in many NDErs is selfless service called *Karma Yoga* (Canda and Furman 1999). The idea of selfless service comes from the *Bhagavad-Gita* (Songs of the Blessed Lord), which is by far the most popular Hindu sacred text.

Hindu beliefs also include *ahimsa*: non-violence (Crim 1981). Many post-NDE character transformations include the adoption of this belief (Ring 1984). The great Mahatma Gandhi introduced ahimsa to the West, asserting that "nonviolence is the greatest force at the disposal of mankind. It is mightier than the mightiest weapon of destruction devised by the in-genuity of man" (Gandhi 1935).

BUDDHISM AND NDEs

Buddhism began in India in the sixth century BCE. From India, it spread to almost all of Asia and is now gaining followers in the West. The founder of Buddhism is Siddhartha Gautama Buddha. After a long quest to find the roots of human suffering, Buddha achieved "enlightenment" and presented a formula for releasing humankind from the cycle of suffering. The essence of Buddha's solution was captured in his "Four Noble Truths" and his "Noble Eightfold Path" (Fisher 2002):

1. Suffering is universal.
2. The cause of suffering is human desire or craving.
3. Suffering will cease when desire ceases.
4. To cease desire or achieve detachment, humankind needs to follow Buddha's Noble Eightfold Path:
   a. Right View,
   b. Right Resolve,
   c. Right Speech,

d. Right Action,
e. Right Livelihood,
f. Right Effort,
g. Right Mindfulness,
h. Right Concentration.

Afterlife in Buddhism

Buddha was a practical teacher who did not show much interest in eschatological, cosmological, or metaphysical questions. He believed that grasping the true nature of these issues was beyond the comprehension of finite human minds. When asked metaphysical or speculative questions, Buddha usually maintained what is often termed "noble silence" (Molloy 2005, 126). Nonetheless, later Buddhists broke Buddha's silence on metaphysical and speculative questions and engaged in discussions of afterlife and its nature. A well-known example is the classic *Tibetan Book of the Dead.*

Like Hinduism, contemporary Buddhism includes the twin doctrines of transmigration and karma. However, Hindu and Buddhist interpretations of the transmigration doctrine differ in major ways. For instance, Buddhists appear to reject the Hindu concept of atman—the human soul, an immortal substance reborn in subsequent lives. According to Buddhism, a person is comprised of five distinct elements: a physical body, feelings, senses, volition, and consciousness. The union of these five elements, called *skandhas*, forms the human personality. Once this union is dissolved, no major entity is left (Hopkins 1971).

Nevertheless, many passages attributed to Buddha acknowledge the survival and immortality of an element within one's personality, often termed as the mind, consciousness, self, or soul:

> The mind takes possession of everything not only on earth, but also in heaven, and immortality is its securest treasure-trove. (Carus 1915, 169)

> The doctrine of the conquest of Self, O Simha, is not taught to destroy the souls of men, but to preserve them ... He who harbors in his heart love of truth will live and not die, for he has drunk the water of immortality. (Carus 1915, 149)

David Noss and John Noss quoted another Buddhist text, *Dighna Nikaya, IV,* in which Buddha defined consciousness—*vijnana*—as that entity which is "invisible, boundless, all-penetrating, and the ground for Rupa (former body), Vedana (sensation), Samjna (perception), and Samskara (will)" (Noss and Noss 1994, 164). Here, the Buddhist element of mind or consciousness seems to replace the Hindu concept of atman as the only immortal substance in humans.

Buddhism includes belief in the existence of a system of retribution in the universe: that every human being will receive rewards or punishments for actions both on earth and in temporary dwellings between rebirths. Among these temporary abodes are numerous heavens and hells that are described graphically in various Buddhist holy texts. The karma of most beings necessitates their rebirth in one of these heavens or hells. Buddhist heavens may be seen as different paradises, whereas the hells might correspond to purgatory in Catholicism. To a Buddhist, the ultimate goal in life is to escape the cycle of rebirths in these heavens and hells by following the Buddha's Noble Eightfold Path to achieve *Nirvana*—the state of total peace, contentment, and detachment (Hopfe and Woodward 2005).

The Tibetan Book of the Dead (Bardo Thodol) *and NDEs*

One of the major Tibetan texts on afterlife is *Bardo Thodol*, "The Great Liberation by Hearing while in the Intermediate State," commonly known as the *Tibetan Book of the Dead*. The founder of Tibetan Buddhism, Padma Sambhava, who lived in the eighth century CE, probably authored this text. In addition to being a major source of Buddhist eschatology, the *Tibetan Book of the Dead* has also garnered great attention in the field of near-death studies, as it provides strong evidence that the many intriguing elements of NDEs were already well-known to ancient Tibetans. However, this work does not include description of the conventional heaven and hell described in other religious scriptures. It is, for the most part, an account of the different experiences the human soul supposedly undergoes in the *bardo,* or the intermediate state between reincarnations (Becker 1985). Essentially, the *Tibetan Book of the Dead* serves as a manual to guide the dead through their dying process so that they can attain Nirvana or, failing to do so, at least to achieve circumstances for a better rebirth (Becker 1985).

The *Tibetan Book of the Dead* identifies three intermediate states or bardos for the soul following physical death:

In the first state, bardo of the moment of death, the soul will have visions of a being of clear light in a beautiful landscape. Upon encountering this light, the soul is advised to abandon all attachments to its former personality and identify itself with the light. If it fails to do so, the soul will then go to the second intermediate state.

In the second state, bardo of the experiencing of reality, it will find itself in the presence of seven divine beings (Buddhas). If it cannot identify with any of these divine beings, the soul will then face seven terrifying deities and is urged to acknowledge these grotesque beings as projections of its own subconscious and watch them without fear.

In the third state, bardo of rebirth, the soul can move about the earth instantaneously and without any effort. It sees its old home and its family mourning, and it attempts, in vain, to convince them it is still alive. But at the end, it realizes that it is dead to other humans. Next, in the presence of Yama, the judge of the dead, the soul's good and evil actions are weighed, "and it feels itself hacked and racked by demons" (Becker 1985, 13).

Many parallels exist between accounts of NDE and those of the *Tibetan Book of the Dead*. Following are two examples.

Out-of-body Experiences (OBEs)   Many NDErs have reported that during their NDEs they could look down on their bodies and see the sadness of their families, the activities of the medical staff, and the environment around these people. These phenomena coincide with descriptions in the *Tibetan Book of the Dead* in which the author says that when the person's "consciousness principle gets outside its body," the person can see and hear friends and relatives who are gathered around the corpse mourning, but he or she cannot communicate with them (Badham 1997).

Being of Light   Many contemporary NDErs have reported seeing a "Being of Light." This being is often described as an extremely bright, loving presence. Some NDErs identify this being as their own higher self. The *Tibetan Book of the Dead* refers to this entity as the "Clear Light" or the *Buddha Amida* (Becker 1985). According to Tibetan Buddhism, by recognizing oneself as this Clear Light, one will attain Nirvana—freedom from transmigration.

Pure Land Holy Scriptures and NDE

In addition to the *Tibetan Book of the Dead,* the scriptures of Pure Land Buddhism contain striking similarities with modern NDE accounts. Following are two examples.

Being of Light   Many NDErs have spoken of an encounter with a Being of Light who welcomed them into the life beyond and had immense compassion and understanding for them. The description and the role of this figure do not correspond with traditional expectations in some religions such as Hinduism. However, it seems to correspond fully with Pure Land vision of Buddha Amida, or "the Buddha of Infinite Light," who has made a vow to appear to the dying at the moment of death. Pure Land Buddhists believe that Amida appears to the dying and leads them into his "Pure Land" paradise (Badham 1997).

The Realm Beyond   Some NDErs have given a description of a realm beyond that is similar to Amida's Pure Land. They described this realm as a place of lakes, pavilions, and wonderful gardens with multicolored flowers and jewels. Likewise, Pure Land Buddhists believe that Amida rules a paradise of jewels, gold, and beautiful fountains and flowers where days are spent in constant repetition of *sutras*—holy texts. In this beautiful realm of no craving and no suffering, the saved people sit on lotuses in the middle of a clear lake (Becker 1981).

The Buddhist Belief System and NDE Aftereffects

Buddhist beliefs and values are similar in some ways to the types of changes most NDErs go through after their NDEs. The most important of these changes are feelings of detachment from worldly matters, compassion toward others—*karuna*—and commitment to nonviolence—*ahimsa*.

One of Buddha's Four Noble Truths is that attachment is the cause of sorrow (Fisher 2002). He taught that it is the human desire or craving for transient things that brings about pain and suffering. Thus, suffering can be eliminated through detachment, which is one of the main values consistently quoted as important to most NDErs (Ring 1984).

Compassion and empathy for others is another fundamental value in Buddhism, which corresponds to most NDErs' beliefs (Canda and Furman 1999; Ring and Valarino 1998). In Mahayana Buddhism, the supreme ideals are the *bodhisattvas*—enlightened ones—who are the embodiments of *karuna*—compassion. The bodhisattvas are beings who have attained enlightenment but have postponed entering Nirvana until all other beings are enlightened. By not entering Nirvana, the bodhisattvas can be reborn on earth to help others. In Korean Buddhism, Kuan Yin is the Bodhisattva of Compassion. In art, this bodhisattva is depicted with many faces, hands, and eyes, symbolizing the ability to perceive the suffering of all beings in all situations and to respond to them. Many Zen Buddhists take a vow of great compassion that entails a commitment to serve all beings.

Yet another important value in Buddhism that characterizes many NDErs is belief in ahimsa. Buddhism is known as a very tolerant and peaceful religion. The significance of peacefulness is much emphasized in many of Buddha's sermons. For example, Buddha acknowledged: "Many do not know we are here in this world to live in harmony. Those who know this do not fight against each other" (*Dhammapada* 1:6). Nancy, an NDEr described in *Heading toward Omega,* heard the same injunction from the Being of Light: "You must all learn to live in peace and harmony with one another on earth" (Ring 1984, 266).

ZOROASTRIANISM AND NDEs

The Persian prophet Zarathushtra, whose name means "Golden Shining Star," founded Zoroastrianism around 1000–600 BCE (Bausani 2000). Among the Greeks, Zarathushtra was known as Zoroaster. His religion appears to be the oldest major belief system to contain an explicit personal and general eschatology (Masumian 2002).

Afterlife in Zoroastrianism

Zoroaster's Gathas (Hymns) are the oldest existing religious document that has references to numerous afterlife concepts found in later religions. Among them are judgment at death, a balance in which the deeds of all deceased are weighed, a bridge over hell that narrows for the wicked and widens for the righteous as they take a mandatory walk over it to heaven, and a vision of God in heaven for the righteous (Noss and Noss 1994).

Many years after Zoroaster's death, such other Zoroastrian sacred texts as the Later Avestan Texts and Pahlavi literature gradually transformed Zoroaster's concise afterlife doctrines into a full-blown eschatology (Ichaporia 2008). These texts present detailed and graphical images of heaven and hell and contain references to other *eschaton*—end of time—events such as a final battle between God, *Ahura Mazda*, and Satan, *Ahriman;* the advent of a Promised Messiah, *Saoshyant;* subsequent universal purification of humankind; and the establishment of the Kingdom of God on earth.

Several commonalities exist between afterlife accounts found in later Zoroastrian texts and certain NDE episodes, as evident in the following examples.

Being of Light   A majority of individuals with NDEs have recollected the presence of a kind, loving being whom they referred to as the "Being of Light" (Zaleski 1987). According the Zoroastrian scriptures, righteous souls will enter heaven, and there they will have a vision of God who is depicted as pure light (Haug and West 1971).

Life Review   Many NDErs speak of a panoramic life review that includes both "righteous" and "unrighteous" actions (Vincent 1994). However, in the Zoroastrian book called the *Book of Arda Viraf,* only wicked souls are said to go through life reviews. These reviews are very frightening because they contain only sins and crimes committed during the person's earthly life (Peterson 1996). According to this source, the purpose of the horrible experiences awaiting the wicked might simply be to attempt to persuade the ungodly to change their ways (Masumian 2002).

Meeting Others   Many NDErs have described encountering deceased relatives in their NDEs (Greyson 2000; Vincent 1994). This idea finds support in the following passage from a ninth-century-CE Zoroastrian source called *Datastan-i-Denik,* in which the author claims the newly arrived soul is greeted by friends who tell of all the delights awaiting the deceased in heaven: "And the righteous in heaven, who have been his intimate friends, of the same religion and like goodness, speak to him of the display of affection, the courteous inquiry, and the suitable eminence from coming to heaven, and his everlasting well-being in heaven" (Peterson 1996, 31: 9).

The Zoroastrian Belief System and NDE Aftereffects

The essence of Zoroaster's teachings is often summed up as "Good Words, Good Deeds, Good Thoughts." This maxim finds parallels in the positive aftereffects of many NDErs whose experiences permanently transform their lives for the better. Countless narratives document such transformations that often lead individuals to a reexamination of their values and a conscious decision to live a moral life of selfless dedication to others.

JUDAISM AND NDEs

Judaism began approximately 4,000 years ago among a nomadic, and later agricultural, people known as the ancient Hebrews (Beversluis 2000). Among the historical figures who shaped this religion were such Hebrew patriarchs as Abraham, Isaac, Jacob, and Moses, as well as such other Jewish prophets as Isaiah, Jeremiah, and Daniel. Judaism is a monotheistic religion that teaches belief in one "mighty and good" Creator whose arena of activity is the earthly world. The main holy scripture of the Jews is the Hebrew Bible comprised of three sections: the Law (the Torah), the Prophets, and the Writings (Wilson 1995). In addition to the Bible, some Jews believe in the Talmud (Oral Torah), a collection of Jewish oral traditions.

Afterlife in Judaism

Afterlife teachings of the Torah are significantly different from those of other world religions. Whereas the Torah does contain references to an afterlife and to paradise, heaven, and hell, these terms do not carry their traditional meanings in the Torah. Also, unlike many religious texts, the Torah does not contain any mention of an immortal soul that conquers death; nor does it give any clear indication of exactly what remains of a person at death. Left instead of a soul is a mysterious, unexplained entity that "goes down" to a dark and gloomy place called *Sheol*—the Pit.

Sheol is a subterranean hollow in the lowest depths of the earth. It is the eternal dwelling of the dead, whether righteous or unrighteous (Psalms 63:9, 86:13; Ezekiel 26:20, 31:14). Life in Sheol is marked by inactivity and stagnation. According to the Torah, the inhabitants of Sheol are in a state of permanent sleep.

The Hebrew Bible and NDEs

Nevertheless, the Torah and NDE accounts share the following common elements.

Tunnel experience. Although not identical, the tunnel experience of many NDErs is somewhat similar to the Torah's description of the afterlife journey of the dead to the lowest depths of the earth to reach Sheol:

But those who seek to destroy my life
Shall go down into the depths of the earth. (Hebrew Bible, Psalms 63:9)

Being of Light. In the Torah, the notion of God as Light occurs several times:

The Lord is my light and my salvation; whom shall I fear? (Hebrew Bible, Psalms 27:1)

The Lord will be your everlasting light.
(Hebrew Bible, Isaiah: 60:20)

Importance of Love   Many NDErs emphasize the significance of love in their NDEs.

This idea finds numerous parallels in the Torah:

I love those who love me, and those who seek me diligently find me. (Hebrew Bible, Proverbs 8:17)

Hatred stirs up strife, but love covers all offenses. (Hebrew Bible, Proverbs 10:12)

Rabbinic Literature and NDEs

In addition to the Torah, Judaism's sacred literature contains a significant body of commentaries composed through the ages by Jewish rabbis. These works are known as rabbinic literature. The best known among them is the Talmud, a record of rabbinic discussions concerning Jewish law, ethics, history, and customs (Hopfe and Woodward 2005).

Although finding parallels between NDE accounts and the Torah is somewhat of a challenge, such commonalities are abundant in rabbinic literature:

Auditory Sensations, Pleasant or Unpleasant   Some NDErs report hearing roaring and banging during their experience (Moody 1975). The Talmud supports this claim: "The noise of the soul departing from the body reverberates throughout the entire world" (Shapiro 1979, 91).

The Tunnel Experience   The NDE tunnel experience (Ring 1984) has its parallel in a Talmudic teaching that claims the bodies of the Jews buried in the Diaspora—the dispersion of the Jews in countries outside Israel from the sixth century BCE to the present time—will, at the time of resurrection, go through caves or tunnels on their way to Israel, where the resurrection takes place (Shapiro 1979, 91).

Meeting Others   Among Talmudic passages that seem to confirm NDE claims of "meeting others" during their experience (Parnia 2006) is the following: "I will explain the Mishnah in accordance with the opinion of R Oshaya, so that when I die, R Oshaya will come forward to meet me" (Shapiro 1979, 92).

Being of Light   The NDE encounter with a Being of Light (Morse and Perry 1994) has its parallel in some of the rabbinic literature: "While man cannot see the glory of God during his lifetime, he can see it at the time of death" (Shapiro 1979, 93).

The Jewish Belief System and NDE Aftereffects

Positive character change is a recurring theme in many NDE accounts. Following their experiences, NDErs often find new significance in spiritual values. The Torah echoes this increased attention to spirituality and right-eousness: "He who pursues righteousness and kindness, will find life and honor" (Hebrew Bible, Proverbs 21:21).

Among other parallels between Jewish values and positive NDE aftereffects are belief in God, an appreciation for earthly life, the sanctity of human nature, and the importance of justice, love, and forgiveness.

Belief in the sanctity of human nature is a deeply rooted biblical teaching that can be traced back to the biblical claim that humans were created in God's image. As such, they are the only species on earth that can engage in deep reflection and contemplation on divine qualities. During the course of their experiences, many NDErs claim they become conscious of the "spark of the Divine" within their inner selves. This self-awareness results in an internal transformation that enables the person to manifest justice, love, and forgiveness toward all (Ring 1984).

Judaism has a strong focus on the concept of a just God who expects humanity to practice justice. The commandment to live a life of justice is echoed in the words of many Jewish prophets, including Amos: "But let justice roll down like waters, and righteousness like an ever-flowing stream" (Hebrew Bible, Amos 5:24).

The value of love is reflected in the biblical passage "Thou shalt love thy neighbor as thyself" (Hebrew Bible, Leviticus 19:18), whereas the quality of forgiveness is represented through the annual celebration of the Jewish New Year, Yom Kippur. On this day, Jews go through a process of asking for forgiveness first from God and then from any friends, relatives, or acquaintances whom they have harmed or insulted over the past year.

Jewish holy texts and NDE accounts include references to belief in the existence of a God. As one NDEr put it, "As I look back at [my NDE], it seems to me that the reason for this happening was for God to come into my life because I wouldn't let Him come in any other way" (Ring 1984, 144).

CHRISTIANITY AND NDEs

Christianity has its roots in Judaism. It is a religion based on the life, teachings, death, and resurrection of Jesus Christ, who was born over 2,000 years ago in Roman-occupied Palestine. Christians believe in the uniqueness of Jesus and that he provided for the redemption of humankind through his death. In general, Christians also believe in baptism as an initiation into Christianity and in a communion meal called the Eucharist (Hopfe and Woodward 2005).

The Christian Bible includes the Old and the New Testaments. The Old Testament (Hebrew Bible) was the holy book of Jesus and his followers. The New Testament contains the Gospels of Matthew, Mark, Luke, and John; the epistles by Paul, Peter, James, John, and others; the Acts of the Apostles; and the Book of Revelation (Wilson 1995).

Afterlife in Christianity

Christianity teaches that human beings have two realities: body and soul. Christians believe that upon the death of the body, the soul of the individual will be rewarded or punished permanently for the way the individual has lived on earth. Heaven is depicted in Christian art as the abode of light, joy, songs, dance, and angels that awaits the righteous, whereas hell is depicted as a place of smoke, fire, and suffering, a place of retribution for the wicked. In addition to heaven and hell, there is in Christian belief a temporary intermediate state of existence in a place known as purgatory. Like Zoroastrians before them, Christians also believe in a general resurrection and final judgment at the end of time (Molloy 2005).

The New Testament and NDEs

Several NDE traits find support in the New Testament (*Holy Bible* 1952):

OBE A main characteristic of an NDE is the OBE, when the individual experiences rising above his or her body and sees it below. This idea finds parallel in an experience of St. Paul in the New Testament:

> I know of a man in Christ who fourteen years ago was caught up to the third heaven—whether in the body or out of the body I do not know, God knows. And I know that this man was caught up into Paradise—whether in the

body or out of the body I do not know, God knows—and he heard things, that can not be told, which man may not utter. (*Holy Bible* 1952, II Corinthians 12:2–4)

Many scholars believe that in the phrase "man in Christ," Paul was referring to himself. Yet, as Paul could not understand or explain his OBE, he left the nature of his experience ambiguous and stated that God knew what had happened because it was God's doing (Bretherton 2004). Interestingly, Paul's experience of near death included an OBE and visions of heaven, both of which are among the main characteristics of modern-day NDEs (Badham 1997).

Spiritual Body (soul)   According to a survey conducted by Bruce Greyson and Ian Stevenson (1980, 1194), 58 percent of NDErs reported that during their NDEs, they felt themselves to be in a new body. Some of these individuals described this body as a spiritual body, a concept that finds support in the following Pauline passage:

> There are celestial bodies and there are terrestrial bodies; but the glory of the celestial is one, and the terrestrial is another … So it is with the resurrection of the dead … It is sown a physical body, it is raised a spiritual body. If there is a physical body, there is also a spiritual body … I tell you this, brethren; flesh and blood can not inherit the kingdom of God, nor does the perishable inherit the imperishable. (*Holy Bible* 1952, I Corinthians 15:32–50)

Being of Light   Many NDErs report an encounter with a Being of Light who knows everything about them (Moody 1975). For Christians, the supreme reward of righteous souls is the unimpeded, luminous sight of God in heaven, as described in the following biblical passages:

> And [God's] servants shall worship him; they shall see his face, and his name shall be on their foreheads. And night shall be no more; they need no light of lamp or sun, for the Lord God will be their light. (*Holy Bible* 1952, Revelation 22:4–5)

> This then is the message which we have heard of him, and declare unto you, that God is light, and in him is no darkness at all. (*Holy Bible* 1952, 1 John 1:5)

> And the city had no need of the sun, neither of the moon, to shine in it: for the glory of God did lighten it, and the Lamb [Jesus] is the light thereof. (*Holy Bible* 1952, Revelation 21:23)

In other passages, Christ designates himself as the light of this world:

> As long as I am in the world, I am the light of the world. (*Holy Bible* 1952, John 9:5)

Again Jesus spoke to them, saying, "I am the light of the world; he who follows me will not walk in darkness, but will have the light of life." (*Holy Bible* 1952, John 8:12)

Life Review   Life reviews are integral parts of many NDEs (Moody 1975). The Christian parallel for such life reviews is the judgment of the dead at Christ's return, or *Parousia*. Matthew (*Holy Bible* 1952, Matthew 25:31–46) provided a detailed account of the judgment scene. Before passing a verdict of heaven or hell on individuals, Christ engages in a life review with them and recounts examples of good and evil deeds they committed in their earthly lives. The author of the Book of Revelation also confirms a postmortem life review for the deceased:

"And the dead were judged by what was written in the books, by what they had done" (*Holy Bible* 1952, Revelation 20: 12).

Importance of Love   The importance of love is emphasized by many NDErs (Ring 1998). Indeed, the New Testament confirms the significance of love: "This is my commandment, that ye love one another, as I have loved you" (*Holy Bible* 1952, John 15:12).

Spiritual Transformation   Many NDErs describe life-changing transformations that result in a shift of focus from pursuit of material gains to a search for spiritual values such as kindness and service to humanity (Greyson 2000; Ring 1984). Countless passages in the New Testament emphasize the importance of such values. For instance, it is written, "Let no one seek his own good, but the good of his neighbor" (*Holy Bible* 1952, 1 Corinthians 10: 24).

The Christian Belief System and NDE Aftereffects

Many Christians with NDEs often wonder if their experience can be accommodated by their religion. They are particularly puzzled by whether such experiences confirm or deny their belief in Jesus as the Son of God and their Savior. Christian writers have written many books on NDEs. However, except for a minority who have regarded NDEs as genuinely spiritual, most of these authors have tended to regard NDEs as a type of demonic deception (Flynn 1986). This latter view may have stemmed from the words of St. Paul in II Corinthians 11:14 (*Holy Bible* 1952), where he notes that Satan can disguise himself as an "angel of light" (Flynn 1986). Today, many evangelical Christian books on NDEs view Raymond Moody, the author of the first book to popularize knowledge of the NDE (1975), as an emissary of that being of light which is to them Satan in disguise (Zaleski 1987). Yet, such a distorted view of the Being of Light "places too much weight on a single Bible verse" (Vincent 2003, 63).

Such biblical passages as Matthew 7:16 emphasize the importance of the "fruits" of one's actions: "Ye shall know them by their fruits" (*Holy Bible* 1952). Galatians 5:22–23 does likewise: "The fruit of the spirit is love, joy, peace, patience, kindness, goodness, faithfulness, gentleness, and self-control. Against such there is no law." If the Being of Light is to be judged by the standards set by Matthew and Galatians, then its effect on NDErs, as evidenced in numerous researchers' studies of NDE aftereffects (Atwater 1988; Grey 1988; Morse and Perry 1992; Ring 1984; Sutherland 1995) seems to be perfectly biblical. In fact, the Being of Light appears to be the antithesis of Satan, who neither prescribes nor generates goodness in others: "A good tree cannot bear bad fruit, and a bad tree cannot bear good fruit" (*Holy Bible* 1952, Matthew 7:18).

Christian values and the values to which NDErs aspire following their experiences hold much in common. These values include love, compassion, care, and service to others. Indeed, Christ's teachings, his life, and his tragic death on the cross present him as the personification of "unconditional love." His selfless life later became a source of inspiration for countless Christian-based social and medical services. Many Christians with NDE experiences often described "Christ-like" transformations in their characters that enabled them to show great care and compassion for the sick, the poor, and the oppressed. Some NDErs even changed careers to become teachers and social service providers (Greyson 2000; Ring 1984).

Furthermore, many Christian NDErs show a distinct preference for the inner attitudes that Jesus emphasized in his sermons about church doctrines, rituals, and dogmas. This new "religious and spiritual orientation following NDEs" (Ring 1984, 154) can be observed in the following account:

> I was brought up in the Bible Belt and when I was a child I was very religious ... I mean I was taught certain things and I believed them as a child and adhered to them ... just out of rote. But *after* [my NDE], it made me *less* religious formally but probably more religious inwardly ... I don't think I was in church one time since [my NDE], but I think I'm spiritually stronger than I ever was before. (Ring 1984, 154)

ISLAM AND NDEs

The term "Islam" literally means "submission." As a religion, the message of Islam is understood to revolve around "submission to the Will of God." Islam is a monotheistic religion with roots in both Judaism and Christianity.

The teachings of Islam are found in the Muslim holy book Qur'an, meaning "the recitation," as well as in the Sunnah, or "trodden path," both of which are collections of the words and deeds of Muhammad, the prophet of Islam. Muhammad was born in 570 CE in Mecca, located in what is now Saudi Arabia (Beversluis 2000). According to the teachings of Muhammad, all Muslims are bound by five obligations:

1. confession of faith in God (called Allah) and in Muhammad as the prophet of God,
2. daily prayers to be said at five appointed times,
3. fasting during the month of Ramadan,
4. almsgiving, and
5. pilgrimage.

Afterlife in Islam

Muslims believe in the immortality of the human soul. The Qur'an (1993) teaches that at the moment of death, the soul is separated from the body by the angel of death, '*Izra'il* (*Qur'an* 1993, 8:52).

Many Muslims believe in an intermediate, postmortem state of being known as *Barzakh*, meaning literally "the grave" or "the barrier." The Qur'an contains no detailed account of the life of the soul in Barzakh, yet the term does occur in a number of places (see, for examples, *Qur'an* 1993, 25:55, 55:20, 23:102). The Barzakh period is the time the soul spends in the grave between physical death and the general resurrection—the *Ma'ad*—of humanity at the end of time.

On the day of resurrection, all souls in Barzakh will rise from their slumbers and appear before Allah for a universal reckoning. The time of the resurrection is believed to be a secret to all but Allah. However, a number of signs indicate its approach. Among the most universally accepted are (1) the coming of the Anti-Christ, whom Muslims call *Al-Dajjal*, literally "the deceiver"; (2) the return of Christ; and (3) the advent of the Promised One, called *Al-Mahdi*, "The Rightly Guided One" (Glasse 1989; Momen 1985). The Qur'an indicates that immediately preceding the general resurrection will be two trumpet blasts by the archangel *Israfil*, a variation of *Raphael* meaning "God Heals."

According to Islamic *hadith*—literally, "traditions" relating to the deeds and words of Muhammad—on the day of resurrection, God will come down with his angels. Human beings and angels will gather before God (*Qur'an* 1993, 25:24). Each person will carry his or her own "book" of deeds. Muslims believe all one's earthly deeds are recorded in one's personal "book of deeds" by two recording angels known as *Kiraamun Kaatibeen*—"Honorable Recorders." Using their individual book of deeds, God will weigh each person's actions in a special balance—*Mizan*. The tipping of the scales will determine each individual's fate.

Following the judgment, all souls must cross a bridge called *Sirat*—literally, "straight." The bridge becomes wide for the righteous, who can then cross it easily, reaching heaven. But for the wicked souls, the bridge becomes sharp like a razor, so that when the wicked step foot on it, they fall down to hell (Johnson and McGee 1986).

The Qur'an also includes the concept of heaven and hell following the judgment. A main feature of the Muslim paradise is flowing water, which makes this place particularly appealing to desert-dwelling Arabs. Islamic heaven also consists of the most exquisite precious metals and stones. However, both the Qur'an and the more reliable hadith indicate that the greatest happiness awaiting the faithful in heaven is not material but spiritual: it is the joy of seeing Allah. "Upon that day faces shall be radiant, gazing upon their Lord" (Arberry 1955, 75:22).

Like the pleasures of heaven, torments of Islamic hell are also portrayed in both the Qur'an and the hadith. As with most hells, fire is the major element of Muslim hell (*Qur'an* 1993, 4:59).

Qur'an, Hadith, and NDEs

Soul (spiritual body)   A majority of NDErs speak of seeing themselves in a new spiritual body that cannot be described (Moody 1975). The idea of soul or spirit as an ineffable entity separate from the body is supported in the Qur'an: "And they will ask thee of the spirit. Say: The spirit proceedeth at my Lord's command; but of [that] knowledge, only a little is given to you" (*Qur'an* 1993, 17:87).

Life Review   Many NDErs claim a life review in the presence of a Being of Light. The following passages in the Qur'an support the notion of a life review; but unlike typical Western NDE accounts, Muslim life reviews include judgment of deeds: "On that day shall every soul find present before it whatever it hath wrought of good. As to what it hath wrought of evil, it will wish that wide were the space between itself and it!" (*Qur'an* 1993, 3:28).

Being of Light   A particular characteristic of many NDE accounts is an encounter with the Being of Light (Moody 1975). The Qur'an also describes Allah as "Light": "God is the light of the heavens and of the earth" (*Qur'an* 1993, 24:35).

The Muslim Belief System and NDE Aftereffects

The beliefs and values NDErs hold dear (Ring 1984) are similar in some ways to Muslim beliefs and values. Among such similarities are belief in God and valuing humility, honesty, and charity, as evident in the following passages:

> Say, "He is God, the One. God, to Whom the creatures turn for their needs. He begets not, nor was He begotten, and there is none like Him." (*Qur'an* 2001, 112:1–4)

And the servants of [Allah] Most Gracious are those who walk on the earth in humility. (*Qur'an* 2001, 25:63)

Allah will say: This is a day on which the truthful will profit from their truth: theirs are gardens, with rivers flowing beneath,—their eternal Home: Allah well-pleased with them, and they with Allah: That is the great salvation. (*Qur'an* 1993, 5:119)

God enjoins justice, kindness, and charity to one's kindred, and forbids indecency, abomination, and oppression. He admonishes you so that you may take heed. (*Qur'an* 1993, 16:90)

Spiritual Transformation   Many NDErs are spiritually transformed as a result of their NDEs. Instead of being concerned with material things, they begin to care more about spiritual values (Ring 1984). Here are examples from the Qur'an and hadith in support of spiritual values:

[Show] kindness unto parents, and unto near kindred, and orphans, and the needy, and unto the neighbor who is of kin (unto you) and the neighbor who is not of kin, and the fellow-traveler. (*Qur'an* 1993, 4:36)

The best of men are those who are useful to others. (*Hadith of Bukhari*, quoted in Wilson 1995, 688)

Significance of Knowledge   NDEs convince many people of the value of knowledge (Moody 1975). This idea is confirmed in Muslim hadith:

Learn to know thyself. He who knows himself, knows his Lord. (Novak 1994, 321)

Seek knowledge from the cradle to the grave. (Novak 1994, 321)

THE BAHÁ'Í FAITH AND NDEs

The Bahá'í Faith is an independent world religion originated in 1844 in Persia—today's Iran. According to the *Encyclopedia Britannica Yearbook*, this faith is now the second most widespread religion in the world (Beversluis 2000). The prophet-herald of this religion was the Báb (literally "Gate"), who announced the advent of the founder of the Bahá'í Faith, Bahá'u'lláh, or "The Light of God," regarded by the Bahá'ís as the Promised One whose advent has been foretold by all the major religions of the past.

Bahá'u'lláh's writings, revealed over a 40-year period, are comprised of many books and thousands of letters (Tablets) written on various subjects. The ultimate goal of the Bahá'í Faith is the unification of humankind into a single global family. The three basic principles of this religion are oneness of God, oneness of humankind, and fundamental unity of religion. Chief among other Bahá'í teachings are independent investigation of truth, abandoning prejudice and superstition, harmony of religion and science, equality of women and men, universal compulsory education, economic justice, need for a spiritual foundation for society, and the significance of prayer and meditation (Hatcher and Martin 1984).

The Bahá'í Faith regards humans as essentially spiritual beings who are going through a temporary physical experience on earth. The purpose of life is to know, love, and worship God, as well as to reflect divine attributes such as love, kindness, generosity, compassion, and trustworthiness that are innately enshrined within the human soul. A spiritually developed person is one who manifests a sanctified character while still on earth and devotes his or her life to the service of others (Hatcher and Martin 1984).

Afterlife in the Bahá'í Faith

Bahá'í eschatology teaches that shortly before death, one's soul begins to experience a sense of impending judgment. Spiritually developed people will begin to experience indescribable joy, whereas erring souls will be seized with fear and consternation (Bahá'u'lláh 1983). Nevertheless, undeveloped souls are not barred from eventual redemption. They, too, can continue to make progress in the afterlife by a variety of spiritual means, including God's forgiveness or prayers and intercession by others and even by themselves (Esslemont 1980).

To Bahá'ís, rewards and punishments of the afterlife are spiritual in nature. Bahá'u'lláh taught that rewards of the afterlife can best be described as a sense of one's soul drawing closer to God and receiving spiritual bounties and everlasting joy from him, whereas punishments of the next world would be a feeling of remoteness from God and being deprived of his spiritual bounties and blessings ('Abdu'l-Bahá 1981).

According to Bahá'í writings, traditional descriptions of heaven and hell as physical places of material delights or punishments are only symbolic and meant to be allusions to ineffable spiritual realities. To Bahá'ís, heaven and hell are "spiritual conditions" that the human soul will experience after separation from the body. "Heaven is the natural consequence of spiritual progress, [whereas] hell represents the results of failure to progress spiritually" (Hatcher and Martin 1984, 111). Bahá'í teachings do not relegate believers to heaven and nonbelievers to hell. All souls will move on to a common spiritual realm. Ultimately, individuals' spiritual development on earth will determine the nature of their spiritual reality in the afterlife (Bryson 1997).

Bahá'í Scriptures and the NDE

Commonalities between NDE accounts and Bahá'í afterlife teachings are quite extensive.

Ineffability As the following passages illustrate, Bahá'í writings support NDErs' accounts of their inability to describe their NDEs in words (Bryson 2003):

> The nature of the soul after death can never be described, nor is it meet and permissible to reveal its whole character to the eye of men ... The world beyond is as different from this world as this world is different from that of the child while still in the womb of its mother. (Bahá'u'lláh 1983, 156–57)

Heavenly (spiritual) Body The idea of a nonmaterial or spiritual body reported by a majority of NDErs (Moody 1975) is confirmed in the Bahá'í writings:

> It is manifest that beyond this material body, man is endowed with another reality ... This other and inner reality is called the heavenly body. ('Abdu'l-Bahá 1982, 464)

Realm of Light Some deep NDErs claim entrance into a realm of light (Bryson 1997). This idea finds parallels in Bahá'í holy texts: "That divine world is manifestly a world of lights" ('Abdu'l-Bahá 1982, 226).

Meeting Others A recurring theme in many NDE accounts is reunion with deceased relatives, friends, and loved ones (Vincent 1994). Bahá'í writings support this phenomenon as well:

> As to the question whether the souls will recognize each other in the spiritual world: This fact is certain; for the Kingdom is the world of vision where all the concealed realities will become disclosed. How much more the well-known souls will become manifest ... how much more will he recognize or discover persons with whom he hath been associated. (Bahá'u'lláh and 'Abdu'l-Bahá 1976, 367)

Life Review Another frequently reported element of both pleasurable and distressing NDEs is the vivid, instantaneous review of the person's earthly life in the presence of the Being of Light. Kenneth Ring referred to this life review as "the ultimate teaching tool" (Ring and Valarino 1998, 169). The idea of a life review finds support in Bahá'í scripture: "It is clear and evident that all men shall, after their physical death, estimate the worth of their deeds, and realize all that their hands have wrought" (Bahá'u'lláh 1983, 171).

Being of Light Many NDErs recollect an encounter with a loving being of pure light (Moody 1975). In the Bahá'í writings, God is frequently

referred to as "the source of light." In fact, the term "Bahá'í" is connected
to the concept of light. Literally, "Bahá'í" means a follower of "light" or
"glory." Translated into English, the title of the Bahá'í prophet,
Bahá'u'lláh, means "The Light" or "The Glory" of God: "I have turned my
face unto Thee, O my Lord! Illumine it with the light of Thy counte-
nance. Protect it, then, from turning to any one but thee" (Bahá'u'lláh,
the Báb, and 'Abdu'l-Bahá 2002, 5).

The Bahá'í Belief System and NDE Aftereffects

Similarities between the Bahá'í value system and positive NDE character transformations are many. Among similarities are a new appreciation of
knowledge and learning, the importance of love, an absence of fear of
death, the importance of physical life on earth, a belief in the sanctity
of human nature, and an emphasis on manifesting such positive attributes
as love, justice, selfless service, unity, and peace (Greyson 2000; Ring
1984). Bahá'í values also uniquely parallel certain NDE aftereffects,
including belief in the essential unity of all religions.

Like many NDErs, Bahá'ís give great importance to life on the material
plane of existence. Yet, they also view earthly life as the "embryonic preparation" for an eternal spiritual journey ('Abdu'l-Bahá 1982b).

Sanctity of Human Nature   The sanctity of human nature that most
NDErs have emphasized (Ring 1984) is an essential teaching of the Bahá'í
Faith. One example is from the Bahá'í writings in which God addresses
humanity in exalted terms:

> Thou art My lamp and My light is in thee. Get thou from it thy radiance
> and seek none other than Me. For I have created thee rich and have bounti-
> fully shed My favor upon thee. (Bahá'u'lláh 1986, 6)

Bahá'ís also believe that every person on the planet has a role to play in
building a peaceful, prosperous global society:

> The honor and distinction of the individual consist in this, that he among
> all the world's multitudes should become a source of social good ... How
> excellent, how honorable is man, if he arises to fulfill his responsibilities ...
> Supreme happiness is man's, ... if he urges on the steed of high endeavor in
> the arena of civilization and justice. ('Abdu'l-Bahá 1979b, 2–4)

Knowledge   Some NDErs seem to have a heightened appreciation of
learning following their experience (Moody 1975). The importance of
acquiring knowledge has been stressed in many Bahá'í writings: "Regard
man as a mine rich in gems of inestimable value. Education can, alone,

cause it to reveal its treasures, and enable mankind to benefit therefrom" (Bahá'u'lláh 1983, 260).

Importance of Love Following their experiences, many NDErs develop a new appreciation for the value of love (Moody 1975). The significance of love is emphasized in many Bahá'í writings. For example, "In the world of existence there is indeed no greater power than the power of love" ('Abdu'l-Bahá 1979a, 179).

No Fear of Death People who have had pleasurable NDEs show no fear of death (Bryson 1997). This idea finds support in the Bahá'í teaching, as this passage shows:

> Sorrow not if, in these days and on this earthly plane, things contrary to your wishes have been ordained and manifested by God, for days of blissful joy, of heavenly delight, are assuredly in store for you. Worlds, holy and spiritually glorious, will be unveiled to your eyes. You are destined by Him, in this world and hereafter, to partake of their benefits, to share in their joys, and to obtain a portion of their sustaining grace. To each and every one of them you will, no doubt, attain. (Bahá'u'lláh 1983, 329)

Essential Unity of All Religions In his book *Heading toward Omega*, Kenneth Ring considered "a belief in the essential underlying unity of all religions" as one of the main elements of the new "religious and spiritual orientation" of many NDErs (Ring 1984, 146). As one NDEr said, "I've had the freedom to investigate many religions, and the only thing that I've been able to really understand is that every religion—that pure religion itself—is the same thing. There's no difference" (Ring 1984, 163). Belief in the oneness of all religions is also one of the fundamental teachings of Bahá'ís: "Religions are many, but the reality of religion is one ... The branches are many, but the tree is one" ('Abdu'l-Bahá 1982b, 126).

Deemphasizing Sectarianism, Dogma, and Doctrinal Disputes NDEs often lead individuals to move away from the confines of narrow, sectarian, and dogmatic religion and, instead, to focus on the perceived true purpose of religion, which is spiritual growth and fulfillment. As one NDEr described her newfound *spiritual orientation*, "[My NDE] made me less religious formally but probably more religious inwardly" (Ring 1984, 154). The following Bahá'í passages confirm this idea:

> All these divisions we see on all sides, all these disputes and oppositions, are caused because men cling to ritual and outward observance, and forget the simple, underlying truth. It is the outward practices of religion that are so different, and it is they that cause disputes and enmity—while the reality is

always the same, and one. The Reality is the Truth, and truth has no division. ('Abdu'l-Bahá 1979a, 120–21)

We should, therefore, detach ourselves from the external forms and practices of religion. We must realize that these forms and practices, however beautiful, are but garments clothing the warm heart of the living limbs of Divine truth. We must abandon the prejudices of tradition if we would succeed in finding the truth at the core of all religions. ('Abdu'l-Bahá 1979a, 136)

CONCLUSION

Near-death experiences are probably as ancient as humans. They cut across the boundaries of time, geography, culture, and religious belief. This chapter has identified parallels between the common features of NDE episodes and the afterlife teachings and the values of seven world religions. Among the many features of typical NDEs that find support in the eschatology of major religions are the OBE, the tunnel experience, life reviews, a blissful existence in a "realm of light" inhabited by the dead, a Being of Light, and association of the NDEr with the deceased in that realm.

Much of what the founders of major religious traditions have long been claiming in the sacred literature of the world is now largely corroborated by countless NDE findings. These parallels demonstrate that the afterlife teachings of various religions are significantly accommodating to the NDEs described by individuals across the world. Some professionals in the scientific community, including medical doctors, who until recently tended to summarily dismiss religious and NDE claims of continuation of life after physical death as wishful thinking, are now showing growing interest in the field of near-death studies.

Historically, prophets' afterlife teachings and exemplary lives have given their followers hope, inspiration, and a blueprint for spiritual living. Scientific investigation of NDEs is now beginning to offer tangible evidence for postmortem survival of some as yet unknown entity in humans. Particularly intriguing are cases involving small children, the blind, and those in coma who were declared brain-dead by their neurologists and neurosurgeons but eventually regained consciousness and gave accurate accounts of what went on during their NDEs (see Chapter 9, this volume). Implications of such research are immense not only for the billions of people all over the world who consider themselves religious or spiritual but also for those in applied sciences and professional services who need to provide counseling to the dying, the suicidal, and their grieving families (Pandarakalam 1990) and hope to the terminally ill (Axelroad 1978).

Testimonies of many NDErs about the transformative nature of their NDEs and the importance of love and living a life of service confirm the age-old teachings of great religious traditions of the world and provide hope to countless billions of people. In the words of one NDEr, "Not everyone can have or needs to have an NDE, but everyone can learn to assimilate these lessons of the NDE into his own life if he chooses to" (Ring 1984, 268).

Today, scriptural evidence of an afterlife can be coupled with positive transformation stories from NDErs to provide prescriptions for a spiritual, service-oriented, and productive life on earth. In the future, the combination of religious guidance and NDE research, particularly studies that focus on the possibility of postmortem consciousness by researchers such as Janice Holden and Leroy Joesten (1990); Peter Fenwick and Elizabeth Fenwick (1997); Sam Parnia, Derek Waller, R. Yeates, and Peter Fenwick (2001); Pim van Lommel, Ruud van Wees, Vincent Meyers, and Ingrid Elfferich (2001); and van Lommel (2005) may eventually provide an answer to the question that has baffled the human mind since the dawn of time: Do we humans survive physical death?

9

Veridical Perception in Near-Death Experiences

Janice Miner Holden

Are near-death experiences (NDEs) the hallucinations of a dying brain, or are they perceptions of reality? Beyond most near-death experiencers' (NDErs) own claims that the experience was as real as or more real than normal physical experience (Fenwick and Fenwick 1995, 26; Miner-Holden 1988, 106; Moody 1975, 77–78; Sabom 1982, 16), beyond theory and logical argument, what has empirical evidence—based on direct observation and scientific investigation—shown so far? The purpose of this chapter is to review critically the professional literature pertinent to these questions.

Following are the key terms used in this chapter. A near-death *episode* is the *physical situation* in which a person survives an actual or perceived close brush with death—typically, an acute medical crisis involving actual or threatened serious physical injury or illness. By contrast, a near-death *experience* is a person's *subjective experience* of consciousness functioning apart from one's physical body during a near-death episode. As explained elsewhere in this volume, only one out of every five or six near-death episoders reports having had a near-death experience during the episode (see Chapter 2).

Here, NDEs are conceptualized as having material and transmaterial aspects. In the *material* aspect, an NDEr perceives phenomena in the physical, "material" world, most often the area in the vicinity of and including the NDEr's physical body, but sometimes not including the body or being away from its vicinity. In the *transmaterial* aspect, an NDEr perceives phenomena in transcendent dimensions beyond the physical world. The word "aspect" rather than "phase" is used here because the latter term implies sequence, whereas NDErs have reported perception of the material world before, during, and after perception of a transmaterial dimension(s). In an example of material and transmaterial commingling, an NDEr saw her own surgery from the ceiling, from where she also saw two angels each infuse a surgeon with light that traveled down the surgeons' arms and through their fingertips into her body, signifying that they were successfully repairing her broken back. Also, readers familiar with the term "out-of-body" experience (OBE)—those experiences in which "people feel that their 'self,' or center of awareness, is located outside of the physical body" (Alvarado 2000, 183)—will notice that the term "material NDE" is used here instead of "ND OBE." On this point, I agree with Sabom (1982): Because even during the *transmaterial* aspect of NDEs, experiencers feel their consciousnesses to be functioning without regard to their physical bodies, the entire NDE is probably best understood as an extended OBE. Thus, I conceptualize NDEs as extended OBEs in which experiencers perceive material and/or transmaterial domains.

Veridical NDE perception refers to any perception—visual, auditory, kinesthetic, olfactory, and so on—that a person reports having experienced during one's NDE and that is later corroborated as having corresponded to material consensus reality. An example from the material domain is an NDEr who reported that while her body was unconscious, she saw her stepfather, whom she had always known to be a health-food devotee, buy a candy bar from a vending machine with the intention to eat it; when the NDEr regained consciousness, she told her mother what she saw, and her mother confirmed the accuracy of her daughter's perception. An example from the transmaterial domain is an NDEr who, upon regaining consciousness, reported having gone in his NDE to a transmaterial realm where he encountered a deceased relative whom the NDEr had presumed to be still living; shortly thereafter, the NDEr received word that the relative had died shortly before the NDEr's near-death episode. Many authors have used the term "veridical perception" to describe or imply that the knowledge gained—the stepfather's atypical eating, the relative's death— could not have been perceived through normal sensory means or deduced from logical inference. However, here, the term is used to refer to any corroborated NDE perception whether or not it might be the result of normal sensory and/or logical processes.

For reasons discussed here later, NDE researchers and others have shown particular interest in what I am calling *apparently nonphysical veridical NDE perception* (AVP). In AVP, NDErs report veridical perception that, considering the positions and/or conditions of their physical bodies during the near-death episodes, apparently could not have been the result of normal sensory processes or logical inference—nor, therefore, brain mediation—either before, during, or after those episodes. Thus, AVP suggests the ability of consciousness to function independent of the physical body. As the previous examples illustrate, AVP can occur in the material and/or transmaterial aspects of NDEs but, as will be discussed, has been reported far more frequently in the material aspect.

Numerous anecdotal descriptions of AVP appear in the near-death literature, and researchers have attempted to study the phenomenon under scientifically controlled conditions. Before delving into these topics, following is a discussion of the importance of AVP research.

THE IMPORTANCE OF AVP

Why should anyone care whether AVP exists? To answer this question and proceed with discussion, one further distinction needs to be made: the difference between reversible and irreversible death.

In this chapter, *reversible death* refers to conditions as extreme as prolonged cardiac and respiratory arrest from which a person, either spontaneously or as a result of other people's efforts, resuscitates and survives. *Irreversible death* refers to the condition in which the dying process has advanced so far that resuscitation cannot occur. In the study of AVP, this distinction is important because from a purely scientific perspective, the nature of a person's consciousness during reversible death may or may not indicate the nature of one's consciousness during irreversible death. The consciousness associated with a body that *has not yet* lost the potential to live may or may not be the same as the consciousness associated with a body that *has* lost that potential.

With this distinction in mind, the answers to the question of the importance of AVP are several. They include that if AVP exists,

- then NDErs themselves could have not only the subjective but also the objective reality of their experiences confirmed;
- then consciousness—perception, thought, memory, and so on—could be considered capable of functioning apart from the reversibly dead—and thus, perhaps, the living—physical body;
- then consciousness could be considered potentially capable of continuing after irreversible physical death; and
- then credibility could be lent to the nonmaterial aspects of NDEs, including the message of most NDErs regarding the meaning and purpose of human existence.

Regarding the first point, although NDErs are usually firmly convinced of the objective reality of their experiences despite what other people believe, one source of their postexperience distress is encountering the disbelief of health care providers, family members, and others (Greyson and Harris 1987). Thus, affirmation of the apparent objective reality of their NDEs would likely promote NDErs' well-being.

Regarding the second point, positive results would support the hypothesis that, at least regarding the living or resuscitated brain, consciousness can function independent of it. Such results would contradict one of the most fundamental current assumptions of Western science: that the brain produces conscious experience and, thus, that consciousness is entirely dependent on brain function (Kelly et al. 2007; Tart 1975). Evidence that contradicts this assumption has the potential to revolutionize human understanding of humanity, with potentially far-reaching implications that are as difficult to envision fully as it would have been for the originators of the Internet to envision its revolutionary impact on human existence worldwide.

One implication of the second point is the third: If consciousness can function apart from the reversibly dead body, perhaps it continues to function beyond irreversible death. However, many authors over the past century have asserted that from a purely scientific perspective, NDEs alone can never prove the *ongoing* survival of consciousness after permanent bodily death. The reason is a clash between the scientific requirement that researchers study their subject directly and the methodological failure of researchers to find reliable, irreversibly dead people to participate in their studies—at least so far. Although AVP cannot prove the survival of consciousness after permanent bodily death, investigations yielding positive results certainly could narrow the gap in the leap of faith about such survival.

Regarding the fourth point, positive AVP research results also could lend credibility to what most NDErs often adamantly assert having learned from usually the transmaterial aspect of their NDEs: that developing the capacity to love and acquiring knowledge are both the purposes and the most appropriate pursuits of human existence. However, for the most scientifically minded people, the credibility of that message is brought into doubt because almost all phenomena that NDErs perceive during the nonmaterial, transcendent aspects of their experiences can be scientifically affirmed in only very limited ways. Thus, a possible—perhaps likely—result of positive findings from AVP research could be greater belief in that message and, consequently, an increasingly widespread human commitment to more humane personal choices and more humanitarian public policy.

Thus, positive AVP results have the potential to benefit NDErs themselves, humanity, and earthly existence at large. Following is a discussion of categories of AVP and means of investigating them.

TYPES OF AVP AND MEANS OF AVP INVESTIGATION

Two potential sources of empirical data on AVP have dominated the professional NDE literature. One is the anecdote, in which an NDEr reports AVP and some amount and quality of subsequent investigation of the near-death episode reveals the degree to which the report is accurate. The other is the field study involving the control of a perceptual target under circumstances in which AVP is most likely to occur. This latter mode of investigation is aimed at "capturing" AVP in ways that enable objective evaluation of the accuracy of the perception; that reduce, as much as possible, alternative physical explanations for the perception; and that yield quantitative results amenable to statistical analysis of the role of chance in the perception.

From a scientific perspective, both sources of AVP data are valuable (Braud and Anderson 1998, 13), and both have advantages and disadvantages. Anecdotes constitute retrospective, qualitative data that, especially when taken collectively, reveal such information as the range of conditions in which NDErs have reported AVP, including characteristics of AVP experiencers and the nature and circumstances of their perceptions. Among the problems with such data are the possibility of inadequate information to confirm or deny the accuracy of an AVP report; the difficulty of ruling out alternative, "material" explanations for the perception; and the possible roles of memory error and/or unconscious bias among witnesses and/or investigators. Conversely, field studies, if designed well, can substantially reduce the problems of anecdotal data, but they cannot reveal, for example, the range of conditions in which NDErs might report AVP. Thus *anecdotes* might be conceptualized as providing *broader yet shallower information* about AVP, and *field studies* as providing *narrower yet deeper information*.

Again, in terms of empirical value, both breadth and depth are important. However, the potential to gather more definitive data regarding the alleged accuracy and nonphysicality of AVP rests more securely in the field study mode of investigation (Holden 1988; Holden and Joesten 1990; Parnia 2006). Nevertheless, any justification for investing the considerable resources necessary for high-quality field studies comes from anecdotes indicating that such an investment holds reasonable promise of "success" in capturing relatively indisputable nonphysical veridical perception.

In light of these understandings, following is a review of AVP accounts and investigations reported in the near-death literature.

Summary of AVP Accounts and Investigation

Anecdotes

History The first indications of AVP in the professional near-death literature came in the form of anecdotes. In the book that opened the contemporary field of near-death studies, Raymond Moody included a section entitled, "Corroboration." In it, he began, "The question naturally arises whether any evidence of the reality of near-death experiences might be acquired independently of the descriptions of the experiences themselves" (Moody 1975, 92–93). He then proceeded to report four cases in which the patients had reported such evidence to him. In one, a patient reportedly told his doctor "everything that had happened" from the onset of respiratory arrest until he began to regain physical consciousness, to which the doctor reportedly responded with "shock," with uncertainty how to respond, and by coming back repeatedly to ask more about the patient's memory during his time of physical unconsciousness (Moody 1975, 94). In another, when a patient regained consciousness after an accident, he told his father the details of his rescue, including the color of the clothes of his rescuer; his father confirmed the accuracy of these details, "yet," the young man said, "my body was physically out this whole time, and there was no way I could have seen or heard these things without being outside of my body" (Moody 1975, 94). Moody also reported that in a few other cases, he had collected independent corroborative testimony from witnesses at the scenes, though he provided no examples and discussed briefly the logistical and philosophical challenges of such cases.

Actually, such cases had appeared in the professional literature decades before Moody's work. The earliest I found was physician A. S. Wiltse's (1889) description of his own NDE in 1880 that occurred during his presumed death from typhoid fever. After lying in apparent cardiac and respiratory arrest for what he estimated was a half hour, he revived spontaneously and subsequently recovered. In 1892, Frederic W. H. Myers reported his investigation of the case that included sworn testimony Wiltse had obtained from the attending physician, family members, and friends on the scene at the presumed deathbed. The attending physician, S. H. Raynes, reported that by every indication, including insertion of a needle at various points in Wiltse's body, the patient was dead. Wiltse reported that he first lost consciousness and then regained it to witness his "spirit" as it "emerged" from his body (Myers 1892, 181). In this material NDE state, he saw, among other things, two women weeping by his bedside. In his sister's sworn testimony, Sarah Wiltse reported that while her brother was still conscious,

> I thought he could feel my touch, and believed he saw my face, and so I would not give way to tears. *It was not until we were sure that all his bodily senses had failed that I allowed myself to cry;* therefore his singularly well remembered train of thought about his soul, and his observance of his weeping wife and sister, must have occurred while he was apparently unconscious, and after the doctor had pronounced life extinct. (Myers 1892, 192; italics original)

Interestingly, this same sister exhibited the circumspection and critical thinking evident in the AVP literature over the next century when she concluded:

> It seems to me that the psychological value of this phenomenon lies in the probable activity of the mind during apparent unconsciousness, and not in any guesses that may be hazarded about relations of life and death which might be based upon it, although one must reverence the opinion of any

who think as some of the good mountain people do, that Dr. Wiltse actually died and came to life again. (Myers 1892, 193)

Over the next century, AVP anecdotes continued to appear in the professional literature. An early, often-cited account was the case of social worker Kimberly Clark, who found a shoe on a hospital window ledge just as an NDEr had told her the NDEr had seen it during the material aspect of her experience (Clark 1984).

One of the most recent accounts is among the most cited because of its evidentiary value. The following description comes from the 1998 book *Light and Death* by cardiologist and NDE researcher Michael Sabom, with interviews of the key players and recreation of key events presented in the 2002 British Broadcasting Corporation documentary, *The Day I Died: The Mind, the Brain, and Near-Death Experiences* (Broome 2002).

In 1991, Atlanta, Georgia, musician Pam Reynolds was diagnosed with a brain aneurysm—the ballooning of a brain artery that threatens to burst. At first, the aneurysm was believed inoperable. But neurosurgeon Robert Spetzler, practiced a radical surgical procedure officially termed "hypothermic cardiac arrest" and nicknamed "standstill" (Sabom 1998, 37) that seemed to be Reynolds's only hope of survival. The surgery "would require that her body temperature be lowered to 60 degrees [Fahrenheit], her heartbeat and breathing stopped, her brain waves flattened, and the blood drained from her head" (Sabom 1998, 37). She would remain in this condition for the length of time it would take Spetzler to repair the aneurysm.

Following are the key events, relevant to the topic of AVP, as documented in Spetzler's report of the surgery on that August 1991 day. Except where otherwise specified, this material is paraphrased from pages 38–47 of Sabom's (1998) book:

7:15 A.M.—   Reynolds was brought into the operating room while still conscious, she was given intravenous pentathol, after which she reported "a loss of time," her eyes were taped shut, and general anesthesia was begun.

    The operating team then instrumented her with numerous monitoring devices, including electroencephalograph (EEG) electrodes taped to her head to monitor the activity of the outer part of her brain, and small speakers molded to and inserted in both of her ears to emit a 95 decibel clicking sound that would register on a monitor of her brainstem, the lowest part of her brain responsible for the most basic bodily functions. They also instrumented her for the surgical procedure.

8:40 A.M.—	Spetzler incised her scalp, exposing the skull bone; activated the bone saw to remove a section of her skull; cut through the outer membrane around her brain; and inserted a tiny surgical microscope into her brain, wending it through to the aneurysm site, where he found that the aneurysm was so large that, indeed, the hypothermic cardiac arrest procedure would be necessary. Meanwhile, a female cardiac surgeon incised Reynolds's right groin and began preparing the femoral artery and vein for the cardiopulmonary bypass, but, finding the blood vessels too small, prepared the left side, instead.
10:50 A.M.—	The team began the blood- and body-cooling cardiopulmonary bypass process.
11:00 A.M.—	Reynolds's core body temperature reached 73 degrees.
11:05 A.M.—	Cardiac arrest was induced. The EEG of her outer brain functioning went flat. The EEG of her inner "brainstem function weakened as the clicks from the ear speakers produced lower and lower spikes on the monitoring electrogram" (Sabom 1998, 43).
11:25 A.M.—	Core body temperature reached 60 degrees. "The clicks from the ear speakers no longer elicited a response. Total brain shutdown" (Sabom 1998, 43). Then "the head of the operating table was tilted up, the cardiopulmonary bypass machine was turned off, and the blood was drained from Pam's body like oil from a car" (Sabom 1998, 43). Any possibility of metabolism to support brain functioning was eliminated.

Spetzler repaired the aneurysm. All surgical body-altering procedures were then reversed and, with them, Reynolds's core temperature and brain functions. |
12:00 noon—	Reynolds's still quiet heart monitor began showing "the disorganized activity of ventricular fibrillation" (Sabom 1998, 45–46). After two rounds of defibrillator shocks, her heart beat normally.
12:32 P.M.—	Body temperature reached 89.6 degrees. Monitoring equipment was removed. Assistants to Spetzler took over the surgical closing procedures.
2:10 P.M.—	The team took Reynolds, in stable condition, to the recovery room.

During this time, Reynolds had a vivid, detailed experience. After having lost consciousness with the intravenous pentathol, she reported having suddenly been brought to consciousness by the piercing sound of the cranial saw. She said the saw emitted a natural D tone and that it pulled her out of the top of her head. She came to rest at a location near Spetzler's shoulder. She described a sense of awareness far greater than she had ever experienced before, as well as greatly enhanced "vision" with which she saw with clarity and detail the cranial saw, her head, the operating room (OR), and OR personnel. She saw things that she had not expected or that contradicted her expectations, such as the appearance of the cranial saw, the interchangeable saw blades in a socket-wrench-type case, and the way her head was shaved (Sabom 1998, 41). She also was somewhat dismayed to see someone conducting a procedure in her groin area when this was supposedly brain surgery (Broome 2002). From that area, she heard a female voice report that the vessels were too small on the right side, and a male voice directing her to try the other side.

At some later point, during a transmaterial aspect, she encountered deceased loved ones. At some yet later point, she returned to the vicinity of her body accompanied by her deceased uncle, but seeing her body's terrible condition, she was frightened and did not want to reenter it. She saw the body "jump" once, then, upon a second "jump" (Broome 2002), recalled her deceased uncle giving her a push back into her body. She described reentry as "like diving into a pool of ice water ... It hurt!" (Sabom 1998, 46).

The AVP aspects of Reynolds's experience have been debated in detail both in print and on the Internet. Yet because her case is the one most widely recognized as containing, to date, the most detailed and objectively corroborated content, it points the most convincingly to the "reality" of NDEs and all that such reality implies.

Analysis   As Kenneth Ring and Evelyn Elsaesser Valarino noted in 1998, AVP accounts "are scattered in some profusion throughout the literature on NDEs" (Ring and Valarino 1998, 59). In addition, AVP critic Keith Augustine (2006) focused on what he termed "hallucinatory" OBE anecdotes, those in which corroboration revealed one or more perceptual errors. Both to remedy the "scatter" of AVP accounts and to analyze their overall accuracy rather than highlight only those involving error, I collected as many accounts as I could find from three types of sources: books published before 1975 when NDEs became widely known, both the scholarly periodical literature and books published between 1975 and early 2006 in which the author(s) described some systematic study of NDEs, and case studies published in the scholarly periodical literature or edited books during those three decades. I excluded post-1975 accounts from the popular periodical literature, from autobiographical books, and from books on NDEs that were not explicitly reporting a systematic study of NDEs, as well as single case studies described outside the peer-reviewed literature. Also, scholars have generally, though not universally, agreed with Celia Green's (1968) assertion that more accurate nonphysical perception occurs in association with near-death episodes than with other circumstances of spontaneous or induced OBEs. For this reason, I included only experiences associated with near-death episodes. I found a total of 107 such cases gleaned from 39 publications by 37 different authors or author teams; see Table 9.1.

Then I analyzed each anecdote for various factors. Categorizing the anecdotes, I found 89 material, 14 transmaterial, and 4 that included

Table 9.1

Sources of Anecdotes Involving Apparently Nonphysical Veridical Perception

Source	No. of cases	Page Numbers
Atwater, P. M. H. 1999	1	96–102
Bonenfant, R. J. 2001	1	89
Brumblay, R. J. 2003	1	214
Clark, K. 1984	1	243
Cobbe, F. P. 1882.	1	297
Cook, E. K., Greyson, B., and Stevenson, I. 1998	10	384, 385, 387–88, 389–90, 391, 391–92, 393–94, 395–98, 398, 399
Crookall, R. 1972	1	386
Ellwood, G. F. 2001	1	25
Fenwick, P., and Fenwick, E. 1995	7	31, 32, 32–33, 33 (2), 35, 193
Green, C. 1968	1	121
Grey, M. 1985	3	37, 37–38, 80–81.
Hampe, J. C. 1979	1	260–61
Hyslop, J. H. 1918	1	620
Jung, C. G. 196.	1	92
Kelly, E. W., Greyson, B., and Stevenson, I. 1999–2000	1	516
Kübler-Ross, E. 1983	1	210
Lawrence, M. 1997	1	117
Lindley, J. H., Bryan, S., and Conley, B. 1981	2	109, 110
Manley, L. K. 1996	1	311
Moody, R. 1975	4	93, 94 (2), 95–102
Moody, R., and Perry, P. 1988	4	170–71, 171, 172, 173
Morris, L. L., and Knafl, K. 2003	2	155, 156
Morse, M. L. 1994	4	62, 67, 67–68, 68

Morse, M. L., and Perry, P. 1990	3	6, 25–26, 152–53
Myers, F. W. H. 1892	2	180-194, 194–200
Near-Death Experiences: The Proof. February 2, 2006	1	
Ogston, A. 1920	1	383
Rawlings, M. 1978	7	5, 56–57, 57–58, 75, 77–78, 79–80, 99
Ring, K. 1980	2	50, 51
Ring, K. 1984	1	44
Ring, K., and Cooper, S. 1999	9	4, 6–7, 7, 51, 61, 83, 101–2, 108–9, 109–20
Ring, K., and Lawrence, M. 1993	3	226–27, 227, 227–28
Ring, K., and Valarino, E. E. 1998	11	59, 60–61 (2), 62, 62–63, 63, 64, 224–25, 226 (3)
Rommer, B. 2000	2	5–7, 7
Sabom, M. 1982	10	64–69, 69–72, 73–74, 87–91, 94, 99, 104, 105–11, 111–13, 116–18
Tutka, M. A. 2001	1	64
Tyrrell, G. N. M. 1946	1	197–99
van Lommel, P., van Wees, R., Meyers, V., and Elfferich, I. 2001	1	2041
Wilson, 1987	1	163–64
Total	107	

195

perception of both aspects. Anecdotes in the material category included a variety of corroborated details of NDErs' rescues, resuscitations, and other events during their NDEs, including NDErs facilitating the recovery of lost objects. Anecdotes in the transmaterial category consisted primarily of the experiencer encountering someone in the NDE whom they did not know at the time was deceased; it also more rarely included cases of acquiring other information, such as the location of secretly hidden documents, and of spontaneous healing.

I took two further steps to analyze the evidentiary strength of the AVP. First, I categorized the anecdotes into those verified only by the experiencer, those verified by outside sources as reported by the experiencer, or those verified by outside sources as reported by the author—believing this sequence to represent weakest to strongest evidentiary value. The latter category included sources such as the testimony of witnesses, typically medical personnel caring for the experiencer at the time of the NDE, and/or medical records. Second, I also categorized the accounts into those that apparently contained no error, those that contained both error and accuracy, and those that were predominantly or completely erroneous. Results appear in Table 9.2.

To Augustine's credit, I found only one case involving apparent error that he had not included in his review. Nevertheless, cases involving AVP clearly outnumbered substantially those involving erroneous perception. In particular, whereas 8 percent of material and 11 percent of transmaterial cases involved even some error, 38 percent of material and 33 percent of transmaterial cases involved complete accuracy of perception that the authors corroborated through objective means.

In reviewing these cases as a whole, it appears to me that the strength of evidence, even among the cases of accurate and objectively corroborated perceptions, ranged from somewhat weak to extremely strong. Many NDE researchers have pointed out that anecdotes are often a flawed source of evidence for the ability of consciousness to function apart from the brain. Most cases have not involved cardiac arrest and, thus, probably involved a still-viable brain. Thus, it is difficult to rule out the possibility that NDErs—probably unknowingly—constructed perceptions based on information they received through normal physiological channels. For example, they might construct visual images on the basis of something they heard. It also is difficult to rule out the possibility that NDErs might have gained information, even unconsciously, before or after their near-death episodes that led to or embellished their "memory." This problem is exacerbated by delay in interview: Among the 107 cases in this review, only 18 involved an interview during the first two days following the NDE. Another potential problem is a phenomenon called *the file drawer effect*, in which NDE perceptions that are mostly or totally inaccurate are labeled hallucinations and are filed away as irrelevant rather than being considered a valid source of information and reported in publication.

Table 9.2

Analysis of Anecdotes of Apparently Nonphysical Veridical Perception (AVP) during Near-Death Experiences (NDEs)

Phenomena Perceived during Material Aspect of NDE

		Corroborated by	
	Experiencer Only	Others per Report of Experiencer	Objective Source(s)
Accurate	13	38	35
Some Error	0	2	4
Completely Erroneous	0	0	1

Phenomena Perceived during Transmaterial Aspect of NDE

		Corroborated by	
	Experiencer Only	Others per Report of Experiencer	Objective Source(s)
Accurate	3	7	6
Some Error	1	0	0
Completely Erroneous	0	0	1

n = 107 anecdotes

Total entries = 111 because 4 anecdotes involved phenomena perceived during both material and transmaterial aspects of NDE.

Yet the sheer volume of AVP anecdotes that a number of different authors over the course of the last 150 years have described suggests AVP is real. In this regard, Ring and Valarino's (1998) assertion is interesting to note: "Although no single instance may be absolutely conclusive in itself, the cumulative weight of these narratives is sufficient to convince most skeptics that these reports are something more than mere hallucinations on the patient's part" (59). Lacking the ability to determine the accuracy of their assertion regarding most skeptics, their reference to some skeptics who remain unconvinced is definitely accurate. Some of the most vocal of these unconvinced skeptics have been Susan Blackmore (1993), Gerald Woerlee (2004), and Augustine (2006).

The crux of these skeptics' arguments is that the AVPs were actually the perceptions of the physical body and the constructions of the still-viable physical brain during the experience and/or the brain through thought processes before and/or after the experience. Augustine (2006) referred to this class of arguments as the "physiological explanation" (21). For example, in the case of Pam Reynolds, he pointed out, the material aspect of her experience occurred before cardiopulmonary bypass began; thus, it was not coincident with her clinical death, which occurred after the bypass procedure was initiated, but was coincident with her having been only under general anesthesia. Consequently, her perceptions could be attributed to "anesthesia awareness," a documented phenomenon in which people continue to perceive despite anesthesia. He said that this phenomenon occurs in one to two patients out of 1,000 who have undergone general anesthesia, which represents at least 20,000 patients in the United States. alone, and that about half of these patients report having been able to hear and one-quarter having felt pain.

Between this phenomenon and the functions of deduction and memory, he asserted physiological explanations for every veridical element in her experience. In his view, she heard the sound of the bone saw and the exchange between the surgeon and cardiologist through normal means. She reconstructed her "memory" of the unique pattern in which her head was shaved once she saw or otherwise learned of it postoperatively. The bone saw's socket-wrench–like case of interchangeable blades was a logical deduction based on previous experience with dental drills. And her description of the bone saw itself contained an important error: that it had a "groove at the top where the saw appeared to go into the handle" (Sabom 1998, 187), whereas the groove was actually located at the tip— the opposite end from where the saw entered the handle. Augustine concluded that "her NDE was entirely expectation-driven" (Sabom 1998, 25) and that he believed that the three-year lapse between her surgery and the time Sabom first interviewed her allowed plenty of time to consolidate a coherent memory based on normally acquired information before, during, and after the surgery.

I question Augustine's arguments and conclusion. Perhaps most notable is how Reynolds could have heard the operating room conversation, given her surgical circumstances. Anesthesia awareness often is attributed to the patient being underanesthetized, but Ms. Reynolds's brain was being monitored three different ways to ensure that she was deeply and consistently anesthetized. One of these ways was the monitoring of her most basic level of brain function by stimulating her hearing with ear speakers. Augustine (2006) did not report that the ear speakers molded into Reynolds' ears emitted clicks throughout her entire period of general anesthesia at a loudness of 90 to 100 decibels and a rate of 11 to 33 clicks per second (Spetzler et al. 1988). That volume has been described as louder than a whistling teakettle and as loud as a lawn mower or a subway when a train is going through it (League for the Hard of Hearing n.d.). The reader is invited to imagine ear speakers molded to fill the ear canals completely and emitting clicks that loud and that rapid, and then to imagine the likelihood of accurately hearing a brief conversation that occurred at an estimated level of 60 decibels—the loudness of normal conversation. In addition, if Reynolds had been hearing through normal means, it is curious that, as Sabom has confirmed (M. Sabom, personal communication, May 1, 2006), she never mentioned even hearing clicks, more or less feeling distracted by them or struggling to hear through them. Her own perception of her accurate hearing was that it occurred through nonphysical processes.

Beyond the details of Reynolds's experience is the testimony of someone present on the scene, someone presumably steeped in the skill of scientific analysis as deduced from his position as director of the Barrow Neurological Institute: Spetzler himself. In a recent interview, he stated:

> At that stage in the operation, nobody can observe, hear, in that state. And I find it inconceivable that your normal senses, such as hearing, let alone the fact that she had clicking modules in each ear, that there was any way to hear [what she heard] through normal auditory pathways.
>
> I don't have an explanation for it. I don't know how it's possible for it to happen, considering the physiological state she was in. At the same time, I have seen so many things that I can't explain, that I don't want to be so arrogant as to be able to say that there's no way it can happen. (Broome 2002)

Stepping back from the specific debate regarding the Reynolds case, and even the volume of evidence from the total collection of AVP anecdotes, the problem of relying on anecdotes for *definitive* evidence supporting or contradicting the hypothesized ability of consciousness to function independent of the brain becomes clear. By their nature, anecdotes are reports of spontaneous occurrences, that is, those that happened in the absence of controlled conditions. In the absence of controls, commentators can debate almost endlessly about the source of the apparently nonphysical perceptions that experiencers reported. That debate has continued (Ebbern, Mulligan, and Beyerstein 1996; for a thorough treatment of this topic, see Chapter 10, this volume), and from a scientific perspective, even winning it would not carry the evidentiary value that would accompany AVP corroborated through systematic study. Such studies are the focus of the next section.

Systematic Studies of AVP

Studies or Aspects of Studies Not Involving Perceptual Targets

In 1975, Moody reported having attempted to verify the accuracy of material NDE perceptions by comparing those reports to hospital records. Without providing the specifics of his method or an illustrative case, he asserted that the accuracy of NDErs' reports were "borne out" (Moody 1975, 148).

Sabom (1982) published findings from the next study of this kind. He used a prospective sampling procedure to conduct retrospective interviews. Over a period of almost five years, Sabom and coinvestigator Sarah

Kreutziger, a social worker, through their hospital positions, approached every patient for interview who came to their attention as having a history of a crisis event "in which the patient had been rendered unconscious and physically near death" (Sabom 1982, 7). Their approach promised to provide a more representative sample of NDErs than had been provided by purely retrospective sampling procedures involving self-selected NDErs whom researchers had solicited by advertisement and word-of-mouth and who had themselves initiated coming forth and being studied. Sabom and Kreutziger found 71 near-death experiencers, 32 of whose NDEs included what here is called perception of the material world—people who "claimed to have 'seen' portions of their own resuscitation ... most ... during cardio-pulmonary resuscitation (CPR) for a cardiac arrest" (Sabom 1982, 83). Except for an experiencer whom they interviewed 12 hours after the crisis event and another two whom they interviewed one month after, they interviewed the remaining 29 between one and 58 years after.

Sabom (1982) found that 26 of the 32 material NDErs could not describe the material aspect of their experiences in enough detail to compare to medical records. Thus, although they did not report specifically accurate details, they also made no identifiable errors in their material NDE accounts. For the remaining six, all of whom suffered cardiac arrest and received CPR, Sabom compared their detailed material NDE accounts with hospital records and found that they conformed, in virtually every detail, to the records, which the patients had never seen. Sabom then found 25 "seasoned" cardiac patients who had "similar backgrounds" to the material experiencers but who had not had NDEs. When he asked them to describe a cardiac resuscitation procedure, 80 percent made major errors in their descriptions. His findings seemed to support the hypothesis that the consciousness of material experiencers, indeed, continued functioning outside of their bodies.

Despite the striking nature of Sabom's results, researchers have criticized his methodology. Blackmore (1985, 79–80) noted what is probably the strongest point: that only four of the 25 patients in the comparison group had actually experienced exactly what the material experiencers had: resuscitation from cardiac arrest (Sabom 1982, 84). Sabom did not provide enough detail to enable a reader to ascertain which five of his comparison group (20% of 25) made no major errors, but the possibility remains that the four who had experienced cardiac arrest were among those five, indicating that some mechanism other than an NDE might be at work in accurate recall of CPR. "A more appropriate [comparison] group would have consisted entirely of [research participants] who had been ... resuscitated from cardiac arrest without an NDE (or at least a [material] NDE)" (Miner-Holden 1988, 52). Presumably, Sabom had access to far more resuscitated non-NDErs than his 71 resuscitated NDErs. It is not known why he did not choose to use this more appropriate control group. The fact that he didn't has, unfortunately, undermined the power of his findings to support the independent consciousness hypothesis.

Interestingly, with regard to the file drawer effect, prospective study researchers would be most likely to document alleged AVP that contained errors and, therefore, be less prone to fall victim to that effect. In fact, none have reported erroneous AVP, and one prospective study report explicitly included a case of AVP with no apparent error: the case of the man who reported having seen where a nurse had put his dentures when the nurse removed them from the comatose patient's mouth during CPR (van Lommel et al. 2001, 2041). Nevertheless, because no prospective studies so far have explicitly involved a comparison of AVP to hospital records, the possibility exists that prospective researchers may have dismissed as hallucination cases that should possibly have been considered erroneous AVP.

A more recent study has the potential to sort out these fine points. Penny Sartori (2004) conducted a five-year prospective hospital study in Wales. The first year, she interviewed every patient who survived admission to the intensive therapy unit—comparable to the intensive care unit in U.S. hospitals. For the remaining four years, she interviewed only those patients who had survived cardiac arrest, who "came so close to death that they were not expected to survive, [and who] spontaneously reported NDEs/OBEs" (Sartori 2004, 36). She also replicated and extended two aspects of Sabom's research.

First, Sartori (2004) specifically documented 12 patients among "many" (Sartori 2004, 38) who reported experiences she labeled hallucinations because of their similarity to hallucinations as generally described and because of their differences from NDEs. Those differences are detailed in Table 9.3.

The differences Sartori (2004) found lend support to the idea that NDEs are not hallucinations as the latter phenomena are typically understood. However, this finding alone does not rule out the possibility that NDEs might constitute a different "class" of hallucinations in which the content is equally unreal while the NDEr experiences it subjectively as decidedly real if not hyperreal. In addition, it isn't clear from the preliminary report of her research how she chose the 12 documented cases out of the "many" cases of hallucination to which she referred. Details of her research protocol would need to be known to determine whether sampling bias may have been involved.

Second, Sartori (Near Death Experiences: The Proof 2006) apparently compared the reports of material NDErs who reported watching their bodies being resuscitated to the reports of material NDErs "who didn't report seeing their own bodies" (2006, 3) and could only speculate about the resuscitation process. I use the term "apparently" because in this report of her study from a popular source, the author(s) did not include details of

Table 9.3
Sartori's (2004) Comparison of Hallucinations and NDEs

Feature / Experience	Hallucination	NDE	Same/ Different
Number	"Many"; 12 documented	15	
Content			
Specificity	Nonspecific	Specific	Different
Organization	Random, unpatterned	Patterned	Different
Relationship to surrounding activities while regaining consciousness	Related	Unrelated	Different
Sense of reality	Patient reasoned that experience was unreal	Patient adamant that experience was real	Different
Recall after elapsed time			
Vividness of images	Some remained vivid	All remained vivid	Different
Degree of degradation	Memory had faded	Memory did not fade	Different
Completeness of recall	Some content omitted	All content included	Different

Sartori's research protocol. The author(s) stated that Sartori found that "patients who see their bodies during their near-death experiences can describe accurately how the medical staff revived or resuscitated them," whereas Sartori was quoted as saying, "The ones who didn't report seeing their own bodies tried to guess what happened and always got it wrong. They usually described scenarios from TV shows like *Casualty* and *ER* and very often thought they had been 'shocked' with a defibrillator even when they hadn't" (2006, 3). If, based on future professional publications, her research protocol withstands scrutiny, then her findings have the potential to clarify distinctions between hallucinations, erroneous conjecture, and apparent veridical perception.

To harken back one last time to Sabom's (1982) investigation, one further criticism of his study is noteworthy and provides a segue to the next section of this chapter.

Gabbard and Twemlow (1984) further criticized that "only six of the 32 [material NDErs] reported observations in sufficient detail to permit some subsequent validation. The probabilities involved in such reports are difficult to figure, but ... chance alone could explain these findings" (Gabbard and Twemlow 1984, 96–97). It is precisely because the probabilities are difficult to figure that a more credible study would utilize a [perceptual] stimulus [that] could be manipulated, thus rendering any results amenable to statistical analysis. (Miner-Holden 1988, 52)

Such control of a perceptual stimulus is the domain of NDE AVP prospective field studies.

Prospective Studies Involving Perceptual Targets

Preliminary Considerations Before embarking on a review of prospective field studies, it is important to clarify why these investigations are being referred to here as field studies and not experiments. In "classical or 'true' experiments" (Heppner, Kavlighan, and Wampold 1999, 40), the researcher controls or changes one variable, called the independent variable, and examines the effect on another variable, the dependent variable; a change in the dependent variable is presumed to be caused by the control or change of the independent variable (Heppner, Kavlighan, and Wampold 1999, 41). The general idea of prospective investigation of AVP is to make present continuously a controlled perceptual stimulus, knowable only to a material NDEr, in a setting in which NDEs are most likely to occur. Although the field researcher has the power to control or change the perceptual stimulus, that control or change does not *cause* the NDEr to perceive it. Research has not yet enabled investigators to know the "cause(s)" of NDEs or of specific perceptions during them: It's not yet possible to predict, even in the relatively clear-cut case of cardiac arrest and respiratory arrest, who will have an NDE; whether any given NDE will include a material aspect; among those that do, the location of the allegedly perceiving consciousness; and whether that consciousness would be able to perceive, or even be inclined to notice, any particular feature of the material environment. Alleged NDE perception is *caused* by factors outside the control of the researcher. Consequently, controlling or changing the nature of the perceptual stimulus will not *cause* it to be perceived, though it might *increase the likelihood* that an NDEr would perceive it. Thus, prospective AVP research involves not experimentation per se but, rather, field study.

Beginning with Moody (1975), numerous authors have suggested, urged, and even exhorted investigators to pursue AVP research (Holden 1988; Lundahl and Gibson 2000; Parnia and Fenwick 2002; Ring and Lawrence 1993). From the beginning, they suggested the basic research protocol: In a place where NDEs are likely to occur, plant some perceptual stimulus and then interview everyone who survives a near-death episode in the vicinity of that stimulus to determine whether they perceived it. Authors provided a few refinements along the way: Place the stimulus so that it is perceivable by an NDEr but not by other people in the area; in fact, to rule out the possibility that an interviewer or others might intentionally or unintentionally convey the content of the stimulus to the NDEr through normal—or even paranormal—means, arrange it so that the stimulus is not known even to the research team or associates. However, beyond these guidelines, investigators still had questions. Fortunately, research provided at least preliminary answers.

For example, under what conditions should AVP field research take place? To best answer the question of consciousness functioning independent of the brain, the research should target times when the brain is not functioning. This condition is most reliably approached or achieved during cardiac arrest. The controllable environment(s) in which cardiac arrest most reliably occurs is hospitals. Thus, the exclusive sites for AVP research so far have been hospitals, most often their cardiac care units.

What kind of perceptual stimulus should be used? NDErs most often report perception through two sensory modalities: sound and sight. Sound stimuli are difficult to isolate: It would be difficult to project a sound in the vicinity of a material experiencer's body that others in the vicinity— not to mention the experiencer's own physical body—couldn't also hear. That leaves visual stimuli.

Where should the visual target be placed? Most material NDEs involve perception in the vicinity of the physical body (Greyson 2000). Even more specifically, in one study (Holden 1989; Miner-Holden 1988) of 63 material NDErs, about 70 percent reported consciousness located above their physical bodies, most located at or near the ceiling. These findings confirmed what other authors had suggested: To isolate the stimulus, it should be located above the eye level of any person in the room, facing toward the ceiling, so as to be potentially visible only from the vantage point of the ceiling.

And what should be the nature of the stimulus? Here, the question becomes a bit more complex. What can material NDErs see, and to what degree does their sight in the material NDE state correspond to physical sight? In anecdotes, AVP NDErs had mentioned visual elements of color, object recognition, movement, and the ability to read monitors and electronic displays. But was physical "red" perceived as "red" in material NDEs? And what about other aspects of "visual" perception?

In the Miner-Holden (1988) study of "visual" perception among material NDErs, about 75 percent said that they saw clearly and without distortion during their material NDEs, that color they perceived in their material NDEs matched physically perceived color, and that material NDE field of vision was as good as or better than their physical field of vision. About 60 percent said they had mostly or totally complete and accurate memories of what they saw during their material NDEs and that they could probably or definitely read during their material NDEs. Somewhat less encouraging was the finding regarding attention to extraneous detail, that is, aspects of the environment other than activity related to their physical bodies: Only slightly more respondents said they would be attentive to such detail as would not. Also less than encouraging was that more said they would not be attracted to attention-getting factors, like motion or changes in brightness, than would be attracted, though the quality of that finding was questionable.

In addition to the preceding questions, respondents reported about such things as their willingness to be interviewed about their material NDE shortly after the event. Results supported several conclusions: Hospital research of AVP was warranted; the visual target should be intensely colored and lighted; reading should include extremely simple number or letter combinations; the visual target should be placed as far below ceiling level as possible while maintaining masked conditions (in which the target is not visible to physical bodies in the room); no potential research participant should be excluded based on any personal or socioeconomic variable; pharmacological factors and a recalled NDE length of less than 10 minutes might interfere with accurate recall of the material NDE; and not all potential participants would necessarily be willing to participate in an interview following shortly after their NDEs. In light of the research that has transpired in the intervening years since 1988, one conclusion of the study now seems rather prophetic—namely, that "the process of accumulating sufficient data in hospital veridicality research may be protracted. Thus it is recommended that such research be conducted simultaneously at more than one hospital" (Miner-Holden 1988, 126).

However, this conclusion was already informed by an attempt at hospital AVP research. That study and the four subsequent studies of this kind are the next focus of attention.

The Studies   Key features of the five AVP studies conducted so far are summarized in Table 9.4. All of the researchers used a "total blind" design in which they intended that no living person would know the exact content of the visual target until after the subject interview had occurred. Controlling this aspect proved to be a challenge. Three studies (Holden and Joesten 1990; Parnia et al. 2001; Sartori 2004) involved static targets, and one (Lawrence 1996, 1997) involved a running electronic target, all of which were displayed continuously and were visible, with some effort, to hospital staff and other persons in the room. In all studies of this kind, the researchers reported problems with the staff and/or visitors looking at the targets and, thus, compromising the masked research protocol. Most of these researchers reported that they had to work intensely and repeatedly with the staff to get their cooperation in not tampering with or peeking at the targets.

The remaining study (Greyson, Holden, and Mounsey 2006) involved a more limited and quasi-randomized display. Just before an electrophysiology (EP) procedure, in which cardiac arrhythmia is induced for the

Table 9.4

Summary of AVP Studies in Hospital through 2005

Key to contractions:

pt = patient

uk = unknown

CCU = Cardiac care unit

ECU/ER = Emergency care unit/room

EP = Electrophysiology lab

ICU/ITU = Intensive care/therapy unit; MCU = Medical care unit

Citation (in chrono-logical order)	Location	Hospital Ward	Study Duration	Type of Stimulus	Projected # of NDEs	Actual # of NDEs	Number of VP Cases	Problems with Staff	Pts.
Holden, J. M., & Joesten, L. (1990). Near-death veridicality research in the hospital setting. *J. Near-Death Studies* 9 (1): 45–54.	Lutheran General Hospital, Park Ridge, IL, USA	ER, ICU, CCU	1 year	8″ square matte board with random combo of 1 of 6 colors, numbers, and symbols. Placed face up in rimmed paper tray mounted 12″ below ceiling corners (chance odds: 1/216)	1 from cardiac arrest per month	1 in study ward (pt declined); 1 in nonstudy ward	0	\<yes\>	\<yes\>
Lawrence, M. (1996, August). Prospective near-death experience studies with AIDS and cardiac patients. Paper presented at the annual North American Conference of the International Association for Near-Death Studies, Oakland, CA. Lawrence, M. (1997). *In a world of their own. West*	Hartford Hospital, Hartford, CT, USA	EP	1 year	Oblong electronic "running text" sign placed face-up on top of cabinet, visible only by standing on ladder, displaying nonsense message such as "The popsicles are in bloom." (chance odds: uk)	7% of EP pts	25 pts; 0 full NDEs; 3 "reported the early stages of an out-of-body experience" (1997, 159).	0	\<yes\>	\<no\>

206

Citation	Location	Setting	Duration	Target	Prevalence	NDEs	Hits	Prospective	Verified
Parnia, S., Waller, D. G., Yeates, R., & Fenwick, P. (2001). A qualitative and quantitative study of the incidence, features and aetiology of near death experiences in cardiac arrest survivors. *Resuscitation* 48:149–56. Parnia, S. (2006). *What happens when we die.* Carlsbad, CA: Hay House.	Southampton General Hospital, Southampton, England, UK	MCU, ECU, CCU	1 year	"Boards suspended from the ceiling … [that] had various figures on the surface facing the ceiling which were not visible from the floor" (2001, 151). (chance odds: uk)	uk; 30% of cardiac arrests	4 NDEs, 0 mNDEs	0	yes	no
Sartori, P. (2004). A prospective study of NDEs in an intensive therapy unit. *Christian Parapsychologist* 16 (2): 34–40. Near-death experiences: The proof. (2006, February 2). *London Daily Express*, 24–25.	Morriston Hospital, Swansea, Wales, UK	ITU	5 years	"Symbols … mounted on brightly coloured day glow paper … placed on the top of [the cardiac] monitor … mounted on the wall … at each patient's bedside … above head height and concealed behind ridges to prevent them being viewed from a standing position	uk	uk; <15 (18% after cardiac arrest). mNDEs: uk; <8 (5% after cardiac arrest)	0: "Not all the patients rose high enough out of their bodies and some reported … a position opposite to where the symbols were situated" (2004, 38).	yes	no

207

(*Continued*)

Table 9.4 (Continued)

Key to contractions:
pt = patient
uk = unknown
CCU = Cardiac care unit
ECU/ER = Emergency care unit/room
EP = Electrophysiology lab
ICU/ITU = Intensive care/therapy unit; MCU = Medical care unit

Citation (in chronological order)	Location	Hospital Ward	Study Duration	Type of Stimulus	Projected # of NDEs	Actual # of NDEs	Number of VP Cases	Problems with Staff	Pts.
				… [and] rotated on a two-monthly basis" during night shift using procedure to protect double blind (2004, 35). (chance odds: uk)					
Greyson, B., Holden, J. M., & Mounsey, P. (2006). Failure to elicit near-death experiences in induced cardiac arrest. *J. Near-Death Studies* 25:85–98.	University of Virginia Hospital, Charlottesville, VA, USA	EP	1 year	Computer opened flat and mounted above eye level on top of monitor; near-random, continuous display of ~20-sec. animation loop displaying color, time, and a simple action cartoon; started just before EP procedure, went off after 90 mins., recorded in code which of 60 animations had been projected (chance odds: 1/60 [12 animations × 5 colors])	7% of pts (Milne 1995)	0 of 50 EP episodes	0	no	no

purposes of diagnosis and treatment of serious cardiac dysrhythmia, a research associate would go to the EP lab, get up on a ladder, and power up the computer that was mounted face up on top of the monitor located near the center of the room. The computer was programmed to select one of 60 animations depending on the second (as in 11 hours, 36 minutes, and *29 seconds*) that the researcher pushed the power button. The computer took 20 seconds to boot up and begin its display—plenty of time for the research associate to get out of visual range of the screen—and it turned off automatically after 90 minutes and made a coded recording of which animation it had displayed. These researchers reported no problem with the blind research condition being compromised.

Even with a well-oriented staff, a continuously displayed visual target makes a masked research protocol vulnerable to compromise. If masked research conditions cannot be maintained, any positive results could be attributed to physical, rather than NDE, sources of knowledge. However, more controlled visual targets are more complex and expensive to design and use. These factors are important considerations for future research.

Another related factor involves a central question that Susan Blackmore (Broome 2002), among others, has asked: When, exactly, does the NDE occur? Specifically for the focus of this chapter, does the material NDE occur when the experiencer's heart has stopped and the brain is presumed not to be functioning? To "capture" this aspect of hypothesized material NDE perception, Bruce Greyson, Janice Holden, and Mounsey (2006) included in each 20-second animation loop a three-second display of the current time, in the hope that a reported time would correspond to the time of cardiac arrest noted in the EP procedure records. This strategy is not the only possible one to address the issue of when the veridical perception occurs, but future AVP researchers will have to grapple with this issue as well as the issue of maintaining masked research conditions.

The bottom line of findings from these five studies is quite disappointing: No researcher has succeeded in capturing even one case of AVP.

Possible explanations are numerous. One possibility is that AVP does not exist. Another is that its rarity in the anecdotal literature indicates its extreme rarity under controlled conditions of investigation; that is, the necessary conditions—someone in cardiac arrest with an NDE involving AVP from a location at which the target can be perceived—are likely to be rare. Yet another explanation involves the nature of perception in the material NDE state, which many NDErs have reported is more a matter of feeling and of personal meaning than is the case with physical perception. If so, what kinds of visual targets would involve feeling and meaning for individuals whose material NDEs cannot, as yet, be predicted? Before returning to this point of the challenges of AVP field research, it may be helpful first to summarize the conclusions, implications, and applications presented in this chapter so far.

SUMMARY AND CONCLUSIONS

Considering sources before 1975, systematic studies, and peer reviewed reports, the professional NDE literature contains probably no more than about 150 anecdotal cases in which NDErs and/or others have attempted to corroborate the NDErs' adamant reports: that during their NDEs, they experienced apparently nonphysical veridical perception (AVP), that is, accurate perception of the material world that should not have been possible given the condition and/or location of their physical bodies.

- Out of approximately 100 of those cases, a small minority involved error or possible error, and the great majority involved anywhere from very weak to extremely strong evidence that the AVP was accurate.
- In a few of these strongly evidential cases, most investigators have ruled out alternate explanations to the hypothesis of nonphysical perception.
- Nevertheless, because of the uncontrolled nature of anecdotal cases, alternate explanations remain open to debate; for these reasons, controlled investigation of AVP has seemed warranted.
- The professional NDE literature contains five reports of controlled investigation of AVP in hospital settings.
- None of these studies yielded a case of AVP.
- If the controlled investigation of AVP is to continue, it will likely be a complex and protracted—and, therefore, costly—process.

CONCLUSION

In an e-mail exchange with Bruce Greyson and me regarding the contemporary state of AVP research, eminent NDE researcher Kenneth Ring said:

> There is so much anecdotal evidence that suggests [experiencers] can, at least sometime, perceive veridically during their NDEs ... but isn't it true that in all this time, there hasn't been a single case of a veridical perception reported by an NDEr under controlled conditions? I mean, thirty years later, it's still a null class (as far as I know). Yes, excuses, excuses—I know. But, really, wouldn't you have suspected more than a few such cases *at least* by now? ...
>
> My (tongue-in-cheek) interpretation: The NDE is governed by The Trickster who wants to tease us, but never give us the straight dope, so people are left to twist in the wind of ambiguity, and meanwhile the search for the elusive white crow in the laboratory ... continues to frustrate researchers and gives ammunition to the skeptics. Maybe Raymond [Moody] is right about there being an imp in the parapsychological closet, and with a sense of humor, too. (personal communication, September 7, 2006)

The trickster is "a cunning or deceptive character appearing in various forms in the folklore of many cultures" (*Merriam-Webster Online Dictionary* 2008). So, in the face of failed attempts to capture veridical perception, yet another explanation is offered: that some force, for some reason, is using trickery to deceive humanity by hiding evidence of nonphysical veridical perception.

Alfred Adler asserted that conclusions become guiding fictions that influence future courses of action. By drawing the skeptical—or, rather, cynical—conclusion that nonphysical veridical perception does not exist, one runs the risk of not seeking evidence of it—and that which is not sought is rarely found or, depending on one's view of reality, is not co-created. For me, the danger of concluding that the trickster is at work is to feel powerless and to assume a passive role, awaiting the whim of this outside force to possibly someday allow the evidence of nonphysical veridical perception to be revealed.

In the matter of failed efforts at controlled AVP research so far, the wisdom of Albert Einstein may be helpful. In 1921, he said, "Raffiniert ist der Herrgott, aber boshaft ist er nicht": God is subtle, but he is not malicious (Clark 1971). When asked what he meant, Einstein replied, "Nature hides her secret because of her essential loftiness, but not by means of ruse" (Pais 1982). What phenomenon could be subtler than the unpredictable NDE in which, reportedly, people often perceive objects based more on emotional characteristics of the objects than on inanimate characteristics? And what aspect of nature could compare in loftiness to the notion of, in Pim van Lommel's (2004) words, "the continuity of consciousness" beyond its physical associations? The pursuit of AVP research may involve a similar degree of subtlety and duration as the undertaking of meditation to achieve enlightenment. Neither cynicism nor resignation aids in the pursuit of that most subtle yet immanent condition. If nonphysical veridical perception is to be confirmed or, depending, again, on the view of reality, realized—it will take researchers with purpose, perseverance, and patience—and one or more backers with abiding interest and substantial financial resources.

Perhaps a fitting ending to this chapter is to echo the question that F. W. H. Myers posed in 1892: "Why should not every deathbed be made the starting point of a long experiment?"

Explanatory Models for Near-Death Experiences

Bruce Greyson, Emily Williams Kelly, and Edward F. Kelly

Although experts on near-death experiences (NDEs) have not reached universal agreement on a definition (Greyson 1999), NDEs are generally understood to be the unusual, often vivid and realistic, and sometimes profoundly life-changing experiences occurring to people who have been physiologically close to death, as in cardiac arrest or other life-threatening conditions, or psychologically close to death, as in accidents or illnesses in which they feared they would die. Frequently recurring features include feelings of peace and joy; an out-of-body experience (OBE) or a sense of being out of one's physical body; a cessation of pain; seeing a dark tunnel or void; seeing an unusually bright light, sometimes experienced as a "Being of Light" that radiates love and may communicate with the person; encountering other beings, often deceased people; experiencing a revival of memories, sometimes accompanied by feelings of judgment; seeing some "other realm," often of great beauty; sensing a border beyond which the person cannot go; and returning to the physical body, often reluctantly.

One particularly noteworthy feature of NDEs is that for many experiencers, an NDE permanently and dramatically alters individuals' attitudes, beliefs, and values, often leading to beneficial personal transformation. Aftereffects most often reported include increases in spirituality, concern for others, and appreciation of life; a heightened sense of purpose; and decreases in fear of death, in materialistic attitudes, and in competitiveness (Bauer 1985; Flynn 1982, 1986; Grey 1985; Greyson 1983, 1992; Noyes 1980; Ring 1980, 1984; Sabom 1982; van Lommel et al. 2001; see Chapter 3, this volume).

The major features associated with NDEs can occur in a wide variety of conditions in which the person is clearly *not* near death. However, despite the wide variety of physiological and psychological conditions under which NDEs occur, many such experiences clearly *do* occur when the brain is severely impaired. The common assumption in neuroscience has been that consciousness is the product of brain processes or that the mind is merely the subjective concomitant of neurological events. Near-death experiences, however, call into question that assumption. An analogy can be drawn with Newtonian dynamics, which appears to explain the physics of everyday life. It was only the investigation of extraordinary circumstances, involving extremely small or large distances, speeds, or mass, that revealed the limits of the Newtonian model and the need for additional explanatory models. So, too, with the question of the mind-brain relationship: Exploration of extraordinary circumstances such as NDEs may reveal limitations of the current model of mind-brain identity and the need for a more comprehensive explanatory model.

EXPLANATORY MODELS

The challenge for explanatory models for NDEs is to take into account the vivid and complex thinking, sensations, and memory formation under conditions in which current neuroscientific models of the mind deem them impossible, such as under general anesthesia and in cardiac arrest. This chapter briefly reviews some of the explanatory models that have been proposed for NDEs, paying special attention to how well they can account for the various features of NDEs (Kelly, Greyson, and Kelly 2007).

Psychological Theories

Expectation

Oskar Pfister (1930) offered one of the earliest psychodynamic interpretations of NDEs, describing them as a defense against the threat of death. Building on Pfister's theory, many other observers of NDEs have proposed a general model of expectancy, which suggests that NDEs are products of the imagination, constructed from one's personal and cultural expectations, to protect oneself when facing the threat of death. Prior beliefs apparently do have some influence on the kind of experience a person will report. The life review and tunnel sensation, for example, are common in some cultures but rare in others (Kellehear 1993; also see Chapter 7, this volume). Such cultural differences lend support to the view that the specific content of NDEs can be colored by the sociocultural context in which they occur (Ehrenwald 1974; Noyes et al. 1977; Noyes and Kletti 1976; Pasricha 1993; Pasricha and Stevenson 1986).

Other data, however, do not support the expectation theory. Experiences often run sharply counter to the individual's specific religious or personal beliefs and expectations about death (Abramovitch 1988; Ring 1984). People who had no prior knowledge about NDEs have described the same kinds of experiences and features as people who were more familiar with the phenomenon (Greyson 1991; Greyson and Stevenson 1980; Ring 1980; Sabom 1982). Experiences that were reported before 1975, when Raymond Moody's first book coined the term "NDE" and made it a well-known phenomenon, do not differ from those that occurred after that date (Athappilly, Greyson, and Stevenson 2006). And young children, who are less likely to have developed expectations about death, have reported NDEs with features similar to those of adults (Bush 1983; Gabbard and Twemlow 1984; Herzog and Herrin 1985; Morse 1983, 1994a, 1994b; Morse, Conner, and Tyler, 1985; Morse et al. 1986; Serdahely 1990).

Even the cross-cultural differences observed suggest that it is not the core experience that differs but the ways in which people interpret what they have experienced. Among both Indian and Western cases, for example, many people have reported being met by discarnate persons, although in the West these persons were usually either identified as deceased loved ones or unrecognized, whereas in India they have often been assumed to be messengers of the god of death. Similarly, in both cultures people have reported that they were sent back because it was "not my time." Whereas in the West people have often reported that they were sent back because of unfinished business, in India they were often sent back because the messengers of death were said to have inadvertently taken the wrong person (Osis and Haraldsson 1977/1997; Pasricha and Stevenson 1986). In short, there seems to be an underlying core experience that is "inevitably cast in the images, concepts and symbols available to the individual" (Roberts and Owen 1988, 611; see also Knoblauch, Schmied, and Schnettler 2001).

Depersonalization

Russell Noyes and Roy Kletti (1976), following Pfister (1930), suggested that NDEs are a type of depersonalization in which feelings of detachment, strangeness, and unreality protect one from the threat of death. However, they acknowledged that such a model fits primarily those NDEs in which the person was psychologically, but not physiologically, near death. Furthermore, Glen Gabbard and Stuart Twemlow (1984, 45–59) demonstrated that there are significant phenomenological differences between most NDEs and depersonalization. For example, in depersonalization, "the feeling of one's own reality is temporarily lost" (46), whereas many NDEs are described as being vividly real; most depersonalization is also unpleasant, in distinct contrast to most NDEs; and in depersonalization the experiencer may feel a certain detachment from the body without feeling actually out of the body.

Birth Models

Carl Sagan (1979, 1984), among others, interpreted NDEs—with a dark tunnel, a bright light, and going to another realm—as a memory of one's birth. Carl Becker (1982) argued, however, that newborns lack the visual, spatial, or mental capacities to register memories of birth experiences. Furthermore, many NDEs do not contain the features of a tunnel or a light, and many other common features of NDEs are not accounted for by these "birth" models. Finally, Susan Blackmore (1983) found that claims of OBEs and of passing through a tunnel to another realm were equally common among persons born by Caesarean section and those born by normal vaginal delivery.

Personality Factors

Attempts to identify personality traits that predict the occurrence of an NDE or its various features have been inconclusive. Near-death experiencers (NDErs) have collectively been found to be as psychologically healthy as people who have not had an NDE, and they do not differ in age, gender, race, religion, religiosity, intelligence, neuroticism, extroversion, anxiety, or Rorschach measures (Gabbard and Twemlow 1984; Greyson 1991; Irwin 1985; Locke and Shontz 1983; Ring 1980; Sabom 1982; see also Chapter 6, this volume).

Some researchers have examined personality variables related to hypnotic susceptibility, dream recall, or imagery, such as dissociation. Kenneth Ring and Christopher Rosing (1990) and Bruce Greyson (2000) found that near-death experiencers (NDErs) scored higher than a comparison group on a dissociative scale, but their scores were much lower than those of patients with pathological dissociation disorders. Near-death experiencers may therefore be persons who respond to serious stress with dissociative behavior that is adaptive, rather than pathological (Greyson 2001).

Related to dissociative tendencies is *absorption*, the ability to screen out certain features of the external world and focus one's attention either on selected sensory experiences or on internal imagery (Tellegen and Atkinson 1974), and *fantasy proneness*, characterized by frequent and vivid fantasies and even hallucinations, intensely vivid sensory experiences, and eidetic imagery (Wilson and Barber 1981, 1983). Empirical data regarding absorption and fantasy proneness among NDErs, however, have been equivocal. In any case, even a strong relationship between fantasy proneness and NDEs would not demonstrate that NDEs are nothing but fantasies. A tendency toward fantasy proneness or absorption might instead reflect an ability to enter more readily into altered states in which the ordinary relationship of consciousness to brain activity and the external environment has changed.

Physiological Theories

Numerous theorists have attempted to explain NDEs in terms of conventional biochemical or neurobiological mechanisms. They have hypothesized changes in the neurochemistry of the brain brought on by the physiological or psychological conditions accompanying a close brush with death and leading to abnormal neuroelectric activity in critical brain areas, usually the limbic system or temporal lobes. As researchers have learned more about the variations and complexities of the conditions under which NDEs can occur, however, they have moved noticeably away from attempting to find a single common mechanism underlying all NDEs and have increasingly recognized that "a multi-leveled interpretation is ... the most useful" (Jansen 1997, 13).

Altered Blood Gas Levels

One of the earliest physiological theories proposed for NDEs is that lowered levels of oxygen—hypoxia or anoxia—have produced hallucinations (Blackmore 1993; Lempert 1994; Rodin 1980). However, NDEs occur without anoxia or hypoxia, as in non-life-threatening illnesses, falls, or other near-accidents. Furthermore, the experiential phenomena associated with hypoxia are only superficially similar to NDEs. James Whinnery (1997), who compared NDEs to what he called "dreamlets" occurring in brief periods of unconsciousness induced in fighter pilots by rapid acceleration, argued that some features common to NDEs are also found in these hypoxic episodes, including tunnel vision, bright lights, brief fragmented visual images, a sense of floating, pleasurable sensations, and, rarely, a sense of leaving the body. The primary features of acceleration-induced hypoxia, however, are rhythmic jerking of the limbs, compromised memory for events just prior to the onset of unconsciousness, tingling in extremities and around the mouth, confusion and disorientation upon awakening, and paralysis (Whinnery 1997), symptoms that do not occur in NDEs. Moreover, contrary to NDEs, the visual images Whinnery reported frequently included living people, but never dead people, and no life review or accurate out-of-body perceptions have been reported in acceleration-induced loss of consciousness.

Other authors have suggested that increased levels of carbon dioxide—hypercarbia—may contribute to NDEs (Blackmore 1996, 74; Jansen 1997, 19). Melvin Morse, David Venecia, and Jerrold Milstein (1989, 48) wrote that "all the reported elements of NDEs can be produced in the office setting" with inhaled carbon dioxide. The only research cited in support of this claim is that of Ladislas Meduna (1950). Although Meduna did mention some features that occur commonly in NDEs, such as a sense of being out of the body, a bright light, a dark void or tunnel, revival of a memory, and a sense of peace, love, or harmony with God, he did not find other typical NDE features, such as meeting deceased persons or a life review. What NDE-like features do occur in hypercarbia seem comparatively rare and isolated. Furthermore, some authors have reported instances in which arterial blood gases in NDErs did not reflect lowered oxygen levels or heightened carbon dioxide levels (Morse, Venecia, and Milstein. 1989, 50; Parnia et al. 2001; Sabom 1982, 178). Finally, if anoxia and related mechanisms play an important role in the generation of NDEs, why do most cardiac arrest patients not report an NDE (van Lommel et al. 2001)? Clearly, anoxia is neither a necessary nor a sufficient condition for NDEs to occur.

Neurochemical Theories

Another proposed mechanism involved in NDEs is the release of endorphins or other endogenous opioids at a time of stress (Blackmore 1993; Carr 1981, 1982; Saavedra-Aguilar and Gómez-Jeria 1989). Endorphins may produce cessation of pain (Oyama, Jin, and Yamaya 1980) as well as feelings of peace and well-being, both of which are common in NDEs. However, most such neurochemicals produce long-lasting effects once they are released; the injection of endorphins produces pain relief for hours (Oyama, Jin, and Yamaya 1980). In contrast, the onset and cessation of the NDE and its associated features are usually quite abrupt, with the pain relief lasting only as long as the NDE itself, which may be only seconds. Furthermore, the release of endorphins fails to account for many other important components of NDEs, such as the OBE, seeing deceased persons, a life review, and the transformative aftereffects.

Other models have been proposed that might be more comprehensive in scope. Perhaps the most important of these has been the suggestion that a ketamine-like endogenous neuroprotective agent may be released in conditions of stress, acting on N-methyl-D-aspartate (NMDA) receptors. Ketamine, an anesthetic agent that selectively occupies NMDA receptors, can at subanesthetic doses produce feelings of being out of the body (Collier 1972; Rogo 1984) and can produce other experiences that resemble NDEs, such as travel through a dark tunnel into light, believing that one has died, or communing with God (Jansen 1997, 9).

However, unlike the vast majority of NDEs, ketamine experiences are usually frightening and involve bizarre imagery, and patients usually express the wish *not* to repeat the experience (Collier 1972; Johnstone 1973; Strassman 1997). Most ketamine users also recognize the illusory character of their experience (Fenwick 1997, 45), whereas NDErs are almost always convinced of the reality of the experience. Many important features of NDEs, such as seeing deceased people or a life review, have not been reported with ketamine. Furthermore, ketamine typically exerts its effects in an otherwise more or less normal brain, whereas many NDEs occur under conditions in which brain function is severely compromised.

Neuroanatomical Models

Behind most physiological theories of NDEs is the belief that abnormal activity of the limbic system or the temporal lobes produces NDE-like experiences. Morse, Venecia, and Milstein (1989), for example, proposed that imbalances in serotonin or other monoamines lead to abnormal activity in the temporal lobes. Juan Saavedra-Aguilar and Juan Gómez-Jeria (1989) proposed that hypoxia and psychological stress produce temporal lobe dysfunction and the release of endogenous neurotransmitters, resulting in analgesia, euphoria, and feelings of detachment. They claimed that "the list of mental phenomena seen in temporal lobe epilepsy and stereotaxic stimulation of the temporal lobe includes all the NDE phenomena" (209), and they described their theory as "a neurophysiological explanation for NDEs that is based on their striking similarity to temporal lobe epilepsy" (217).

Many people cite electrical stimulation studies, particularly those of the neurosurgeon Wilder Penfield, as justifying this belief in the "striking similarity" between NDEs and temporal lobe epilepsy. Morse and his colleagues (1989, 47), for example, wrote of "activation of areas of the temporal lobe that have been documented to cause mystical visions, out-of-body sensations, panoramic memories, and vivid hallucinations," citing Penfield (1955) and Penfield and Theodore Rasmussen (1950) as authority for this statement.

However, electrical stimulation of the cortex is *not* like physiological electrical activity and does *not* result simply in a localized "activation" of the stimulated region. As Penfield (1975) himself clearly recognized, its predominant effects are disruption of electrical activity in the immediate vicinity of the electrode, accompanied by abnormal patterns of discharge into additional cortical or subcortical areas to which the stimulated cortex itself is linked. These remote influences, moreover, may be *either* excitatory *or* inhibitory in character. The net result of electrical stimulation, as with epileptic seizures, is a poorly controlled, poorly characterized, and spatially widespread pattern of abnormal electrical activity.

Second, the experiences reported by Penfield's subjects, during electrical stimulation or epileptic seizures, do not show a "striking similarity" to NDEs. Most of the experiences Penfield reported consisted of hearing bits of music or singing, seeing isolated and repetitive scenes that seemed familiar, hearing voices, experiencing fear or other negative emotions, or seeing bizarre imagery that was often described as dreamlike (Penfield 1955; Penfield and Perot 1963, 611–65). Subsequent researchers have found similar experiential phenomena, especially fear and fragmented, distorted experiences quite unlike NDEs (Gloor 1990; Gloor et al. 1982).

Michael Persinger (1989) also claimed that "a vast clinical and surgical literature ... indicates that floating and rising sensations, OBEs, personally profound mystical and religious encounters, visual and auditory experiences, and dream-like sequences are evoked, usually as single events, by electrical stimulation of deep, mesiobasal temporal lobe structures" (Persinger 1989, 234). His sole reference for this strong claim was a paper by Janice Stevens (1982); that paper, however, was confined entirely to physiological observations of epileptic patients and included no mention of any subjective experiences or of electrical stimulation studies, much less of "a vast clinical and surgical literature" supporting Persinger's claim. Persinger went on to claim that using transcranial magnetic stimulation, he and his colleagues had produced "all of the major components of the NDE, including out-of-body experiences, floating, being pulled towards a light, hearing strange music, and profound meaningful experiences" (Persinger 1989, 234). However, the brief descriptions he has published of these experiences bear little resemblance to NDEs (for example, Persinger 1994, 284–85). His participants completed a questionnaire of items that Persinger called "the classic types of experiences associated with these experiments" (Persinger 1999, 96). Nearly all these items were completely unlike typical NDE features, and the few that might resemble them ("I felt the presence of someone"; "I felt as if I left my body"; "I experienced thoughts from childhood") were too vague to judge their similarity to NDEs. Furthermore, Pehr Granqvist, Mats Fredrikson, Patrik Unge, Andrea Hagenfeldt, Sven Valind, Dar Larhammar, and Marcus Larsson (2005; see also Larsson et al. 2005) were unable to replicate Persinger's results using Persinger's own equipment, and they concluded, "Suggestibility may account for previously reported effects" (Granqvist et al. 2005, 1).

The experiences reported in other brain stimulation studies inspired by Penfield's work also bear little resemblance to NDEs (Horowitz and Adams 1970, 19). Neurologist Ernst Rodin (1989) stated bluntly: "In spite of having seen hundreds of patients with temporal lobe seizures during three decades of professional life, I have never come across that symptomatology [of NDEs] as part of a seizure" (Rodin 1989, 256).

Out-of-body Experiences

The OBE, in which a person's consciousness is experienced as separated from the physical body, is a frequent feature of NDEs and may represent an early stage of the NDE (Lange, Greyson, and Houran 2004, 167). As with other NDE features, theories about OBEs have become polarized between conventional psychophysiological theories and a transcendental model in which consciousness functions outside the body. Psychophysiological theories generally suggest that abnormal activation of areas of the brain, usually the temporal lobes, produce alterations in body perceptions, leading to depersonalization and OBEs. As mentioned earlier, research frequently cited in support of a model in which temporal lobe stimulation produces an OBE is that of Penfield (Penfield 1955, 1958a, 1958b; Penfield and Erickson 1941; Penfield and Perot 1963), in which, in the course of stimulating various points in the exposed brains of awake epileptic patients being prepared for surgery, Penfield is said to have produced NDE-like phenomena (Blackmore 1993, 212–13; Morse et al. 1989, 47; Neppe 1989, 247; Tong 2003). Only two out of his 1,132 patients, however, reported anything that *might* be said to *resemble* an OBE. One patient said, "Oh God! I am leaving my body" (Penfield 1955, 458), and another patient said only, "I have a queer sensation as if I am not here ... as though I were half and half here" (Penfield and Rasmussen 1950, 174). Such experiences would hardly seem to be phenomenologically equivalent to OBEs.

Saavedra-Aguilar and Gómez-Jeria similarly claimed that OBEs "appear frequently in TLE [temporal lobe epilepsy]" (Gómez-Jeria 1989, 214), and they cited J. A. M. Frederiks (1969) as the reference for this statement. However, Frederiks made no mention at all of OBEs in connection with temporal lobe epilepsy. Indeed, in his discussion of disorders of the body schema, Frederiks specifically denied that such phenomena have been localized: "No well-defined anatomical localization has yet been established nor is any likely to be established because in most cases a large, bilateral or diffuse cerebral damage is present or diffuse cerebral dysfunction can be assumed" (Frederiks 1969, 233).

More recently, Olaf Blanke and his colleagues (Blanke et al. 2002; Blanke et al. 2004) have provided detailed neuroimaging results for six neurological patients, three of whom had experiences associated with seizure activity of verifiable origin or with direct electrical stimulation of the exposed cortex. Blanke and his colleagues described these experiences as OBEs. The imaging and stimulation results suggested involvement of a common cortical region encompassing the junction of temporal and parietal cortex (TPJ), a region that is thought normally to be involved in the integration of vestibular information with tactile, proprioceptive, and visual information regarding the body and its location in perceptual space. On this basis, the authors hypothesized that *all* such experiences involve failures of this integration, caused by "paroxysmal cerebral dysfunction of the TPJ in a state of partially and briefly impaired consciousness" (Blanke et al. 2004, 243).

The interpretation of the empirical findings of Blanke and his colleagues is controversial. First, the purported localization of neurologic abnormalities is less than clear. The identified region, the TPJ, is only a region of "mean overlap" of individual lesions that are distributed much more widely. Furthermore, the appearance of localization derives partly from mapping results from the very different brains of all five patients onto the left hemisphere of only one of them (Blanke et al. 2004, Figures 2 and 4). In one patient, no overt anatomical or functional defect could even be identified. Among the 29 additional patients for whom any information was available, the seizures of two were specifically localized to the anterior temporal lobe (which does not involve the TPJ), and only about a dozen were characterized in terms even loosely consistent with the hypothesis of Blanke and colleagues. Furthermore, there was no clear evidence of lateralization; among Blanke and colleagues' patients, the location of identifiable foci was almost evenly split between the left and right hemispheres.

Second, the generalization from these few patients with neurological problems to all persons experiencing an OBE, most of whom have no known neurological problem, is purely conjectural. Abnormal activity in the TPJ region or some other location may sometimes be *sufficient* for occurrence of an OBE; to conclude that any such activity pattern is *necessary* is dubious. Five of the six patients of Blanke and his colleagues (2004) suffered moderate to severe neurological pathology, but such pathology appears generally to be absent in the vast majority of persons spontaneously experiencing OBEs. A special OBE subject studied by Charles Tart (1968), for example, was specifically found to have a normal clinical electroencephalography (EEG).

Furthermore, even if we assume that cortex in the vicinity of the TPJ is involved somehow in the production of at least some OBEs, that cortex itself is probably not *producing* them. This is because both seizure activity and direct electrical stimulation of a particular region of association cortex typically disrupt whatever patterns of neuroelectric activity would otherwise be going on there. That is, seizure activity and direct electrical stimulation could explain the failure of the normal integration, but not the production of the abnormal one (the OBE).

Moreover, the vast majority of patients with seizures do *not* experience OBEs. In Orrin Devinsky, Edward Feldmann, Kelly Burrowes, and Edward Bromfield's prospective study (1989), only 6 percent of seizure patients described OBEs or other body image anomalies. Furthermore, although these patients had suffered numerous seizures, often over a period of many years, the majority who described OBEs reported only one experience. Only two of Penfield's 1,132 patients reported OBE-like phenomena. These findings suggest that localized abnormal activity in the brain is neither *necessary* nor, in general, *sufficient* to produce an OBE.

Finally, even if OBEs were shown to be associated with a certain region of the brain—something that is far from established—such localization cannot account for the occurrence of any complex perception or mentation at a time when the abnormalities in brain functioning would ordinarily abolish consciousness. As Devinsky, Feldmann, Burrowes, and Bromfield themselves cautioned, "An unresolved problem involves ... the paradox of apparent consciousness during the seizure" (Devinsky, Feldmann, Burrowes, and Bromfield 1989, 1087–88). To equate OBEs with pathological "body illusions," as Blanke and colleagues did, ignores the complexity of their physiological, psychological, and phenomenological aspects.

The cases that present the most serious challenge to explaining OBEs in conventional terms are those that involve the veridical perception of some event happening at a distance. Clearly, not all OBEs are veridical in nature, and most provide no evidence that they are anything more than subjective experiences. Nonetheless, some OBEs do include corroborated reports of perception of events at a distance (Cook, Greyson, and Stevenson 1998; Kelly, Greyson, and Stevenson 1999–2000). Hornell Hart (1954) analyzed 288 published OBE cases in which persons reported perceiving events that they could not have perceived in the ordinary way. In 99 of these cases, the events in question had been verified as having occurred, and the experience had been reported to someone else *before* that verification occurred.

In a few individuals, OBEs occur repeatedly or voluntarily, which makes their experiences amenable to observation under controlled conditions. Tart (1968) studied a woman who reported frequent sleep-related OBEs, monitoring her EEG in a sleep lab and asking her to try, if she had an OBE, to read a five-digit number randomly selected and placed on a shelf out of the range of her normal sight. She succeeded completely on one occasion, in which her OBE occurred in conjunction with a fairly well defined physiological pattern, developing out of Stage 1 sleep and consisting primarily of low-voltage "alphoid" EEG dominated by slow alpha frequencies, in the absence of the rapid eye movements characteristic of dreaming.

Karlis Osis and Donna McCormick (1980), working with a person who claimed to induce OBEs at will, conducted an experiment involving a specific task. While reclined with eyes closed and purportedly out-of-body, the subject was to view a randomly generated target in a remotely located optical image device in which the target appeared as an illusion visible only from a position directly in front of the viewing window; at that position, a strain gauge sensor was situated in a shielded chamber to measure changes in electrical resistance. Out of 197 trials, there were 114 accurate "hits," and strain gauge activation was significantly higher during "hits" than during "misses," suggesting that the subject had influenced the strain gauge remote from his physical body at the only point from which the target could be seen.

Results of the OBE research of Hart (1954) and Osis and McCormick (1980) suggest that veridical OBE perception may be not only subjectively but also objectively real. (This topic is further discussed in this chapter, but see also Chapter 9, this volume.)

Rapid Eye Movement Intrusion

Recently, Kevin Nelson and his colleagues (Nelson et al. 2006) suggested an association between NDEs and rapid eye movement (REM) intrusion, the intrusion into waking consciousness of mentation typical of rapid eye movement sleep. Nelson and colleagues noted that NDEs and REM intrusion share common elements of extraordinary light and a sense of being immobilized and alert to the surroundings, with a sense of being dead. They claimed that some aspects of NDEs, including autoscopy, light, visual experience, pleasant feelings, and transcendent qualities, can also occur in other conditions with an established association with REM intrusion.

To answer the question of whether NDErs have a greater lifetime prevalence of REM intrusion than other people, Nelson conducted a study involving a survey of an NDE group and a comparison group. For the NDE group, he invited self-reported NDErs, who had posted their NDEs on an Internet Web site, by e-mail, to participate in a study. For the comparison group, he interviewed people recruited from medical center personnel or their contacts who matched the NDEr group in age and sex. The survey consisted of four questions about REM intrusion symptoms: visual hypnagogic or hypnopompic hallucinations (seeing things as you fall asleep or wake up), auditory hypnagogic or hypnopompic hallucinations (hearing things as you fall asleep or wake up), sleep paralysis (finding yourself partially awake but unable to move), and cataplexy (sudden buckling of the legs).

Near-death experiencers said yes to three of these four questions more often than did the comparison group members, and the number of NDErs who said yes to a total of one or more questions also was greater. Nelson concluded that REM intrusion was more common in NDErs. However, the interpretation of this finding is not straightforward. Nelson's NDE sample, drawn from volunteers who shared their NDE on the Internet, may be atypical of most NDErs in their willingness to acknowledge unusual experiences publicly. Moreover, it is likely that questions about hallucinations imbedded for the NDE sample in an anonymous Internet survey of unusual experiences would elicit more positive responses than identical questions asked in face-to-face interviews with the control sample. Furthermore, the control group, "recruited from medical center personnel or their contacts," may have had reservations about endorsing hallucinations and related symptoms they would likely identify as pathological. This suspicion is bolstered by the control group's endorsement rate of only 7 percent for hypnagogic hallucinations, about one-fourth of that in the general population (Ohayon et al. 2002).

Data arguing against the contribution of REM intrusion to NDEs include many features, such as fear, typical in sleep paralysis but rare in NDEs, and the occurrence of typical NDEs under general anesthesia and other drugs that inhibit REM (Cronin et al. 2001). Finally, a correlation between REM intrusion and NDEs would not establish that REM intrusion contributes to NDEs. These researchers did not ask whether the REM intrusion symptoms had occurred before or after the NDE. It is equally plausible that NDEs enhance subsequent REM intrusion. Rapid eye movement intrusion is increased in post-traumatic stress disorder (Husain, Miller, and Carwile 2001), and post-traumatic stress symptoms are increased following NDEs (Greyson 2001). In light of these concerns, the association of REM intrusion and NDEs must be regarded as speculative, and any causal role of REM intrusion in NDEs must be regarded as doubtful.

PROBLEMS WITH PHYSIOLOGICAL MODELS

Despite the shaky foundations for assertions that NDEs are similar to experiences associated with abnormal temporal lobe activity, anoxia, ketamine, or endorphins, several multifactorial theories, based on these foundations, combine these putative causes at will to account for whatever constellation of features is observed in any given NDE. Blackmore (1984, 1993) and John Palmer (1978), for example, suggested that sensory isolation or increasing malfunction of the body threatens the patient's body image, leading the person to feel detached from the body, producing the illusion of watching what is going on around the physical body. The release of endorphins leads to analgesia and feelings of joy and peace. With increasing cerebral anoxia, the visual system may be compromised, producing the illusion of a tunnel and lights. Temporal lobe seizures may stimulate a revival of memories. Visions of deceased persons and of another realm are simply hallucinations produced by expectations of what will happen at death.

Although physiological, psychological, and sociocultural factors may indeed interact in complicated ways in conjunction with NDEs, theories proposed thus far consist largely of unsupported speculations about what might be happening during an NDE. *None* of the proposed neurophysiological mechanisms have been shown to occur in NDEs. A naturally occurring ketamine-like substance, for example, has *not* been identified in humans (Strassman 1997, 31). Moreover, some of these proposals, such as the role of expectation or the presence and effects of anoxia, are *inconsistent* with what few data we do have.

Near-death experiences were reported by only 12 percent of the cardiac arrest patients in the study of Pim van Lommel and his colleagues (2001), 10 percent in Greyson's study (2003), and 6 percent in the study of Sam

Parnia and his colleagues (2001). One may ask why most people, under conditions that may precipitate an NDE, do *not* report such experiences.

Part of the answer may be that many people who have NDEs are reluctant to talk about them. Additionally, in some cardiac arrest patients, physiological consequences may have blocked memory for any experience. Van Lommel and his colleagues (2001) noted that generalized memory defects were significantly more frequent (14%) among those who did not report an NDE than among those who did (2%). Among the remaining patients who appeared capable of reporting an NDE, what might distinguish those who did from those who did not? Van Lommel and colleagues (2001) found no significant effect on NDE reports of the resuscitation procedures themselves, that is, of factors such as the use of medications, intubation, and defibrillation. The occurrence of NDEs to only some people under apparently sufficient physiological conditions suggests the involvement of psychological factors.

Biological naturalism views the neuroelectric substrate for conscious experience as coherent high-frequency EEG oscillations linking widely separated regions of the brain. Empirical evidence supports these mind-brain correlations under normal conditions. However, the conventional *interpretation* of this correlation—that the neuroelectric activity itself generates (or *is*) the conscious experience—cannot explain how, in both general anesthesia and cardiac arrest, the neuroelectric conditions that are held to be necessary for conscious experience are abolished, and yet vivid, even heightened, awareness, thinking, and memory formation can still occur.

General Anesthesia

In our collection of NDEs, 127 out of 578 NDE cases (22%) occurred under general anesthesia, and they included such features as OBEs that involved experiencers' watching medical personnel working on their bodies, an unusually bright or vivid light, meeting deceased persons, and thoughts, memories, and sensations that were clearer than usual.

E. Roy John and his colleagues (2001) studied EEG correlates of consciousness and their changes during general anesthesia. They found that unconsciousness is associated with a shift toward lower frequencies in the delta and low theta range, with a more frontal distribution and higher power, and that high-frequency gamma-type EEG rhythms lost power and became decoupled across the brain when patients lost consciousness. These changes were reversed with return of consciousness, a pattern consistent with current neurophysiological theories reflecting disabling of the mind under anesthesia (Baars 2001).

This conclusion has also been supported by studies of blood flow, glucose metabolism, or other indicators of cerebral activity under general anesthesia (Alkire 1998; Alkire, Haier, and Fallon 2000; Fiset et al. 1999;

Shulman, Hyder, and Rothman 2003; Veselis et al. 1997; White and Alkire 2003). In these studies, auditory stimuli still activated their primary receiving areas in the cortex because the sensory pathways remain relatively unimpaired, but they no longer ignited the cooperative network interactions that accompany normal conscious experience.

Cardiac Arrest

Reports of NDEs in cardiac arrest, like those that occur with general anesthesia, include vivid or even enhanced sensation and mentation. However, in cardiac arrest, cerebral functioning shuts down within a few seconds. Whether the heart actually stops beating entirely or goes into ventricular fibrillation, there is instantaneous circulatory arrest, with blood flow and oxygen uptake in the brain plunging swiftly to near-zero levels. The EEG signs of cerebral ischemia are detectable within 6 to 10 seconds and progress to flat-line EEGs within 10 to 20 seconds. Cardiac arrest leads rapidly to the three major clinical signs of death—absence of cardiac output, absence of respiration, and absence of brainstem reflexes—and provides the best model we have of the dying process (DeVries et al. 1998; Parnia and Fenwick 2002; van Lommel et al. 2001; Vriens et al. 1996). Nevertheless, in five published studies alone, more than 100 cases of NDEs occurring under conditions of cardiac arrest have been reported (Greyson 2003; Parnia et al. 2001; Sabom 1982; Schwaninger et al. 2002; van Lommel et al. 2001).

Even with a flat-lined EEG, undetected brain activity could be occurring, as the EEG detects only activity common to large populations of neurons in the cerebral cortex. Certain electrical events, such as highly localized epileptic spikes, may not appear in scalp recordings (Niedermeyer and Lopes da Silva 2004; Pacia and Ebersole 1997). Moreover, recordings under anesthesia have shown that activity can appear subcortically or near the ventricles, even with an essentially flat scalp EEG (Karasawa et al. 2001). The issue is not, however, whether there is *any* brain activity, but whether there is the type of brain activity that is considered necessary for conscious experience. Such activity *is* detectable by EEG, and it is abolished both by anesthesia and by cardiac arrest. In cardiac arrest, even neuronal action potentials, the ultimate physical basis for coordination of neural activity between widely separated brain regions, are rapidly abolished (van Lommel 2004). Moreover, cells in the hippocampus, essential for memory formation, are especially vulnerable to the effects of anoxia (Vriens et al. 1996). Thus it is not plausible that NDEs under anesthesia or in cardiac arrest can be accounted for by a hypothetical residual capacity of the brain to process and store complex information under those conditions.

This is the most important objection to current psychophysiological theories: that mental clarity, vivid sensory imagery, a clear memory of the experience, and a conviction that the experience seemed more real than ordinary consciousness are the norm for NDEs, even when they occur under conditions of drastically altered cerebral physiology. As Sam Parnia and Peter Fenwick (2002) pointed out, "Any acute alteration in cerebral physiology such as occurring in hypoxia, hypercarbia, metabolic, and drug induced disturbances and seizures leads to disorganised and compromised cerebral function ... [and] impaired attention," whereas "NDEs in cardiac arrest are clearly not confusional and in fact indicate heightened awareness, attention and consciousness at a time when consciousness and memory formation would not be expected to occur" (8). Moreover, experiencers of NDEs in connection with cardiac arrest almost invariably retain vivid memories of their experience that change little with the passage of time (van Lommel et al. 2001), despite the fact that memory under such conditions is ordinarily seriously impaired. Most patients with temporal lobe epilepsy also have no memory afterward for what happened during a seizure (Fenwick 1997, 48). In brief,

> abnormal discharges in the temporal lobe may produce confusional fragments of phenomena sometimes seen in NDEs ... This is a very long way from arguing that seizure discharges in those areas, resulting from brain catastrophe, can give rise to the clearly remembered, highly structured NDE. (Fenwick 1997, 48)

Near-death experiences seem instead to provide direct evidence for a type of mental functioning that varies "inversely, rather than directly, with the observable activity of the nervous system" (Myers 1891, 638). Such evidence fundamentally conflicts with the conventional doctrine that brain processes produce consciousness, and it supports the alternative view that brain activity normally serves as a kind of filter, selecting material that is allowed to emerge into waking consciousness. On this latter view, the "relaxation" of the filter under certain poorly understood circumstances may lead to drastic alterations of the normal mind-brain relation and an associated enhancement of consciousness. We now turn to the empirical evidence for this interpretation of NDEs.

Transcendental Model

Many NDErs are convinced that during the NDE they temporarily separated from their physical bodies. The idea that some level of reality transcends the ordinary physical world is not inherently unscientific. Although it contradicts the assumptions of many contemporary psychologists and neuroscientists that the ordinary physical world *is* the only reality, several

NDE features suggest caution in making assumptions about the scope and fundamental character of the natural world.

Enhanced Mentation

Perhaps the most important of these features, because it is so commonly reported in NDEs, is the occurrence of normal thought processes, and even enhanced mental activity, at times when the mind-brain identity model would expect such activity to be severely diminished, if not impossible. Near-death experiencers often describe their mental processes during the NDE as remarkably clear and lucid and their sensory experiences as unusually vivid, surpassing those of their normal waking state. An analysis of 520 cases in our collection showed that 80 percent of experiencers described their thinking during the NDE as "clearer than usual" or "as clear as usual." Furthermore, in our collection, people reported enhanced mental functioning significantly *more* often when they were actually physiologically close to death than when they were not (Owens, Cook, and Stevenson 1990).

Another example of enhanced mental functioning during an NDE is the rapid revival of memories. In contrast to the isolated, often single, brief memories evoked during cortical stimulation, memories revived during NDEs are frequently described as being "many" or as an instantaneous "panoramic" review of the person's entire life. In our collection, 57 percent of those reporting memories said they had experienced many memories or a review of their entire life. Additionally, in an analysis of 68 published life review cases *not* from our collection, we found that in 71 percent of these the experience had involved memories of many events or of the person's whole life (Stevenson and Cook 1995, 455).

Veridical Out-of-body Perceptions

Near-death experiencers often report that during the NDE, they viewed their bodies as if from a different point in space. An analysis of 452 cases in our collection showed that 47 percent reported seeing their physical bodies from a different visual perspective. Many experiencers also reported witnessing events going on in the vicinity of their physical body, such as resuscitation attempts.

Most of these out-of-body perceptions are subjective phenomena, providing no evidence that the person had separated from the physical body and observed contemporaneous circumstances. Some commentators (Blackmore 1993; Saavedra-Aguilar and Gómez-Jeria 1989; Woerlee 2004) have argued that apparent OBEs are retrospective imaginative reconstructions based upon a persisting ability to hear, even when unconscious, or upon the memory of objects glimpsed before losing consciousness or while regaining consciousness, or upon expectations about what was likely to have occurred.

However, memory of events occurring just before or after loss of consciousness is usually confused or completely absent (Aminoff et al., 1988; Parnia and Fenwick 2002; van Lommel et al. 2001). Second, claims that adequately anesthetized patients retain significant capacity to be aware of their environment in more than rudimentary ways—let alone to hear and understand—have not been substantiated (Ghoneim and Block 1992, 1997). Despite occasional anecdotal reports of memory in anesthesia, usually attributable to insufficient anesthesia (Cheek 1959, 1964; Levinson 1965, 1990), controlled studies provide no convincing evidence that adequately anesthetized patients retain any conscious memory of events during surgery.

Partial awakening does occur in about 0.1 to 0.3 percent of general surgical procedures (Heier and Steen 1996; Sandin et al. 2000), but these awakenings are altogether different from NDEs and are generally extremely unpleasant, frightening, and painful (Osterman et al. 2001; Spitelli, Holmes, and Domino 2002). The experiences are typically brief and fragmentary, and they are primarily auditory or tactile, but not visual. Explanations of NDEs involving sensory awareness during anesthesia are even less credible when, as commonly happens, the sensory channels involved in the reported experience have been blocked, as when visual experiences are reported by patients whose eyes were taped shut during the surgical procedure.

Michael Sabom (1982) carried out a study specifically to examine the hypothesis that accurate out-of-body perceptions were retrospective reconstructions. Sabom had interviewed 32 patients, mostly cardiac patients undergoing cardiopulmonary resuscitation (CPR), who reported NDEs in which they seemed to be watching what was going on around their physical body. Sabom then interviewed a comparison group of 25 "seasoned cardiac patients" who had *not* had NDEs, asking them to describe a cardiac resuscitation procedure as if they were watching from a third-person perspective. In that study, 80 percent of the comparison patients made at least one major error in their descriptions, whereas none of the NDE patients made any but, in fact, related accurate details of idiosyncratic or unexpected events during their resuscitations (Sabom 1982, 87–115).

Another challenge to ordinary psychological or physiological theories of NDEs comes from experiencers' reports that while out of the body, they became aware of events occurring beyond the reach of their ordinary senses even if they had been conscious. In our collection, 60 people reported being aware of events occurring outside the range of their physical senses. Kimberly Clark (1984) and Justine Owens (1995) each reported a case of this type, and we have reported 15 cases, including 7 previously published ones and 8 from our own collection (Cook, Greyson, and

Stevenson 1998; Kelly, Greyson, and Stevenson 1999–2000). Some of these accurate perceptions included unexpected or unlikely details. In addition, Ring and Sharon Cooper (1997, 1999) reported 31 cases of blind individuals, nearly half of them blind from birth, who experienced during their NDEs quasi-visual and sometimes veridical perceptions of objects and events.

A frequent criticism of these reports of perceptions of events at a distance from the physical body is that they often depend on the experiencer's testimony alone. However, some cases *have* been corroborated by others (Clark 1984; Hart 1954; Ring and Lawrence 1993; Sartori, Badham, and Fenwick 2006; van Lommel et al. 2001, 2041). We have previously reported a case of this type in which the patient described leaving his body and watching the cardiac surgeon "flapping his arms as if trying to fly." The surgeon verified this detail by explaining that after scrubbing in, to keep his hands from becoming contaminated before beginning surgery, he had flattened his hands against his chest, rapidly giving instructions by pointing with his elbows (Cook, Greyson, and Stevenson 1998, 399–400).

Visions of Deceased Acquaintances

Many people who approach death and recover report that during the time they seemed to be dying, they met deceased relatives and friends. An analysis of 250 cases in our collection showed that 44 percent reported meeting deceased acquaintances during the NDE. Such experiences have been attributed by some commentators to hallucinations or to expectations or wishes to be reunited with deceased loved ones.

However, people close to death are more likely to perceive deceased persons than are healthy people, who, when they hallucinate, are more likely to perceive *living* persons (Osis and Haraldsson 1977/1997). Near-death experiencers whose medical records document their proximity to death were also more likely to perceive deceased persons than experiencers who were ill but less close to death (Kelly 2001). Moreover, many people also perceive unrecognized figures during the NDE. If expectation played a significant role, people would probably recognize the hallucinatory figures more often than was the case. In our collection, few people reported perceiving living persons, even though many of them commented that it was the thought of living people whom they were leaving that made them return to their bodies. Furthermore, although NDErs often perceive deceased people with whom they were emotionally close, consistent with the expectation theory, in one-third of the cases the deceased person was either someone with whom the experiencer had a distant or even poor relationship or someone whom the experiencer had never met (Kelly 2001). For example, van Lommel (2004, 122) reported the case of a man who had an NDE during cardiac arrest in which he saw an unknown adult male. He later learned from his dying mother that he had been born out of an extramarital affair with a man killed during war. Shown a picture of his biological father, he immediately recognized him as the man he had seen in his NDE, 10 years previously.

Converging Lines of Evidence

When examined in isolation, the features described in this section may seem potentially explainable by some psychological or physiological hypothesis, even though very little evidence exists that supports any of these hypotheses. When several features occur together, however, and when increasing layers of explanation must be added on to account for them, these hypotheses become increasingly strained.

A case that conspicuously exemplifies numerous features difficult to explain in conventional psychophysiological terms was reported in detail by Sabom (1998, 37–51). This case is also particularly important because Sabom was able to obtain verification from participating medical personnel concerning some critical details of the operation the patient reported observing during her experience.

This patient underwent hypothermic cardiac arrest (Spetzler et al. 1988; Weiss et al. 1998; Williams et al. 1991) for removal of a deep cerebral aneurysm that would have been fatal if it ruptured and that was inaccessible by ordinary neurosurgical techniques. Her eyes were first taped shut; then, following induction of anesthesia, her vital functions were constantly monitored, including EEG, electrocardiogram (EKG), arterial blood pressure and flow, and temperature from various sites, including her brain. Molded speakers placed in her ears, occluding the ear canals, were used to deliver loud clicks that permitted monitoring of her brainstem auditory-evoked potentials. After about 90 minutes, her skull was opened, and she was connected to a cardiopulmonary bypass machine. The circulating blood was chilled, her core temperature dropping 25° in about 10 minutes. At this point her heart was deliberately stopped and her EEG went flat. At 60°, her brainstem evoked responses ceased entirely, indicating "total brain shutdown." At this point, the surgical table was tilted up and the blood was drained from her brain so that the aneurysm could be safely removed. Following repair of the aneurysm, her blood was warmed and returned to her body. During the rewarming procedure, she went into ventricular fibrillation and had to be cardioverted twice.

By all conventional criteria this patient could be considered clinically dead during the main part of this procedure: Her EEG was totally flat, her brainstem auditory-evoked potentials had ceased, and blood was completely absent from her brain. Nevertheless, the patient reported an unusually detailed, prolonged, and continuous NDE that included some verifiable features: First, despite having speakers in her ears that blocked all external sounds with 95 decibel clicks, the experience began when she heard the sound of the special saw used to cut into her skull. She then seemed to leave her body and was able to see and subsequently describe the saw itself. She also noted the unexpected way in which her head had been shaved, and she heard a female voice commenting that her femoral vessels were too small for the cardiopulmonary bypass shunt. At some point, she felt herself being pulled along a "tunnel vortex" toward a light, she heard her deceased grandmother's voice, and then she saw numerous deceased relatives. Told by her relatives that she had to go back, and thinking about the young children she would be leaving, she reluctantly returned to her body. She also reported, "When I came back, they were playing 'Hotel California' and the line was 'You can check out anytime you like, but you can never leave'"—a choice of music that she later told one of her doctors had been "incredibly insensitive" (Sabom 1998, 47).

Her description of the unusual saw was verified by the neurosurgeon and by photographs of it that Sabom obtained. As the patient had heard, at the time the cardiopulmonary bypass procedure was being started, the cardiac surgeon, a woman, had commented that the right femoral vessels were too small to support the bypass, so that she had to prepare the left leg. Equally important, the patient reported that during her experience she was not only aware, but "the most aware that I think I have ever been in my life" (Sabom 1998, 41). She further commented that her vision "was not like normal vision. It was brighter and more focused and clearer than normal vision" (Sabom 1998, 41) and that her hearing "was a clearer hearing than with my ears" (Sabom 1998, 44).

The verifiable events this patient reported observing occurred when she was anesthetized and her eyes and ears isolated, but before and after she was clinically "dead." It is impossible to tell exactly when during the procedure she had the experience of going into a tunnel, seeing a bright light, and conversing with her deceased relatives, and we cannot say with certainty that any part of her NDE actually occurred during the period when she was clinically dead. Even so, the extremity of her condition and her heavily anesthetized state throughout the entire procedure cast serious doubt on any view of consciousness as totally dependent on intact physiological functioning.

The NDE just described occurred under both deep general anesthesia and cardiac arrest. Even if we assume that her entire experience occurred during the early stages of the procedure, when she was not yet "brain dead" but already deeply anesthetized, brain activity at that time was inadequate to support organized thinking, according to current theories.

Many physiological or psychological models of NDEs presume that NDEs occur, not during the actual episodes of brain shutdown, but just before or just after it, when the brain is more or less functional. However, unconsciousness produced by cardiac arrest typically leaves people amnesic and confused for events immediately preceding and following (Aminoff et al. 1988; Parnia and Fenwick 2002; van Lommel et al. 2001), and the confusional experiences recalled by people as they lose or regain consciousness do not have the life-transforming impact so characteristic of NDEs.

Furthermore, many NDEs contain apparent time "anchors," that is, verifiable reports of events occurring during the period of brain shutdown. For example, a cardiac arrest victim described by van Lommel and his colleagues (2001) had been brought to the emergency room comatose and cyanotic, and yet a week later, having recovered, he was able to describe accurately various circumstances occurring during the ensuing resuscitation procedures in the hospital.

One response of skeptics to verifiable time-anchor events is to dismiss the reports as mere "anecdotes," without value as scientific evidence. Many reports of veridical perception during NDEs are not simply vague or general statements, however, but contain very specific details, and the correspondence of these details with remote events is highly unlikely to have occurred by chance. Another skeptical response is to suggest that verifiable NDEs are inadvertent misreporting by the experiencers themselves or by investigators. That is always a possibility in individual cases. However, when this claim is cited repeatedly, *without supporting evidence, as a blanket defense against all such accounts,* it amounts to an unwillingness to examine that evidence in a scientific spirit.

CONCLUSION

The real challenge of explanatory models of NDEs lies in examining how complex consciousness, including thinking, sensory perception, and memory, can occur under conditions in which current physiological models of mind deem it impossible (Kelly, Greyson, and Kelly 2007). This conflict between neuroscientific orthodoxy and the occurrence of NDEs under conditions of general anesthesia or cardiac arrest is profound and inescapable. If scientific discourse on the mind-brain problem is to be intellectually responsible, it *must* take these data into account. Only when researchers approach the study of NDEs with this question firmly in mind will we progress in our understanding of NDEs beyond unsatisfactory neuroscientific conjectures. Similarly, only when neuroscientists examine current models of mind in light of NDEs will we progress in our understanding of consciousness and its relation to the brain.

11

Practical Applications of Research on Near-Death Experiences

Ryan D. Foster, Debbie James, and Janice Miner Holden

Integration of evidence-based practices is an increasing trend in the fields of medicine (Friedland 1998), nursing (DiCenso, Cullum, and Ciliska 1998), and mental health (Norcross, Koocher, and Garofalo 2006). Evidence-based practice is based on the assumption that practitioners in health care professions can provide the most effective and efficient care to patients or clients through the use of scientifically supported methods. If research into transpersonal phenomena—those that transcend the usual limits of space and/or time—is to be taken seriously by the mainstream scientific community, then researchers of these phenomena must follow the trend toward increasing empiricism (Scotton, Chinen, and Battista 1996).

In light of the movement toward scientifically based practice, this chapter reviews 30 years of near-death experience (NDE) research regarding practical applications in medical, spiritual, and mental health care settings with a specific focus on the scientific support for such applications. Then discussed are the therapeutic effects of the NDE on non-near-death experiencers (NDErs), followed by a section on incorporating NDEs into educational settings. Finally, the chapter concludes with a brief summary and implications for future research.

MEDICAL HEALTH CARE PROVIDERS

Medical practitioners and researchers have been reporting the NDEs of patients since the 19th century (Greyson 1998). In one hospital-based study, between 9 percent and 18 percent of patients who had come close to death subsequently reported an NDE (Greyson 1998). In another, more recent incidence study, Bruce Greyson (2003) investigated NDEs of hospital patients subsequent to cardiac arrest and other cardiac events. He interviewed them and administered the NDE Scale (Greyson 1983), a measure developed to distinguish NDErs from non-NDErs and to assess the nature and depth of NDEs. Greyson reported an incidence of 2 percent of the total sample of 1,595 patients. He also found that upon admission to the hospital, 10 percent of patients diagnosed with cardiac arrest reported having had NDEs. Other studies have reported similar incidences of NDEs in cardiac arrest survivors (Parnia et al. 2001; Schwaninger et al. 2002; van Lommel et al. 2001).

Greyson (2003) argued that incidence studies are limited in that they reflect only those patients who report NDEs and do not necessarily include everyone who has actually experienced NDEs. Near-death experiencers are often reluctant to report their experiences to health care providers, suggesting that the incidence of NDEs may be higher than has been reported. Though exact incidence is unclear, it is clear that a substantial number of patients have and disclose NDEs in hospital and other medical health care settings. Thus, medical care providers need to be aware of patients' needs when they report these experiences (Fremit 1989; Moody 1977, 1980; Moore 1994; Oakes 1981; Parnia and Fenwick 2002; Walker 1989).

One aspect of preparedness to respond constructively to NDEr patients is the medical health care providers' knowledge and attitudes toward NDEs. The primary instrument researchers have used to assess this domain is Nina Thornburg's (1988) Near-Death Phenomena Knowledge and Attitudes Questionnaire, designed originally for use with nurses. Thornburg designed her questionnaire also to assess the effect of nurses' attitudes on their care of patients who reported NDEs. Analysis of the 15-item instrument revealed acceptable reliability: Cronbach's alphas of .83 for the knowledge subscale, .84 for the attitude toward NDEs subscale, and .81 for the attitude toward patient care subscale. Reliability was not reported for the entire instrument. It also revealed acceptable construct and content validity but limited criterion validity. Whereas Thornburg asserted that no previous study provided a criterion reference (1988, 237–38), Roberta Orne's (1986) study had provided such a reference. Whether Thornburg not referencing Orne's study was an oversight in her literature review or was the result of a lapse in time to develop an instrument and publish results of its analysis cannot be known. As evident in the following sections, researchers have used this instrument not only with nurses but also with physicians and with spiritual and mental health providers.

Physicians

How can physicians adequately help patients who report NDEs? Raymond Moody (1977) conceptualized this question as "the essential clinical dilemma" (690). The first step that physicians must undertake is to become knowledgeable about NDEs (Fremit 1989; Moody 1977; Parnia and Fenwick 2002). Physicians' knowledge of NDEs, as well as their attitudes toward them, has been the focus of only two studies (Hayes and Waters 1989; Moore 1994). In a study of physicians, clergy, and nurses, Evelyn Hayes and Linda Waters found that 66 percent of 85 physicians surveyed reported themselves to be familiar with NDEs; these researchers did not assess participants' knowledge objectively.

In a survey of 143 hospital staff physicians (Moore 1994), participants completed Thornburg's (1988) Near-Death Phenomena Knowledge and Attitudes Questionnaire. Fifty-one percent of participants indicated that they had cared for a patient who reported an NDE. The majority of participants lacked adequate knowledge about NDEs: Only 16 percent met Linda Moore's criterion score of 11 out of 15 items that indicated sufficient knowledge about the phenomenon. However, inadequate knowledge aside, 65 percent of the participants indicated positive attitudes toward NDEs, and 51 percent of the participants reported that they would like to attend an educational offering on the topic of NDEs.

Moore (1994) acknowledged that a major limitation to the study was a return rate of 11 percent. Although she encouraged future researchers to use larger samples to explore physicians' knowledge and attitudes, her results from this study were promising. Whereas the majority of surveyed physicians lacked well-grounded knowledge about NDEs, a majority also wanted to learn more about the phenomenon. Forty-seven percent of the participants from Moore's study indicated that one of the ways future generations of physicians should learn about NDEs was through a course in medical school. (The inclusion of the topic of NDEs in medical school curricula is explored later in this chapter.)

After gaining an accurate and well-grounded knowledge base about NDEs, a physician is then adequately prepared to share with NDEr patients that other patients have reported similar experiences (Fremit 1989; Moody 1977; Parnia and Fenwick 2002). Simply acknowledging the existence of NDEs—normalization—is likely to help the patient feel a sense of comfort and relief. In addition, by validating patients' NDEs, a physician may instill in patients greater courage and willingness to share their NDEs with such others as family and other loved ones. Conversely, a physician who ignores patients' NDEs or dismisses them as meaningless hallucinations is likely to engender in those patients a sense of rejection and could even contribute to depression (Moody 1980; Ring 1984; Walker 1989). This felt sense of rejection may inhibit patients from any further disclosure of their NDEs.

As well as acknowledging patients' NDEs, a physician should actively listen to patients' verbalizations in a nonjudgmental manner (Moody 1980; Morse 1994; Walker 1989). This process includes demonstrating genuine concern for NDEr patients' emotional well-being by acknowledging and accepting the typically intense emotions associated with NDEs and the typically profound sense of meaning these experiences hold for NDErs. This validation is likely to lead to a sense of acceptance for patients. Finally, a physician's best practice is to listen and not to attempt to apply his or her own spiritual or personal meaning to patient NDErs. Rather, a physician can encourage patients to discover their own meaning from the experience. The somewhat more detailed recommendations nursing professionals have developed, described next, both correspond to and expand on recommendations directed to physicians, and the absence of empirical support for all such recommendations is important for health care providers to keep in mind.

Special Considerations for Children

According to Fremit (1989), physicians "often fail to give proper attention to the potential emotional impact of [NDEs] on children" (47). Children who report NDEs may have unique needs that physicians, especially pediatricians, need to consider.

Some pediatricians have suggested that physicians should give special consideration to the emotional state of child patients who report NDEs (Herzog and Herrin 1985). Because even adults consistently report their NDEs to be ineffable and report feeling challenged to convey adequately their experience in the limited medium of human language, the challenge for children is presumably that much greater. In addition, children may be apprehensive about verbalizing their NDEs because of conflicting emotions surrounding such experiences (Morse 1994a, 1994b). One of the reasons for such conflicting emotions may be related to the inability of children under 10 years of age to adequately understand the concept of death (Herzog and Herrin 1985). Children may be more likely to experience an NDE as a form of separation or abandonment. Because of the strong emotional impact that NDEs can have on children, child patients may need additional emotional support from their physicians.

One child verbalized her NDE to her pediatrician-interviewer only after illustrating pictures that depicted her NDE (Morse 1983). This single reported case of a specific intervention hints at the kind of clinical flexibility physicians may need to employ when working with child NDErs.

Nurses

Nurses are often the primary health care providers with whom patients come into contact (Oakes 1981) and the primary resources for patients with both medical and psychosocial needs (Milne 1995). The roles that nurses assume may explain why patients prefer to disclose their NDEs to nurses over other health care providers (Oakes 1981). Therefore, nurses, like physicians, must be accurately informed about NDEs and how to respond to patients who report their experiences (Barnett 1991; Bucher et al. 1997; Cunico 2001; McEvoy 1990; Orne 1986; Thornburg 1988; Trevelyan 1989).

In several studies, investigators have examined nurses' attitudes toward and knowledge of NDEs (Barnett 1991; Bucher et al. 1997; Cunico 2001; Orne 1986). In the first of these studies, Orne (1986) found that out of 912 participants, 70 percent reported being familiar with NDEs. Interestingly, of these, 89 percent did not respond accurately on tests assessing knowledge of NDEs. However, whether or not the participants had accurate knowledge about NDEs, they reported positive attitudes toward NDEs, suggesting a likely openness to learn more accurate information. Other researchers have found similar results (Bucher et al. 1997; Hayes and Orne 1990).

One limitation of Orne's study was the way she addressed one of the research questions she had posed: "Do knowledge and attitude influence nursing care?" (419). For this specific research question, she operationalized knowledge as "a patient's report of an NDE" (419) rather than as participant nurses' scores on tests of knowledge about NDEs. Therefore, the question of the relationship between degree of accurate knowledge of NDEs and quality of care of NDErs remained unanswered.

Linda Barnett (1991) used Thornburg's (1988) questionnaire in her investigation of hospice nurses. Barnett argued that hospice nurses "need adequate knowledge and attitudes in order to help clients deal with their emotional and spiritual feelings about the dying process and/or the NDE" (226). Out of 60 respondents, 63 percent reported having provided care for at least one patient who had disclosed an NDE. Barnett found that 52 percent of her participants had sufficient knowledge of NDEs. In addition, 100 percent reported positive attitudes toward NDEs. As in previous studies addressing the attitudes of physicians, most of Barnett's respondents stated that nursing education programs should include a required course on NDEs. (The application of NDEs in nursing education programs is addressed later in this chapter.)

Laura Cunico (2001) also used Thornburg's (1988) questionnaire in her study of nurses from three hospitals in Italy. Overall, the participants in the study scored poorly in their knowledge of NDEs. Cunico argued that because near-death research in Italy began roughly a decade after research in the United States, nurses in Italy may not have had as much opportunity to be informed as U.S. nurses. In addition, she pointed out that NDEs were not yet addressed in any nursing education programs in Italy. Clearly, the issue of adequate preparation in NDE-related knowledge is not limited to nursing education programs in the United States.

Nursing researchers and practitioners have reported best practices for assisting patients who report NDEs (Byl 1988; Callanan 1994; Cole 1993;

Corcoran 1988; Freeman 1985; Hayes et al. 1998; Lee 1978; Oakes 1981; Orne 1995; Sommers 1994; Trevelyan 1989; Vinter 1994; Wimbush, Hardie, and Hayes 2001). Overwhelmingly, nurses have acknowledged that NDErs should be allowed the freedom to report their experiences to nurses and other health care professionals. The following list represents a compilation of suggestions along with the frequency with which authors made each recommendation, beginning with the most frequent and ending with the least frequent:

- Be nonjudgmental toward patients as they explain their NDEs. (11)
- Pay attention to long-term impacts of NDEs on patients and make appropriate referrals to professionals who are familiar with NDEs. (9)
- Be alert to common signs of NDEs, such as changes in the patient's affect following an acute health crisis. (8)
- Be aware of personal attitudes toward NDEs. (7)
- Universalize and normalize the experience for patients; let them know they are not alone. (7)
- During resuscitation or painful procedures, touch the patient's hand. (7)
- Allow patients to tell their stories at their own pace; avoid probing. (7)
- Allow patients to express their emotions and to ask questions. (6)
- While patients are unconscious, do not use threatening or harsh language. (5)
- While a patient is unconscious, assign a nurse to stand near the patient's head and narrate what is happening to the patient. (5)
- As patients regain consciousness, begin reality orientation. (5)
- Discuss with patients how they want to reveal their NDEs to their families, including whether patients want nurses to be present at that time. (5)
- Support families of NDErs and refer them to appropriate resources. (5)
- Reinforce confidentiality. (5)
- Do not label patients or their experiences. (4)
- Provide accurate information about NDEs. (4)
- Avoid explaining or interpreting the meaning of NDEs. (3)
- Do not touch patients' heads, necks, or faces while they are unconscious. (3)
- As patients regain consciousness, provide reassurance. (3)
- Discuss patients' periods of unconsciousness in order to establish a climate for additional discussion if patients need to talk about their experiences. (3)
- Listen attentively and allow patients to complete their narratives. (3)
- Document patients' experiences on their charts. (2)
- Be attentive to the impact of NDEs on patients' immediate behaviors. (2)
- Be honest. (2)

Annalee Oakes (1981) suggested that NDErs seeking to disclose their experiences typically selected nurses whom they could trust. Based on the preceding list, however, only moderate consistency has existed among nursing researchers on how best to respond to patients who report NDEs. In addition, none of the preceding suggestions have been validated through empirical research. Furthermore, only two research teams have actually addressed the views of patients regarding nurses' supportive responses to NDEs (Morris and Knafl 2003; Schoenbeck and Hocutt 1991).

In a study of patients who underwent cardiopulmonary resuscitation, Susan Schoenbeck and Gerald Hocutt (1991) explored NDErs' perspectives of supportive nursing responses. The researchers used an interview format to ask participants questions about possible responses to their NDEs. To determine whether participants' experiences met the criterion for an NDE, the researchers administered the NDE Scale (Greyson 1983). Only one participant met the criterion of a score of seven or higher on the 16-item scale. From this one patient's perspective, a supportive nursing response included reassurance, universalization of NDEs, and active listening, where the nurse was open to listening to the patient's story and helped the NDEr understand the experience.

Linda Morris and Kathleen Knafl (2003) asked five patients who experienced NDEs what suggestions they had for health care professionals. The patients stated that labeling the experience as a symptom of psychopathology, such as hallucination, was not helpful. Additionally, patients recommended that health care professionals validate patients' experiences. The patients also wanted health care professionals to be aware that seemingly unconscious patients could often hear what nurses said. Therefore, according to these patients, nurses should avoid using provocative or inappropriate language during surgical or resuscitation procedures, in case patients are experiencing NDEs. Clearly, the patients' statements reflected some of what nursing researchers have included in their recommendations for nursing responses to NDErs.

SPIRITUAL HEALTH CARE PROVIDERS

In addition to physicians and nurses, NDErs in hospitals disclose their experiences to spiritual health care providers, such as clergy and hospital chaplains (Bechtel et al. 1992; Royse 1985). After release from hospital, parishioners who have experienced NDEs call upon spiritual care providers for counsel. David Royse (1985) surveyed clergy who represented 20 denominations of Christian affiliations from conservative through liberal theologies; the largest groups of respondents were Methodist (53%) and Catholic (9%). Of his sample of 174 spiritual health care providers, 65 percent reported having counseled at least one parishioner who had disclosed an experience that matched Moody's (1975) description of the

NDE. In a later study of 320 midwestern and northeastern clergy of Protestant, Catholic, Jewish, and unspecified Eastern faiths, 85 percent indicated having counseled parishioners that had reported NDEs (Bechtel et al. 1992). Limited in number and geographic representation, these two studies nevertheless provide an indication that clergy do and should expect to hear NDE accounts from their constituents. It is probably fair to say that NDErs are represented in every congregation; and as survival of medical and other crises continues, new NDErs will continue to present themselves.

To provide the most helpful service to NDErs, spiritual health care providers, like medical health care providers, must first become adequately knowledgeable about NDEs (Axelrod 1978; Bechtel et al. 1992; Royse 1985). Our extensive review of the near-death literature revealed only three studies that addressed clergy knowledge of and attitudes toward NDEs (Bechtel et al. 1992; Hayes and Waters 1989; Royse 1985). In the Royse study (1985), 52 percent of participants had read at least one book about NDEs. Unfortunately, Royse did not investigate the degree to which the participants were accurately knowledgeable about NDEs. Hayes and Waters (1989) surveyed clergy of unreported religions and found a slightly larger result: Of their sample of 103 clergy, 76 percent indicated familiarity with NDEs.

Lori Bechtel and others (1992) used Thornburg's (1988) questionnaire with their sample of 320 religiously diverse clergy. Ninety-eight percent of the participants reported having heard of NDEs. However, participants' average score on the knowledge scale was 7.8 out of a possible 15. The researchers concluded that this sample of clergy "lack[ed] a comprehensive understanding" (166) of NDEs. It also indicated that these clergy either overestimated their knowledge or considered incomplete knowledge adequate. Generally, however, the participants had positive attitudes toward NDEs, and half of them indicated interest in learning more about NDEs in formal settings, such as workshops. These results indicated that spiritual care providers both needed and were moderately willing to become more knowledgeable about NDEs in order to better counsel their constituents.

One well-established NDE aftereffect is potentially of particular relevance to spiritual health care providers: changes in NDErs' spirituality and/or religiosity (see Chapter 3, this volume). Several researchers have found that many NDErs experience profound changes in their spiritual experiences and/or beliefs, and that they may either greatly increase or decrease—even desist—in involvement in organized religion. In response to these aftereffects, NDErs may seek spiritual or religious guidance. Therefore, spiritual care providers should become knowledgeable about NDEs and how to respond when constituents report these experiences.

How should clergy and other spiritual care providers respond when a parishioner reports an NDE? In their survey of religiously diverse clergy,

Bechtel and others (1992) found 47 percent of respondents suggested that clergy should actively listen, without interruption, to constituents who report NDEs. Other authors agreed with this view (Axelrod 1978; Royse 1985; Sabom 1980). Other than this suggestion, however, we were unable to find further suggestions for clergy responses to NDEs in the professional literature. In addition, the research literature lacks sufficient scientific evidence to support any sort of clergy response whatsoever. This absence is a matter of particular concern because of certain NDE-related challenges specific to the spiritual health care domain. For example, a member of the clergy whom an NDEr has sought for counseling may feel challenged about how best to respond when the NDEr begins to explore disaffiliation from the clergyperson's religion—or organized religion altogether. For these and other reasons, it is particularly unfortunate that research on the practical applications of NDEs in religious and spiritual arenas is so severely lacking.

MENTAL HEALTH CARE PROVIDERS

It seems safe to assume that because a substantial minority of people who survive a health crisis or other precipitating event later report an NDE, NDErs likely are represented among counseling and psychotherapy clients and that a variety of factors may influence the incidence and depth with which NDErs disclose their experiences to their mental health care providers. Another safe assumption is that mental health care practitioners can provide a psychologically safe, nonjudgmental environment in which NDErs may feel free to disclose, process, and integrate their experiences. However, the NDE literature does not extensively indicate the incidence or depth with which NDErs actually disclose their experiences to mental health care providers. In fact, only one study included incidence of NDE disclosure (Walker and Russell 1989): Out of 117 surveyed psychologists who were registered with the State of Illinois Department of Registration and Education, 19 percent reported that they had counseled NDErs. The lack of recent scientific evidence regarding disclosure incidence is of concern because NDE "clients being seen in psychotherapy may have special needs" (Groth-Marnat and Summers 1998, 122); and those needs cannot be met, or even assessed, if clients do not disclose their NDEs and mental health practitioners are unaware of the presence of NDErs among their constituents and of factors related to whether NDErs will even disclose their experiences.

Another area in the NDE literature has received little attention: the extent to which mental health care providers are knowledgeable about NDEs. Barbara Walker and Robert Russell (1989) administered Thornburg's (1988) questionnaire to their sample. Eighty-one percent of participants were clinical psychologists, and 38 percent saw clients in private practice settings. The mean knowledge score was 7.5, indicating that most of the participants had incomplete knowledge of NDEs. In addition, whereas 88 percent of the participants self-reported familiarity with the NDE, many of them identified only one of Moody's (1975) 15 dimensions as aspects of NDEs. However, the participants generally reported a positive attitude toward NDEs, and many of them expressed the desire to learn more about the application of NDEs in clinical settings. Although this study contributed to an understanding of psychologists' knowledge of and attitudes toward NDEs, no researchers have as yet addressed these dimensions among such other mental health care practitioners as counselors, clinical social workers, and psychiatrists.

Addressing NDE Aftereffects in Mental Health Care

Numerous researchers have affirmed patterns of both intra- and interpersonal reaction, change, and even transformation among NDErs in the aftermaths of their NDEs (see Chapter 3, this volume). Intrapersonally, both immediate and long-term emotional aftereffects include sorrow, anger, confusion, self-doubt, and isolation. Psychological aftereffects include deep changes in NDErs' value systems, enhanced self-worth, and loss of fear of death. Spiritual changes include, as noted, changes in sense of spirituality and in spiritual or religious practices; they also include such enhanced psychic phenomena as empathic hypersensitivity to others, telepathy, precognition, and healing of both self and others. Physical aftereffects include a sense of having been physically transformed with such outcomes as a reduced need for sleep and the malfunctioning of electrical devices in the vicinity of NDErs. For a variety of reasons, some NDErs appear to integrate their experiences with relatively little difficulty, whereas others have reported that their lives were severely disrupted—sometimes for years—in the process of integrating their NDEs.

These intrapersonal changes can affect NDErs' interpersonal relationships in a variety of ways. Numerous mental health care practitioners and NDE researchers have asserted that qualified mental health care providers can help NDErs who seek counseling (Bonenfant 2001; Christian 2005; Greyson 1997, 2003; Groth-Marnat and Summers 1998; Insinger 1991; Musgrave 1997; Raft and Andresen 1986; Ring 1984). Providers can serve both NDErs and the people with whom NDErs have relationships by offering individual, family, group, or couple counseling (Greyson 1997). Following is a discussion of various studies in which the results held implications for mental health providers working with NDEr clients and patients.

Intrapersonal Aftereffects

David Raft and Jeffry Andresen (1986) conducted in-depth case studies of two NDErs. They found that both clients "wished to incorporate aspects of themselves that they had discovered" (330) as a result of their NDEs. However, both clients also expressed a need to grieve the elements of themselves they no longer wished to integrate into their senses of self after their NDEs. This finding supports similar views (Greyson 1997; Rosen 1976) that bereavement counseling may be a part of the therapeutic process for clients who have experienced NDEs, because they may need to grieve the loss of former aspects of themselves and/or profoundly pleasurable aspects of their NDEs. Because researchers have not yet studied this grieving process in NDErs, a full understanding of how any specific form of bereavement counseling can be integrated into mental health care settings does not currently exist.

Cassandra Musgrave (1997) conducted a quantitative study of 51 participants' life changes following their NDEs, with results that pertained to the issue of psychological distress for which NDErs might seek counseling and the issue of disclosure. The majority of participants reported that they became more helpful, compassionate, open-minded, and purposeful. However, 8 percent indicated that they were more depressed, and 2 percent reported that they had become more fearful. In addition, the participants revealed an interesting dichotomy. Whereas most of them reported life-enhancing NDE aftereffects, 76 percent reported fear of sharing their NDEs with others out of concern for being ridiculed or rejected. These results support the contention that part of mental health care practitioners' responsibilities toward NDErs is to be prepared to facilitate any emotions surrounding NDErs' fears of sharing their experiences with others—possibly including the mental health practitioners themselves.

In a study of 52 participants who reported having had NDEs, Gary Groth-Marnat and Roger Summers (1998) empirically studied changes in attitudes, beliefs, and behaviors. Compared to a control group of 27 participants who had come close to death but had not reported NDEs, the results indicated that experimental group members were less fearful of death and experienced increased levels of self-esteem. These results corresponded to other studies regarding psychological aftereffects of NDEs (Flynn 1982; Greyson 2000; Musgrave 1997). Thus, mental health practitioners might be less likely to encounter issues of low self-esteem and fear of death among their NDEr clients, perhaps especially those whose NDEs were predominantly pleasurable.

Other researchers have also found specific changes in attitudes and beliefs following NDEs related to preexisting psychopathology. Greyson (1981, 1992–93) found that people who experienced NDEs during suicide attempts subsequently underwent reductions in risk for further suicide attempts. Similarly, Greyson (2001) reported that symptoms of post-traumatic stress decreased in participants after NDEs. Also, Janet Colli and Thomas Beck (2003) presented a case study in which the recollection of an NDE resulting from an attempted suicide may have contributed to a woman's recovery from post-traumatic stress and bulimia nervosa. Thus, mental health care practitioners might expect the NDE to be in some ways an ally in clients' movement toward enhanced psychological health.

Distressing NDEs are of special concern because of their typically stressful aftereffects (Bonenfant 2001; Bush 2002; Greyson and Bush 1992). Richard Bonenfant presented a case study of a six-year-old boy who experienced a distressing NDE following an automobile accident. Afterward, the boy's parents "reported that their son suffered from restlessness, anxiety, and nightmares for months following his NDE" (93). In addition, Bonenfant indicated that the boy and his parents experienced post-traumatic stress in the aftermath of the boy's NDE. Other researchers have indicated that distressing NDEs can increase fearfulness in experiencers, requiring special consideration by mental health care providers (Bush 2002; Greyson and Bush 1992). (These special considerations are reviewed later in the chapter.)

Interpersonal Aftereffects

Because of the many intrapersonal transformations and emotional aftereffects that NDErs often experience, NDEs can also influence interpersonal relationships. Musgrave (1997) found that 78 percent of participants in her study indicated life-enhancing changes in their relationships, but she provided no additional information. Other researchers have investigated the effect of NDEs on family and spousal relationships (Christian 2005; Groth-Marnat and Summers 1998; Insinger 1991; Sutherland 1992).

Cherie Sutherland (1992) reported that the divorce rate of participants who had experienced NDEs in her study was nearly three times that of the general population of Australia. Mori Insinger (1991), in his qualitative analysis of the aftereffects of NDEs on spousal and family relationships, found similar results. Participants in his study reported that their spousal relationships terminated as a result of the inability of their spouses to cope with the NDErs' changes and the subsequent effect that the value differences had on their relationships.

Sandra Rozan Christian (2005) found an even larger quantitative connection between relationship termination and NDEs. In her empirical study of marital relationships, she compared a group of NDErs who used their NDEs as past referents to a comparison group of people who used their most profound non-NDE life-changing events (LCEs) as past referents. She found that 65 percent of the NDErs' marriages ended in divorce following their NDEs, compared to 19 percent of the marriages of LCE experiencers (LCErs). She also found low marital satisfaction, low marriage stability, and lack of shared meaning in the marital relationship as negative aftereffects among most NDEr participants. Near-death experiencers who divorced tended to report that their post-NDE values had resulted in a values divergence from their spouses. A minority of NDErs reported that their post-NDE value changes had resulted in a values convergence with their spouses, resulting in marriages they reported to be more satisfying and stable than before the NDE. Despite a flaw in the sampling procedure—more LCErs used more recent events as referents, thus allowing for less time for distress and divorce to occur—Christian's findings lend support to other investigators' research into greater incidence of primary relationship dissolution in the aftermath of NDEs.

Only one study conflicted with the contention that NDEs often lead to problems in spousal relationships. Whereas Groth-Marnat and Summers (1998) compared changes in marital status, researchers found no significant difference between NDErs and participants who underwent a life-threatening event without an NDE. However, the authors noted that this result could have been the result of the post-traumatic stress that can often accompany life-threatening experiences. Therefore, both groups of participants could have had marital problems but for different reasons.

Based on these results, mental health practitioners might expect NDEr clients who were in committed relationships at the time of their NDEs to report changes in those relationships as a result of the NDEs. The weight of evidence suggests that most NDErs would report greater distress, but some might report greater satisfaction. The results do not indicate how to treat couple relationship distress, but it is worth noting that empirically based marriage therapist John Gottman (1999) identified divergent core values, which he referred to as incompatible life dreams, to be one of the few cases in which divorce seemed to be indicated.

Near-death experiencers have also reported post-NDE conflicts with children, other relatives, and friends—the latter including a major or complete turnover in social relationships (Greyson 2000). Clearly, these conflicts could be NDErs' foci in counseling and psychotherapy.

Another likely focus is career change. It appears to be common for NDErs who were not engaged in social service careers prior to their NDEs to change to those careers following their NDEs (see Chapter 3, this volume). The impact of such a shift—especially if it involves the personal, interpersonal, and financial costs of reeducation—might reasonably become a probable focus in NDErs' counseling and psychotherapy.

Process Issues in the Mental Health Care of NDErs

Working from a single guiding theory of psychotherapy is generally an accepted practice among mental health practitioners (Fall, Holden, and Marquis 2004). Greyson (1983) argued that this practice should be no different when working with clients who report NDEs. The mental health practitioner's theoretical conceptualization of the NDE has "significance for our understanding of the individual's adaptation to the experience and its subsequent effects" (380). Theoretical conceptualization enables the mental health care provider to understand the "underlying dynamics" (380) of the NDE without attributing the experience to fantasy or hallucination. Theoretical interpretation does not mean that the mental health practitioner is labeling the client; conceptualization acts as a way for the clinician to understand, within a consistent framework, the ineffable experience of the NDE. Ultimately, theoretical interpretation benefits the client, because it also provides the mental health practitioner a way of conceptualizing healthy and holistic integration of the NDE.

Bette Furn (1987) introduced a cross-cultural model to conceptualize NDErs when she worked with this client population. She viewed the primary psychological issue that NDErs experienced in the context of adjustment. Viewed from a cross-cultural perspective, adjustment is a continuous process and has no determinable endpoint. Furn stated that the "common denominator" (13) among NDErs is that their worldviews transformed as a result of their experiences. As NDErs began to examine their changed worldviews, they experienced a form of culture shock. Eventually, through cross-cultural counseling, NDErs learned to respect and accept the qualities of their newfound worldviews as well as the worldviews of their dominant cultures, which were, in her experience, Western.

However, Furn's (1987) cross-cultural model drew some criticism. For example, Judith Miller (1987) argued for a client-centered approach in which NDErs and their mental health care practitioners would set no specific therapeutic goals. Miller disagreed with Furn's use of the concept of adjustment because it implied psychopathology. Finally, Miller denied Furn's assertion that the majority of mental health care providers already had the required proficiencies to work with NDErs. Instead, Miller suggested that "therapists identifying with different theoretical disciplines will necessarily have different values and will use different styles and techniques when working with NDErs" (36); she also suggested that these variations might prove to be more or less helpful to NDErs.

Indeed, guiding theories of counseling range from those that explicitly do not address subjective experiences like NDEs, such as classical behaviorism; to those that honor subjective experience without explicitly addressing transpersonal experiences, such as person-centered theory; to those that explicitly address experiences in the transpersonal domain, such as Ken Wilber's integral theory (Fall, Holden, and Marquis 2004). Hypothetically, therapists with a classical behavioral orientation would be least prepared to address process and psychoeducational aspects of NDEr care, those with a person-centered orientation would be prepared to provide process but not psychoeducational aspects, and those with an integral orientation would be most prepared to provide both; this possibility remains for future researchers to investigate. Although the debate about which theory or model of psychotherapy is the most appropriate fit for clients who report NDEs continues, one point is likely to be true: The adoption of a consistent, guiding theory for all of a mental health practitioner's clients, NDErs or not, and referral when the practitioner is limited in knowledge of or ability to address any phenomena, including NDEs, seems to be the most beneficial course of action.

Differential Diagnosis

Although theoretical conceptualization is important when counseling NDErs, attributing psychological causation to NDEs is unhelpful to clients seeking psychotherapy (Greyson and Harris 1987; Noble 1987) and can often lead to misdiagnosis of psychopathology. Therefore, mental health care providers must be aware of differential diagnosis of NDEs (Bates and Stanley 1985). During the development of the *Diagnostic and Statistical Manual of Mental Disorders, 4th edition* (American Psychiatric Association 1994), researchers proposed a new "Z Code" diagnostic category—addressing phenomena that do not involve psychopathology per se but do call for clinical attention—to incorporate issues stemming from spiritual or religious experiences. They designated these issues psychoreligious or psychospiritual problems (Lukoff, Lu, and Turner 1992). They argued that the diagnosis of adjustment disorder was inappropriate because many of the aftereffects of transpersonal experiences, such as NDEs, were "normal and expectable reactions" (679). Furthermore, they asserted that unsettling spiritual or religious experiences were not being addressed appropriately in training programs or by practitioners.

Near-death experiences have often been wrongly attributed to psychopathology (Greyson and Harris 1987). To further differentiate NDEs from psychopathology, Greyson (2003) incorporated an empirical research design in his study of aftereffects in a psychiatric outpatient population. A group comprised of 61 participants who had come close to death and had experienced NDEs was compared to a group of 211 participants who had come close to death but had not experienced NDEs. The participants completed the SCL-90-R (Derogatis 1992), an instrument designed to measure overall psychological distress in the week prior to completing the instrument. Participants who had come close to death but not had NDEs reported more psychological distress than did participants who had come close to death and had NDEs. The results indicated that NDEs were not causally related to psychological distress.

Greyson and Liester (2004) further separated the aftereffects of NDEs from psychological disorders in their investigation of auditory hallucinations. They compared NDErs who reported aftereffects that included auditory hallucinations to a sample of psychiatric patients with auditory hallucinations. Near-death experiencers had significantly more positive attitudes toward their auditory hallucinations than did psychiatric patients.

These results indicated that NDErs' auditory hallucinations may not always be pathological; thus, for mental health care practitioners to assume that auditory hallucinations are in all cases would be inappropriate.

Counseling Interventions

Mental health practitioners and researchers have published several suggestions for specific techniques when working with NDErs. In addition to advising individual, group, couple, and family counseling (Greyson 1997), many practitioners have encouraged the use of experiential techniques. Some practitioners successfully used hypnosis to assist NDErs in fuller recollection of their clients' NDEs (Colli and Beck 2003; Holden and MacHovec 1993). Though acknowledging the vast majority of NDErs who considered their NDEs real rather than dreamlike, Bush (2002) suggested that dreamwork techniques might be useful in helping NDErs come to deeper experiences and clearer interpretations of their NDEs. In response to the virtually universal report of NDErs that their NDEs were ineffable, Greyson (1997) encouraged the use of guided imagery or art to help NDE clients express emotions or thoughts that they are unable to communicate in words.

Aside from specific techniques, following are some general guidelines for mental health care providers when working with clients who report NDEs (Greyson 1997; MacHovec 1994; Noble 1987):

1. Avoid the assumption that clients' NDEs are symptomatic of pathology.
2. Provide a safe, nonjudgmental environment in which clients can freely discuss their experiences and emotions surrounding their NDEs.
3. Avoid projecting your own value system.
4. Normalize the experience for clients without taking away the uniqueness of the NDE. Practitioners have often recommended bibliotherapy (Noble 1987) or psychoeducation (Greyson 1997) for this process.
5. Assist clients with integrating their NDEs into their daily lives.
6. Refer clients to local NDE-focused groups, such as any of the more than 55 International Association for Near-Death Studies (IANDS) groups, most in the United States but a few in various countries around the world (www.iands.org).

These suggestions are specific to mental health practitioners and are probably best considered along with the overlapping suggestions presented in the earlier discussion on medical health care providers.

Conducting studies of NDErs' disclosure habits and needs, Regina Hoffman (1995a, 1995b) was the first to provide scientific support for the general guidelines listed earlier. Hoffman interviewed 50 NDErs in her qualitative study of disclosure. The results indicated that disclosure needs of NDErs are often stagelike. Near-death experiencers underwent an initial varying degree of shock or surprise, followed by a need for validation of the experience. Then, NDErs began to notice the effects of their experiences on their daily lives. In the next stage, active exploration, experiencers investigated the philosophical, spiritual, and psychological implications of their experiences. Finally, they reached the integration stage, where they were increasingly able to own and apply their experiences to their lives in a holistic manner. Hoffman asserted that mental health care providers must be prepared to assist clients in their struggles and successes during any or all of these stages.

In addition, Hoffman (1995a) found several commonalities among NDErs when they decided with whom to share their NDEs. Her research participants indicated that rejection of their experiences was especially detrimental during initial disclosures. Participants also reported that catharsis was an important beneficial aspect of their disclosures. Finally, these NDErs looked for several qualities when considering to whom they would disclose their NDEs: willingness to consider serious thanatological matters, open-mindedness, nonjudgmental respect, and appreciation for the value of their experiences. These results support many of the general guidelines for mental health practitioners listed earlier.

Special Considerations for Distressing Near-Death Experiences

Nancy Evans Bush (2002) presented special considerations when working with clients who reported distressing NDEs. Because distressing NDEs can be terrifying or frightening experiences, clients may have an intense need to find meaning from their experiences. One of the ways therapists can assist in this process is by using archetypes and symbols to make connections between clients' intrapersonal conflicts and their transpersonal experiences. Bush suggested, "If the experience can expand fully, a positive [therapeutic] experience is likely to emerge" (124). She also argued, however, that no value judgments should be made about clients' frightening experiences. Ultimately, clients may need to work through any preexisting intrapersonal or interpersonal issues to fully and meaningfully integrate their NDEs into their daily lives (see also Chapter 4, this volume).

THE THERAPEUTIC EFFECTS OF NDEs ON NON-NDErs

Authors have suggested that NDEs could have therapeutic effects on non-NDErs by reducing suicidal ideation (Ring and Franklin 1981–82; Winkler 2003), providing "supportive preparation for those facing combat" (Sullivan 1984, 151), comforting people with terminal illnesses (Vinter 1994), and assisting in the grief process (Horacek 1997; McDonagh 2004).

Anecdotal evidence that supports the therapeutic effects of NDEs on non-NDErs does exist in the literature. Bruce Horacek presented seven case studies in which personal knowledge of NDEs assisted in the bereavement processes of surviving loved ones of people who had died. Three categories related to non-NDErs emerged: In the first category were NDErs who just before dying shared their NDEs with loved ones, which helped the loved ones through the grieving process when the NDErs actually died; in the second, general knowledge of NDEs was found to reduce death anxiety; and in the third, general knowledge of NDEs assisted the grieving processes of loved ones of non-NDErs who had died.

John McDonagh (2004) offered similar results in a review of his experiences as a therapist using NDEs psychoeducationally. He often presented videotaped interviews of NDErs to clients grieving the losses of loved ones. He found that this process not only comforted his clients but also "generate[d] movement on personal issues that [went] beyond the grieving process" (272). McDonagh also used these videotapes with clients who presented suicidal ideation, and he reported profound reductions in such thoughts and behaviors.

In addition, Engelbert Winkler (2003) presented a case study of a nine-year-old boy, Patrick, who was suicidal as a result of his father's recent suicide. Winkler compiled an illustrated book about NDEs written for children, and he shared it with the boy. Subsequently, Patrick's suicidal ideation disappeared.

However, in a study of the effect of NDEs on college students, Kenneth Ring (1995) published a bold statement regarding the state of NDE research:

> It's curious that for all the work that has so far been reported on the effects of near-death experiences on the experiencers themselves, there has been almost nothing published in the literature concerning how nonexperiencers are affected by their exposure to information about NDEs. (223)

Ring called for more research regarding the utilization of NDEs for non-NDErs. Yet, over 10 years after the publication of Ring's small-scale study, little scientific evidence exists in the NDE literature regarding this area.

The lack of empirical research is surprising, given the results of Ring's study (1995) and a similar study by Charles Flynn (1986). Flynn included reference to NDEs among students in his undergraduate sociology classes at Miami University of Ohio: Of 428 undergraduates, over 80 percent reported an increased sense of compassion, and 65 percent reported an increased sense of self-worth—effects that in follow-up assessment one year later tended to persist with some reduction.

Ring (1995) summarized findings from three sections of two undergraduate courses specifically on the topic of NDEs: two sections at the University of Connecticut and one at Montana State University. At the end of the courses, most of the total 111 students indicated being more convinced of the authenticity of NDEs, reported a decrease in their fear of death, affirmed they had a more positive view of death, indicated they were more convinced of "some form of conscious existence following physical death" (229), indicated they were more spiritually oriented, said that their ideas about God had changed—some specifically stating their view of God had strengthened and either zero or one student in each class reporting it had weakened—and indicated an increase in their belief in the purposefulness of life. Despite some methodological issues, the results from this study and other anecdotal evidence presented in this section indicate that the effects of NDEs on non-NDErs, whether in educational, therapeutic, or other settings, is a fruitful subject for future empirical research.

EDUCATIONAL SETTINGS

As noted earlier in this chapter, results from surveys of professionals from a variety of disciplines have indicated support for inclusion of curricula on near-death experiences into such professional educational settings as medical schools (Moore 1994), nursing programs (Barnett 1991), schools of theology (Bechtel et al. 1992), and mental health training programs (Walker and Russell 1989). Results from a study of physicians, clergy, and nurses indicated that 75 percent of the participants wanted to learn more information about NDEs (Hayes and Waters 1989). Regarding nonprofessional educational settings, Glenn Richardson (1979) reported a case in which a high school health course included the topic of NDEs in the curriculum, and as previously described, Ring (1995) and Flynn (1986) reported on their inclusion of NDE-related curricula in undergraduate education. Although researchers have encouraged educators to include NDEs in courses related to death education, as of 1989, at least, Hayes and Waters (1989) found that NDEs were rarely taught in secondary, undergraduate, or graduate health care programs.

If educators were to consider including an NDE curriculum in their course offerings, what would they include? In Ring's (1995) semester-long undergraduate course on NDEs, which he taught from 1985 to 1994 at the University of Connecticut, he instructed students to write a journal throughout the course to maintain a record of their reactions to the class lectures and assignments. In the beginning of the course, Ring provided general information about NDEs in a lecture format, followed by videos of interviews with NDErs. Next, three NDErs came to class and shared their experiences, after which students participated in small-group discussions. Later in the semester, Ring presented didactic material regarding NDE-related transpersonal experiences and NDE aftereffects. Three additional NDErs came to class to discuss their aftereffects, and NDE researchers also visited the class.

Although most universities likely do not have the faculty resources that the University of Connecticut had with Kenneth Ring, some of his methods of teaching about the NDE could be introduced into similar courses. Departments of psychology, sociology, and counseling could integrate brief learning sections on the NDE in courses related to loss and grief, religion or spirituality, and multiculturalism. Coauthor of this chapter Ryan D. Foster, in a recent counseling program graduate course that included the topic of NDEs, found the NDEr panel the most emotionally impactful of a four-hour class that included the movie *The Day I Died: The Mind, the Brain, and Near-Death Experiences* (Broome 2002; Holden 2005; Holden, MacLurg, and James 2006); didactic material provided in the class notes packet; and class discussion. However, generalizations about the relative value of various educational activities on various aspects of knowledge and attitudes toward NDEs remain the foundation of future research.

One reason that the helping professions have apparently not yet extensively integrated NDEs into educational settings may be because few teaching models exist. In the past 30 years, only two articles have included guidelines for teaching about NDEs to students in professional training programs. Whereas in the literature no teaching models exist for schools of theology, psychology, social work, or counselor education, there are clear models for schools of nursing (McEvoy 1990) and schools of medicine (Sheeler, 2005).

Mary Dee McEvoy (1990) presented a model of teaching NDEs in schools of nursing. Included in her model was the objective to teach nurses a "pragmatic way of talking with patients about it" (53). Her recommended guidelines are simple:

1. The student should have an understanding of the nature of the near-death experience and subsequent impact on patients.
2. The student should have an understanding of his or her personal beliefs and attitudes relating to the paranormal and transcendental aspects of the NDE.
3. The student should develop strategies to assist the patient in discussion of the NDE. (54)

McEvoy encouraged schools of nursing to integrate NDEs into courses that address the topic of death and dying.

Robert Sheeler (2005) developed and tested a teaching model for NDEs in medical schools. His teaching model included a media component, a lecture component, and a discussion component. During the media component, Sheeler showed students a videotaped interview of an NDEr describing his experience. Next, he gave an in-class lecture about common elements of NDEs and their aftereffects. Finally, he provided students with two discussion opportunities: in-class and online. In the class discussions, he divided students into groups and instructed them to discuss several scenarios that involved NDEs. In the online discussions, students individu-ally posted discussion responses on a university-based online Internet fo-rum. After testing the model for two years, Sheeler concluded that "from a faculty standpoint the exercise was successful" (246), because the students reported a greater understanding of the "patient-centered approach."

As previously mentioned, the British Broadcasting Corporation docu-mentary *The Day I Died: The Mind, the Brain, and Near-Death Experiences* (Broome 2002) is available for purchase to use in educational settings in the United States. To the present authors' knowledge, it is the only NDE-related teaching resource to date that includes an instructor's guide (Holden 2005) and that health professionals have reviewed with special attention to its possible inclusion in general professional preparatory and educational settings (Holden, MacLurg, and James 2006). The value of this particularly promising resource remains to be established through future research.

Considering together these few reports in the professional literature, a curriculum about NDEs can include didactic material in print as well as lecture form; media including commercial productions as well as noncom-mercial interviews of NDErs; guest speakers with content knowledge of NDEs; NDEr guest speakers; and class discussion, both in-class and online. Numerous Internet sources now exist on NDEs, including several NDEr testimonials. Preliminary studies have indicated the value of various approaches in both general and professional educational settings, and fur-ther investigation remains opportune.

SUMMARY AND IMPLICATIONS FOR FUTURE RESEARCH

In 1981, Craig Lundahl proposed that the clinical application of NDE research should be one of NDE researchers' major foci. Other researchers soon echoed this assertion (Serdahely, Drenk, and Serdahely 1988). Nearly 30 years later, this admonition still holds true. With the increasing trend toward empirically validated practices in medicine, nursing, and mental health care settings, NDE researchers must support practical applications of NDE research with sound scientific evidence.

Following the 1984 International Association for Near-Death Studies (IANDS) Conference, experts in the field of near-death studies drew on personal experience and anecdotal reports to produce several general guidelines for helping professionals to follow when caring for NDErs (Greyson and Harris 1987). They concurred that helping professionals should act and react sensitively by following these guidelines:

1. Explore their own attitudes toward NDEs.
2. Avoid forcing their own value systems onto NDErs.

3. Respect the profound nature of these experiences as well as the individuality of each experiencer.
4. Avoid labeling NDEs and NDErs with pathological diagnoses.
5. Maintain an honest, nonjudgmental attitude toward NDErs.
6. Provide a safe, confidential atmosphere.
7. Encourage NDErs to express their emotions surrounding both their NDEs and any precipitating events.

The collaborators also outlined many specific interventions for both short-term care providers and long-term care providers.

Although the preceding list of general guidelines appears to be quite useful when caring for NDErs in medical, spiritual, or mental health care settings, relatively few researchers have focused on scientifically testing these guidelines or any other specific interventions. In the case of the guidelines, one reason for the absence of research may be that they seem to reflect common sense. However, rarely do scholars and educators in health care professions teach scientists- and practitioners-in-training to function based on common sense. If the mainstream scientific community is to incorporate clinical interventions with NDErs, this rarity of research on both general approaches to and specific interventions with NDErs must be remedied through future research.

Whether or not the NDE research community prefers mainstream status is not the only reason behind our encouragement of future empirical investigation. Another, even greater reason is that NDErs are likely to receive the best care when the effectiveness of that care has been scientifically validated. In addition, NDEs are so profound in nature that non-NDErs could likely benefit from learning, understanding, and applying these experiences to their own lives. If the greatest source of information about NDEs is such mass media as television, nonscholarly publications, Internet forums, and fringe skeptics, inaccurate and unsubstantiated knowledge will likely continue to propagate.

The review presented in this chapter provides some evidence that medical and spiritual health care providers are only somewhat familiar with NDEs and that what they do know seems only partially accurate. Overall, those professionals seem to have positive attitudes toward NDEs and want to learn more about them. Providing a high-quality knowledge base for those helping professionals who yearn for more accurate information is the job of NDE researchers.

The evidence that exists about medical and spiritual health care providers' knowledge and attitudes toward NDEs is not current, however, and researchers have not yet investigated those domains among such key health care providers as chaplains and mental health professionals. Thus those research foci are ripe for investigation. Also lacking is knowledge of the incidence of attention to NDEs in spiritual care and mental health care settings. The coauthors of this chapter encourage future researchers to perform knowledge, attitude, and incidence studies in these populations and settings.

Professional preparatory schools of medicine, nursing, and mental health are increasingly teaching from a scientist-practitioner model. Thus, professional educators in these settings are looking to NDE research for the most rigorous empirical research to guide them in evidence-based health care of their constituents who have disclosed these singularly profound experiences. Although the physician, nursing, and mental health literature contains suggestions for best practices, research on the efficacy of these suggestions is virtually absent. In addition, suggestions for clergy and chaplains are nonexistent. All those areas are potential sources of inquiry for NDE researchers.

Even more specifically, counselors and psychologists must know how to carry out the process of psychotherapy with clients who report NDEs. Researchers should perform outcome studies on the most effective and beneficial methods to assist clients in holistically understanding and integrating NDEs into their daily lives. One promising topic of investigation is the grieving process that NDErs sometimes experience as a result of assuming new value systems and shedding old ones. Also, more exploration is needed on the effects of NDEs on experiencers' loved ones and relational systems. Intervention studies on methods to help systems assimilate and accommodate healthful change could reveal highly useful information.

Another future focus for NDE researchers is the therapeutic effects of NDEs on non-NDErs. Understanding NDEs might help a variety of people, such as the terminally ill, the bereaved, soldiers preparing for combat, the aging, and people contemplating suicide—as well as members of the general public, all of whom face death. Anecdotal evidence supports a need for empirical research in all these domains.

Finally, what little evidence exists about including the topic of NDEs in undergraduate curricula is encouraging regarding its potential benefits. This evidence justifies further investigation into the incidence and effects of attention to NDEs in not only undergraduate but also public school and graduate education. In addition, researchers could contribute by investigating the effects of such existing educational tools as video productions and by developing and investigating yet such others as additional video productions and lecture materials. One question is whether any video production of NDErs' testimonials can hold equivalent impact to hearing those testimonials and talking with NDErs in person. These questions apply equally, if not even more pressingly, to professional education settings.

The future of practical applications of NDE research is wide open for development. Researchers interested in contributing to this area of inquiry might take their inspiration from the majority of NDErs who report increases in such characteristics as open-mindedness, sense of meaning, and desire to impact others' inner and outer worlds positively. Researchers who embrace these qualities have 30 years of promising research to support the next level of scientific inquiry. It is our hope that they embark on the next 30 years with a grand vision of how the world could be changed for the good through the application of methodologically sound NDE research.

References

CHAPTER 1

Athappilly, G. K., Greyson, B., and Stevenson, I. 2006. Do prevailing societal models influence reports of near-death experiences? *Journal of Nervous and Mental Disease* 194:218–22.

Barrow, J. 1847. Admiral Beaufort's letter to Dr. W. H. Wollaston. In *An autobiographical memoir of Sir John Barrow*, 398–403. London: John Murray.

Cardeña, E., Lynn, S. J., and Krippner, S. (Eds.). 2000. *Varieties of anomalous experience: Examining the scientific evidence*. Washington, DC: American Psychological Association.

Clarke, E. H. 1878. *Visions: A study of false sight (pseudopia)*. Boston: Houghton, Osgood & Co.

Cobbe, F. P. 1882. *Peak in Darien*. Boston: George H. Ellis.

Cozzens, S. W. 1873. *The marvelous country: Three years in Arizona and New Mexico*. Boston: Shepard & Gill.

Douglas, M., and Bieber, R. (Producers), and Schumacher, J. (Director). 1990. *Flatliners* [motion picture]. Hollywood, CA: Columbia Pictures.

Fenwick, P., and Fenwick, E. 1995. *The truth in the light*. New York: Berkley Books.

Grey, M. 1985. *Return from death*. London: Arkana.

Greyson, B. 1983. The Near-Death Experience Scale: Construction, reliability, and validity. *Journal of Nervous and Mental Disease* 171:369–75.

Greyson, B. 2007. Consistency of near-death experience accounts over two decades: Are reports embellished over time? *Resuscitation* 73:407–11.

Greyson, B., and Bush, N. E. 1992. Distressing near-death experiences. *Psychiatry* 55:95–110.

Greyson, B., and Flynn, C. P. (Eds.). 1984. *The near-death experience: Problems, prospects, perspectives*. Springfield, IL: Charles C. Thomas.

Hampe, J. C. 1979. *To die is gain: The experience of one's own death*. Trans. M. Kohl. Atlanta, GA: John Knox Press.

Heim, A. 1892. Notizen über den Tod durch Absturz [Remarks on fatal falls]. *Jahrbuch der Schweizerischen Alpclub* [Yearbook of the Swiss Alpine Club] 21:327–37.

Holden, J. M., and Christian, R. 2005a. *Near-death experiences: Index to the periodical literature through 2001*. East Windsor Hill, CT: International Association for Near-Death Studies.

Holden, J. M., and Christian, R. 2005b. The field of near-death studies through 2001: An analysis of the periodical literature. *Journal of Near-Death Studies* 24:21–34.

Hyslop, J. H. 1907. Visions of the dying. *Journal of the American Society for Psychical Research* 1:45–55.

Hyslop, J. H. 1918. Death visions. *Journal of the American Society for Psychical Research* 12 (6): 375–91.

Hyslop, J. H. 1918. Visions of the dying: Class I. *Journal of the American Society for Psychical Research* 12 (10): 585–626.

Hyslop, J. H. 1918. Visions of the dying: Class II. *Journal of the American Society for Psychical Research* 12 (10): 626–37.

Kelly, E. F., Kelly, E. W., Crabtree, A., Gauld, A., Grosso, M., and Greyson, B. 2007. *Irreducible mind: Toward a psychology for the 21st century*. Lanham, MD: Rowman & Littlefield.

Lange, R., Greyson, B., and Houran, J. 2004. A Rasch scaling validation of a "core" near-death experience. *British Journal of Psychology* 95:161–77.

Little, J. A. 1881. *Jacob Hamlin, a narrative of his personal experiences as a frontiersman, missionary to the Indians and explorer*. Salt Lake City: Juvenile Instructor Office.

Livingstone, D. 1872. *Adventures and discoveries in the interior of Africa*. Philadelphia: Hubbard Brothers.

Lundahl, C. R. 1979. Mormon near-death experiences. *Free Inquiry in Creative Sociology* 7:101–4, 107.

Lundahl, C. R. 1993–94. A nonscience forerunner to modern near-death studies in America. *Omega* 28:63–78.

Moody, R. 1975. *Life after life*. Atlanta: Mockingbird Books.

Morse, M., with Perry, P. 1990. *Closer to the light: Learning from the near-death experiences of children*. New York: Ballantine.

Munck, W. 1887. *Euthanasia: Or, medical treatment in aid of an easy death*. London: Longmans, Green.

Noyes, R. 1971. Dying and mystical consciousness. *Journal of Thanatology* 1 (1): 25–41.

Noyes, R. 1972. The experience of dying. *Psychiatry* 35:174–84.

Noyes, R. 1981. The encounter with life-threatening danger: Its nature and impact. *Essence* 5 (1): 21–32.

Parnia, S. 2006. *What happens when we die*. Carlsbad, CA: Hay House.

Ring, K. 1980. *Life at death: A scientific investigation of the near-death experience*. New York: Coward, McCann & Geoghegan.

Ring, K. 1984. *Heading toward omega: In search of the meaning of the near-death experience*. New York: Quill.

Ring, K., and Cooper, S. 1999. *Mindsight: Near-death and out-of-body experiences in the blind*. Palo Alto, CA: William James Center for Consciousness Studies.

Ring, K., and Valarino, E. E. 1998. *Lessons from the light: What we can learn from the near-death experience*. New York: Plenum.

Rommer, B. 2000. *Blessing in disguise: Another side of the near-death experience.* St. Paul, MN: Llewellyn.

Sabom, M. 1982. *Recollections of death: A medical investigation.* New York: Simon & Schuster.

Sabom, M. 1998. *Light and death.* Grand Rapids, MI: Zondervan.

Schoolcraft, H. 1825. *Travels in the central portion of the Mississippi Valley.* New York: Collins & Hannay.

Sheils, D. 1978. A cross-cultural study of beliefs in out-of-the-body experiences, waking and sleeping. *Journal of the Society for Psychical Research* 49:697–741.

Spetzler, R. F., Hadley, M. N., Rigamonti, D., Carter, L. P., Raudzens, P. A., Shedd, S. A., and Williams, E. 1988. Aneurysms of the basilar artery treated with circulatory arrest, hypothermia, and barbiturate cerebral protection. *Journal of Neurosurgery* 68:868–79.

Sutherland, C. 1992. *Transformed by the light: Life after near-death experiences.* Sydney: Bantam.

Teilhard de Chardin, P. 1964. *The future of man.* Trans. N. Denny. New York: Harper & Row. (Orig. pub. 1959.)

Thalbourne, M. A. 2000. Transliminality: A review. *International Journal of Parapsychology* 11 (2): 1–34.

White, J. W. 1990. *The meeting of science and spirit: Guidelines for a new age.* St. Paul, MN: Paragon House.

Wiltse, A. S. 1889. A case of typhoid fever with subnormal temperature and pulse. *Saint Louis Medical and Surgical Journal* 57:355–64.

Winslow, F. 1868. *On obscure diseases of the brain, and disorders of the mind.* London: John Churchill.

CHAPTER 2

Alvarado, C. S. 1997. Mapping the characteristics of out-of-body experiences. *Journal of the American Society for Psychical Research* 91:15–32.

Alvarado, C. S. 2001. Features of out-of-body experiences in relation to perceived closeness to death. *Journal of Nervous and Mental Disease* 189:331–32.

Alvarado, C. S., and Zingrone, N. L. 1997. Out-of-body experiences and sensations of "shocks" to the body. *Journal of the Society for Psychical Research* 61:304–13.

Alvarado, C. S., and Zingrone, N. L. 1997–98. Factors related to the depth of near-death experiences: Testing the "embellishment over time" hypothesis. *Imagination, Cognition and Personality* 17:339–44.

Alvarado, C. S., and Zingrone, N. L. 1999. Out-of-body experiences among readers of a Spanish New Age magazine. *Journal of the Society for Psychical Research* 63:65–85.

Athappilly, G. K., Greyson, B., and Stevenson, I. 2006. Do prevailing societal models influence reports of near-death experiences? A comparison of accounts reported before and after 1975. *Journal of Nervous and Mental Disease* 194:218–22.

Audette, J. 1979. Denver cardiologist discloses findings after 18 years of near-death research. *Anabiosis* [East Peoria] 1(1):1–2.

Bozzano, E. 1937. *Les phénomènes de bilocation* [The phenomena of bilocation]. Trans. G. Gobron. Paris: Jean Meyer. (Orig. pub. 1934.)

Chari, C. T. K. 1982. Parapsychological reflections on some tunnel experiences. *Anabiosis: The Journal for Near-Death Studies* 2:110–31.

Cook, E. W., Greyson, B., and Stevenson, I. 1998. Do any near-death experiences provide evidence for the survival of human personality after death? Relevant features and illustrative case reports. *Journal of Scientific Exploration* 12:377–406.

Crookall, R. 1961. *The study and practice of astral projection.* London: Aquarian Press.

Crookall, R. 1964. *More astral projections.* London: Aquarian Press.

Crookall, R. 1967. *Events on the threshold of the after life.* Moradabad, India: Darshana International.

Egger, V. 1896. Le moi des mourants [The self of the dying]. *Revue philosophique de la France et de l'étrangere* 21:26–38.

Fenwick, P., and Fenwick, E. 1995. *The truth in the light.* New York: Berkley Books.

Finkelmeier, B. A., Kenwood, N. J., and Summers, C. 1984. Psychologic ramifications of survival from sudden cardiac death. *Critical Care Quarterly* 7:71–79.

Gabbard, G. O., and Twemlow, S. W. 1991. Do "near death experiences" occur only near-death?—Revisited. *Journal of Near-Death Studies* 10:41–47.

Gabbard, G. O., Twemlow, S. W., and Jones, F. C. 1981. Do "near death experiences" only occur near death? *Journal of Nervous and Mental Disease* 169:374–77.

Gallup, G., Jr., and Proctor, W. 1982. *Adventures in immortality: A look beyond the threshold of death.* New York: McGraw-Hill.

Green, C. E. 1968. *Out-of-the-body experiences.* London: Hamish Hamilton.

Green, J. T. and Friedman, P. 1983. Near-death experiences in a Southern California population. *Anabiosis: The Journal for Near-Death Studies* 3:77–95.

Grey, M. 1985. *Return from death: An exploration of the near-death experience.* Boston: Arkana.

Greyson, B. 1983. The Near-Death Experience Scale: Construction, reliability, and validity. *Journal of Nervous and Mental Disease* 171:369–75.

Greyson, B. 1985. A typology of near-death experiences. *American Journal of Psychiatry* 142:967–69.

Greyson, B. 1986. Incidence of near-death experiences following attempted suicide. *Suicide and Life Threatening Behavior* 16:40–45.

Greyson, B. 1998. The incidence of near-death experiences. *Medicine & Psychiatry* 1:92–99.

Greyson, B. 2000. Dissociation in people who have near-death experiences: Out of their bodies or out of their minds? *Lancet* 355:460–63.

Greyson, B. 2003. Incidence and correlates of near-death experiences in a cardiac care unit. *General Hospital Psychiatry* 25:269–76.

Greyson, B., Holden, J. M., and Mounsey, J. P. 2006. Failure to elicit near-death experiences in induced cardiac arrest. *Journal of Near-Death Studies* 25:85–98.

Greyson, B., and Stevenson, I. 1980. The phenomenology of near-death experiences. *American Journal of Psychiatry* 137:1193–96.

Heim, A. 1892. Notizen über den Tod durch Absturz [Remarks on fatal falls]. *Jahrbuch der Schweitzerischen Alpclub* [Yearbook of the Swiss Alpine Club] 21:327–37.

Holden, J. M., Christian, R., Foster, R., Forest, L., and Oden, K. 2008. *Near-death experiences: Index to the periodical literature through 2005* (internet access via www.iands.org/bibcd). Durham, NC: International Association for Near-Death Studies.

Holden, J. M. 1988. Visual perception during naturalistic near-death out-of-body experiences. *Journal of Near-Death Studies* 7:107–20.

Irwin, H. J., and Bramwell, B. A. 1988. The devil in heaven: A near-death experience with both positive and negative facets. *Journal of Near-Death Studies* 7:38–43.

Kelly, E. W. 2001. Near-death experiences with reports of meeting deceased people. *Death Studies* 25:229–49.

Knoblauch, H., Schmied, I., and Schnettler, B. 2001. Different kinds of near-death experience: A report on a survey of near-death experiences in Germany. *Journal of Near-Death Studies* 20:15–29.

Lai, C. F., Kao, T. W., Wu, M. S., Chiang, S. S., Chang, C. H., Lu, C. S., Yang, C. S., Yang, C. C., Chang, H. W., Lin, S. L., Chang, C. J., Chen, P. Y., Wu, K. D., Tsai, T. J., and Chen, W. Y. 2007. Impact of near-death experiences on dialysis patients: A multicenter collaborative study. *American Journal of Kidney Diseases* 50:124–32.

Lange, R., Greyson, B., and Houran, J. 2004. A Rasch validation of a "core" near-death experience. *British Journal of Psychology* 95:161–77.

Lawrence, M. 1995a. Paranormal experiences of previously unconscious patients. In L. Coly and J. D. S. McMahon (Eds.), *Parapsychology and thanatology: Proceedings of an international conference held in Boston, November 6–7, 1993,* 122–48. New York: Parapsychology Foundation.

Lawrence, M. 1995b. The unconscious experience. *American Journal of Critical Care* 4:227–32.

Lindley, J. H., Bryan, S., and Conley, B. 1981. Near-death experiences in a Pacific Northwest American population: The Evergreen Study. *Anabiosis: The Journal for Near-Death Studies* 1:104–24.

Locke, T. P., and Shontz, G. C. 1983. Personality correlates of the near-death experience: A preliminary study. *Journal of the American Society for Psychical Research* 77:311–18.

Lundahl, C. R. 1992. Angels in near-death experiences. *Journal of Near-Death Studies* 11:49–56.

Milne, C. T. 1995. Cardiac electrophysiology studies and the near-death experience. *CCACN: Journal of the Canadian Association of Critical Care Nurses* 6:16–19.

Moody, R. 1975. *Life after life*. Atlanta: Mockingbird Books.

Morris, L. L., and Knafl, K. 2003. The nature and meaning of the near-death experience for patients and critical care nurses. *Journal of Near-Death Studies* 21:139–67.

Morse, M. L., Castillo, P., Venecia, D., Milstein, J., and Tyler, D. 1986. Childhood near-death experiences. *American Journal of Diseases of Childhood* 140:1110–14.

Morse, M. L., Conner, D., and Tyler, D. 1985. Near-death experiences in a pediatric populations: A preliminary report. *American Journal of the Disease of Childhood* 139:595–600.

Morse, M., and Perry, P. 1990. *Closer to the light: Learning from the near-death experiences of children*. New York: Villard.

Muldoon, S. J. 1936. *The case for astral projection*. Chicago: Ariel Press.

Myers, F. W. H. 1892. On indications of continued terrene knowledge on the part of phantasms of the dead. *Proceedings of the Society for Psychical Research* 8:170–252.

Noyes, R., Jr., Hoenk, P. R., Kuperman, S., and Slymen, D. J. 1977. Depersonalization in accident victims and psychiatric patients. *Journal of Nervous and Mental Disease* 164:401–7.

Noyes, R., Jr., and Kletti, R. 1976. Depersonalization in the face of life-threatening danger: A description. *Psychiatry* 39:19–27.

Noyes, R., and Slymen, D. J. 1978–79. The subjective response to life-threatening danger. *Omega* 9:313–21.

Olson, M., and Dulaney, P. 1993. Life satisfaction, life review, and near-death experiences in the elderly. *Journal of Holistic Nursing* 11:368–82.

Orne, R. 1995. The meaning of survival: The early aftermath of a near-death experience. *Research in Nursing & Health* 18:239–47.

Owens, J. E., Cook, E. W., and Stevenson, I. 1990. Features of "near-death experience" in relation to whether or not patients were near death. *Lancet* 336:1175–77.

Pacciolla, A. 1996. The near-death experience: A study of its validity. *Journal of Near-Death Studies* 14:179–85.

Parnia, S. 2006. *What happens when we die*. Carlsbad, CA: Hay House.

Parnia, S., Waller, D. G., Yeates, R., and Fenwick, P. 2001. A qualitative and quantitative study of the incidence, features and aetiology of near death experiences in cardiac arrest survivors. *Resuscitation* 48:149–56.

Pasricha, S. 1992. Near-death experiences in South India: A systematic survey in Channapatna. *National Institute of Mental Health & Neurosciences Journal* 10:111–18.

Pasricha, S. 1993. A systematic survey of near-death experiences in South India. *Journal of Scientific Exploration* 7:161–71.

Ring, K. 1979. Further studies of the near-death experience. *Theta* 7:1–3.

Ring, K. 1980. *Life at death: A scientific investigation of the near-death experience*. New York: Coward, McCann & Geoghegan.

Ring, K. 1982. Precognitive and prophetic visions in near-death experiences. *Anabiosis: The Journal for Near-Death Studies* 2:47–74.

Ring, K., and Franklin, S. 1981–82. Do suicide survivors report near-death experiences? *Omega* 12:191–208.

Ring, K., and Lawrence, M. 1993. Further evidence for veridical perception during near-death experiences. *Journal of Near-Death Studies* 11:223–29.

Rosen, D. H. 1975. Suicide survivors: A follow-up study of persons who survived jumping from the Golden Gate and San Francisco–Oakland Bay Bridges. *Western Journal of Medicine* 122:289–94.

Sabom, M. 1982. *Recollections of death: A medical investigation*. New York: Harper & Row.

Sabom, M. B., and Kreutziger, S. A. 1978. Physicians evaluate the near death experience. *Theta* 6:1–6.

Sartori, P., Badham, P., and Fenwick, P. 2006. A prospectively studied near-death experience with corroborated out-of-body perceptions and unexplained healing. *Journal of Near-Death Studies* 25:69–84.

Schnaper, N., and Panitz, H. L. 1990. Near-death experiences: Perception *is* reality. *Journal of Near-Death Studies* 9:97–104.

Schoenbeck, S. B., and Hocutt, G. D. 1991. Near-death experiences in patients undergoing cardiopulmonary resuscitation. *Journal of Near-Death Studies* 9:211–19.

Schwaninger, J., Eisenberg, P. R., Schechtman, K. B., and Weiss, A. N. 2002. A prospective analysis of near-death experiences in cardiac arrest patients. *Journal of Near-Death Studies* 20:215–32.

Stevenson, I., and Cook, E. W. 1995. Involuntary memories during severe physical illness or injury. *Journal of Nervous and Mental Disease* 183:452–58.

Stevenson, I., Cook, E. W., and McClean-Rice, N. 1989–90. Are persons reporting near-death experiences really near death? A study of medical records. *Omega* 20:45–54.

Sutherland, C. 1995. *Reborn in the light.* New York: Bantam. (Orig. pub. 1992.)

Thomas, L. E., Cooper, P. A., and Suscovich, D. J. 1982–83. Incidence of near-death and intense spiritual experiences in an intergenerational sample: An interpretation. *Omega* 13:35–41.

Tosch, P. 1988. Patients' recollections of their posttraumatic coma. *Journal of Neuroscience Nursing* 20:223–28.

Twemlow, S. W., Gabbard, G. O., and Coyne, L. 1982. A multivariate method for the classification of preexisting near-death conditions. *Journal of Near-Death Studies* 2:132–39.

van Lommel, P., van Wees, R., Meyers, V., and Elfferich, I. 2001. Near-death experience in survivors of cardiac arrest: A prospective study in the Netherlands. *Lancet* 358:2039–45.

Walker, B. A., Serdahely, W. J., and Bechtel, L. L. 1991. Three near-death experiences with premonitions of what could have been. *Journal of Near-Death Studies* 9:189–98.

White, R. L., and Liddon, S. C. 1972. Ten survivors of cardiac arrest. *Psychiatry in Medicine* 3:219–25.

Zhi-ying, F., and Jian-xun, L. 1992. Near-death experiences among survivors of the 1976 Tangshan earthquake. *Journal of Near-Death Studies* 11:39–48.

CHAPTER 3

American Psychiatric Association. 2000. *Diagnostic and statistical manual of mental disorders.* 4th ed., rev. Washington, DC: Author.

Atwater, P. M. H. 1988. *Coming back to life: The after-effects of the near-death experience.* Rev. ed. New York: Citadel.

Bauer, M. 1985. Near-death experiences and attitude change. *Anabiosis: The Journal for Near-Death Studies* 5:39–47.

Blackmore, S. 1993. *Dying to live: Near-death experiences.* New York: Prometheus Books.

Bonenfant, R. J. 2004. A comparative study of near-death experience and non-near-death experience outcomes in 56 survivors of clinical death. *Journal of Near-Death Studies* 22:155–78.

Brewin, C. R., Andrews, B., and Valentine, J. D. 2000. Meta-analysis of risk factors for posttraumatic stress disorder in trauma-exposed adults. *Journal of Consulting and Clinical Psychology* 68:748–66.

Britton, W., and Bootzin, R. 2004. Near-death experience and the temporal lobe. *Psychological Science* 15:254–58.

Bush, N. E. 1991. Is ten years a life review? *Journal of Near-Death Studies* 10:5–9.

Bush, N. E. 2002. Afterward: Making meaning after a frightening near-death experience. *Journal of Near-Death Studies* 21:99–133.

Christian, S. R. (2005). Marital satisfaction and stability following a near-death experience of one of the marital partners. *Dissertation Abstracts International,* A 66/11. (UMI No. 3196139.)

Corazza, O. (2008). *Near-death experiences: Exploring the mind-body connection.* Oxford, UK: Routledge.

Council, J. R., and Greyson, B. 1985. Near-death experiences and the "fantasy prone" personalities: Preliminary findings. Presented at the annual meeting of the American Psychological Association, Los Angeles, CA.

Ehlers, A. 2000. Post-traumatic stress disorder. In M. G. Gelder, J. J. Lopez-Ibor, and N. C. Andreasen (Eds.), *New Oxford Textbook of Psychiatry,* 758–71. New York: Oxford University Press.

Fenwick, P., and Fenwick, E. 1995. *The truth in the light.* New York: Berkley Books.

Flynn, C. P. 1982. Meanings and implications of near-death experience transformation. *Anabiosis: The Journal for Near-Death Studies* 2:3–14.

Flynn, C. P. 1986. *After the beyond: Human transformation and the near-death experience.* Englewood Cliffs, NJ: Prentice-Hall.

Furn, B. G. 1987. Adjustment and the near-death experience: A conceptual and therapeutic model. *Journal of Near-Death Studies* 6:4–19.

Gabbard, G. O., Twemlow, S. W., and Jones, F. C. 1981. Do "near-death experiences" occur only near death? *Journal of Nervous and Mental Disease* 169:374–77.

Gallup, G., and Proctor, W. 1982. *Adventures in immortality: A look beyond the threshold of death.* New York: McGraw-Hill.

Granja, C., Cabral, G., Pinto, A., and Costa-Pereira, A. 2002. Quality of life six months after cardiac arrest. *Resuscitation* 55:37–44.

Grey, M. 1985. *Return from death.* London: Arkana.

Greyson, B. 1983a. Near-death experiences and personal values. *American Journal of Psychiatry* 140:618–20.

Greyson, B. 1983b. Increase in psychic phenomena following near-death experiences. *Theta* 11:26–29.

Greyson, B. 1983c. Near-Death Experience Scale: Construction, reliability, and validity. *Journal of Nervous and Mental Disease* 171:369–75.

Greyson, B. 1986. Incidence of near-death experiences following attempted suicide. *Suicide and Life-Threatening Behavior* 16:40–45.

Greyson, B. 1989. Can science explain the near-death experience? *Journal of Near-Death Studies* 8:77–92.

Greyson, B. 1992. Reduced death threat in near-death experiencers. *Death Studies* 16:523–36.

Greyson, B. 1992–93. Near-death experiences and anti-suicidal attitudes. *Omega* 26:81–89.

Greyson, B. 1993a. Near-death experiences and the physio-kundalini syndrome. *Journal of Religion and Health* 32:277–90.

Greyson, B. 1993b. Varieties of near-death experience. *Psychiatry* 46:390–99.

Greyson, B. 1994. Near-death experiences and satisfaction with life. *Journal of Near-Death Studies* 13:103–8.

Greyson, B. 1997. The near-death experience as a focus of clinical attention. *Journal of Nervous and Mental Disease* 185:327–34.

Greyson, B. 1998. Biological aspects of near-death experiences. *Perspectives in Biology and Medicine* 42:14–32.

Greyson, B. 1999. Defining near-death experiences. *Mortality* 4:7–19.

Greyson, B. 2000a. Near-death experiences. In E. Cardeña, S. J. Lynn, and S. Krippner (Eds.), *Varieties of anomalous experience: Examining the scientific evidence*, 315–52. Washington, DC: American Psychological Association.

Greyson, B. 2000b. Dissociation in people who have near-death experiences. *Lancet* 355:460–63.

Greyson, B. 2001. Posttraumatic stress symptoms following near-death experiences. *American Journal of Orthopsychiatry* 71:368–78.

Greyson, B. 2003a. Near-death experiences in a psychiatric outpatient clinic population. *Psychiatric Services* 54:1649–51.

Greyson, B. 2003b. Incidence and correlates of near-death experiences in cardiac care. *General Hospital Psychiatry* 25:269–76.

Greyson, B., and Bush, N. E. 1992. Distressing near-death experiences. *Psychiatry* 55:95–110.

Greyson, B., and Harris, B. 1987. Clinical approaches to the near-death experiencer. *Journal of Near-Death Studies* 6:41–52.

Greyson, B., and Liester, M. B. 2004. Auditory hallucinations following near-death experiences. *Journal of Humanistic Psychology* 44:320–36.

Greyson, B., and Ring, K. 2004. The Life Changes Inventory–Revised. *Journal of Near-Death Studies* 23:41–54.

Greyson, B., and Stevenson, I. 1980. The phenomenology of near-death experiences. *American Journal of Psychiatry* 137:1193–96.

Grof, S., and Grof, C. 1980. *Beyond death: The gates of consciousness*. London: Thames & Hudson.

Grof, S., and Halifax, J. 1977. *The human encounter with death*. New York: Dutton.

Grosso, M. 1981. Toward an explanation of near-death phenomena. *Journal of the American Society for Psychical Research* 75:37–60.

Groth-Marnat, G., and Summers, R. 1998. Altered beliefs, attitudes, and behaviors following near-death experiences. *Journal of Humanistic Psychology* 38:110–25.

Hastings, A. 2002. The resistance to belief. *Journal of Near-Death Studies* 21:77–98.

Hay, D. 1994. "The Biology of God": What is the current status of Hardy's hypothesis? *International Journal for the Psychology of Religion* 4:1–23.

Hay, D., and Morisy, A. 1985. Secular society/religious meanings: A contemporary paradox. *Review of Religious Research* 26:213–27.

Hoffman, R. M. 1995. Disclosure needs and motives after a near-death experience. *Journal of Near-Death Studies* 13:137–266.

Holeva, V., and Tarrier, N. 2001. Personality and peritraumatic dissociation in the prediction of PTSD in victims of road accidents. *Journal of Psychosomatic Research* 51:687–92.

Holy Bible, Revised Standard Version. 1972. Iowa Falls, IA: World Bible Publishers.

Insinger, M. 1991. The impact of a near-death experience on family relationships. *Journal of Near-Death Studies* 9:141–81.

International Association for Near-Death Studies. 2006. *Near-death experiences: Index to the periodical literature through 2001*. East Windsor Hill, CT: International Association for Near-Death Studies.

Irwin, H. J. 1993. The near-death experience as a dissociative phenomenon: An empirical assessment. *Journal of Near-Death Studies* 12:95–103.

Jansen, K. 1990. Neuroscience and the near-death experience: Roles for the NMDA-PCP receptor, the sigma receptor and the endopsychosins. *Medical Hypotheses* 31:25–29.

Kalish, R. A. 1969. Experiences of people reprieved from death. In A. H. Kutscher (Ed.), *Death and bereavement*, 84–96. Springfield, IL: Charles C. Thomas.

Kellehear, A. 1990. The near-death experience as a status passage. *Social Science and Medicine* 31:933–39.

Kellehear, A. 1996. *Experiences near death: Beyond medicine and religion*. New York: Oxford University Press.

Knoblauch, H., Schmied, I., and Schnettler, B. 2001. Different kinds of near-death experience: A report on a survey of near-death experiences in Germany. *Journal of Near-Death Studies* 10:15–29.

Kohr, R. L. 1982. Near-death experience and its relationship to psi and various altered states. *Theta* 10:50–53.

Kohr, R. L. 1983. Near-death experiences, altered states, and psi sensitivity. *Anabiosis: The Journal for Near-Death Studies* 3:157–76.

Krupitski, E. M., and Grinenko, A. Y. 1997. Ketamine psychedelic therapy (KPT): A review of the results of 10 years of research. *Journal of Psychoactive Drugs* 29:165–83.

Lifton, R. J. 1979. *The broken connection: On death and the continuity of life*. Washington, DC: American Psychiatric Press.

Lindley, J. H., Bryan, S., and Conley, B. 1981. Near-death experiences in a Pacific Northwest American population: The Evergreen study. *Anabiosis: The Journal for Near-Death Studies* 1:104–25.

McLaughlin, S. A., and Malony, H. N. 1984. Near-death experiences and religion: A further investigation. *Journal of Religion and Health* 23:149–59.

McMillen, J. C. 1999. Better for it: How people benefit from adversity. *Social Work* 44:455–68.

Moody, R. 1975. *Life after life: The investigation of a phenomenon—the survival of bodily death*. Atlanta: Mockingbird Books.

Morris, L. L., and Knafl, K. 2003. The nature and meaning of the near-death experience for patients and critical care nurses. *Journal of Near-Death Studies* 21:139–67.

Morse, M. L., and Perry, P. 1992. *Transformed by the light: The powerful effect of near-death experiences on people's lives*. New York: Villard Books.

Musgrave, C. 1997. The near-death experience: A study of spiritual transformation. *Journal of Near-Death Studies* 15:187–201.

Nelson, K. R., Mattingley, M., Lee, S. A., and Schmitt, F. A. 2006. Does the arousal system contribute to near-death experience? *Neurology* 66:1003–9.

Nemeroff, C. B., Bremner, J. D., Foa, E. B., Mayberg, H. S., North, C. S., and Stein, M. B. 2006. Posttraumatic stress disorder: A state-of-the-science review. *Journal of Psychiatric Research* 40:1–21.

Nielo, J. C. 1997. *Religious experience and mysticism: Otherness as experience of transcendence*. New York: University Press of America.

Noyes, R. 1971. Dying and mystical consciousness. *Journal of Thanatology* 1:25–41.

Noyes, R. 1973. Seneca on death. *Journal of Religion and Health* 12:223–40.

Noyes, R. 1979. Near-death experiences: Their interpretation and significance. In R. Kastenbaum (Ed.), *Between life and death*, 73–88. New York: Springer.

Noyes, R. 1980. Attitude change following near-death experiences. *Psychiatry* 43:234–42.

Noyes, R. 1982–83. The human experience of death or, what can we learn from near-death experiences? *Omega* 13:251–59.

Noyes, R., and Kletti, R. 1976. Depersonalization in the face of life-threatening danger: An interpretation. *Omega* 7:103–14.

Orne, R. M. 1995. The meaning of survival: The early aftermath of a near-death experience. *Research in Nursing and Health* 18:239–47.

Park, C. L., Cohen, L. H., and Murch, R. 1996. Assessment and prediction of stress-related growth. *Journal of Personality* 64:71–105.

Parkes, C. M. 1971. Psycho-social transitions: A field for study. *Social Science and Medicine* 5:101–15.

Pennachio, J. 1986. The near-death experience as a mystical experience. *Journal of Religion and Health* 25:64–72.

Pfohl, B., Blum, N., and Zimmerman, M. 1997. *Structural interview for DSM-IV personality*. Washington, DC: American Psychiatric Press.

Raft, D., and Andresen, J. J. 1986. Transformations in self-understanding after near-death experiences. *Contemporary Psychoanalysis* 22:319–46.

Reker, G. T. 1992. *Life Attitude Profile–Revised procedures manual*. Peterborough, Ontario: Student Psychologists Press.

Richards, W., Grof, S., Goodman, L., and Kurland, A. 1972. LSD-assisted psychotherapy and the human encounter with death. *Journal of Transpersonal Psychology* 4:121–50.

Ring, K. 1980. *Life at death: A scientific investigation of the near-death experience*. New York: Coward, McCann & Geoghegan.

Ring, K. 1984. *Heading toward omega: In search of the meaning of the near-death experience*. New York: William Morrow.

Ring, K. 1992. *The Omega Project: Near-death experiences, UFO encounters, and mind at large*. New York: William Morrow.

Ring, K. 1993. A new Book of the Dead: Reflections on the near-death experience and the Tibetan Buddhist tradition regarding the nature of death. *Journal of Near-Death Studies* 12:75–84.

Ring, K., and Franklin, S. 1981–82. Do suicide survivors report near-death experiences? *Omega* 12:191–208.

Ring, K., and Rosing, C. J. 1990. The Omega Project: An empirical study of the NDE-prone personality. *Journal of Near-Death Studies* 8:211–39.

Ring, K., and Valarino, E. E. 1998. *Lessons from the light: What we can learn from the near-death experience*. New York: Plenum.

Roberts, G., and Owen, J. 1988. The near-death experience. *British Journal of Psychiatry* 153:607–17.

Rosen, D. H. 1975. Suicide survivors: A follow-up study of persons who survived jumping from the Golden Gate and San Francisco–Oakland Bay bridges. *Western Journal of Medicine* 122:289–94.

Sabom, M. B. 1982. *Recollections of death: A medical investigation*. New York: Harper & Row.

Sabom, M. B., and Kreutziger, S. 1978. Physicians evaluate the near-death experience. *Theta* 6:1–6.

Schwaninger, J., Eisenberg, P. R., Schechtman, K. B., and Weiss, A. N. 2002. A prospective analysis of near-death experiences in cardiac arrest patients. *Journal of Near-Death Studies* 20:215–32.

Seneca. 1928. Seneca moral essays. Trans. J. W. Basore. In *The Loeb Classic Library*, vol. 3. Cambridge, MA: Harvard University Press.

Smith, D. W. 1979. Survivors of serious illness. *American Journal of Nursing* 79:441–46.

Sutherland, C. 1989. Psychic phenomena following near-death experiences: An Australian study. *Journal of Near-Death Studies* 8:93–102.

Sutherland, C. 1990. Changes in religious beliefs, attitudes, and practices following near-death experiences: An Australian study. *Journal of Near-Death Studies* 9:21–31.

Sutherland, C. 1992. *Transformed by the light: Life after near-death experiences*. New York: Bantam Books.

Sutherland, C. 1995. *Reborn in the light: Life after near-death experiences*. New York: Bantam Books.

Tedeschi, R., and Calhoun, L. 1996. The post-traumatic growth inventory: Measuring the positive legacy of trauma. *Journal of Traumatic Stress* 9:455–71.

Tedeschi, R. G., Park, C. L., and Calhoun, L. G. (Eds.). 1998. *Posttraumatic growth: Positive changes in the aftermath of crisis*. London: Erlbaum.

Tiberi, E. 1988. Extrasomatic emotions. *Journal of Near-Death Studies* 11:149–70.

Twemlow, S., and Gabbard, G. 1984–85. The influence of demographic/psychological factors and pre-existing conditions on the near-death experience. *Omega* 15:223–35.

van Lommel, P., van Wees, R., Meyers, V., and Elfferich, I. 2001. Near-death experience in survivors of cardiac arrest: A prospective study in the Netherlands. *Lancet* 358:2039–45.

Weiss, J. M. A. 1957. The gamble with death in attempted suicide. *Psychiatry* 20:17–25.

Wells, A. D. 1993. Reincarnation beliefs among near-death experiencers. *Journal of Near-Death Studies* 12:17–34.

White, P. R. 1997. The anatomy of a transformation: An analysis of the psychological structure of four near-death experiences. *Journal of Near-Death Studies* 15:163–85.

Wren-Lewis, J. 1994. Aftereffects of near-death experiences: A survival mechanism hypothesis. *Journal of Transpersonal Psychology* 26:107–15.

Yalom, I. D. 1980. *Existential psychotherapy.* New York: Basic Books.

Zalesky, C. 1987. *Otherworld journeys: Accounts of near-death experience in medieval and modern times.* New York: Oxford University Press.

CHAPTER 4

Atwater, P. M. H. 1992. Is there a hell? Surprising observations about the near-death experience. *Journal of Near-Death Studies* 10:149–60.

Atwater, P. M. H. 1994. *Beyond the light: What isn't being said about the near-death experience.* New York: Birch Lane Press.

Bache, C. 1994. A perinatal interpretation of frightening near-death experiences: A dialogue with Kenneth Ring. *Journal of Near-Death Studies* 13:25–45.

Bache, C. 1996. Expanding Grof's concept of the perinatal: Deepening the inquiry into frightening near-death experiences. *Journal of Near-Death Studies* 15:113–39.

Basford, T. 1990. *Near-death experiences: An annotated bibliography* (Garland Reference Library of Social Science Vol. 481). New York: Garland.

Bonenfant, R. 2001. A child's encounter with the devil: An unusual near-death experience with both blissful and frightening elements. *Journal of Near-Death Studies* 20:87–100.

Bush, N. E. 1983. The near-death experience in children: Shades of the prison-house reopening. *Anabiosis: The Journal for Near-Death Studies* 3:177–94.

Bush, N. E. 1994. The paradox of Jonah: Response to "Solving the riddle of frightening near-death experiences." *Journal of Near-Death Studies* 13:47–54.

Bush, N. E. 2002. Afterward: Making meaning after a frightening near-death experience. *Journal of Near-Death Studies* 21:99–133.

Clark, K. 1984. Clinical interventions with near-death experiencers. In B. Greyson and C. P. Flynn (Eds.), *The near-death experience: Problems, prospects, perspectives,* 242–55. Springfield, IL: Charles C. Thomas.

Corbett, L. 1996. *The religious function of the psyche.* London: Routledge.

Couliano, I. P. 1991. *Out of this world: Otherworld journeys from Gilgamesh to Albert Einstein.* Boston: Shambhala.

Cressy, J. 1994. *The near-death experience: Mysticism or madness?* Hanover, MA: Christopher Publishing House.

Ellwood, G. F. 1996. Distressing near-death experiences as photographic negatives. *Journal of Near-Death Studies* 15:83–114.

Ellwood, G. F. 2001. *The uttermost deep: The challenge of near-death experiences.* New York: Lantern Books.

Farr, S. S. 1993. *What Tom Sawyer learned from dying.* Norfolk, VA: Hampton Roads.

Fox, M. 2003. *Religion, spirituality, and the near-death experience.* London: Routledge.

Flynn, C. P. 1986. *After the beyond*. Englewood Cliffs, NJ: Prentice-Hall.

Fox, M. 1983. *Original blessing: A primer in creation spirituality*. Santa Fe, NM: Bear.

Gallup, G., Jr., and Proctor, W. 1982. *Adventures in immortality: A look beyond the threshold of death*. New York: McGraw-Hill.

Garfield, C. 1979. More grist for the mill: Additional near-death research findings and discussion. *Anabiosis* [East Peoria] 1(1):5–7.

Grey, M. 1985. *Return from death: An exploration of the near-death experience*. London: Arkana.

Greyson, B. 1991. Near-death experiences precipitated by suicide attempt: Lack of influence of psychopathology, religion, and expectations. *Journal of Near-Death Studies* 9:182–88.

Greyson, B. 1996. Editor's foreword. *Journal of Near-Death Studies* 15:81.

Greyson, B., and Bush, N. E. 1992. Distressing near-death experiences. *Psychiatry* 55:95–110.

Greyson, B., and Flynn, C. P. (Eds.). 1984. *The near-death experience: Problems, prospects, perspectives*. Springfield, IL: Charles C. Thomas.

Grof, S. 1980. *Beyond death*. New York: Viking.

Grof, S., with Bennett, H. Z. 1993. *The holotropic mind: The three levels of human consciousness and how they shape our lives*. San Francisco: HarperCollins.

Grosso, M. 1983. Jung, parapsychology, and the near-death experience: Toward a transpersonal paradigm. *Anabiosis: The Journal for Near-Death Studies* 3:3–38.

Hastings, A. 2002. The resistance to belief. *Journal of Near-Death Studies* 21:77–98.

Hoffman, R. 1995. Disclosure habits after near-death experiences: Influences, obstacles, and listener selection. *Journal of Near-Death Studies* 13:29–48.

Jambor, M. 1997. The mystery of frightening transcendent experiences: A rejoinder to Nancy Evans Bush and Christopher Bache. *Journal of Near-Death Studies* 16:163–76.

James, W. 1902. *Varieties of religious experience*. New York: Simon & Schuster.

Knoblauch, H., Schmied, I., and Schnettler, B. 2001. Different kinds of near-death experience: A report on a survey of near-death experiences in Germany. *Journal of Near-Death Studies* 20:15–30.

Lindley, J. H., Bryan, S., and Conley, B. 1981. Near-death experiences in a Pacific Northwest American population: The Evergreen study. *Anabiosis: The Journal for Near-Death Studies* 1:104–25.

Matlock, J. 1989. Review of Carol Zaleski's *Otherworld Journeys*. *Journal of the American Society for Psychical Research* 83:168-73.

McClenon, J. 1994. *Wondrous events: Foundations of religious belief*. Philadelphia: University of Pennsylvania Press.

Moody, R. A., Jr. 1975. *Life after life*. Atlanta: Mockingbird Books.

Moody, R. A., Jr. 1977. *Reflections on life after life*. St. Simon's Island, GA: Mockingbird Books.

Murphy, T. 1999. Recreating near-death experiences: A cognitive approach. *Journal of Near-Death Studies* 17:261–65.

Murphy, T. 2001. The structure and function of near-death experiences: An algorithmic reincarnation hypothesis. *Journal of Near-Death Studies* 20:101–18.

Murphy, T. 2002. Forgetting about enlightenment. Retrieved March 22, 2008, from http://www.shaktitechnology.com/enlightenment.htm.

Parnia, S., Waller, D. G., Yeates, R., and Fenwick, P. 2001. A qualitative and quantitative study of the incidence, features and aetiology of near death experiences in cardiac arrest survivors. *Resuscitation* 48:149–58.

Rawlings, M. 1978. *Beyond death's door*. Nashville: Thomas Nelson.

Rawlings, M. 1993. *To hell and back*. Nashville: Thomas Nelson.

Ritchie, G. 1978. *Return from tomorrow*. Waco, TX: Chosen Books.

Ring, K. 1980. *Life at death: A scientific investigation of the near-death experience*. New York: Coward, McCann & Geoghegan.

Ring, K. 1984. *Heading toward omega: In search of the meaning of the near-death experience*. New York: William Morrow.

Ring, K. 1994. Solving the riddle of frightening near-death experiences: Some testable hypotheses and a perspective based on A Course in Miracles. *Journal of Near-Death Studies* 13:5–24.

Ring, K. 1996. A note on anesthetically-induced frightening "near-death experiences." *Journal of Near-Death Studies* 15:17–24.

Rommer, B. 2000. *Blessing in disguise: Another side of the near-death experience*. St. Paul, MN: Llewellyn Publications.

Rosen, D. H. 1975. A follow-up study of persons who survived jumping from the Golden Gate and San Francisco–Oakland Bay bridges. *Western Journal of Medicine* 122 (4): 289–94.

Sabom, M. 1979. Review of *Beyond Death's Door*. *Anabiosis* [East Peoria] 1(3):9.

Sabom, M. 1982. *Recollections of death: A medical investigation*. New York: Harper & Row.

Sabom, M. 1996. Review of *To Hell and Back*. *Journal of Near-Death Studies* 14:197–209.

Schwaninger, J., Eisenberg, P., Schechtman, K., and Weiss, A. 2002. A prospective analysis of near-death experiences in cardiac arrest patients. *Journal of Near-Death Studies* 20:215–32.

Serdahely, W. 1995. Variations from the prototypic near-death experience: The "individually tailored" hypothesis. *Journal of Near-Death Studies* 13:185–96.

Sutherland, C. 1992. *Transformed by the light: Life after near-death experiences*. Sydney: Bantam Books.

van Lommel, P., van Wees, R., Meyers, V., and Elfferich, I. 2001. Near-death experience in survivors of cardiac arrest: A prospective study in the Netherlands. *Lancet* 358:2039–45.

Young, S. 2005. *The science of enlightenment*, Experience 6 [audio CD]. Louisville, CO: Sounds True.

Zaleski, C. 1987. *Otherworld journeys: Accounts of near-death experience in medieval and modern times*. New York: Oxford University Press.

Zimdars-Swartz, S. 1990. Book review: *Otherworld Journeys*. *Journal of Religion* 70:507-8.

CHAPTER 5

Atwater, P. M. H. 1992. Is there a hell? Surprising observations about the near-death experience. *Journal of Near-Death Studies* 10:149–60.

Atwater, P. M. H. 1995. A call to reconsider the field of near-death studies. *Journal of Near-Death Studies* 14:5–15.

Atwater, P. M. H. 1996. Children and the near-death phenomenon: Another viewpoint. *Journal of Near-Death Studies* 15:5–16.

Atwater, P. M. H. 2003. *The new children and near-death experiences.* Rochester, VT: Bear.

Bonenfant, R. J. 2001. A child's encounter with the devil: An unusual near-death experience with both blissful and frightening elements. *Journal of Near-Death Studies* 20:87–100.

Bonenfant, R. J. 2004. A comparative study of near-death experience and non-near-death experience outcomes in 56 survivors of clinical death. *Journal of Near-Death Studies* 22:155–78.

Bush, N. E. 1983. The near-death experience in children: Shades of the prison-house reopening. *Anabiosis: The Journal for Near-Death Studies* 3:177–93.

Colli, J. E., and Beck, T. E. 2003. Recovery from bulimia nervosa through near-death experience: A case study. *The Journal of Near-Death Studies* 22:33–55.

Corcoran, D. K. 1988. Helping patients who've had near-death experiences. *Nursing* 18:34–39.

DenBesten, L. 1978. The dying experience. *The Reformed Journal* 28:17–21.

Enright, R. 2004. Silent journeys: The discovery of the near-death experience of a nonverbal adolescent. *Journal of Near-Death Studies* 22:195–208.

Fenwick, P., and Fenwick, E. 1995. *The truth in the light: An investigation of over 300 near-death experiences.* London: Headline.

Flynn, C. P. 1986. *After the beyond: Human transformation and the near-death experience.* Englewood Cliffs, NJ: Prentice-Hall.

Gabbard, G. O., and Twemlow, S. W. 1984. *With the eyes of the mind: An empirical analysis of out-of-body states.* New York: Praeger.

Greyson, B. 1983. The Near-Death Experience Scale: Construction, reliability, and validity. *Journal of Nervous and Mental Disease* 171 (6): 369–75.

Greyson, B. 1997. The near-death experience as a focus of clinical attention. *Journal of Nervous and Mental Diseases* 185 (5): 327–34.

Greyson, B. 2003. Incidence and correlates of near-death experiences on a cardiac care unit. *General Hospital Psychiatry* 25:269–76.

Greyson, B., and Bush, N. E. 1992. Distressing near-death experiences. *Psychiatry* 55:95–110.

Herzog, D. B., and Herrin, J. T. 1985. Near-death experiences in the very young. *Critical Care Medicine* 13 (12): 1074–75.

Hoffman, E. 1998. Peak experiences in childhood: An explanatory study. *Journal of Humanistic Psychology* 38 (1): 109–20.

Holden, J. M., and Joesten, L. 1990. Near-death veridicality research in the hospital setting: Problems and promise. *Journal of Near-Death Studies* 9:45–54.

Horacek, B. J. 1997. Amazing grace: The healing effects of near-death experiences on those dying and grieving. *Journal of Near-Death Studies* 16:149–61.

Irwin, H. J. 1989. The near-death experience in childhood. *Australian Parapsychological Review* 14:7–11.

Irwin, H. J. 1993. The near-death experience as a dissociative phenomenon: An empirical assessment. *Journal of Near-Death Studies* 12:95-103.

Irwin, H. J., and Bramwell, B. A. 1988. The devil in heaven: A near-death experience with both positive and negative facets. *Journal of Near-Death Studies* 7:38–43.

Kübler-Ross, E. 1983. *On children and death*. New York: Macmillan.

Liester, M. B. 1998. Inner communications following the near-death experience. *Journal of Near-Death Studies* 16:233–48.

Moody, R. A. 1975. *Life After life*. Atlanta: Mockingbird Books.

Morse, M. L. 1983. A near-death experience in a 7-year-old child. *American Journal of Diseases of Children* 137 (10): 959–61.

Morse, M. L. 1994a. Near-death experiences and death-related visions in children: Implications for the clinician. *Current Problems in Pediatrics* 24:55–83.

Morse, M. L. 1994b. Near-death experiences of children. *Journal of Pediatric Oncology Nursing* 11 (4): 139–44.

Morse, M. L., Castillo, P., Venecia, D., Milstein, J., and Tyler, D. C. 1986. Childhood near-death experiences. *American Journal of Diseases of Children* 140 (11): 1110–14.

Morse, M. L., Conner, D., and Tyler, D. 1985. Near-death experiences in a pediatric population: A preliminary report. *American Journal of Diseases of Children* 139 (6): 595–600.

Morse, M. L., and Perry, P. 1990. *Closer to the light: Learning from the near-death experiences of children*. New York: Villard Books.

Morse, M. L., and Perry, P. 1992. *Transformed by the light: The powerful effect of near-death experiences on people's lives*. New York: Villard Books.

Parnia, S., Waller, D. G., Yeates, R., and Fenwick, P. 2001. A qualitative and quantitative study of the incidence, features and aetiology of near-death experiences in cardiac arrest survivors. *Resuscitation* 48:149–56.

Quiller-Couch, A. (Ed.). 1919. *The Oxford book of English verse: 1250–1900*. Oxford, England: Clarendon.

Rawlings, M. 1978. *Beyond death's door*. Nashville: Thomas Nelson.

Ring, K. 1980. *Life at death: A scientific investigation of the near-death experience*. New York: Coward, McCann & Geoghegan.

Ring, K. 1984. *Heading toward omega: In search of the meaning of the near-death experience*. New York: William Morrow.

Ring, K. 1991. Amazing grace: The near-death experience as a compensatory gift. *Journal of Near-Death Studies* 10:11–39.

Ring, K. 1992. *The Omega Project: Near-death experiences. UFO encounters, and mind at large*. New York: William Morrow.

Ring, K., and Rosing, C. J. 1990. The Omega Project: An empirical study of the NDE-prone personality. *Journal of Near-Death Studies* 8:211–39.

Ring, K., and Valarino, E. E. 2000. *Lessons from the light: What we can learn from the near-death experience*. Needham, MA: Moment Point Press.

Rosen, D. H. 1975. Suicide survivors: A follow-up study of persons who survived jumping from the Golden Gate and San Francisco–Oakland Bay Bridges. *Western Journal of Medicine* 122 (4): 289–94.

Sabom, M. B. 1982. *Recollections of death: A medical investigation*. New York: Harper & Row.

Schwaninger, J., Eisenberg, P. R., Schechtman, K. B., and Weiss, A. N. 2002. A prospective analysis of near-death experiences in cardiac arrest patients. *Journal of Near-Death Studies* 20:215–32.

Serdahely, W. J. 1987–88. The near-death experience: Is the presence always the higher self? *Omega* 18 (2): 129–34.

Serdahely, W. J. 1989–90. A pediatric near-death experience: Tunnel variants. *Omega* 20 (1): 55–62.

Serdahely, W. J. 1990. Pediatric near-death experiences. *Journal of Near-Death Studies* 9 (1): 33–39.

Serdahely, W. J. 1991. A comparison of retrospective accounts of childhood near-death experiences with contemporary pediatric near-death experience accounts. *Journal of Near-Death Studies* 9:219–24.

Serdahely, W. J. 1992. Similarities between near-death experiences and multiple personality disorder. *Journal of Near-Death Studies* 11:19–38.

Serdahely, W. J. 1993. Near-death experiences and dissociation: Two cases. *Journal of Near-Death Studies* 12:85–94.

Serdahely, W. J. 1995. Variations from the prototypic near-death experience: The "individually-tailored" hypothesis. *Journal of Near-Death Studies* 13:185–96.

Serdahely, W. J., and Walker, B. A. 1990a. The near-death experience of a non-verbal person with congenital quadriplegia. *Journal of Near-Death Studies* 9:91–96.

Serdahely, W. J., and Walker, B. A. 1990b. A near-death experience at birth. *Death Studies* 14:177–83.

Shears, D., Elison, S., Garralda, M. E., and Nadel, S. 2005. Near-death experiences with meningococcal disease. *Journal of the American Academy of Child and Adolescent Psychiatry* 44:630–31.

Steiger, B., and Steiger, S. H. 1995. *Children of the light: The startling and inspiring truth about children's near-death experiences and how they illumine the beyond.* New York: Signet.

Sutherland, C. 1990. Changes in religious beliefs, attitudes, and practices following near-death experiences: An Australian study. *Journal of Near-Death Studies* 9:21–31.

Sutherland, C. 1992. *Transformed by the light: Life after near-death experiences.* Sydney: Bantam Books. (U.S. ed. pub. 1995: *Reborn in the light: Life after near-death experiences.* New York: Bantam Books.)

Sutherland, C. 1993. *Within the light.* Sydney: Bantam Books. (U. S. ed. pub. 1995: *Within the light.* New York: Bantam Books.)

Sutherland, C. 1995. *Children of the light: The near-death experiences of children.* Sydney: Bantam Books.

Sutherland, C. 1997. *Beloved visitors: Parents tell of after-death visits from their children.* Sydney: Bantam Books.

Valent, P. 1993. *Child survivors: Adults living with childhood trauma.* Port Melbourne, Victoria: William Heinemann Australia.

van Lommel, P., van Wees, R., Meyers, V., and Elfferich, I. 2001. Near-death experience in survivors of cardiac arrest: A prospective study in the Netherlands. *Lancet* 358:2039–45.

Walker, B. A., Serdahely, W. J., and Bechtel, L. J. 1991. Three near-death experiences with premonitions of what could have been. *Journal of Near-Death Studies* 9:189–96.

CHAPTER 6

Atwater, P. M. H. 1996. Children and the near-death phenomenon: Another viewpoint. *Journal of Near-Death Studies* 15:5–16.

Atwater, P. M. H. 2000. *The complete idiot's guide to near-death experiences.* Indianapolis: Macmillan.

Audain, L. 1999. Gender and trauma in the near-death experience: An epidemiological and theoretical analysis. *Journal of Near-Death Studies* 18:35–49.

Beeghley, L. 2004. *The structure of social stratification in the United States.* Boston: Pearson, Allyn & Bacon.

Bonenfant, R. J. 2001. A child's encounter with the devil: An unusual near-death experience and both blissful and frightening elements. *Journal of Near-Death Studies* 20:87–100.

Bonenfant, R. J. 2004. A comparative study of near-death experience and non-near-death experience outcomes in 56 survivors of clinical death. *Journal of Near-Death Studies* 22:155–78.

Brinkley, D., and Perry, P. 1994. *Saved by the light.* New York: Villard.

Britton, W., and Bootzin, R. 2004. Near-death experiences and the temporal lobe. *Psychological Science* 15:254–58.

Buehlman, K. T., Gottman, J. M., and Katz, L. F. 1992. How a couple views their past predicts their future: Predicting divorce from an oral history interview. *Journal of Family Psychology* 5:295–318.

Bush, N. 1983. The near-death experience in children: Shades of the prison-house reopening. *Anabiosis: The Journal for Near-Death Studies* 3:177–93.

Carr, C. 1993. Death and near-death: A comparison of Tibetan and Euro-American experiences. *Journal of Transpersonal Psychology* 25:59–110.

Christian, S. R. 2005. Marital satisfaction and stability following a near-death experience of one of the marital partners. University of North Texas dissertation. Retrieved June 15, 2008, from http://www.unt.edu/etd/all/August2005/Open/christian_sandra_rozan/index.htm.

Council, J., and Greyson, B. 1985. Near-death experiences and the "fantasy-prone" personality: Preliminary findings. Paper presented at the 93rd Annual Convention of the American Psychological Association, Los Angeles.

Dale, L. 2001. *Crossing over and coming home: Twenty-one authors discuss the gay near-death experience as spiritual transformation.* Houston: Emerald Ink.

Enright, R. 2004. Silent journey: The discovery of the near-death experience of a nonverbal adolescent. *Journal of Near-Death Studies* 22:195–208.

Fenwick, P., and Fenwick, E. 1995. *The truth in the light: An investigation of over 300 near-death experiences.* London: Headline.

Gabbard, G., and Twemlow, S. 1984. *With the eyes of the mind: An empirical analysis of out-of body states.* New York: Praeger.

Gow, K., Lane, A., and Chant, D. 2003. Personality characteristics, beliefs, and the near-death experience. *Australian Journal of Clinical and Experimental Hypnosis* 31:128–52.

Grey, M. 1985. *Return from death: An exploration of the near-death experience.* London: Arkana.

Greyson, B. 1983. The Near-Death Experience Scale: Construction, reliability, and validity. *Journal of Nervous and Mental Disease* 171:369–75.

Greyson, B. 1990. Near-death encounters with and without near-death experiences: Comparative NDE scale profiles. *Journal of Near-Death Studies* 8:151–61.

Greyson, B. 1991. Near-death experiences precipitated by suicide attempt: Lack of influence of psychopathology, religion, and expectations. *Journal of Near-Death Studies* 9:183–88.

Greyson, B. 1993. Varieties of near-death experience. *Psychiatry* 56:390–99.

Greyson, B. 2000a. Dissociation in people who have near-death experiences: Out of their bodies or out of their minds? *Lancet* 355:460–73.

Greyson, B. 2000b. Near-death experiences. In E. Cardeña, S. J. Lynn, and S. Krippner (Eds), *Varieties of anomalous experience: Examining the scientific evidence*, 315–52. Washington, DC: American Psychological Association.

Greyson, B. 2001. Posttraumatic stress symptoms following near-death experiences. *American Journal of Orthopsychiatry* 71:358–73.

Greyson, B. 2003. Incidence and correlates of near-death experiences in a cardiac care unit. *General Hospital Psychiatry* 25:269–76.

Greyson, B., and Liester, M. 2004. Auditory hallucinations following near-death experiences. *Journal of Humanistic Psychology* 44:320–36.

Greyson, B., and Stevenson, I. 1980. The phenomenology of near-death experiences. *American Journal of Psychiatry* 137:1193–96.

Groth-Marnat, G., and Summers, R. 1998. Altered beliefs, attitudes, and behaviors following near-death experiences. *Journal of Humanistic Psychology* 38:110–25.

Herzog, D., and Herrin, J. 1985. Near-death experiences in the very young. *Critical Care Medicine* 13:1074–75.

IANDS (International Association for Near-Death Studies). 2003. Kircher, P., Holden, J., Atwater, P. M. H., and Morse, M. *Children's Near-Death Experiences.* Retrieved April 19, 2008, from http://www.iands.org/nde_index/ndes/child.html.

Irwin, H. 1985. *Flight of mind: A psychological study of the out-of-body experience.* Metuchen, NJ: Scarecrow Press.

Irwin, H. J. 1993. The near-death experience as a dissociative phenomenon: An empirical assessment. *Journal of Near-Death Studies* 12:95–103.

Irwin, H. J., and Bramwell, B. A. 1988. The devil in heaven: A near-death experience with both positive and negative facets. *Journal of Near-Death Studies* 7:38–43.

Karnofsky, D., and Burchenal, J. 1949. The clinical evaluation of chemotherapeutic agents in cancer. In C. M. MacLeod (Ed.), *Evaluation of chemotherapeutic agents*, 191–205. New York: Columbia University Press.

Kelly, E. 2001. Near-death experiences with reports of meeting deceased people. *Death Studies* 25:229–49.

Locke, T., and Shontz, F. 1983. Personality correlates of the near-death experience: A preliminary study. *Journal of the American Society for Psychical Research* 77:311–17.

Lundahl, C. 1981–82. The perceived other world in Mormon near-death experiences: A social and physical description. *Omega* 12:319–27.

Lynn, S., and Rhue, J. 1986. The fantasy-prone person: Hypnosis, imagination, and creativity. *Journal of Personality and Social Psychology* 51:404–8.

Lynn, S., and Rhue, J. 1988. Fantasy proneness: Hypnosis, developmental antecedents, and psychopathology. *American Psychologist* 43:35–44.

McLaughlin, S. A., and Malony, H. N. 1984. Near-death experiences and religion: A further investigation. *Journal of Religion and Health* 23 (2): 119–59.

Moody, R. 1975. *Life after life*. Atlanta: Mockingbird Books.

Morse, M. 1983. A near-death experience in a 7-year-old child. *American Journal of Diseases of Children* 137:959–61.

Morse, M., Castillo, P., Venecia, D., Milstein, J., and Tyler, D. C. 1984. Childhood near-death experiences. *American Journal of Diseases of Children* 140:1110–14.

Morse, M., and Perry, P. 1992. *Transformed by the light*. New York: Villiard Books.

Near-Death Experience Research Foundation. 2008a. Jody R's NDE. Retrieved April 19, 2008, from http://www.nderf.org/jody_r's_nde.htm.

Near-Death Experience Research Foundation. 2008b. Non-Western NDEs Log. Retrieved April 19, 2008, from http://www.nderf.org/non_western_ndes.htm.

Noyes, R., and Kletti, R. 1976. Depersonalization in the face of life-threatening danger: An interpretation. *Omega* 7:103–14.

Owens, J., Cook, E., Stevenson, I. 1990. Features of "near-death experience" in relation to whether or not patients were near death. *Lancet* 336:1175–77.

Pacciolla, A. 1996. The near-death experience: A study of its validity. *Journal of Near-Death Studies* 14:179–85.

Pasricha, S., and Stevenson, I. 1986. Near-death experiences in India: A preliminary report. *Journal of Nervous and Mental Disease* 174:165–70.

Parnia, S., Waller, D., Yeates, R., and Fenwick, P. 2001. A qualitative and quantitative study of the incidence, features, and aetiology of near death experiences in cardiac arrest survivors. *Resuscitation* 48:149–56.

Ring, K. 1980. *Life at death: A scientific investigation of the near-death experience*. New York: Coward, McCann & Geoghegan.

Ring, K. 1992. *The Omega Project: Near-death experiences, UFO encounters, and mind at large*. New York: William Morrow.

Ring, K., and Cooper, S. 1998. Near-death and out-of-body experiences in the blind: A study of apparent eyeless vision. *Journal of Near-Death Studies* 16:101–47.

Ring, K., and Cooper, S. 1999. *Mindsight: Near-death and out-of-body experiences in the blind*. Palo Alto, CA: Institute of Transpersonal Psychology.

Ring, K., and Rosing, C. J. 1990. The Omega Project: An empirical study of the NDE-prone personality. *Journal of Near-Death Studies* 8:211–39.

Rommer, B. 2000. *Blessing in disguise: Another side of the near-death experience*. St. Paul, MN: Llewellyn Publications.

Sabom, M. 1982. *Recollections of death: A medical investigation*. New York: Harper & Row.

Schoenbeck, S., and Hocutt, G. 1991. Near-death experience in patients undergoing cardiopulmonary resuscitation. *Journal of Near-Death Studies* 9:211–18.

Schorer, C. 1985–86. Two Native American near-death experiences. *Omega* 16 (2): 111–13.

Schwaninger, J., Eisenberg, P., Schechtman, K., and Weiss, A. 2002. A prospective analysis of near-death experiences in cardiac arrest patients. *Journal of Near-Death Studies* 20:215–32.

Serdahely, W. J., and Walker, B. A. 1990. The near-death experience of a nonverbal person with congenital quadriplegia. *Journal of Near-Death Studies* 9 (2): 91–96.

Serdahely, W. J. 1991. A comparison of retrospective accounts of childhood near-death experiences with contemporary pediatric near-death experience accounts. *Journal of Near-Death Studies* 9:219–24.

Social Security Online. Period Life Table. 2004. Retrieved April 19, 2008, from http://www.ssa.gov/OACT/STATS/table4c6.html.

Suliman, A. 2004. *A passage to eternity*. Calgary, Alberta: Amethyst.

Sullivan, R. M. 1984. Combat-related near-death experiences: A preliminary investigation. *Anabiosis: The Journal for Near-Death Studies* 4:143–52.

Sutherland, C. 1989. Psychic phenomena following near-death experiences: An Australian study. *Journal of Near Death Studies* 8:93–102.

Sutherland, C. 1992. *Transformed by the light: Life after near-death experiences*. Sydney: Bantam Books. (U.S. ed. pub. 1995: *Reborn in the light: Life after near-death experiences*. New York: Bantam Books.)

Sutherland, C. 1995. *Children of the light: The near-death experiences of children*. Sydney: Bantam Books.

Tellegen, A., and Atkinson, G. 1974. Openness to absorbing and self-altering experiences ("absorption"), a trait related to hypnotic susceptibility. *Journal of Abnormal Psychology* 83:268–77.

Tiberi, E. 1993. Extrasomatic emotions. *Journal of Near-Death Studies* 11:149–70.

van Lommel, P., van Wees, R., Meyers, V., and Elfferich, I. 2001. Near-death experience in survivors of cardiac arrest: A prospective study in the Netherlands. *Lancet* 358:2039–45.

Wilson, S., and Barber, T. 1981. Vivid fantasy and hallucinatory abilities in the life histories of excellent hypnotic subjects ("somnambules"): Preliminary report with female subjects. In E. Klinger (Ed.), *Imagery*. Vol. 2, *Concepts, results, and applications*, 133–49. New York: Plenum.

Wilson, S. C., and Barber, T. X. 1983. The fantasy-prone personality: Implications for understanding imagery, hypnosis, and parapsychological phenomena. In A. A. Sheikh (Ed.), *Imagery: Current theory, research, and application*, 340–90. New York: Wiley.

Zhi-ying, F., and Jian-xun, L. 1992. Near-death experiences among survivors of the 1976 Tangshan earthquake. *Journal of Near-Death Studies* 11:39–48.

CHAPTER 7

Athappilly, G. K., Greyson, B., and Stevenson, I. 2006. Do prevailing societal models influence reports of near-death experiences? *Journal of Nervous and Mental Disease* 194:218–22.

Atwater, P. M. H. 1988. *Coming back to life: The after-effects of the near-death experience*. New York: Ballantine.

Bailey, L. W. 2001. A "little death": The near-death experience and Tibetan *delogs*. *Journal of Near-Death Studies* 19:139–59.

Becker, C. 1981. The centrality of near-death experiences in Chinese Pure Land Buddhism. *Anabiosis: The Journal for Near-Death Studies* 1:154–71.

Becker, C. 1984. The Pure Land re-visited: Sino-Japanese meditations and near-death experiences of the next world. *Anabiosis: The Journal for Near-Death Studies* 4:51–68.

Bellah, R. N. 1976. *Beyond belief: Essays on religion in a post-traditional world*. New York: Harper & Row.

Berndt, R. M., and Berndt, C. H. 1989. *The speaking land: Myth and story in Aboriginal Australia*. Harmondsworth, England: Penguin.

Blackmore, S. J. 1993. Near-death experiences in India: They have tunnels too. *Journal of Near-Death Studies* 11:205–17.

Blackmore, S. J., and Troscianko, T. S. 1989. The physiology of the tunnel. *Journal of Near-Death Studies* 8:15–28.

Butler, R. N. 1963. The life review: An integration of reminiscence in the aged. *Psychiatry* 26:65–76.

Carroll, L. 1965. *Alice's adventures in wonderland*. New York: Airmont. (Original work published 1865.)

Counts, D. A. 1983. Near-death and out-of-body experiences in a Melanesian society. *Anabiosis: The Journal for Near-Death Studies* 3:115–35.

Douglas, M. 1966. *Purity and danger*. London: Routledge & Kegan Paul.

Drab, K. J. 1981. Unresolved problems in the study of near-death experiences: Some suggestions for research and theory. *Anabiosis: The Journal for Near-Death Studies* 1:126–52.

Gómez-Jeria, J. S. 1993. A near-death experience among the Mapuche people. *Journal of Near-Death Studies* 11:219–22.

Green, J. T. 1984. Near-death experiences in a Chommorro culture. *Vital Signs* 4(1–2): 6–7.

Grey, M. 1985. *Return from death: An exploration of the near-death experience*. London: Arkana.

Greyson, B., and Stevenson, I. 1980. The phenomenology of near-death experiences. *American Journal of Psychiatry* 137:1193–96.

Grosso, M. 1981. Toward an explanation of near-death phenomena. *Journal of the American Society for Psychical Research* 8:19–63.

Kellehear, A. 1993. Culture, biology, and the near-death experience: A reappraisal. *Journal of Nervous and Mental Disease* 181:148-56.

Kellehear, A. 1996. *Experiences near death: Beyond medicine and religion*. New York: Oxford University Press.

Kellehear, A. 2001. An Hawaiian near-death experience. *Journal of Near-Death Studies* 20:31–35.

Kellehear, A. 2007. *A social history of dying*. Cambridge, England: Cambridge University Press.

Kellehear, A., Heaven, P., and Gao, J. 1990. Community attitudes toward near-death experiences: A Chinese study. *Journal of Near-Death Studies* 8:163–73.

Kellehear, A., Stevenson, I., Pasricha, S., and Cook, E. 1994. The absence of tunnel sensation in near-death experiences from India. *Journal of Near-Death Studies* 13:109–13.

King, M. 1985. *Being Pakeha: An encounter with New Zealand and the Maori Renaissance*. Auckland, New Zealand: Hodder & Stoughton.

Knoblauch, H., Schmied, I., and Schnettler, B. 2001. Different kinds of near-death experience: A report on a survey of near-death experiences in Germany. *Journal of Near-Death Studies* 20:15–29.

Lai, W. 1996. Tales of rebirths and the later Pure Land tradition in China. In J. Foard, M. Solomon, and R. K. Payne (Eds.), *The Pure Land tradition: History and development* (Berkeley Buddhist Studies, Series 3). Berkeley, CA: Institute of Buddhist Studies.

Lundahl, C. R. 1981–82. The perceived otherworld in Mormon near-death experiences: A social and physical description. *Omega* 12:319–27.

Moody, R. A. 1975. *Life after life*. Atlanta: Mockingbird Books.

Morse, M., and Perry, P. 1990. *Closer to the light*. New York: Villiard.

Morse, M., and Perry, P. 1993. *Transformed by the light*. New York: Villiard.

Murphy, T. 2001. Near-death experiences in Thailand. *Journal of Near-Death Studies* 19:161–78.

Noyes, R., and Kletti, R. 1977. Depersonalization in the face of life threatening danger: A description. *Psychiatry* 39:19–27.

Ogasawara, S. 1963. *Chugoku kinsei jodokyoshi no kenkyu* [Research on the history of Pure Land Buddhism in recent China]. Kyoto, Japan: Hyakkaen.

Osis, K., and Haraldsson, E. 1977. *At the hour of death*. New York: Avon.

Oxford English Dictionary. 1989. Oxford, England: Oxford University Press.

Panoff, M. 1968. The notion of the double self among the Maenge. *Journal of the Polynesian Society* 77:275–95.

Pasricha, S. 1992. Near-death experiences in South India: A systematic survey in Channapatna. *National Institute of Mental Health & Neuroscience Journal* 10:111–18.

Pasricha, S. 1993. A systematic survey of near-death experiences in South India. *Journal of Scientific Exploration* 7:161–71.

Pasricha, S., and Stevenson, I. 1986. Near-death experiences in India: A preliminary report. *Journal of Nervous and Mental Disease* 174:165–70.

Pommaret, F. 1989. *Les revenants de l'au-delà dans le monde Tibétain: Sources littéraires et tradition vivante* [Those who return from the hereafter in the Tibetan world: Literary sources and living tradition]. Paris: Editions du Centre National de le Recherche Scientifique.

Roheim, G. 1932. Psychoanalysis of primitive cultural types. *International Journal of Psychoanalysis* 13:1–224.

Sabom, M. 1982. *Recollections of death: A medical investigation*. New York: Harper & Row.

Schoolcraft, H. R. 1825. *Travels in the central portion of the Mississippi Valley*. New York: Collins & Henry.

Schorer, C. E. 1985. Two Native American near-death experiences. *Omega* 1:111–13.

Schwaninger, J., Eisenberg, P. R., Schechtman, K. B., and Weiss, A. N. 2002. A prospective analysis of near-death experiences in cardiac arrest patients. *Journal of Near-Death Studies* 20:215–32.

Sheils, D. 1978. A cross-cultural study of beliefs in out-of-body experiences, waking and sleeping. *Journal of the Society of Psychical Research* 49:697–741.

Smith, W. R. 1970. *Myths and legends of the Australian Aboriginals*. London: George G. Harrap [Johnson Reprint Corp.].

Sutherland, C. 1992. *Transformed by the light*. Sydney: Bantam Books.

Thrum, T. 1907. *Hawaiian folk tales: A collection of native legends*. Chicago: A. C. McClurg.

Wade, J. 2003. In a sacred manner we died: Native American near-death experiences. *Journal of Near-Death Studies* 22:82–114.

Walker, B. A., and Serdahely, W. J. 1990. Historical perspectives on near-death phenomena. *Journal of Near-Death Studies* 9:105–21.

Warner, W. L. 1937. *A black civilization: A social study of an Australian tribe*. New York: Harper & Brothers.

Weber, M. 1965. *The sociology of religion*. London: Methuen.

Zaleski, C. 1987. *Otherworld journeys: Accounts of near-death experiences in medieval and modern times*. New York: Oxford University Press.

Zhi-ying, F., and Jian-xun, L. 1992. Near-death experiences among survivors of the 1976 Tangshan earthquake. *Journal of Near-Death Studies* 11:39–48.

Zinberg, N. 1984. *Drug, set and setting: The basis for controlled intoxicant use*. New Haven, CT: Yale University Press.

CHAPTER 8

'Abdu'l-Bahá. 1979a. *Paris talks: Addresses given by 'Abdu'l-Bahá in Paris in 1911–12*. 11th ed. London: Bahá'í Publishing Trust.

'Abdu'l-Bahá. 1979b. *The secret of divine civilization*. Wilmette, IL: Bahá'í Publishing Trust.

'Abdu'l-Bahá. 1981. *Some answered questions*. Rev. ed. Comp. and trans. L. C. Barney. Wilmette, IL: Bahá'í Publishing Trust.

'Abdu'l-Bahá. 1982b. *Promulgation of universal peace*. Wilmette, IL: Bahá'í Publishing Trust.

Arberry, A. J. 1995. *Qur'an (The Koran Interpreted)*. New York: MacMillan.

Atwater, P. M. H. 1988. *Coming back to life*. New York: Dodd, Mead.

Axelrod, B. 1978. Pastoral implications of *Life after Life*. *Soul Searcher* 1 (3): 11–14.

Badham, P. 1997. Religious and near-death experience in relation to belief in a future life. *Mortality* 2 (1): 7–21.

Bahá'u'lláh. 1983. *Gleanings from the writings of Bahá'u'lláh*. Trans. S. Effendi. Wilmette, IL: Bahá'í Publishing Trust.

Bahá'u'lláh. 1986. *The hidden words of Bahá'u'lláh*. Oxford, England: Oneworld.

Bahá'u'lláh, and 'Abdu'l-Bahá. 1976. *Bahá'í world faith: Selected writings of Bahá'u'lláh and 'Abdu'l-Bahá.* Wilmette, IL: Bahá'í Publishing Trust.

Bahá'u'lláh, the Báb, and 'Abdu'l-Bahá. 2002. *Bahá'í prayers: A selection of prayers revealed by Bahá'u'lláh, the Báb, and 'Abdu'l-Bahá.* Wilmette, IL: Bahá'í Publishing Trust.

Bausani, A. 2000. *Religion in Iran: From Zoroaster to Baha'u'llah.* New York: Bibliotheca Persica Press.

Becker, C. B. 1981. The centrality of near-death experiences in Chinese Pure Land Buddhism. *Anabiosis: The Journal for Near-Death Studies* 1:154–71.

Becker, C. B. 1985. Views from Tibet: NDEs and the Book of the Dead. *Anabiosis: The Journal for Near-Death Studies* 5(1):3–20.

Beversluis, J. 2000. *Sourcebook of the world religions: An interfaith guide to religion and spirituality.* Novato, CA: New World Library.

Bretherton, D. 2004. NDEs and the Christian hope. *Christian Parapsychologist* 16 (2): 41–47.

Bryson, A. 1997. *Light after death: A comparison of the near-death experience and the teachings of the Bahá'í faith on life after death.* New Delhi, India: Sterling.

Canda, E., and Furman, L. 1999. *Spiritual diversity in social work practice: The heart of helping.* New York: Free Press.

Carus, P. 1915. *The gospel of Buddha.* Chicago: Open Court.

Crim, K. 1981. *Abingdon dictionary of living religions.* Nashville: Parthenon Press.

Dhammapada: The path to perfection. 1973. Trans. J. Mascaro. New York: Penguin.

Ellwood, G. F. 2000. Religious experience, religious worldviews, and near-death studies. *Journal of Near-Death Studies* 19:5–21.

Esslemont, J. 1980. *Bahá'u'lláh and the new era.* Wilmette, IL: Bahá'í Publishing Trust.

Fenwick, P. 2005. Science and spirituality: A challenge for the 21st century [The Bruce Greyson lecture from the International Association for Near-Death Studies 2004 annual conference]. *Journal of Near-Death Studies* 23:131–57.

Fenwick, P., and Fenwick, E. 1997. *The truth in the light: An investigation of over 300 near-death experiences.* New York: Berkley Books.

Fisher, M. 2002. *Living religions.* Upper Saddle River, NJ: Prentice Hall.

Flynn, C. 1986. *After the beyond.* Engelwood Cliffs, NJ: Prentice-Hall.

Gandhi, M. 1935, July 20. *Harijan.* Quotation retrieved January 14, 2007, from http://www.quotedb.com/quotes/2066.

Glasse, C. 1989. *The concise encyclopedia of Islam.* San Francisco: Harper & Row.

Grey, M. 1988. *Return from death: An exploration of the near-death experience.* New York: Penguin.

Greyson, B. 2000. Near-death experiences. In E. Cardeña, S. J. Lynn, and S. Krippner (Eds.), *Varieties of anomalous experience: Examining the scientific evidence,* 315–52. Washington, DC: American Psychological Association.

Greyson, B., and Stevenson, I. 1980. The phenomenology of near-death experiences. *American Journal of Psychiatry* 137:1193–96.

Griffith, R. 1926. *Hymns of the Rigveda.* Benares, India: Medical Hall Press.

Haug, M., and West, E. 1971. *The Book of Arda Viraf.* Amsterdam: Oriental Press.

Hatcher, W. S., and Martin, J. D. 1984. *The Bahá'í faith: The emerging global religion.* San Francisco: Harper & Row.

Holden, J. M., and Joesten, L. 1990. Near-death veridicality research in the hospital setting. *Journal of Near-Death Studies* 9:45–54.

Holmes, E. 1919. *The creed of Buddha*. 2nd ed. Retrieved March 28, 2008, from http://www.sacred-texts.com/bud/cob/index.htm.

Holy Bible, Revised Standard Version. 1952. New York: Thomas Nelson & Sons.

Hopfe, L., and Woodward, M. 2005. *Religions of the world*. Upper Saddle River, NJ: Pearson Prentice Hall.

Hopkins, T. 1971. *The Hindu religious tradition*. Encino, CA: Dickenson.

Ichaporia, P. R. n.d. The doctrine of after life in avesta and pahlavi. Retrieved March 28, 2008, from http://tenets.zoroastrianism.com/after33.html.

Johnson, C., and McGee, M. 1986. *Encounters with eternity: Religious views of death and life after death*. New York: Philosophical Library.

Keith, A. 1971. *The religion and philosophy of the Veda and Upanishads*. Westport, CT: Greenwood Press.

Kellehear, A. 1993. Culture, biology, and the near-death experience: A reappraisal. *Journal of Nervous and Mental Disease* 181 (3): 148–56.

Masumian, F. 2002. *Life after death: A study of afterlife in world religions*. Los Angeles: Kalimat Press.

Masumian, F., and Masumian, B. 2005. *Divine educators*. Oxford, England: George Ronald.

Molloy, M. 2005. *Experiencing the world's religions*. Boston: McGraw Hill.

Momen, M. 1985. *An introduction to Shi'i Islam: The history and doctrine of Twelver Shi'ism*. Oxford, England: George Ronald.

Moody, R. 1975. *Life after life: The investigation of a phenomenon—survival of bodily death*. Atlanta: Mockingbird Books.

Morse, M., and Perry, P. 1994. *Parting visions: Uses and meanings of pre-death, psychic, and spiritual experiences*. New York: Villard Books.

Morse, M., and Perry, P. 2001. *Transformed by the light*. New York: Villiard.

Nigosian, S. 1994. *World faiths*. New York: St. Martin's Press.

Noss, D., and Noss, J. 1994. *A history of the world's religions*. New York: Macmillan College.

Novak, P. 1994. *The world's wisdom: Sacred texts of the world's religions*. New York: Harper San Francisco.

Pandarakalam, J. P. 1990. Enigma of the near-death experience. *Indian Journal of Psychological Medicine* 13 (1): 131–36.

Parnia, S. 2006. *What happens when we die: A groundbreaking study into the nature of life and death*. Carlsbad, CA: Hay House.

Parnia, S., Waller, D. G., Yeates, R., and Fenwick, P. 2001. A qualitative and quantitative study of the incidence, features and aetiology of near death experiences in cardiac arrest survivors. *Resuscitation* 48 (2): 149–56.

Pasarow, R. 1981. A personal account of an NDE: Reinee Pasarow. *Vital Signs* 1 (3): 11, 14.

Pasricha, S., and Stevenson, I. 1986. Near-death experiences in India: A preliminary report. *Journal of Nervous and Mental Disease* 174 (3): 165–70.

Peterson, J. H. 1996. *Dadestan-i denig* [Religious decisions]. Trans. E. W. West. Available at http://www.avesta.org/mp/dd.htm.

Qur'an: Text, translation, and commentary. 2001. Trans. A. Y. Ali. New York: Tah-rike Tarsile Qur'an.

Qur'an (The Koran). 1993. Trans. J. M. Rodwell. New York: Ivy Books.

Ring, K. 1980. *Life at death: A scientific investigation of the near-death experience.* New York: Coward, McCann & Geoghegan.

Ring, K. 1984. *Heading toward omega.* New York: William Morrow.

Ring, K. 1993. A new Book of the Dead: Reflections on the near-death experience and the Tibetan Buddhist tradition regarding the nature of death. *Journal of Near-Death Studies* 12:75–84.

Ring, K., and Valarino, E. 1998. *Lessons from the light: What we can learn from the near-death experience.* New York: Plenum Press.

Shapiro, D. S. 1979. Death experiences in rabbinic literature. *Judaism* 28:90–94.

Sutherland, C. 1995. *Within the light.* New York: Bantam Books.

van Lommel, P. 2004. About the continuity of our consciousness. *Advances in Experimental Medicine and Biology* 550: 115–32.

van Lommel, P., van Wees, R., Meyers, V., and Elfferich, I. 2001. Near-death experience in survivors of cardiac arrest: A prospective study in the Netherlands. *Lancet* 358:2039–45.

Vincent, K. R. 1994. *Visions of God: From the near-death experience.* New York: Larson.

Vincent, K. R. 2003. The near-death experience and Christian universalism. *Journal of Near-Death Studies* 22:57–71.

Wilson, A. (Ed.). 1995. *World scripture: A comparative anthology of sacred texts.* New York: Paragon House.

Zaleski, C. 1987. *Otherworld journeys: Accounts of near-death experience in medieval and modern times.* New York: Oxford University Press.

CHAPTER 9

Alvarado, C. 2000. Out-of-body experiences. In E. Cardeña, S. J. Lynn, and S. Krippner (Eds.), *Varieties of anomalous experience: Examining the scientific evidence,* 183–218. Washington, DC: American Psychological Association.

Atwater, P. M. H. 1999. *Children of the new millenium.* New York: Three Rivers Press.

Augustine, K. 2006. Hallucinatory near-death experiences. Retrieved September 15, 2006, from http://www.infidels.org/library/modern/keith_augustine/HNDEs. html#OBE%20discrepancies.

Blackmore, S. 1985. Susan Blackmore replies [Letter to the editor]. *Journal of Near-Death Studies* 5:79–82.

Blackmore, S. 1993. *Dying to live: Science and the near-death experience.* London: Grafton/HarperCollins.

Bonenfant, R. J. 2001. A child's encounter with the devil: An unusual near-death experience with both blissful and frightening elements. *Journal of Near-Death Studies* 20:87–100.

Braud, W., and Anderson, R. 1998. *Transpersonal research methods for the social sciences: Honoring human experience.* Thousand Oaks, CA: Sage.

Broome, K. (Producer). 2002. *The day I died* [Motion picture]. Glasgow, Scotland: British Broadcasting Corporation.

Brumblay, R. J. 2003. Hyperdimensional perspectives in out-of-body and near-death experiences. *Journal of Near-Death Studies* 21:201–21.

Clark, K. 1984. Clinical interventions with near-death experiencers. In B. Greyson and C. P. Flynn (Eds.), *The near-death experience: Problems, prospects, perspectives*, 242–55. Springfield, IL: Charles C. Thomas.

Clark, R. W. 1971. *Einstein*. New York: World.

Cobbe, F. P. 1882. *The peak in Darien*. London: Williams & Norgate.

Cook, E. W., Greyson, B., and Stevenson, I. 1998. Do any near-death experiences provide evidence for the suvival of human personality after death? Relevant features and illustrative case reports. *Journal of Scientific Exploration* 12:377–406.

Crookall, R. 1972. *Case-book of astral projection*. Secaucus, NJ: University Books.

Ebbern, H., Mulligan, S., and Beyerstein, B. L. 1996. Maria's near-death experience: Waiting for the other shoe to drop. *Skeptical Inquirer* 20:27–33.

Ellwood, G. F. 2001. *The uttermost deep: The challenge of near-death experiences*. New York: Lantern Books.

Fenwick, P. 2005. Science and spirituality: A challenge for the 21st century. *Journal of Near-Death Studies* 23:131–57.

Fenwick, P., and Fenwick, E. 1995. *The truth in the light: An investigation of over 300 near-death experiences*. London: Headline.

Fuller, J. G. 1969. *The great soul trial*. New York: MacMillan.

Gabbard, G. O., and Twemlow, S. W. 1984. *With the eyes of the mind: An empirical analysis of out-of-body states*. New York: Praeger.

Green, C. 1968. *Out-of-the-body experiences*. Oxford, England: Institute of Psychophysical Research.

Grey, M. 1985. *Return from death*. New York: Arkana.

Greyson, B. 2000. Near-death experiences. In E. Cardeña, S. J. Lynn, and S. Krippner (Eds.), *Varieties of anomalous experience: Examining the scientific evidence*, 315–52. Washington, DC: American Psychological Association.

Greyson, B., and Harris, B. 1987. Clinical approaches to the near-death experiencer. *Journal of Near-Death Studies* 6:41–52.

Greyson, B., Holden, J. M., and Mounsey, J. P. 2006. Failure to elicit near-death experiences in induced cardiac arrest. *Journal of Near-Death Studies* 25:85–98.

Hampe, J. C. 1979. *To die is gain: The experience of one's own death* Trans. M. Kohl. Atlanta: John Knox Press.

Heppner, P. P., Kavlighan, D. M., Jr., and Wampold, B. E. 1999. *Research design in counseling*. New York: Wadsworth.

Holden, J. M. 1988. Rationale and considerations for proposed near-death research in the hospital setting. *Journal of Near-Death Studies* 7:19–31.

Holden, J. M. 1989. Visual perception during naturalistic near-death out-of-body experiences. *Journal of Near-Death Studies* 7:107–20.

Holden, J. M., and Joesten, L. 1990. Near-death veridicality research in the hospital setting. *Journal of Near-Death Studies* 9:45–54.

Hyslop, J. H. 1918. Visions of the dying: Class I. *Journal of the American Society for Psychical Research* 12 (10): 585–626.

Jung, C. G. 1969. Synchronicity: An acausal connecting principle. Trans. R. F. C. Hull. In H. Read, M. Fordham, G. Adler, and W. McGuire (Eds.), *The collected works of C. G. Jung.* 2nd ed. Vol. 8, *The structure and dynamics of the psyche,* 417–531. Princeton, NJ: Princeton University Press. (Orig. pub. 1952.)

Kelly, E. W., Greyson, B., and Stevenson, I. 1999–2000. Can experiences near death furnish evidence of life after death? *Omega* 40 (4): 513–19.

Kelly, E. F., Kelly, E. W., Crabtree, A., Gauld, A. Grosso, M., and Greyson, B. 2007. *Irreducible mind: Toward a psychology for the 21st century.* Lanham, MD: Rowman & Littlefield.

Kübler-Ross, E. 1983. *On children and death.* New York: Simon & Schuster.

Lawrence, M. 1996, August. Prospective NDE studies with AIDS and cardiac patients. Paper presented at the International Association for Near-Death Studies North American Conference, Oakland, CA.

Lawrence, M. 1997. *In a world of their own: Experiencing unconsciousness.* Westport, CT: Praeger.

League for the Hard of Hearing. n.d. Noise levels in our environment fact sheet. Retrieved October 8, 2006, from http://www.lhh.org/noise/decibel.htm.

Lindley, J. H., Bryan, S., and Conley, B. 1981. Near-death experience in a Pacific Northwest American population: The Evergreen study. *Anabiosis: The Journal for Near-Death Studies* 1:104–24.

Lundahl, C. R., and Gibson, A. S. 2000. Near-death studies and modern physics. *Journal of Near-Death Studies* 18:143–79.

Manley, L. K. 1996. Enchanting journeys: Near-death experiences and the emergency nurse. *Journal of Emergency Nursing* 22 (4): 311–16.

Merriam-Webster Online Dictionary. 2008. Trickster. Retrieved August 20, 2008, from http://www.merriam-webster.com/dictionary/trickster.

Miner-Holden, J. 1988. *Visual perception during the naturalistic near-death out-of-body experience.* PhD dissertation. (UMI No. 8822373.)

Moody, R. 1975. *Life after life.* Atlanta: Mocking bird Books.

Moody, R. A., and Perry, P. 1988. *The light beyond.* New York: Bantam Books.

Morris, L. L., and Knafl, K. 2003. The nature and meaning of the near-death experience for patients and critical care nurses. *Journal of Near-Death Studies* 21:139–67.

Morse, M. L. 1994. Near death experiences and death-related visions in children: Implications for the clinician. *Current Problems in Pediatrics* 24:55–83.

Morse, M. L., and Perry, P. 1990. *Closer to the light: Learning from the near-death experiences of children.* New York: Villard Books.

Myers, F. W. H. 1892. On indications of continued terrene knowledge on the part of the phantasms of the dead. *Proceedings of the Society for Psychical Research* 8:170–252.

Near-death experiences: The proof. 2006, February 2. Article scanned from *Daily Express,* London. Retrieved February 2006 from http://farshores.org/p06ndetp.htm.

Ogston, A. 1920. *Reminiscences of three campaigns.* London: Hodder & Stoughton.

Osis, K. 1975. Perceptual experiments on out-of-body experiences. In J. D. Morris, W. G. Roll, and R. L. Morris (Eds.), *Research in parapsychology, 1974,* 53–55. Metuchen, NJ: Scarecrow.

Pais, A. 1982. *Subtle is the Lord: The science and the life of Albert Einstein*. New York: Oxford University.

Parnia, S. 2006. *What happens when we die*. Carlsbad, CA: Hay House.

Parnia, S., and Fenwick, P. 2002. Near death experiences in cardiac arrest: Visions of a dying brain or visions of a new science of consciousness. *Resuscitation* 52 (1): 5–11.

Parnia, S., Waller, D. G., Yeates, R., and Fenwick, P. 2001. A qualitative and quantitative study of the incidence, features and aetiology of near death experiences in cardiac arrest survivors. *Resuscitation* 48:149–56.

Rawlings, M. 1978. *Beyond death's door*. Nashville: Thomas Nelson.

Ring, K., and Cooper, S. 1999. *Mindsight: Near-death and out-of-body experiences in the blind*. Palo Alto, CA: William James Center for Consciousness Studies.

Ring, K., and Lawrence, M. 1993. Further evidence for veridical perception during near-death experiences. *Journal of Near-Death Studies* 11:223–29.

Ring, K., and Valarino, E. E. 1998. *Lessons from the light*. New York: Plenum.

Rogo, D. S. 1986. *Life after death: The case for survival of bodily death*. Wellingborough, Northamptonshire, England: Aquarian.

Rommer, B. 2000. *Blessing in disguise: Another side of the near-death experience*. St. Paul, MN: Llewellyn Publications.

Sabom, M. 1982. *Recollections of death: A medical investigation*. New York: Simon & Schuster.

Sabom, M. 1998. *Light and death: One doctor's fascinating account of near-death experiences*. Grand Rapids, MI: Zondervan.

Sartori, P. 2004. A prospective study of NDEs in an intensive therapy unit. *Christian Parapsychologist* 16 (2): 34–40.

Sartori, P., Badham, P., and Fenwick, P. 2006. A prospectively studied near-death experience with corroborated out-of-body perceptions and unexplained healing. *Journal of Near-Death Studies* 25:69–84.

Spetzler, R. F., Hadley, M. N., Rigamonti, D., Carter, L. P., Raudzens, P. A., Shedd, S. A., and Wilkinson, E. 1988. Aneurysms of the basilar artery treated with circulatory arrest, hypothermia, and barbiturate cerebral protection. *Journal of Neurosurgery* 68:868–78.

Tart, C. 1975. Some assumptions of orthodox, Western psychology. In C. Tart (Ed.), *Transpersonal psychologies*, 57–111. New York: Harper & Row.

Trickster. 2006. Retrieved October 8, 2006, from http://en.wikipedia.org/wiki/Trickster.

Tutka, M. A. 2001. Near-death experiences: Seeing the light. *Nursing* 31 (5): 62–63.

van Lommel, P. 2004. About the continuity of our consciousness. In C. Machado and D. A. Shewmon (Eds.), *Brain death and disorders of consciousness*, 115–32. New York: Springer.

van Lommel, P., van Wees, R., Meyers, V., and Elfferich, I. 2001. Near-death experience in survivors of cardiac arrest: A prospective study in the Netherlands. *Lancet* 358:2039–45.

Wilson, I. 1987. *The after death experience: The physics of the non-physical*. New York: William Morrow.

Wiltse, A. S. 1889. A case of typhoid fever with subnormal temperature and pulse. *Saint Louis Medical and Surgical Journal* 57:355–64

Woerlee, G. M. 2004. Cardiac arrest and near-death experiences. *Journal of Near-Death Studies* 22:235–49.

CHAPTER 10

Abramovitch, H. 1988. An Israeli account of a near-death experience: A case study of cultural dissonance. *Journal of Near-Death Studies* 6:175–84.

Alkire, M. T. 1998. Quantitative EEG correlations with brain glucose metabolic rate during anesthesia in volunteers. *Anesthesiology* 89:323–33.

Alkire, M. T., Haier, R. J., and Fallon, J. H. 2000. Toward a unified theory of narcosis: Brain imaging evidence for a thalamocortical switch as the neurophysiologic basis of anesthetic-induced unconsciousness. *Consciousness and Cognition* 9:370–86.

Aminoff, M. J., Scheinman, M. M., Griffin, J. C., and Herre, J. M. 1988. Electrocerebral accompaniments of syncope associated with malignant ventricular arrhythmias. *Annals of Internal Medicine* 108:791–96.

Athappilly, G. K., Greyson, B., and Stevenson, I. 2006. Do prevailing societal models influence reports of near-death experiences? A comparison of accounts reported before and after 1975. *Journal of Nervous and Mental Disease* 194:218–22.

Baars, B. J. 2001. The brain basis of a "consciousness monitor": Scientific and medical significance. *Consciousness and Cognition* 10:159–64.

Bauer, W. 1985. Near-death experiences and attitude change. *Journal of Near-Death Studies* 5:39–47.

Becker, C. B. 1982. The failure of Saganomics: Why birth models cannot explain near-death phenomena. *Journal of Near-Death Studies* 2:102–9.

Blackmore, S. 1983. Birth and the OBE: An unhelpful analogy. *Journal of the American Society for Psychical Research* 77:229–38.

Blackmore, S. 1984. A psychological theory of the out-of-body experience. *Journal of Parapsychology* 48:201–18.

Blackmore, S. 1993. *Dying to live: Near-death experiences.* Buffalo, NY: Prometheus.

Blackmore, S. 1996. Near-death experiences. *Journal of the Royal Society of Medicine* 89:73–76.

Blanke, O., Ortigue, S., Landis, T., and Seeck, M. 2002. Stimulating illusory own-body perceptions. *Nature* 419:269–70.

Blanke, O., Landis, T., Spinelli, L., and Seeck, M. 2004. Out-of-body experience and autoscopy of neurological origin. *Brain* 127:243–58.

Bush, N. E. 1983. The near-death experience in children: Shades of the prison-house reopening. *Journal of Near-Death Studies* 3:177–93.

Carr, D. 1981. Endorphins at the approach of death. *Lancet* 1:390.

Carr, D. 1982. Pathophysiology of stress-induced limbic lobe dysfunction: A hypothesis for NDEs. *Journal of Near-Death Studies* 2:75–89.

Cheek, D. B. 1959. Unconscious perception of meaningful events during surgical anesthesia as revealed under hypnosis. *American Journal of Clinical Hypnosis* 1:101–13.

Cheek, D. B. 1964. Surgical memory and reaction to careless conversation. *American Journal of Clinical Hypnosis* 6:237.

Clark, K. 1984. Clinical interventions with near-death experiencers. In B. Greyson and C. P. Flynn (Eds.), *The near-death experience: Problems, prospects, perspectives*, 242–55. Springfield, IL: Charles C Thomas.

Collier, B. B. 1972. Ketamine and the conscious mind. *Anaesthesia* 27:120–34.

Cook, E. W., Greyson, B., and Stevenson, I. 1998. Do any near-death experiences provide evidence for the survival of human personality after death? Relevant features and illustrative case reports. *Journal of Scientific Exploration* 12:377–406.

Cronin, A. J., Keifer, J. C., Davies, M. F., King, T. S., and Bixler, E. O. 2001. Postoperative sleep disturbance: Influences of opioids and pain in humans. *Sleep* 24:39–44.

Crookall, R. 1966. *The study and practice of astral projection*. New Hyde Park, NY: University Books. (Orig. pub. 1960.)

Devinsky, O., Feldmann, E., Burrowes, K., and Bromfield, E. 1989. Autoscopic phenomena with seizures. *Archives of Neurology* 46:1080–88.

DeVries, J. W., Bakker, P. F. A., Visser, G. H., Diephuis, J. C., and van Huffelen, A. C. 1998. Changes in cerebral oxygen uptake and cerebral electrical activity during defibrillation threshold testing. *Anesthesiology and Analgesia* 87:16–20.

Ehrenwald, J. 1974. Out-of-the-body experiences and the denial of death. *Journal of Nervous and Mental Disease* 159:227–33.

Fenwick, P. 1997. Is the near-death experience only *N*-methyl-*D*-aspartate blocking? *Journal of Near-Death Studies* 16:43–53.

Fiset, P., Paus, T., Daloze, T., Plourde, G., Meuret, P., Bonhomme, V., Hajj-Ali, N., Backman, S. B., and Evans, A. C. 1999. Brain mechanisms of propofol-induced loss of consciousness in humans: A positron emission tomographic study. *Journal of Neuroscience* 19:5506–13.

Flynn, C. P. 1982. Meanings and implications of NDEr transformations: Some preliminary findings and implications. *Anabiosis: Journal for Near-Death Studies* 2:3–14.

Flynn, C. P. 1986. *After the beyond: Transformation and the near-death experience*. Englewood Cliffs, NJ: Prentice-Hall.

Frederiks, J. A. M. 1969. Disorders of the body schema. In P. J. Vinken and G. W. Bruyn (Eds.), *Handbook of clinical neurology*. Vol. 4, *Disorders of speech, perception, and symbolic behavior*, 207–40. Amsterdam: North-Holland Publishing.

Gabbard, G. O., and Twemlow, S. W. 1984. *With the eyes of the mind: An empirical analysis of out-of-body states*. New York: Praeger.

Ghoneim, M. M., and Block, R. I. 1992. Learning and consciousness during general anesthesia. *Anesthesiology* 76:279–305.

Ghoneim, M. M., and Block, R. I. 1997. Learning and memory during general anesthesia: An update. *Anesthesiology* 87:387–410.

Gloor, P. 1990. Experiential phenomena of temporal lobe epilepsy. *Brain* 113:1673–94.

Gloor, P., Olivier, A., Quesney, L. F., Andermann, F., and Horowitz, S. 1982. The role of the limbic system in experiential phenomena of temporal lobe epilepsy. *Annals of Neurology* 12:129–44.

Granqvist, P., Fredrikson, M., Unge, P., Hagenfeldt, A., Valind, S., Larhammar, D., and Larsson, M. 2005. Sensed presence and mystical experiences are predicted by suggestibility, not by the application of transcranial weak complex magnetic fields. *Neuroscience Letters* 379:1–6.

Grey, M. 1985. *Return from death*. London: Arkana.

Greyson, B. 1983. Near-death experiences and personal values. *American Journal of Psychiatry* 140:618–20.

Greyson, B. 1991. Near-death experiences precipitated by suicide attempt: Lack of influence of psychopathology, religion, and expectations. *Journal of Near-Death Studies* 9:183–188.

Greyson, B. 1992. Reduced death threat in near-death experiences. *Death Studies* 16:533–46.

Greyson, B. 1999. Defining near-death experiences. *Mortality, 4*, 7–19.

Greyson, B. 2000. Dissociation in people who have near-death experiences: Out of their bodies or out of their minds? *Lancet* 355:460–63.

Greyson, B. 2001. Posttraumatic stress symptoms following near-death experiences. *American Journal of Orthopsychiatry* 71:358–73.

Greyson, B. 2003. Incidence and correlates of near-death experiences in a cardiac care unit. *General Hospital Psychiatry* 25:269–76.

Greyson, B., and Stevenson, I. 1980. The phenomenology of near-death experiences. *American Journal of Psychiatry* 137:1193–96.

Hart, H. 1954. ESP projection: Spontaneous cases and the experimental method. *Journal of the American Society for Psychical Research* 48:121–46.

Heier, T., and Steen, P. A. 1996. Awareness in anaesthesia: Incidence, consequences and prevention. *Acta Anaesthesiologica Scandinavica* 40:1073–86.

Herzog, D. B., and Herrin, J. T. 1985. Near-death experiences in the very young. *Critical Care Medicine* 13:1074–75.

Horowitz, M. J., and Adams, J. E. 1970. Hallucinations on brain stimulation: Evidence for revision of the Penfield hypothesis. In W. Keup (Ed.), *Origin and mechanisms of hallucinations*, 13–22. New York: Plenum.

Husain, A. M., Miller, P. P., and Carwile, S. T. 2001. REM sleep behavior disorder: Potential relationships to post-traumatic stress disorder. *Journal of Clinical Neurophysiology* 18:148–57.

Irwin, H. J. 1985. *Flight of mind: A psychological study of the out-of-body experience*. Metuchen, NJ: Scarecrow Press.

Jansen, K. L. R. 1997. The ketamine model of the near-death experience: A central role for the N-methyl-D-aspartate receptor. *Journal of Near-Death Studies* 16:5–26.

John, E. R., Prichep, L. S., Kox, W., Valdés-Sosa, P., Bosch-Bayard, J., Aubert, E., Tom, M., diMichele, F., and Gugino, L. D. 2001. Invariant reversible QEEG effects of anesthetics. *Consciousness and Cognition* 10:165–83.

Johnstone, R. E. 1973. A ketamine trip. *Anesthesiology* 39:460–61.

Karasawa, H., Sadaida, K., Noguchi, S., Hatayama, K., Naito, H., Hirota, N., Sugiyama, K., et al. 2001. Intracranial electroencephalographic changes in deep anesthesia. *Clinical Neurophysiology* 112:25–30.

Kellehear, A. 1993. Culture, biology, and the near-death experience: A reappraisal. *Journal of Nervous and Mental Disease* 181:148–56.

Kelly, E. W. 2001. Near-death experiences with reports of meeting deceased people. *Death Studies* 25: 229–49.

Kelly, E. W., Greyson, B., and Kelly, E. F. 2007. Unusual experiences near death and related phenomena. In E. F. Kelly, E. W. Kelly, A. Crabtree, A. Gauld, M. Grosso, and B. Greyson, *Irreducible mind: Toward a psychology for the 21st century*, 367–421. Lanham, MD: Rowman & Littlefield.

Kelly, E. W., Greyson, B., and Stevenson, I. 1999–2000. Can experiences near-death furnish evidence of life after death? *Omega* 40:513–19.

Knoblauch, H., Schmied, I., and Schnettler, B. 2001. Different kinds of near-death experiences: A report on a survey of near-death experiences in Germany. *Journal of Near-Death Studies* 20:15–29.

Lange, R., Greyson, B., and Houran, J. 2004. A Rasch scaling validation of a "core" near-death experience. *British Journal of Psychology* 95:161–77.

Larsson, M., Larhammar, D., Fredrikson, M., and Granqvist, P. 2005. Reply to M. A. Persinger and S. A. Koren's response to Granqvist et al., "Sensed presence and mystical experiences are predicted by suggestibility, not by the application of transcranial weak magnetic fields." *Neuroscience Letters* 380:348–50.

Lempert, T. 1994. Syncope and near-death experience. *Lancet* 344:829–30.

Levinson, B. W. 1965. States of awareness during general anaesthesia: Preliminary communication. *British Journal of Anaesthesia* 37:544–46.

Levinson, B. W. 1990. The states of awareness in anaesthesia in 1965. In B. Bonke, W. Fitch, and K. Millar (Eds.), *Memory and awareness in anaesthesia*, 11–18. Amsterdam: Swets & Zeitlinger.

Locke, T. P., and Shontz, F. C. 1983. Personality correlates of the near-death experience: A preliminary study. *Journal of the American Society for Psychical Research* 77:311–18.

Meduna, L. J. 1950. *Carbon dioxide therapy: A neurophysiological treatment of nervous disorders*. Springfield, IL: Charles C Thomas.

Moody, R. A. 1975. *Life after life*. Atlanta: Mockingbird Books.

Morris, R. L., Harary, S. B., Janis, J., Hartwell, J., and Roll, W. G. 1978. Studies of communication during out-of-body experiences. *Journal of the American Society for Psychical Research* 72:1–21.

Morse, M. 1983. A near-death experience in a 7-year-old child. *American Journal of Diseases in Children* 137:959–61.

Morse, M. 1994a. Near death experiences and death-related visions in children: Implications for the clinician. *Current Problems in Pediatrics* 24:55–83.

Morse, M. 1994b. Near-death experiences of children. *Journal of Pediatric Oncology Nursing* 11:139–44.

Morse, M., Castillo, P., Venecia, D., Milstein, J., and Tyler, D. C. 1986. Childhood near-death experiences. *American Journal of Diseases of Children* 140:1110–14.

Morse, M., Conner, D., and Tyler, D. 1985. Near-death experiences in a pediatric population. *American Journal of Diseases of Children* 139:595–600.

Morse, M. L., Venecia, D., and Milstein, J. 1989. Near-death experiences: A neurophysiological explanatory model. *Journal of Near-Death Studies* 8:45–53.

Myers, F. W. H. 1891. Science and a future life. *Nineteenth Century* 29:628–47.

Nelson, K. R., Mattingly, M., Lee, S. A., and Schmitt, F. A. 2006. Does the arousal system contribute to near death experience? *Neurology* 66:1003–9.

Neppe, V. M. 1989. Near-death experiences: A new challenge in temporal lobe phenomenology? Comments on "A neurobiological model for near-death experiences." *Journal of Near-Death Studies* 7:243–48.

Niedermeyer, E., and Lopes da Silva, F. 2004. *Electroencephalography: Basic principles, clinical applications, and related fields.* 5th ed. Baltimore: Lippincott Williams and Wilkins.

Noyes, R. 1980. Attitude change following near-death experience. *Psychiatry* 43:234–42.

Noyes, R., Hoenk, P. R., Kuperman, S., and Slymen, D. J. 1977. Depersonalization in accident victims and psychiatric patients. *Journal of Nervous and Mental Disease* 164:401–7.

Noyes, R., and Kletti, R. 1976. Depersonalization in the face of life-threatening danger: An interpretation. *Omega* 7:103–14.

Ohayon, M. M., Priest, R. G., Zully, J., Smirne, S., and Paiva, T. 2002. Prevalence of narcolepsy symptomatology and diagnosis in the European general population. *Neurology* 58:1826–33.

Osis, K., and Haraldsson, E. 1997. *At the hour of death.* 3rd ed. Norwalk, CT: Hastings House. (Orig. pub. 1977.)

Osis, K., and McCormick, D. 1980. Kinetic effects at the ostensible location of an out-of-body projection during perceptual testing. *Journal of the American Society for Psychical Research* 74:319–29.

Osterman, J. E., Hopper, J., Heran, W. J., Keane, T. M., and van der Kolk, B. A. 2001. Awareness under anesthesia and the development of posttraumatic stress disorder. *General Hospital Psychiatry* 23:198–204.

Owens, J. E. 1995. Paranormal reports from a study of near-death experience and a case of an unusual near-death vision. In L. Coly and J. D. S. McMahon (Eds.), *Parapsychology and thanatology*, 149–67. New York: Parapsychology Foundation.

Owens, J. E., Cook, E. W., and Stevenson, I. 1990. Features of "near-death experience" in relation to whether or not patients were near death. *Lancet* 336:1175–77.

Oyama, T., Jin, T., and Yamaya, R. 1980. Profound analgesic effects of beta-endorphins in man. *Lancet* 1:122–24.

Pacia, S. V., and Ebersole, J. S. 1997. Intracranial EEG substrates of scalp ictal patterns from temporal lobe foci. *Epilepsia* 38:642–54.

Palmer, J. 1978. The out-of-the-body experience: A psychological theory. *Parapsychology Review* 9 (5): 19–22.

Parnia, S., and Fenwick, P. 2002. Near death experiences in cardiac arrest: Visions of a dying brain or visions of a new science of consciousness. *Resuscitation* 52:5–11.

Parnia, S., Waller, D. G., Yeates, R., and Fenwick, P. 2001. A qualitative and quantitative study of the incidence, features and aetiology of near death experiences in cardiac arrest survivors. *Resuscitation* 48:149–56.

Pasricha, S. 1993. A systematic survey of near-death experiences in South India. *Journal of Scientific Exploration* 7:161–71.

Pasricha, S., and Stevenson, I. 1986. Near-death experiences in India. *Journal of Nervous and Mental Disease* 174:165–70.

Penfield, W. 1955. The role of the temporal cortex in certain psychical phenomena. *Journal of Mental Science* 101:451–65.

Penfield, W. 1958a. *The excitable cortex in conscious man.* Liverpool, England: Liverpool University Press.

Penfield, W. 1958b. Functional localization in temporal and deep Sylvian areas. *Research Publications of the Association for Research in Nervous and Mental Disorders* 36:210–26.

Penfield, W. 1975. *The mystery of the mind: A critical study of consciousness and the human brain.* Princeton, NJ: Princeton University Press.

Penfield, W., and Erickson, T. C. 1941. *Epilepsy and cerebral localization.* Springfield, IL: Charles C. Thomas.

Penfield, W., and Perot, P. 1963. The brain's record of auditory and visual experience: A final discussion and summary. *Brain* 86:595–96.

Penfield, W., and Rasmussen, T. 1950. *The cerebral cortex of man: A clinical localization of function.* New York: Macmillan.

Persinger, M. A. 1989. Modern neuroscience and near-death experiences: Expectancies and implications. Comments on "A neurobiological model for near-death experiences." *Journal of Near-Death Studies* 7:233–39.

Persinger, M. A. 1994. Near-death experiences: Determining the neuroanatomical pathways by experiential patterns and simulation in experimental settings. In L. Bessette (Ed.), *Healing: Beyond suffering or death,* 277–86. Chabanel, Canada: Publications MNH.

Persinger, M. A. 1999. Near-death experiences and ecstasy: A product of the organization of the human brain? In S. Della Sala (Ed.), *Mind myths: Exploring popular assumptions about the mind and brain,* 85–99. Chichester, England: John Wiley.

Pfister, O. 1930. Shockdenken und Shockphantasien bei höchster Todesgefahr [Shock thoughts and fantasies in extreme mortal danger]. *International Zeitschrift für Psychoanalyse* 16:430–55.

Ring, K. 1980. *Life at death: A scientific investigation of the near-death experience.* New York: Coward, McCann & Geoghegan.

Ring, K. 1984. *Heading toward omega: In search of the meaning of the near-death experience.* New York: William Morrow.

Ring, K., and Cooper, S. 1997. Near-death and out-of-body experiences in the blind: A study of apparent eyeless vision. *Journal of Near-Death Studies* 16:101–47.

Ring, K., and Cooper, S. 1999. *Mindsight: Near-death and out-of-body experiences in the blind.* Palo Alto, CA: William James Center/Institute of Transpersonal Psychology.

Ring, K., and Lawrence, M. 1993. Further evidence for veridical perception during near-death experiences. *Journal of Near-Death Studies* 11:223–29.

Ring, K., and Rosing, C. J. 1990. The Omega Project: An empirical study of the NDE-prone personality. *Journal of Near-Death Studies* 8:211–39.

Roberts, G., and Owen, J. 1988. The near-death experience. *British Journal of Psychiatry* 153:607–17.

Rodin, E. 1980. The reality of death experience: A personal perspective. *Journal of Nervous and Mental Disease* 168:259–63.

Rodin, E. 1989. Comments on "A neurobiological model for near-death experiences." *Journal of Near-Death Studies* 7:255–59.

Rogo, D. S. 1984. Ketamine and the near-death experience. *Journal of Near-Death Studies* 4:87–96.

Saavedra-Aguilar, J. C., and Gómez-Jeria, J. S. 1989. A neurobiological model for near-death experiences. *Journal of Near-Death Studies* 7:205–22.

Sabom, M. 1982. *Recollections of death: A medical investigation.* New York: Harper & Row.

Sabom, M. 1998. *Light and death: One doctor's fascinating account of near-death experiences.* Grand Rapids, MI: Zondervan.

Sagan, C. 1979. *Broca's brain: Reflections on the romance of science.* New York: Random House.

Sagan, C. 1984. The amniotic universe. In B. Greyson and C. P. Flynn (Eds.), *The near-death experience: Problems, prospects, perspectives,* 140–53. Springfield, IL: Charles C. Thomas.

Sandin, R. H., Enlund, G., Samuelsson, P., and Lennmarken, C. 2000. Awareness during anaesthesia: A prospective case study. *Lancet* 355:707–11.

Sartori, P, Badham, P., and Fenwick, P. 2006. A prospectively studied near-death experience with corroborated out-of-body perceptions and unexplained healing. *Journal of Near-Death Studies* 25: 69–84.

Schwaninger, J., Eisenberg, P. R., Schechtman, K. B., and Weiss, A. N. 2002. A prospective analysis of near-death experiences in cardiac arrest patients. *Journal of Near-Death Studies* 20:215–32.

Serdahely, W. J. 1990. Pediatric near-death experiences. *Journal of Near-Death Studies* 9:33–39.

Shulman, R. G., Hyder, F., and Rothman, D. L. 2003. Cerebral metabolism and consciousness. *Comptes Rendus Biologies* 326:253–73.

Spetzler, R. F., Hadley, M. N., Rigamonti, D., Carter, L. P., Raudzens, P. A., Shedd, S. A., and Wilkinson, E. 1988. Aneurysms of the basilar artery treated with circulatory arrest, hypothermia, and barbiturate cerebral protection. *Journal of Neurosurgery* 68:868–79.

Spitelli, P. H., Holmes, M. A., and Domino, K. B. 2002. Awareness during anesthesia. *Anesthesiology Clinics of North America* 20:555–70.

Stevens, J. R. 1982. Sleep is for seizures: A new interpretation of the role of phasic events in sleep and wakefulness. In M. B. Sternman, M. N. Shouse, and P. Passount (Eds.), *Sleep and epilepsy,* 249–64. New York: Academic Press.

Stevenson, I., and Cook, E. W. 1995. Involuntary memories during severe physical illness or injury. *Journal of Nervous and Mental Disease* 183:452–58.

Strassman, R. 1997. Endogenous ketamine-like compounds and the NDE: If so, so what? *Journal of Near-Death Studies* 16:27–41.

Tart, C. T. 1968. A psychophysiological study of out-of-the-body experiences in a selected subject. *Journal of the American Society for Psychical Research* 62:3–27.

Tellegen, A., and Atkinson, G. 1974. Openness to absorbing and self-altering experiences ("absorption"), a trait related to hypnotic susceptibility. *Journal of Abnormal Psychology* 83:268–77.

Thalbourne, M. A. 1998. Transliminality: Further correlates and a short measure. *Journal of the American Society for Psychical Research* 92:402–19.

Thalbourne, M A., and Delin, P. S. 1994. A common thread underlying belief in the paranormal, creative personality, mystical experience and psychopathology. *Journal of Parapsychology* 58:2–38.

Tong, F. 2003. Out-of-body experiences: From Penfield to present. *Trends in Cognitive Science* 7:104–6.

van Lommel, P. 2004. About the continuity of our consciousness. *Advances in Experimental Medicine and Biology* 550:115–32.

van Lommel, P., van Wees, R., Meyers, V., and Elfferich, I. 2001. Near-death experiences in survivors of cardiac arrest: A prospective study in the Netherlands. *Lancet* 358:2039–45.

Veselis, R. A., Reinsel, R. A., Beattie, B. J., Mawlawi, O. R., Feshchenko, V. A., DiResta, G. R., Larson, S. M., and Blasberg, R. G. 1997. Midazolam changes cerebral blood flow in discrete brain regions: An H sub 2 sup 15 O positron emission topography study. *Anesthesiology* 87:1106–17.

Vriens, E. M., Bakker, P. F. A., DeVries, J. W., Wieneke, G. H., and van Huffelen, A. C. 1996. The impact of repeated short episodes of circulatory arrest on cerebral function. Reassuring electroencephalographic (EEG) findings during defibrillation theshold testing at defibrillator implantation. *Electroencephalography and Clinical Neurophysiology* 98:236–42.

Weiss, L., Grocott, H. P., Rosanaia, R. A., Friedman, A., Newman, M. F., and Warner, D. S. 1998. Case 4: 1998. Cardiopulmonary bypass and hypothermic circulatory arrest for basilar artery aneurysm clipping. *Journal of Cardiothoracic and Vascular Anesthesia* 12:473–79.

Whinnery, J. E. 1997. Psychophysiologic correlates of unconsciousness and near-death experiences. *Journal of Near-Death Studies* 15:231–58.

White, N. S., and Alkire, M. T. 2003. Impaired thalamocortical connectivity in humans during general-anesthetic-induced unconsciousness. *NeuroImage* 19:402–11.

Williams, M. D., Rainer, W. G., Fieger, H. G., Murray, I. P., and Sanchez, M. L. 1991. Cardiopulmonary bypass, profound hypothermia, and circulatory arrest for neurosurgery. *Annals of Thoracic Surgery* 52:1069–75.

Wilson, S. C., and Barber, T. X. 1981. Vivid fantasy and hallucinatory abilities in the life histories of excellent hypnotic subjects ("somnambules"): Preliminary report with female subjects. In E. Klinger (Ed.), *Imagery*. Vol. 2, *Concepts, results, and applications*, 133–49. New York: Plenum.

Wilson, S. C., and Barber, T. X. 1983. The fantasy-prone personality: Implications for understanding imagery, hypnosis, and parapsychological phenomena. In A. A. Sheikh (Ed.), *Imagery: Current theory, research, and application*, 340–90. New York: Wiley.

Woerlee, G. M. 2004. Cardiac arrest and near-death experiences. *Journal of Near-Death Studies* 22:235–49.

CHAPTER 11

American Psychiatric Association. 1994. *Diagnostic and statistical manual of mental disorders.* 4th ed. Washington, DC: American Psychiatric Association.

Axelrod, B. 1978. Pastoral implications of *Life after Life*. *Soul Searcher: Quarterly Journal of Christian Psychical Research* 1 (3): 11–14.

Barnett, L. 1991. Hospice nurses' knowledge and attitudes toward the near-death experience. *Journal of Near-Death Studies* 9:225–32.

Bates, B. C., and Stanley, A. 1985. The epidemiology and differential diagnosis of near-death experience. *American Journal of Orthopsychiatry* 55 (4): 542–49.

Bechtel, L. J., Chen, A., Pierce, R. A., and Walker, B. A. 1992. Assessment of clergy knowledge and attitudes toward near-death experiences. *Journal of Near-Death Studies* 10:161–70.

Bonenfant, R. J. 2001. A child's encounter with the devil: An unusual near-death experience with both blissful and frightening elements. *Journal of Near-Death Studies* 20:87–100.

Broome, K. (Producer). 2002. *The day I died: The mind, the brain, and near-death experiences* [motion picture]. Glasgow, Scotland: British Broadcasting Corporation. Available for purchase at http://ffh.films.com/id/11685.

Bucher, L., Wimbush, F. B., Hardie, T., and Hayes, E. R. 1997. Near death experiences: Critical care nurses' attitudes and interventions. *Dimensions of Critical Care Nursing* 16 (4): 194–201.

Bush, N. E. 2002. Afterward: Making meaning after a frightening near-death experience. *Journal of Near-Death Studies* 21:99–133.

Byl, P. 1988. The near-death experience—moving toward enlightenment. *Kansas Nurse* 63:8.

Callanan, M. 1994. Back from "beyond." *American Journal of Nursing* 94 (3): 20, 22–23.

Christian, S. R. 2005. *Marital satisfaction and stability following a near-death experience of one of the marital partners*. Unpublished doctoral dissertation. University of North Texas, Denton.

Cole, E. J. 1993. The near-death experience. *Intensive and Critical Care Nursing* 9 (3): 157–61.

Colli, J. E., and Beck, T. E. 2003. Recovery from bulimia nervosa through near-death experience: A case study. *Journal of Near-Death Studies* 22:33–55.

Corcoran, D. K. 1988. Helping patients who've had near-death experiences. *Nursing* 18 (11): 34–39.

Cunico, L. 2001. Knowledge and attitudes of hospital nurses in Italy related to near-death experiences. *Journal of Near-Death Studies* 20:37–50.

Derogatis, L. R. 1992. *SCL-90-R administration, scoring, and procedures manual–II*. Towson, MD: Clinical Psychometric Research.

DiCenso, A., Cullum, N., and Ciliska, D. 1998. Implementing evidence-based nursing: Some misconceptions. *Evidence-Based Nursing* 1:38–40.

Fall, K. A., Holden, J. M., and Marquis, A. 2004. *Theoretical models of counseling and psychotherapy*. New York: Brunner-Routledge.

Flynn, C. P. 1982. Meanings and implications of NDEr transformations: Some preliminary findings and implications. *Anabiosis: The Journal for Near-Death Studies* 2:3–13.

Flynn, C. P. 1986. *After the beyond: Human transformation and the near-death experience*. Englewood Cliffs, NJ: Prentice-Hall.

Freeman, C. 1985. Near-death experiences: Implications for medical personnel. *Occupational Health Nursing* 33 (7): 349–59.

Fremit, M. R. (1989). Near-death experiences: A new understanding. *Physician Assistant* 13 (8): 42–50.

Friedland, D. J. 1998. *Evidence-based medicine: A framework for clinical practice.* New York: McGraw-Hill Medical.

Furn, B. G. 1987. Adjustment and the near-death experience: A conceptual and therapeutic model. *Journal of Near-Death Studies* 6:4–19.

Gottman, J. 1999. *The marriage clinic: A scientifically based marital therapy.* New York: W. W. Norton.

Greyson, B. 1981. Near-death experiences and attempted suicide. *Suicide and Life-Threatening Behavior* 11 (1): 10–16.

Greyson, B. 1983. The psychodynamics of near-death experiences. *Journal of Nervous and Mental Disease* 171 (6): 376–81.

Greyson, B. 1992–93. Near-death experiences and antisuicidal attitudes. *Omega* 26 (2): 81–89.

Greyson, B. 1997. The near-death experience as a focus of clinical attention. *Journal of Nervous and Mental Disease* 185 (5): 327–34.

Greyson, B. 1998. The incidence of near-death experiences. *Medicine and Psychiatry* 1:92–99.

Greyson, B. 2000. Near-death experiences. In E. Cardeña, S. J. Lynn, and S. Krippner (Eds.), *Varieties of anomalous experience: Examining the scientific evidence,* 315–52. Washington, DC: American Psychological Association.

Greyson, B. 2001. Posttraumatic stress symptoms following near-death experiences. *American Journal of Orthopsychiatry* 71:368–73.

Greyson, B. 2003. Near-death experiences in a psychiatric outpatient clinic population. *Psychiatric Services* 54 (12): 1649–51.

Greyson, B., and Bush, N. E. 1992. Distressing near-death experiences. *Psychiatry* 55:95–110.

Greyson, B., and Harris, B. 1987. Clinical approaches to the near-death experiencer. *Journal of Near-Death Studies* 6:41–52.

Greyson, B., and Liester, M. B. 2004. Auditory hallucinations following near-death experiences. *Journal of Humanistic Psychology* 44 (3): 320–36.

Groth-Marnat, G., and Summers, R. 1998. Altered beliefs, attitudes, and behaviors following near-death experiences. *Journal of Humanistic Psychology* 38 (3): 110–25.

Hayes, E. R., Hardie, T., Bucher, L., and Wimbush, F. 1998. Near death: Back from beyond. *RN* 61 (12): 54–59.

Hayes, E. R., and Orne, R. M. 1990. A study of the relationship between knowledge and attitudes of nurses in practice related to the near-death experience. *Loss, Grief, and Care* 4 (1–2): 71–80.

Hayes, E. R., and Waters, L. D. 1989. Interdisciplinary perceptions of the near-death experience: Implications for professional education and practice. *Death Studies* 13:443–53.

Herzog, D. B., and Herrin, J. T. 1985. Near-death experiences in the very young. *Critical Care Medicine* 13 (12): 1074–75.

Hoffman, R. M. 1995a. Disclosure habits after near-death experiences: Influences, obstacles, and listener selection. *Journal of Near-Death Studies* 14:29–48.

Hoffman, R. M. 1995b. Disclosure needs and motives after a near-death experience. *Journal of Near-Death Studies* 13:237–66.

Holden, J. M. 2005. *Instructor's/Viewing guide for* The Day I Died: The Mind, the Brain, and Near-Death Experiences. Princeton, NJ: Films for the Humanities and Sciences. Available at http://www.films.com/id/11685 under "related resources" and at http://www.iands.org/news/latest/the_ultimate_nde_video. html.

Holden, J. M., and MacHovec, F. 1993. Risk management in hypnotic recall of near-death experiences. *American Journal of Clinical Hypnosis* 36 (1): 38–46.

Holden, J. M., MacLurg, J., and James, D. 2006. Media review: *The Day I Died: The Mind, the Brain, and Near-Death Experiences* [videorecording]. *Journal of Near-Death Studies* 25:121–28.

Horacek, B. J. 1997. Amazing grace: The healing effects of near-death experiences on those dying and grieving. *Journal of Near-Death Studies* 16:149–61.

Insinger, M. 1991. The impact of a near-death experience on family relationships. *Journal of Near-Death Studies* 9:141–81.

Lee, A. 1978. The Lazarus syndrome: Caring for patients who've "returned from the dead." *RN* 41 (6): 53–64.

Lukoff, D., Lu, F., and Turner, R. 1992. Toward a more culturally sensitive DSM-IV: Psychoreligious and psychospiritual problems. *Journal of Nervous and Mental Disease* 180 (11): 673–82.

Lundahl, C. R. 1981. Directions in near-death research. *Death Education* 5:135–42.

MacHovec, F. 1994. Near-death experiences: Psychotherapeutic aspects. *Psychotherapy in Private Practice* 13 (3): 99–104.

McDonagh, J. M. 2004. Introducing near-death research findings into psychotherapy. *Journal of Near-Death Studies* 22:269–73.

McEvoy, M. D. 1990. The near-death experience: Implications for nursing education. *Loss, Grief & Care* 4 (1–2): 51–55.

McLaughlin, S. A., and Malony, H. N. 1984. Near-death experiences and religion: A further investigation. *Journal of Religion and Health* 23 (2): 149–59.

Miller, J. S. 1987. A counseling approach to assist near-death experiencers: A response to Bette Furn's paper. *Journal of Near-Death Studies* 6:30–36.

Milne, C. T. 1995. Cardiac electrophysiology studies and the near-death experience. *CCACN: Journal of the Canadian Association of Critical Care Nurses* 6 (1): 16–19.

Moody, R. A., Jr. 1975. *Life after life.* Atlanta: Mockingbird Books.

Moody, R. A., Jr. 1977. Near-death experiences: Dilemma for the clinician. *Virginia Medical* 104:687–90.

Moody, R. A., Jr. 1980. Commentary on "The Reality of Death Experiences: A Personal Perspective" by Ernst Rodin. *Journal of Nervous and Mental Disease* 168 (5): 264–65.

Moore, L. H. 1994. An assessment of physicians' knowledge of and attitudes toward the near-death experience. *Journal of Near-Death Studies* 13:91–102.

Morse, M. 1983. A near-death experience in a 7-year-old child. *American Journal of Diseases of Children* 137:959–61.

Morse, M. L. 1994a. Near death experiences and death-related visions in children: Implications for the clinician. *Current Problems in Pediatrics* 24:55–83.

Morse, M. L. 1994b. Near-death experiences of children. *Journal of Pediatric Oncology Nursing* 11 (4): 139–44.

Musgrave, C. 1997. The near-death experience: A study of spiritual transformation. *Journal of Near-Death Studies* 15:187–201.

Noble, K. D. 1987. Psychological health and the experience of transcendence. *Counseling Psychologist* 15 (4): 601–14.

Norcross, J. C., Koocher, G. P., and Garofalo, A. 2006. Discredited psychological treatments and tests: A Delphi poll. *Professional Psychology: Research and Practice* 37 (5): 515–22.

Oakes, A. 1981. Near-death events and critical care nursing. *Topics in Clinical Nursing* 3:62–77.

Orne, R. M. 1995. The meaning of survival: The early aftermath of a near-death experience. *Research in Nursing & Health* 18 (3): 239–47.

Parnia, S., and Fenwick, P. 2002. Near death experiences in cardiac arrest: Visions of a dying brain or visions of a new science of consciousness. *Resuscitation* 52:5–11.

Parnia, S., Waller, D. G., Yeates, R., and Fenwick, P. 2001. A qualitative and quantitative study of the incidence, features and aetiology of near death experiences in cardiac arrest survivors. *Resuscitation* 48:149–56.

Raft, D., and Andresen, J. J. 1986. Transformations in self-understanding after near-death experiences. *Contemporary Psychoanalysis* 22 (3): 319–45.

Richardson, G. E. 1979. The life-after-death phenomenon. *Journal of School Health* 49 (8): 451–53.

Ring, K. 1984. *Heading toward omega: In search of the meaning of the near-death experience*. New York: William Morrow.

Ring, K. 1995. The impact of near-death experiences on persons who have not had them: A report of a preliminary study and two replications. *Journal of Near-Death Studies* 13:223–35.

Ring, K., and Franklin, S. 1981–82. Do suicide survivors report near-death experiences? *Omega* 12 (3): 191–208.

Royse, D. 1985. The near-death experience: A survey of clergy's attitudes and knowledge. *Journal of Pastoral Care* 39:31–42.

Sabom, M. 1982. *Recollections of death: A medical investigation*. New York: Harper & Row.

Sabom, W. S. 1980. Near-death experience: A review from pastoral psychology. *Journal of Religion and Health* 19 (2): 130–40.

Scotton, B. W., Chinen, A. B., and Battista, J. R. 1996. Integration and conclusion. In B. W. Scotton, A. B. Chinen, and J. R. Battista (Eds.), *Textbook of transpersonal psychiatry and psychology*, 409–15. New York: Basic Books.

Schwaninger, J., Eisenberg, P. R., Schechtman, K. B., and Weiss, A. N. 2002. A prospective analysis of near-death experiences in cardiac arrest patients. *Journal of Near-Death Studies* 20:215–32.

Serdahely, W., Drenk, A., and Serdahely, J. J. 1988. What carers need to understand about the near-death experience. *Geriatric Nursing* 9 (4): 238–41.

Sheeler, R. D. 2005. Teaching near death experiences to medical students. *Journal of Near-Death Studies* 23:239–47.

Sommers, M. S. 1994. The near-death experience following multiple trauma. *Critical Care Nurse* 14 (2): 62–66.

Sullivan, R. M. 1984. Combat-related near-death experiences: A preliminary investigation. *Anabiosis: The Journal for Near-Death Studies* 4:143–52.

Sutherland, C. 1992. *Reborn in the light: Life after near-death experiences*. New York: Bantam Books.

Thornburg, N. R. 1988. Development of the Near-Death Phenomena Knowledge and Attitudes Questionnaire. *Journal of Near-Death Studies* 6: 223–39.

Trevelyan, J. 1989. Near death experiences. *Nursing Times* 85 (28): 39–41.

van Lommel, P., van Wees, R., Meyers, V., Elfferich, I. 2001. Near-death experience in survivors of cardiac arrest: A prospective study in the Netherlands. *Lancet* 358:2039–45.

Vinter, M. 1994. An insight into the afterlife: Informing patients about near death experiences. *Professional Nurse* 10 (3): 171–73.

Walker, B. A. 1989. Health care professionals and the near-death experience. *Death Studies* 13:63–71.

Walker, B. A., and Russell, R. D. 1989. Assessing psychologists' knowledge and attitudes toward near-death phenomena. *Journal of Near-Death Studies* 8:103–10.

Wimbush, F. B., Hardie, T., and Hayes, E. 2001. Supporting your patient after a near-death experience. *Nursing* 31 (10): 48.

Winkler, E. J. 2003. The Elias Project: Using the near-death experience potential in therapy. *Journal of Near-Death Studies* 22:78–81.

Subject Index

—demographic of NDEr, 110–18, 120–22, 130–31
—practical applications, 14
—spirituality and religion, 14, 118–20
—veridical perception, 15, 22, 193–9, 203–10
type, by:
—anecdotal, 121, 191, 193–7, 204, 209, 210, 230, 255, 257
—prospective, 28, 34, 112, 113, 115–19, 205–10
—retrospective, 7, 34, 42, 112–5, 117, 119, 126, 129, 200
thanatology and NDEs, 61, 251, 253
Tibetan Book of the Dead, 2, 163, 164, 165
Transformed by the Light, 147

tunnel experiences in NDEs, 22, 25, 27, 66, 88, 90, 95, 97–98, 135, 138, 139–48, 150–52, 154, 155, 169, 233

Uttermost Deep: The Challenge of Near-Death Experiences, The, 75

veridical perception, 15, 22–24, 37, 93, 97, 185, 223, 229–31, 232–4; accounts of, 189–192; apparently non-physical veridical perception (AVP), definition of, 186; definition of, 186; studies, 22, 205–209

Web sites, 4–5, 74, 110, 224
With the Eyes of the Mind, 88

Name Index (*See also* References section of this book)

About the Editors and Contributors

Editors

BRUCE GREYSON, M.D., is the Chester F. Carlson Professor of Psychiatry & Neurobehavioral Sciences at the University of Virginia where he is the Director of the Division of Perceptual Studies. A founder and past president of the International Association for Near-Death Studies, he edited the association's scholarly *Journal of Near-Death Studies* for 27 years. His research for the past three decades has focused on near-death experiences and has resulted in more than 100 publications in academic medical and psychological journals, three edited books, and several research grants and awards.

JANICE MINER HOLDEN, Ed.D., LPC, LMFT, NCC, is Professor of Counseling at the University of North Texas in Denton, TX, where she serves currently as Interim Chair of the Department of Counseling and Higher Education. She has been a scholar of near-death experiences for over 20 years, speaking and publishing both nationally and internationally; has served on the Board of Directors of the International Association for Near-Death Studies and as the organization's president for three years; and serves currently as editor of the *Journal of Near-Death Studies*.

DEBBIE JAMES, MSN, RN, CCRN, is a Senior Instructor in The University of Texas M. D. Anderson Cancer Center's Nursing Education Department. She supervises orientation of nursing instructors and developing nursing clinical coaches, enhancing critical thinking skills to maximize quality patient care. A former director on the International Association for Near-Death Studies (IANDS) Board, Ms. James founded IANDS's San Antonio chapter. Among her many honors is the American Heart Association Nurse Image Maker Award. In 2000, Ms. James was a panelist on the PBS Bill Moyers show, "Dying in America."

Contributors

CARLOS S. ALVARADO, Ph.D., is Assistant Professor of Research in the Department of Psychiatry and Neurobehavioral Sciences at the University of Virginia. He has conducted research on the psychology and the features of out-of-body experiences and has published papers about the history of parapsychology. Alvarado has been twice president of the Parapsychological Association. Currently he is adjunct faculty at the Institute of Transpersonal Psychology, associate editor of the *Journal of Scientific Exploration,* and a member of the editorial board of the *Journal of the Society for Psychical Research.*

NANCY EVANS BUSH, M.A., has been with the International Association for Near-Death Studies since 1982, first as its executive director and later as president, board member, and editor of the quarterly newsletter *Vital Signs.* Author of the first study of children's near-death experiences, she is best known for her research on harrowing NDEs. She is a retired teacher and technical writer.

SANDRA ROZAN CHRISTIAN, Ph.D., LPC, earned her doctoral degree in counseling from the University of North Texas (UNT). At the 2005 International Association for Near-Death Studies conference, she presented her dissertation research on how a near-death experience (NDE) affects married couples' relationships. She is co-developer of *Near-Death Experiences: Index to the Periodical Literature through 2005.* Dr. Christian serves as adjunct professor of counseling at UNT and maintains a private practice in Dallas, TX, where she draws on her research on NDEs and life-changing events to assist her clients through life transitions.

PETER FENWICK, MB, BChir, FRCPsych, is a neuropsychiatrist who for many years ran the neuropsychiatry epilepsy service at the Maudsley Hospital in London, UK. He holds honorary consultant appointments at the Institute of Psychiatry, Kings College London, and at the University of Southampton. He has a special interest in consciousness, particularly the near-death experience and how it challenges prevailing views of brain function. His most recent research has focused on the phenomena that both the dying and their relatives see and experience around the actual time of death.

RYAN D. FOSTER, M.A., NCC, LPC-Intern, is a doctoral student in the Counseling Program at the University of North Texas where he is currently planning dissertation research on the role of near-death experiences (NDEs) in bereavement counseling. He assisted in developing *Near-Death Experiences: Index to the Periodical Literature through 2005*, the most comprehensive NDE literature research tool, published at the International Association for Near-Death Studies Web site. His research and clinical interests include NDEs, grief and loss, and assessment across the lifespan.

ALLAN KELLEHEAR, Ph.D., is professor of Sociology and chair of the Department of Social & Policy Sciences at the University of Bath, UK. His recent books include *Compassionate Cities: Public Health and End of Life Care* (Routledge, 2005) and *A Social History of Dying* (Cambridge University Press, 2007). He is co-editor with Glennys Howarth of *Mortality*, an international journal of interdisciplinary studies of death, dying, and bereavement, published by Taylor & Francis. His book-length study of near-death experiences appeared as *Experiences Near Death: Beyond Medicine and Religion* (Oxford University Press, 1996).

EDWARD F. KELLY, Ph.D., is research professor in the Department of Psychiatry and Neurobehavioral Sciences at the University of Virginia and lead author of *Irreducible Mind: Toward a Psychology for the 21st Century*. Originally trained in psycholinguistics and cognitive science, he worked in experimental parapsychology at Duke University and in somatosensory neurophysiology at the University of North Carolina-Chapel Hill before coming to Virginia where he established a state-of-the-art EEG laboratory. His long-term research interest centers on the functional neuroimaging of psi phenomena and altered states of consciousness.

EMILY WILLIAMS KELLY, Ph.D., research assistant professor in the Department of Psychiatry and Neurobehavioral Sciences at the University of Virginia, has conducted research in the Division of Perceptual Studies for 30 years on near-death experiences, cases of the reincarnation type, and other experiences related to the question of survival after death. Her current research interests include deathbed experiences, apparitions, and mediumship. Co-author of *Irreducible Mind: Toward A Psychology for the 21st Century* (2007), she contributed chapters on F. W. H. Myers, how mental factors influence physiological states, and near-death and related experiences.

JEFFREY LONG, M.D., is a radiation oncologist practicing in Gallup, NM. He is founder of the Near-Death Experience Research Foundation (www.nderf.org) Web site that serves as a public service and for research, has written a number of scholarly papers and participated in numerous regional and national media presentations on near-death experience, and has served on the Board of Directors of the International Association for Near-Death Studies.

B. JASON MacLURG, M.D., is a private-practice psychiatrist in Seattle, Washington, with over 20 years of clinical experience with adult and geriatric patients. Currently on staff at Swedish Medical Center and the immediate past-president of the Washington State Psychiatric Association, he has served on the International Association for Near-Death Studies (IANDS) Board of Directors and has spoken at several IANDS conferences. He has found near-death experiences to be inexplicable yet deeply meaningful and profound, affirming life and love and transforming both experiencers and those who listen openly to their stories.

FARNAZ MASUMIAN, M.A., teaches world religions in the School of Social Work at the University of Texas at Austin. A lecturer of world religions at institutions of higher education since 1992, she has also published in the area of near-death experiences (NDEs). Her first book, *Life After Death: A Study of the Afterlife in World Religions* (Oneworld Publications: Oxford, England, 1995) included a comparative analysis of the afterlife teachings of seven world religions with prominent NDE characteristics.

RUSSELL NOYES, JR., M.D., is Emeritus Professor of Psychiatry at the University of Iowa. He became interested in near-death experiences early in his career and published more than a dozen articles based on interviews with over 200 people involved in accidents of various kinds. He, along with Roy Kletti, showed that such people's experiences can be investigated systematically and that responses, both during and after life-threatening events, follow a meaningful pattern. In 2006 he received the Bruce Greyson Research Award from the International Association for Near-Death Studies for his work.

CHERIE SUTHERLAND, Ph.D., is a sociologist, educator, researcher, speaker, workshop facilitator, and author of five books on near-death experiences and related subjects. For over 15 years she has been a shamanic practitioner and maintains a private counseling practice in Byron Bay, Australia.

NANCY L. ZINGRONE, Ph.D., is Assistant Professor of Research in the Department of Psychiatry and Neurobehavioral Sciences at the University of Virginia. She has conducted experimental ESP research and survey studies of psychic experiences, and she has examined texts in parapsychology from a science studies point of view. Zingrone has been twice president of the Parapsychological Association. She is the associate editor of the series *Advances in Parapsychological Research*.